Memorial Book of Radzivilov
(Radyvyliv, Ukraine)

Translation of
Radzivilov: Sefer Zikaron

Originally in Hebrew and Yiddish
Edited by Ya'acov Adini

Translated by Elizabeth Kessin Berman,
Danielle Charak, Judith Fixler,
Tina Lunson, Ros Romem,
Rivka Schiller, Mary Jane Shubow, and
Yaacov David Shulman

Translation edited by Ellen Garshick

Published by JewishGen
An Affiliate of the Museum of Jewish Heritage - A Living Memorial to the Holocaust
New York

Cover Credits:

Cover Design by Nina Schwartz

Front Cover:

Soviet-era memorial at the Radzivilov massacre site, ©2007 by Dan Frenkel. Courtesy of D. Frenkel, FlameofZion@gmail.com.

Radziwillow Kibbutz Group, 4 July 1935. Courtesy of Dan Frenkel, FlameofZion@gmail.com. Girl in top row, second from left, is Mr. Frenkel's aunt, Pnina Cimbler.

Back cover:

Sign at Radyvyliv Outskirts, ©2007 by Mary Jo Kirschman, courtesy of Steve Luxenberg, author of Annie's Ghosts: A Journey Into a Family Secret.

House that in 1942 bordered the Radziwillow Ghetto, ©2007 by Mary Jo Kirschman, courtesy of Steve Luxenberg, author of Annie's Ghosts: A Journey Into a Family Secret.

1915 Topographic Map showing Radziwillow, Topographic Maps of Eastern Europe, courtesy of mapywig.org.

Memorial Book of Radzivilov
Translation of *Radzivilov: Sefer Zikaron*

Copyright © 2018 by Kremenets District Research Group
All rights reserved.
First Printing: Septmeber 2018, Elul 5778
Second Printing: March 2020, Adar 5780

Editor: Ellen Garshick (Silver Spring, Maryland, USA)
Translators: Elizabeth Kessin Berman, Danielle Charak, Judith Fixler, Tina Lunson, Ros Romem, Rivka Schiller, Mary Jane Shubow, and Yaacov David Shulman
Layout: Ellen Garshick
Cover Design: Nina Schwartz, Impulse Graphics LLC
Indexed by: Diane Salman

Published by JewishGen, Inc.
An Affiliate of the Museum of Jewish Heritage
A Living Memorial to the Holocaust
36 Battery Place, New York, NY 10280

The mission of the JewishGen organization is to produce a translation of the original work and we cannot verify the accuracy of statements or alter facts cited.

Printed in the United States of America by Lightning Source, Inc.

Library of Congress Control Number (LCCN): 2018944199

ISBN: 978-1-939561-69-5 (hard cover: 560 pages, alk. paper)

JewishGen and the Yizkor-Books-in-Print Project

This book has been published by the **Yizkor-Books-in-Print Project,** as part of the **Yizkor Book Project** of **JewishGen, Inc.**

JewishGen, Inc. is a non-profit organization founded in 1987 as a resource for Jewish genealogy. Its website [www.jewishgen.org] serves as an international clearinghouse and resource center to assist individuals who are researching the history of their Jewish families and the places where they lived. JewishGen provides databases, facilitates discussion groups, and coordinates projects relating to Jewish genealogy and the history of the Jewish people. In 2003, JewishGen became an affiliate of the **Museum of Jewish Heritage - A Living Memorial to the Holocaust** in New York.

The **JewishGen Yizkor Book Project** was organized to make more widely known the existence of Yizkor (Memorial) Books written by survivors and former residents of various Jewish communities throughout the world. Later, volunteers connected to the different destroyed communities began cooperating to have these books translated from the original language— usually Hebrew or Yiddish—into English, thus enabling a wider audience to have access to the valuable information contained within them. As each chapter of these books was translated, it was posted on the JewishGen website and made available to the general public.

The **Yizkor-Books-in-Print Project** began in 2011 as an initiative to print and publish Yizkor Books that had been fully translated, so that hard copies would be available for purchase by the descendants of these communities and also by scholars, universities, synagogues, libraries, and museums.

These Yizkor books have been produced almost entirely through the volunteer effort of researchers from around the world, assisted by donations from private individuals. The books are printed and sold at near cost, so as to make them as affordable as possible. Our goal is to make this important genre of Jewish literature and history available in English in book form, so that people can have the personal histories of their ancestral towns on their bookshelves for themselves and for their children and grandchildren.

A list of all published translated Yizkor Books in the project with prices and ordering information can be found at:

http://www.jewishgen.org/Yizkor/ybip.html

Lance Ackerfeld, Yizkor Book Project Manager

Joel Alpert, Yizkor-Book-in-Print Project Coordinator

JewishGen
Yizkor Book Project

This book is presented by the
Yizkor Books in Print Project
Project Coordinator: Joel Alpert

Part of the
Yizkor Books Project of JewishGen, Inc.
Project Manager: Lance Ackerfeld

These books have been produced solely through volunteer effort
of individuals from around the world. The books are printed and
sold at near cost, so as to make them as affordable as possible.

Our goal is to make this history and important genre of Jewish
literature available in English in book form so that people can have
the near-personal histories of their ancestral towns on their bookshelves for themselves and for their children and grandchildren.

Any donations to the Yizkor Books Project are appreciated.

Please send donations to:
Yizkor Book Project
JewishGen
36 Battery Place
New York, NY 10280

JewishGen, Inc. is an affiliate of the
Museum of Jewish Heritage
A Living Memorial to the Holocaust

Foreword to the Translation

Radzivilov: Sefer zikaron is the Yizkor (memorial) Book for the Jewish community of Radzivilov, in present-day Ukraine. This translated edition contains 546 pages. It contains information on the town's institutions, organizations, buildings, and families as recounted by survivors and prewar emigrants, in addition to firsthand reports by survivors of the massacre and Jews who immigrated to Israel, sketches of the town's notable Jewish residents, and all the photographs and illustrations from the original yizkor book.

This translation was coordinated by the Kremenets Shtetl CO-OP (http://kehilalinks. jewishgen.org/Kremenets). A worldwide group of people who trace their ancestors to the towns of the Kremenets District in present-day Ukraine, the CO-OP is part of Jewish Records Indexing—Poland (JRI-Poland) and a project of the Kremenets District Research Group (co-coordinators: Ron Doctor and Sheree Roth).

The Kremenets Shtetl CO-OP translates records, yizkor books, cemetery gravestones, and other documents. When a translation is completed, we add all personal names, town names, and source information to the Indexed Concordance of Personal Names and Town Names, available at the website above.

Support Our Projects

The CO-OP is volunteer-based, but we use paid professional translators to accelerate some projects. You can help by donating time, money, or both. If you can read (or at least recognize) the Cyrillic and/or Hebrew alphabets and would like to help, please contact KremenetsDRG@gmail.com. To support our yizkor book projects, please see http://www.jewishgen.org/JewishGen-erosity and click the Yizkor Book Translation link. To support our records translation projects, please see http://jri-poland.org/support.htm.

Translation Acknowledgments

We are thankful to Marilyn Urwitz, who conceived of the idea of translating this book, funded many of the translations, and inspired her family members to join her in contributing to the project. We also thank the volunteer translators, especially Elizabeth Kessin Berman, who translated many of the Hebrew sections of the book. Ros Romem also contributed Hebrew translations, and Danielle Charak contributed a translation of the Yiddish table of contents. Tina Lunson did the bulk of the Yiddish translation, and Rivka Schiller (with aid from Judy Fixler), Mary Jane Shubow, and Yaacov David Shulman translated Hebrew sections.

We are indebted to all of them for their devoted work on the project. I take full responsibility for changes made and any damage done to their work.

Ellen Garshick
Board Member and Yizkor Book Translation Coordinator
Kremenets Shtetl CO-OP
A project of the Kremenets District Research Group

Map of Ukraine with Radzivilov Indicated

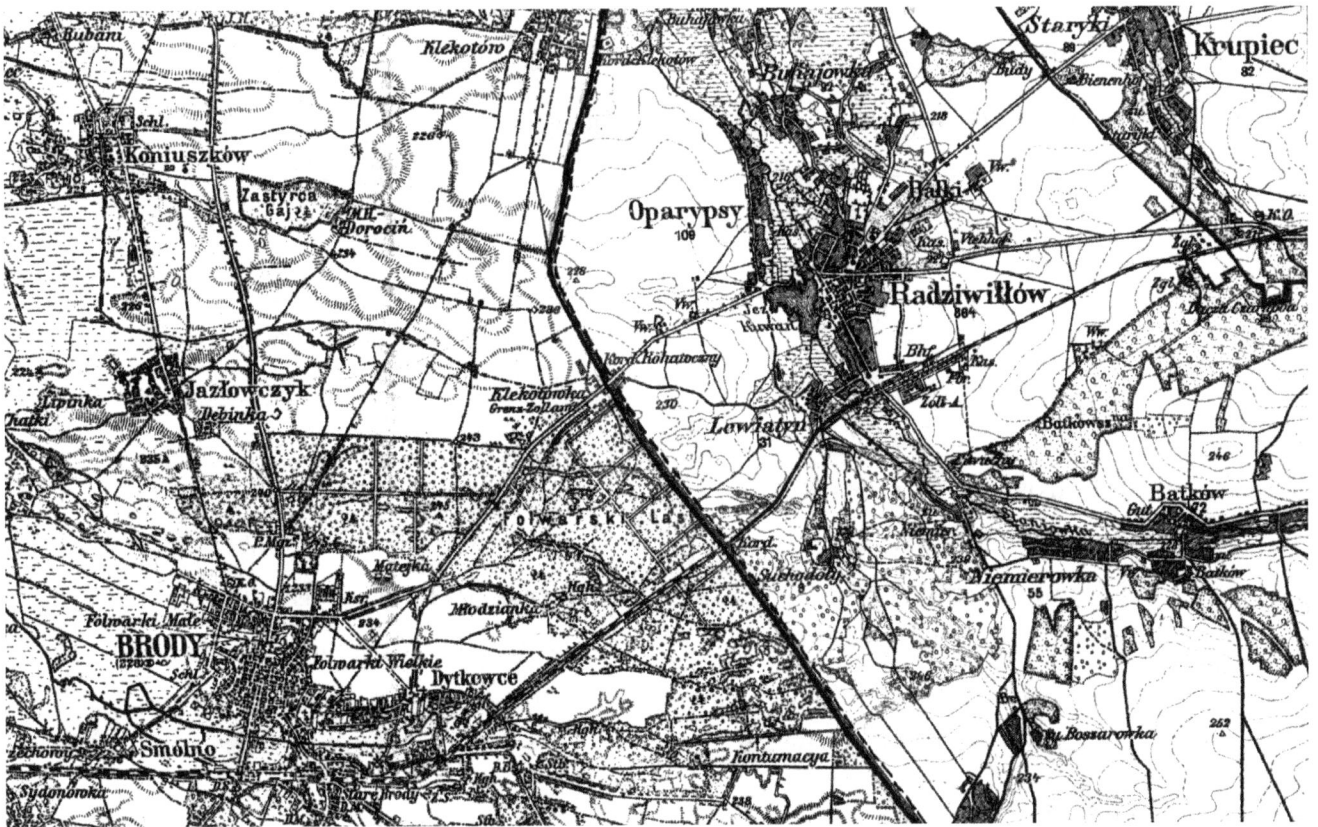

1915 Topographic Map showing Radziwillow. Topographic Maps of Eastern Europe, courtesy of mapywig.org.

Geopolitical Information

Radzivilov is located in present-day Ukraine (50°08' N 25°15' E), 29 miles southwest of Dubno, 21 miles west of Kremenets, and 6 miles northeast of Brody.

Alternate names for the town are Radyvyliv (Ukrainian), Chervonoarmeysk (Ukrainian), Chervonoarmeisk (Russian), Radziwiłłów (Polish), Rodvil (Yiddish), Radevil, Radvil, Radivil, Radzhivilov, Radzivilluv, and Radywyliw.

	Town	District	Province	Country
Before WWI (c. 1900)	Radzivilov	Kremenets	Volhynia	Russian Empire
Between the wars (c. 1930)	Radziwiłłów	Dubno	Wołyń	Poland
After WWII (c. 1950)	Chervonoarmeisk			Soviet Union
Today (c. 2000)	Radyvyliv			Ukraine

Nearby Jewish Communities:

Brody 6 miles SW

Leshniv 10 miles NW

Pochayev 13 miles SE

Shchurovychi 13 miles NW

Kozin 13 miles NE

Pidkamin 14 miles SSE

Stanislavchyk 16 miles W

Berestechko 16 miles NNW

Stremil'che 16 miles NNW

Velikiye Berezhtsy 16 miles E

Zavidche 18 miles NW

Lopatyn 19 miles WNW

Sokolivka 19 miles WSW

Mikolayuv 19 miles NW

Verba 19 miles ENE

Demydivka 20 miles N

Olesko 20 miles SW

About the Jewish Community of Radzivilov

The town's name indicates that it was connected to the Polish Prince of Radzivil's family, but it is not known when or by whom the town was founded. In 1775, there were 298 Jews there. By 1888, the number of residents was approximately 7,400, half of whom were Jewish. In 1897, there were 7,313 residents, including 4,322 Jews, who supported 2 synagogues and 14 small houses of prayer, a Jewish hospital, and a home for invalids. In 1921, Radzivilov's 4,240 residents included 2,036 (48%) Jews. In 1935, the entire population came to about 12,000, of which two thirds were Jews.

After the German occupation of the town in July 1941, a ghetto was established and divided into two parts: one for "useful" Jews and one for "not-use" Jews (those who were unable to work). The latter was liquidated by June 1942, and the former in October 1942. When Radzivilov was liberated in March 1944, only about 50 Jews had survived.

Notes to the Reader

We have tried to be consistent in transliterating Hebrew and Yiddish names in a way that allows the reader to work backward to the original spelling. We take full responsibility for changes to our translators' work.

We apologize ahead of time for the poor quality of images in the book. Often these images were scanned from the original yizkor books and were of poor quality to begin with, being copies of old photographs. Each transfer results in loss of quality. We have done our best given the original material and the resources and technology at hand. Even though images often appear of higher quality on computer screens, that does not transfer to high-quality images in print. The original scans are available on the web sites listed below.

Please note that all page number references within the text of the book refer to the page numbers of the original Yizkor Book. Within the text, "[page 34]" standing before a paragraph indicates that the material below is on page 34 of the original book. However, when a sentence is split between two pages in the original book, the marker is placed after the end of the sentence for ease of reading.

The original book can be seen online at the New York Public Library site:

http://yizkor.nypl.org/index.php?id=1872

or at the Yiddish Book Center site:

https://www.yiddishbookcenter.org/search/collection/%22NYPL-

Ydish%2520Book%2520Center%2520Yizkor%2520Book%2520Collection%22

To obtain a list of all Shoah victims from Radzivilov, please see the Yad Vashem web site listed below; one can also search for specific family names there. Much valuable information is available on this web site, including Pages of Testimony and other documents.

These lists are continually updated by Yad Vashem, so it is worthwhile to search them periodically.

http://yvng.yadvashem.org

A list of all books available in the Yizkor-Book-In-Print Project, along with prices, is available at:

http://www.jewishgen.org/Yizkor/ybip.html

Title Page of the Radzivilov Yizkor Book

ראדזיווילוב

ספר זכרון

הוצאת ארגון יוצאי ראדזיווילוב בישראל

תל־אביב תשכ״ז — 1966

Translation of the Title Page of the Radzivilov Yizkor Book

Radzivilov

Memorial Book

Published by the Organization of Radzivilov Emigrants in Israel

Tel Aviv 5727—1966

Table of Contents

Hebrew Section

Yiddish Section

[page 2]

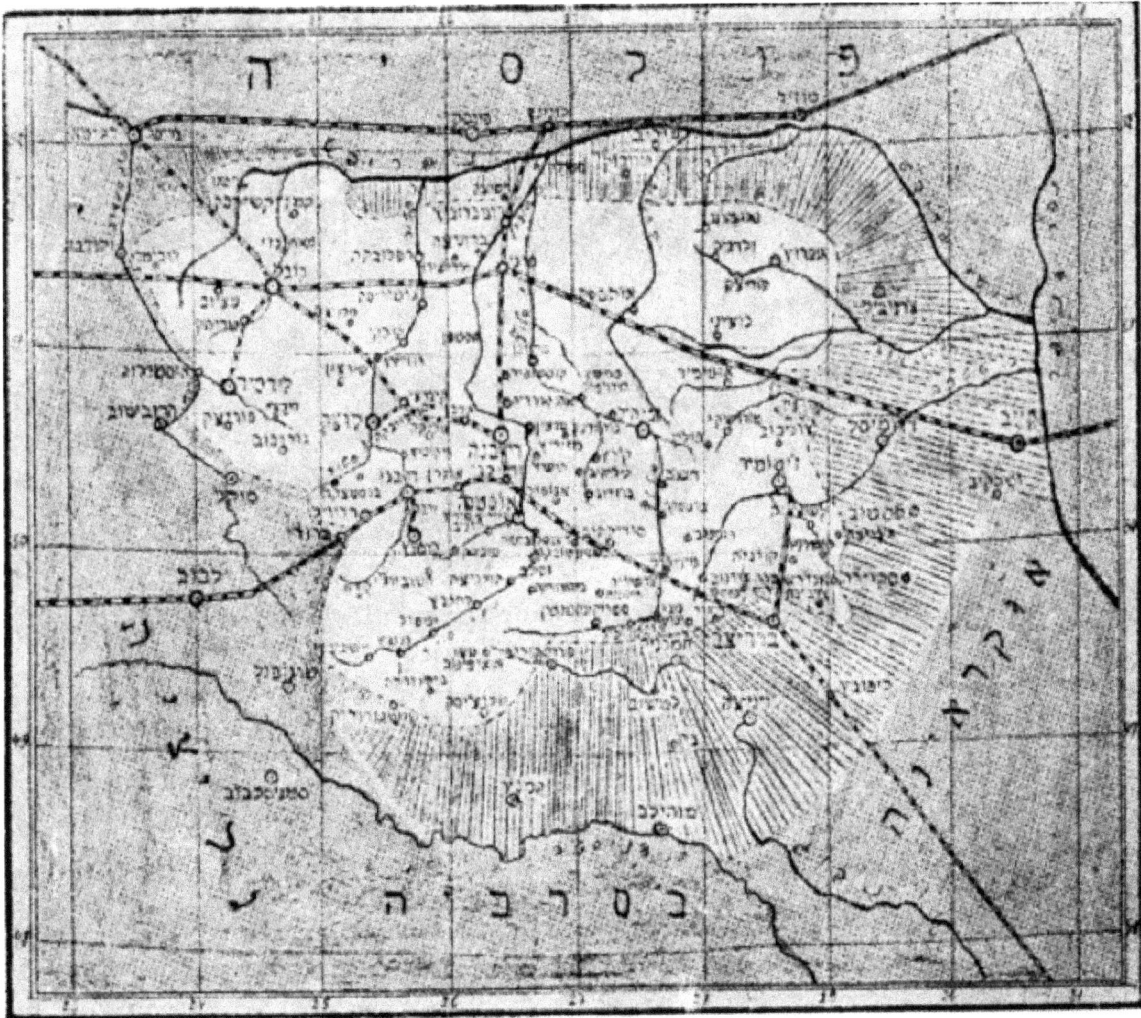

Map of Volhynia

In the Cemetery on Trumpeldor Street in Tel Aviv

[page 9]

Introduction*

The Editorial Board
25 Tishri 5727

When the first survivors of the massacre in our town arrived in the Land, they were like charred remnants from the flames. As with other communities of Israel in the Diaspora, the community of Jews from Radzivilov—Chervonoarmeysk, after it was conquered by the Soviets—an idea arose in the hearts of some of the townspeople who had settled in the Land to establish a memorial for our town's martyrs, those who were tortured and died at the hands of the cursed impure, the German Nazis and the Ukrainians who carried out their orders, many of whom were from the place and its surroundings, may their name and memory be obliterated forever.

In 1950, after many attempts, a monument was erected in the old cemetery on Trumpeldor Street in Tel Aviv in memory of Radzivilov's martyrs. Since then, every year, on 25 Tishri, the day of the community's final extermination in year 5703 on the Hebrew calendar, a memorial service is conducted there for the town's martyrs. (The first "action" was carried out on 13 Sivan 5702.)

But the monument is silent, its agony locked up within the marble. Jewish Radzivilov was a town that was full of life and bustling with activity. Even though it was not counted among the big cities of Volhynia, because of its location on a main thoroughfare, not walled and open, it stood out with its own uniqueness. We can say that the east and west winds converged there. Until World War I broke out, it served as a frontier and bridge town that connected Great Russia with the Kaiser's Austria, may his name be praised. During World War I, the town served as a frontline for different warring armies and was almost totally destroyed and burned down. Later it became an arena for the "Red" military battles in the war with "White"

---

* Translated from Hebrew by Mary Jane Shubow.

gangs and nationalistic Ukrainian plunderers. It went from hand to hand innumerable times until the Polish government was established there and refugees began to return, trying to build their lives anew. It was no longer the same Radzivilov from before the war. Nevertheless, a rehabilitation of new Jewish life occurred at that time with the establishment of cultural, social, and charitable institutions, and our young people gained an awareness of realizing the Zionist idea through pioneering activity and immigrating to Israel.

[page 10]

Suddenly, it was once again a town of mainly Jewish life, until it was wiped out when Poland was crushed under the feet of the bloodthirsty invader.

Here in the Land, there were a few people from Radzivilov who could not rest until they tried to revive memories of the community, insofar as they could, in a book of perpetual memory. When it was decided in 1960, Duvid Sheyn, of blessed memory, took the task on. Unfortunately, despite his strong will and great devotion to the matter, only a few of the 200 families who were related to those from our town lent a hand to the project, whether in spirit or materially. One year followed another, and the gap between the vision and its realization remained wide. When Duvid Sheyn fell to his knees on Rosh Hashanah 5725, still in his prime, his friends swore on his grave to realize his big dream, which was closer to his heart than anything else was.

A small group of friends prepared themselves and became the Publication Committee for Radzivilov's memorial book. They began to work with a stubborn determination to keep working until the book was published. Two years have passed since then, and now we have it. We have fulfilled our sacred duty to our martyrs' memory as much as we could and as much as possible. The pages of this book bear witness and put into words the blood-pact between us and our dear ones, whose blood was absorbed into the killing pits. No monument marks their burial site; there is no grave.

We know, yes we know, that more is missing from the book than is in it. The period between the two wars was neglected—the time under Polish rule, when most of those who came from the town and are living with us were actually there. Some of them left as children, and some grew up there. It is for them and their descendants that this book has been created. That is why we were pained that only a few answered our repeated requests to write down their memories of their days and deeds. And even though that part is missing, many chapters were written in their place about public institutions, ideological movements, and personal experiences, including descriptions of activities that blessed our town. It is appropriate that all of this is memorialized in the book.

As for the list of martyrs, we are certain that many names are missing. There are two reasons for this: one is the great number of families from which no one remained, neither here in Israel nor in any other country; and the other, despite our repeated requests, is that only a few responded and gave us lists of their relatives who perished in the massacre.

[page 11]

Therefore, the one who must be blessed is our friend Arye-Leyb Ayzen, whose amazing memory retrieved a great many names from everlasting oblivion, memorializing them in the book. Their names will reside forever beneath the heavenly throne, along with those anonymous ones who were also wiped out with them in the pits.

We hereby express our gratitude to all those who contributed, both spiritually and materially, to everyone who was generous of heart on behalf of this valuable and holy deed: to Mr. Tsvi Zagoroder, without whose determination this project would not have been possible. We are grateful to him for his limitless devotion, his handling of everything big and small, and his concern over the years. We are grateful to Mr. Arye-Leyb Ayzen, who was active and faithfully assisted us in this work; to Mrs. Rachel Gurman; to Mr. M. Korin; to Mr. M. Landis; to Mr. B. Felman, who guided us with his advice and collected and edited some of the material; to Mr. Tsvi Saley, who translated manuscripts written in Yiddish; and to Mr. Yakov Adini, editor of the book, who lent his vitality to make something whole from pieces and fragments and whose good taste stood him in good stead in the work he did with a loving heart—may everyone be blessed.

Soviet-era memorial at site of the Radzivilov massacre,
©2010 by Ryszard Antolak,
https://poetrania.blogspot.com/2010/10/return-to-radziwillow.html.
Courtesy of the photographer.

[This photo was not in the original Yizkor Book]

[page 12]

Chapters from the Past

Rabbi Yisrael Ba'al Shem Tov*

Amir Gilboa

Rabbi Yisrael Ba'al Shem Tov
By the clay pits

the One above had no pity.
Therefore, Israel returned to the clay pits.

The snow covered the clay pits already
and covered the horse and covered the carriage
and there is no longer a clay pit. And his voice swiftly
and soon, like a wheel
in the snowy wilderness, enveloping like a prayer shawl
a single nation in the land.

He will cover his face in the flap of his cloak;
in the snowy wilderness, enveloping like a prayer shawl.
And his tears fall. And roses blossom
and their image is like that of a temple. And their image is like that of
doves.
And their image is like that of Hannah on [her] seven sons.†
And their image is like that of a candelabra with its seven branches.
And their image is like that of red rubies within the prayer shawl
that envelopes the nation, who worships happily
an incorporeal deity
who fades into the oblivion.

From his eye, a boiling tear
falls into the clay pits.

And his fingers knead, knead the clay.

[Blank]

---

* Translated from Hebrew by Rivka Schiller with Judy Fixler.

† *Translator's note:* This refers to Chana in the Book of Maccabees, who martyred
herself along with her seven sons.

[page 15]

History of the Jews in Radzivilov*

Dr. N. M. Gelber

The town's name points to the fact that its beginning was connected to the Prince of Radzivil's family, but it is not known when or by whom the town was founded.

The proximity of Brody hampered Radzivilov's growth. It is known that Ignacy Malchevsky was the town's owner in 1775, and Miyonchinsky inherited the town afterward. General Gaetan Miyonchinsky, a member of this family, obtained a permit to establish a printing house for Hebrew and Yiddish books on February 19, 1787.

During General Miyonchinsky's lifetime, the town owed the Warszawa banker Shults considerable sums, and after the town became his, he did a great deal to further its growth. When he owned the town, the renowned tannery was founded by Parisot, based on a permit from King Stanislaw August dated July 24, 1789.

The ownership of the town passed from Shults to the nobleman Gorzhynski.

In 1775 there were 298 Jews in the town.

In 1772, when Brody was transferred to Austrian possession, the trade route, which until then had gone through Brody, went to Radzivilov for only a brief time, even though Poland made every effort to draw tradesmen from Brody to Radzivilov by giving them all kinds of incentives. Only after some time did the tradesmen of Brody begin to send large quantities of merchandise via Radzivilov. And so Yitschak Tishminitski and Moshe Danovits of Brody sent large quantities of salt from Brody via Radzivilov, and from there they brought crops to Brody that they sent to Germany. Also, Brody whole-

---

* Translated from Hebrew by Mary Jane Shubow.
Note in original: See also "The Town and Its History," page 19.

salers Leyzer Bik and Fayvel Herts sent large quantities of salt to Lithuania via Radzivilov.

[page 16]

In 1788, some Jews from Brody, among them Duvid Asherovich, who was known as a lead, medical products, and graphite merchant, founded a gunpowder factory. It is not known how long this factory existed.

The first printing house already existed in 1818, when *Haredim, A New Collection*, by Rabbi Yosef, son of Mordekhay of Kremenets, and *Midrash Shmuel* on *Ethics of the Fathers* were both published.

At the beginning of 1819, the printer Yehonatan left the town, leaving his place open "for the famous, exalted rabbinic exalted person," our teacher the rabbi Pinchas son of Asher Zelig Barats. He purchased typographic material for the printer in the town of Poritzk and then enriched it with various letters. With the help of expert workers, he completed the printing of five sections of *Chok L'Yisrael* during 1819.[*] After completing this book, he published an expensive edition of *The Kuzari* and also a second section of *Sifre* with *Zera Avraham*'s commentary.

Due to competition from printers in Slavuta, the printer had to stop working, and he sold the rights to publish the book *Chok L'Yisrael* to the printer R' Aharon son of Yone. He sold the typographic material to Rabbi Yakov Finkelman of Berdichev. In one of the two printing houses that existed in this town, a prayer book containing Hasidic prayers and intentions was printed under the supervision of Rabbi Avraham Yehoshue Heshil of Opatów.[†]

---

[*] *Translation editor's note:* Chok L'Yisrael (Law of Israel) is a compendium of Jewish texts designed for daily or weekly study. *The Kuzari* is a work of the medieval Spanish Jewish philosopher and poet Rabbi Yehuda Halevi, completed around 1140. *Sifre* (books) refers to either of two works of classical Jewish legal Biblical exegesis. *Zera Avraham* is a commentary on *Sifre* by Avraham Lichtstein, rabbi of Plonsk in the 18th century.

[†] *Note in original:* See also "The Printing House in Radzivilov," page 35.

During the Polish rebellion of 1830-1831, General Dvernitski's army corps operated in the vicinity of Radzivilov, with the support of the Radzivilov Jews.

In the years 1832–1835, merchandise worth approximately 15,000 rubles passed through Radzivilov, which benefited from the free city of Brody, a commercial center.

In 1870, 1,077 houses and 2,864 residents were counted in the town, but the number of Jews among them is not known. By 1888, the number of residents had grown to approximately 7,400, half of whom were Jewish. In 1897, there were 7,313 residents, including 4,322 Jews.

In 1910, there was a Jewish school in the town that included a class for crafts, a women's school, a Talmud Torah, and a number of cheders run by private teachers. There were also 2 synagogues and 14 houses of prayer, a Jewish hospital, and a home for invalids.

Most of the Jews, who owned 124 stores, worked in commerce. They also owned three candle factories, a brick factory, a lime furnace, and a flour-mill. Twenty-four different craftsmen were counted in the town—all of whom were Jews.

[page 17]

Market Street in Radzivilov before World War I

With the outbreak of World War I in 1914, Cossacks from a border corps conducted searches among the Jews, and while they were at it, they robbed and looted everything in their way. They also beat and arrested Jews, and some Jewish families were exiled to Siberia.

The town, which went back and forth between the Russians and the Austrians several times, suffered during the war years. A large part of the town was destroyed, and only a few Jewish residents remained. It was easier for the Jews during the Austrian occupation. The occupation authorities let them choose a community leader. At that time, Mr. Zaks was chosen as the head.

After the revolution, the Jews began to return to the town, and life began to return to normal. A democratic community was organized, and Mr. Moshe-Duvid Balaban was chosen as its chairman. Public life continued to develop—and then uprisings and changes in authority harmful to the Jews began. A group called Haganah [self-defense] was set up to protect the Jewish residents' property and honor. And indeed, the Haganah was very effective in carrying out its mission, especially when the authorities were changing, times that were always a cause of concern and constant fear.

This situation continued until the Polish armies conquered the region. The Jews hoped that now a stable and progressive government would arrive, but they were quickly disappointed. General Haller's soldiers began to torture the Jews, cutting off their sidecurls and beards, hitting and insulting them, humiliating and degrading them.

[page 18]

Fortunately, this situation lasted for only a short time. With the stabilization of the government, things improved, and life returned to normal for the most part.

In 1921, when Poland was independent, the number of Radzivilov residents was 4,240, including 2,036 (48%) Jews. In 1935, the entire population came to about 12,000, of which two thirds were Jews.

[page 19]

The Town and Its History[*]

Radzivilov is a border town on the Slovenya (Slonuvka) River, Kremenets district, 26 versts[†] from Pochayev, 5 versts from Krupets, 3 versts southwest of the Radzivilov train station, and 283 versts from Zhitomir, situated on a straight line with the city of Brody.

In 1870, there were 1,077 households in Radzivilov and 2,864 residents, of whom 79% were Jews (today the population is more than 7,400). There were a Pravoslavic church and a small chapel, a Catholic church, two Jewish synagogues, nine study halls, a grade-A customs house, a postal and telegraph office, three candle factories, a brick factory, a lime furnace, a flourmill, 124 stores, 248 craftsmen, and two market areas.

In 1876, merchandise worth 4,377,224 rubles was exported abroad via the local customs house, and merchandise worth 3,323,190 rubles was imported. In the past, local tradesmen had carried out smuggling deals on a large scale ....

The train station is on the railroad line that goes from Zdolbunov up to the Galician border and connects with the Galician Karl Ludwig Road, 85 versts from Zdolbunov.

Radzivilov, the town's name, shows that its beginning is connected to the noblemen of the House of Radzivil, who had family connections with King John III and possessed considerable estates in Ukraine. It is not known who placed the town's foundations or why. In any event, it is clear that the settlement is not from ancient times, and its proximity to Brody allowed the town to grow as it should have. In 1775, when the town had 146 houses, its

---

[*] Translated from Hebrew by Mary Jane Shubow.
Note in original: From Geographical *Dictionary of the Kingdom of Poland and other Slavic Countries,* edited by Bronisław Chlebowski, Władysław Walewski, volume 9, page 76, Warszawa 1888.

[†] *Note in original:* Verst—a Russian measurement of length equivalent to 1.06 kilometers.

owner was Ignacy Malchevsky, head of the ministerial office. Afterward, it was inherited by the sons of Ignacy Malchevsky. One of them, General Kayetan Miyonchinsky, received a permit to establish a printing house for Hebrew and Yiddish books on February 10, 1787.

[page 20]

General Miyonchinsky's property was repossessed by his creditors during his lifetime after he lost and wasted it all on card games and drinking. Radzivilov fell to his primary lender, the Warszawa banker Karl Shults, who did a great deal to contribute to its growth. At that time, the famous tannery was founded here by Piotr Parisot in accordance with a permit of July 24, 1789, which he received from King Stanisław August. Radzivilov went from Shults's ownership to the Turan family, and then to today's owner, Graf Gorzynski. On July 1, 1863, a military battalion struck camp near Radzivilov under Jozef Vysotsky's command. Vysotsky had come from Galicia with the intention of penetrating Volhynia.

[page 21]

Radzivilov, My Hometown*

Duvid Sheyn, of Blessed Memory

I recall vividly my childhood in the town of Radzivilov. So much so that my family tells me that I remember things that occurred even before I was born. I don't know if this is true, but the town, its appearance, its surroundings, and its lifestyle are rooted deeply in my heart and have sustained me since my childhood.

I imagine that, to get a correct understanding of Radzivilov's unique significance, it is important to know two things about the town. First, Radzivilov was a border town, and it had a central customs house. In czarist Russia, there were six customs houses, and one of them was in Radzivilov. Because of its geographic location, it was a convenient place for foreign trade. Goods, in particular grain, chickens, eggs, and similar products, were sent from Russia to western lands in great quantities. Many wealthy Jews were involved in this type of export, and they prospered greatly. They not only exported goods, but they were also involved in importing all sorts of products, particularly manufactured goods. The town also supported many agencies that were devoted to trade and tax issues, and these compatibly employed many clerks. Twice a day, from 10:00 to12:00 AM and from 6:00 to 8:00 PM, the railroad station would quake with a rumble of noise.

[page 22]

Trains would come and go with the flow of riders. Many Jews were associated either directly or indirectly with this stream of activity, making their living this way. In addition to the train station, there was also what was called the "small" border, with only a four-kilometer separation between

---

* Translated from Hebrew by Elizabeth Kessin Berman.

Radzivilov and the Austrian border; and from there to Brody was another five kilometers. And so many Jews found they could earn a living there, too. Because the surrounding area was relatively small, travelers would engage in the free flow of trade, and this, too, was a good source of income.

Because our town was a border town until World War I, there was always a large border patrol, a patrol of Cossacks and regular army. Of course, their presence offered another source of income, as well as a sense of security for Jewish merchants and their workers. So Radzivilov was a place of prosperity, peace, and culture.

The second reason for Radzivilov's importance was that the Radzivilov Jews benefited from the presence of a very wealthy man named Moshe-Mendil Ginzberg. He actually lived in Petersburg (Leningrad, today), but his aging mother lived in Radzivilov, and he was very attached to her. His brother, Shmuel Mes, and his family also lived in Radzivilov, as did additional relatives. Ginzberg, or simply "Moshe-Mendil," as they called him, would visit his family frequently, and his visits were considered festivals in Radzivilov. Although his mother, Rosye, of blessed memory, would frequently give charity with outstretched arms, and many families would exist exclusively on her charity, when Moshe-Mendil came to the town, the charity and aid were even greater. It is correct to say that Moshe-Mendil supported many families.

Therefore, the two circumstances described above were the reasons for the economic stability of the Jews of Radzivilov. But in this town, which was not very large, there were also important factories, such as a button factory, founded by the sons of Ginzberg's brothers; a chair factory owned by Zundel Zaks; two candle factories—one belonging to Goldgardt-Liberman and the other to Stroyman-Brandvayn; and also a brewery.

It appears that this was a town with a very good economy. There were also beautiful houses, not only on the main street, Alifov Street, but also on the rest of the streets. There were beautiful boulevards with carriages in the current fashion. All this influenced the public spirit, and even humble Jews were not considered beggars.

[page 23]

Button Factory

Interior of the Button Factory

[page 24]

In the town, there were also two clubs: one social club called "Grozhdin-sky," in Mokhan the pharmacist's home, and the other for chess, in Yone Sheyn's home. But these were not the only places for culture in the town.

Even before World War I, there were many active Zionist organizations, which sold *shekalim*;[*] shares for the Colonial Bank; Zionist literature, including the newspaper called *Hatsefira;* and other publications in Hebrew. And in connection with our accounting of the Jewish residents who were not quite so famous, we must mention the town's Hebrew teachers: Sender Sefarim, who was known by the nickname Sender the Reader because of his work as the Torah reader at the Great Synagogue; R' Ayzik Shtof, a pedagogical wonder; Katz (whose first name I don't remember), who was considered the best modern teacher; Binyamin Finkelshteyn; and Avigdor Melman, also known as Avigdor the Writer, who primarily taught young girls. A little later, Avraham-Yehuda Polak came to the town from Berestechko. Binyamin Finkelshteyn and Avraham-Yehuda were both pioneers in establishing Hebrew courses for adults.

Numerous children continued their education in larger cities in the area: Dubno, Kremenets, Rovno. Other parents sent their children to cities farther afield to study at special Jewish schools. For example, I traveled to Warszawa to study in a school of trade run by Krinski, while Moshe Goldgardt's sons studied at the Kagan Gymnasium in Vilna. After the outbreak of World War I, the Kagan Gymnasium moved to Yekaterinoslav, and I got my diploma there. One fellow from Radzivilov even studied at the Hertzeliya High School in Tel Aviv.[†] There was a great emphasis on continuing education according to the social politics of the day. The general cultural level of the whole population was so high that it naturally created a strong desire to educate the young. If you take into account the small number of young people in relation to the general Jewish population in the town, there were a great many institutions for the young. There were, for example, two elementary schools that were free for all students, one for boys and one for girls,

---

[*] *Translation editor's note: Shekalim* were tokens of membership in the Zionist Organization.

[†] *Note in original:* That was Mordekhay Peker, of blessed memory, who has since left the country and was a member of Degania.—Translator

under the direction of Mrs. Sverska. It is obvious that any child could receive a basic education.

Because the level of literacy in the town was so high, there was a flurry of activity relating to the question of political socialism. In this small community, there were, apart from the Zionists, many different factions devoted to varying degrees of political interest, including the Bund, the Labor Zionists, and others. The youth of the town did not much follow these other groups in great numbers, calling them the "black shirts," but they would read and consider them and even weigh their political theories.

[page 25]

And in fact, a story about one "Bundovka" (Bundist) was spread by the heart and soul of the movement. It says that during a lengthy dispute, the simple fellow said, "Woe is me because of my hatred of Nicholas (meaning the Russian czar)—he is my father and my mother."

Elementary School before World War I

Let us not forget to praise the scholars who instructed us and greatly influenced our understanding of Israel. It was out of the question that any young boy would not start out in a cheder for beginners. Two of them, I recall, were with R' Mikhel the Teacher (with whom I studied) and the other, with R' Zalman-Hirsh. After that, together with my friend Beni Gili, I went to R' Yisrael-Yone's cheder, and in this cheder we learned Torah and Rashi. At this level there was also R' Aba, whose teaching was a little more modern, as in a modern cheder. After that I went to R' Mordekhay Naftali's, who was the second cantor, or as they say, the deputy cantor, at the Great Synagogue. He taught Bible. After him, I studied Talmud and commentary with R' Dotsi the Teacher, who was considered a modern teacher. I studied with him in the summer months when I would come home from Warszawa for my yearly vacation. For sure, I had already acquired a good education, and I couldn't have learned more from these teachers, but I recalled in later years who the most important teachers were considered to be: R' Aharele, who in his last years lived in the community home for the poor, with his students supporting him.

[page 26]

I remember him because my brother Fayvish was one of his students, and I was dispatched to bring him packages from our home; and R' Ayzik-Leyb, the most honored sage, whose dwelling was adjacent to Great Synagogue, on the other side of R' Itsikel the righteous, of blessed memory.

Trade School before World War I

Social Aid Organizations

Although Ginzberg founded many welfare organizations, much of the effort for social welfare fell on the shoulders of the many town residents, and both simple folks and people of means and prestige avidly opened their hearts, rising admirably to support the aid organizations. An example was the community home for the poor. The home had a bad reputation in many Diaspora towns, but not in Radzivilov. The old and the poor believed strongly in this type of aid agency.

[page 27]

But because Radzivilov was a border town, we had a particular challenge to social aid: our town had become a transit point for the great numbers of émigrés streaming to America. They stole across the border to Brody in Austrian Galicia, and from Brody, the way would be clear straight to Hamburg or Antwerp. There they would connect with aid agencies, which would help them continue on to their chosen destination. But many of the emigrants were sick—eye conditions in particular—and the destination countries prohibited them from entering. Many of them returned to Brody, where the Austrian police apprehended them and transferred them to the Russian police in Radzivilov. And from there they were sent to "Atap," or in other words, under guard from place to place, most of the time on foot, apart from the elderly and the ill, who were carried in wagons. The elderly naturally would remember this suffering as a punishment worse than death (for themselves), especially for weak children. There were cases in which a family's children had applied for and received entry visas, but one child was refused entry. Certainly, in Radzivilov people tried to help those who had been left behind as orphans. But we often had to request entry visas from governments that were very far way, and we also had to petition governments that had blocked their emigration. They were put up in homes—singles and sometimes entire families. I remember that for an extended time a young girl of about six to eight years old stayed with us until we could connect with her grandfather, who eventually came to collect her.

Religious Life

We revered religious life. But we were not as sophisticated as those who came from Poland and their towns. Most of our residents followed traditional Judaism. Sources confirm that the Great Synagogue had stood for 104 years, from its founding in 1811 to 1915, when an explosion was set off by the command of an Austrian officer during World War I. After the war, Ginzberg erected a stone building on the same foundation. But it wasn't like the original building. The original building was quite magnificent. It was created in the style of wooden synagogues, but it rivaled that of buildings made of mortar. It rose four stories high and had a dazzling ark, a large and high pulpit, fancy and solid furniture, and a huge chandelier with many branches shimmering like silver. This was raised and lowered, and in the middle of it all was a large, luxurious candelabrum. On the two sides of the ark were special seats of honor, separated from everything else. There was one for the "government" rabbi, and one for the "new" rabbi. On the walls were paintings taken from Biblical subjects.

[page 28]

The cupola was devoted to the 12 signs of the zodiac. It was truly a Solomon's temple.

There is a special place for the holidays in my memory. In particular, I recall the Days of Awe and the image of Kol Nidre evening, when the joyous and reverent worshipers prepared themselves for the Day of Judgment. Cantor Yankel Zvihiler* would ascend the pulpit looking entirely like an angelic messenger, his beard full and white, looming large among the congregation. The entire congregation was gathered and waiting in anticipation. Suddenly, a loud knock like Solomon's thunder was heard from the *prots*† in his hand, and the cantor's voice intoned Kol Nidre. Certainly, the Kol Ni-

---

* *Note in original:* That is, he was from Zvihil, or Novograd Volynskiy.
† *Note in original:* A kind of heavy bat with a handle made especially for this purpose.

dre prayer was chanted everywhere, but in the Great Synagogue of Radzivilov, it was something spectacular.

There were many study halls in town. First, there was the Spanish Synagogue, which was very close to the ancient burial ground, where the old Jewish settlement existed many hundreds of years ago, even before the Spanish expulsion. Mainly "aristocrats" worshipped there. And there were the Great Synagogue, the Barani synagogue, the Ostra *kloyz,*[*] the Tailors' Synagogue, the Zamd Synagogue, and many other houses of worship associated with rabbis: R' Chayim the righteous, of blessed memory (the "old" rabbi); R' Itsikel; R' Levi; R' Yosele; the Turiysk Hasidim; the Olik Hasidim; R' Zisi Kopf (I don't know the origin of this name); and more. These, then, are the many synagogues and study halls of Radzivilov, and they all were always full of worshipers.

This is what was going on until 1914, when World War I broke out.

Girls' high school, possibly *pro-gymnasium*, summer 1917. Background banner has socialist slogans ("Long live the Democratic Republic. Long live the 8-hour work day. Long live the Socialist International," from the February Revolution of 1917. Banner at right says, "Proletarians of all countries unite," and is signed "Jewish Social-Democratic Workers' Party Poalei Zion."
Courtesy of David Kushner. Kushner's mother, Sarah Zimmerman, is the girl in second row, just behind the short lady with the straw hat. [This photograph as not in the original book.]

---

* *Translation editor's note: Kloyz is Yiddish for a small study hall or synagogue.*

The Life of the Jews in Radzivilov*

Tsvi Zagoroder

The town of Radzivilov, whose name the Soviets changed to "Krasno Armeysk," was located three kilometers from the Austrian border and about eight kilometers from Brody in eastern Galicia. In 1765, about 300 Jews lived there. The official census from 1875 counted the Jewish community of Radzivilov as 3,054 souls, and according to the residents' census of 1887, there were 4,322 Jews in the town among a population of 7,312 residents.

Group of Hebrew School Teachers and Students

After World War I, when the town's refugees returned to their homes, the population of Radzivilov grew to about 12,000, of whom about two thirds were Jewish.

Radzivilov served for a long time as a gate of Jewish immigration from Czarist Russia to the larger world, primarily to the United States of America. Because of the pogroms of 1882–1883—storms in the *negev*†—and the

---

* Translated from Hebrew by Mary Jane Shubow.

† *Translation editor's note:* Jews referred to these pogroms as "storms in the *negev*," *negev* meaning south.

pogroms of 1904–1907, the flow of emigration kept increasing, and many fled through the town across the border to continue on to their destinations. Many were also revolutionaries, liberal authors, and others who fled the persecution of the reactionary czarist government in their country.

The Jewish community always constituted the majority of the town's residents, and among them were families of distinguished lineage who were deeply rooted in the life of the place.

[page 30]

The First Zionist Youth Organization in Radzivilov in 1910. Seated, right to left: 1) Finkelshteyn, 2) Marder, 3) ..., 4) Rayzer, 5) .... Standing, row A: 1) Grinberg, 2) Menachem Goldgart, 3) Ben-Tsion Betlin, 4) sister Gluzman, 5) Finkelshteyn, 6) .... Standing, row B: 1) ..., 2) Zilberman, 3) Tsvi Gluzman, 4) Gluzman, 5) Leviten.

The local intelligentsia was nourished by big cities nearby in both Russia and Galicia. Commerce was well developed, and most of it belonged to the Jews. The central customs house in the town served as a source of abundant income for many families, some of whom had great wealth.

In Radzivilov there were a few cheders, where the children of Israel learned Hebrew and Jewish studies, and two Jewish government schools: one for young boys and one for young girls, and also a progymnasium for girls. Some wealthy people used to send their children to study in Dubno, Kremenets, and Rovno.

[page 31]

Radzivilov also had an active political life. A Zionist Organization was established in the town at the beginning of the current century. It operated underground in the days of the czar, but from 1917 on, when the revolution broke out, the organization appeared in the open among the rest of the parties, which increased their activities in Jewish areas. Zionist activity continued to grow, primarily under Polish rule: movements and parties multiplied—Youth Guard, Freedom, the Revisionists, and many others appeared. A farm for training pioneers in agriculture was also established in town.

As part of the Zionist endeavor, the Tarbut School's establishment must be mentioned, in which instruction was totally in Hebrew from 1924 on. Many of its students received special training and immigrated to the Land.

There were also many important public institutions in town, such as a hospital and an invalid home, and 16 synagogues, including our glorious and grand Great Synagogue.

Rabbi Itsikel of Radzivil[*]

Ben-Chayim

(From the book *Israel's Right—Ten Lights* by Yisrael son of Yitschak Simche. Petrikov Printing, 5667.)

Rabbi Yechiel Mikhel, the *magid* of Złoczów (born in 5486 [1726]), passed away on 25 Elul 5546 [1786]), was the son of the righteous R' Yitschak Drobitsher, and was one of the BEShT's young students.[†] After the BEShT's death, he traveled to the *magid* of Mezhirichi. He had five sons, all eminent Torah scholars. Hasidim called them the *magid*'s Five Books of the Torah.

---

[*] Translated from Hebrew by Mary Jane Shubow.

[†] *Translation editor's note:* BEShT stands for Baal Shem Tov (master of the good Name), Rabbi Yisrael son of Eliezer, a Jewish mystical rabbi who is considered to founder of Hasidic Judaism.

They are R' Volf of Zbaraz, **R' Yitschak of Radzivil**, R' Moshe of Zvihil, R' Mordekhay of Kremenets, and R' Yosef of Yampol.

Some of R' Yitschak of Radzivil's interpretations of Ethics of the Fathers and works, collected under the name *Or Yitschak* [Light of Yitschak], appear in the prayer book *Harei Besamim*, by R' Yeshaye Moshkat, head of the rabbinical court of the Holy Community of Praga near Warszawa, and son-in-law of R' Itsikel, the righteous one, of blessed memory.

[page 32]

During a third Shabbat meal, when R' Itsikel was sitting with others around the table, he said that his father, the holy rabbi and teacher Yechiel Mikhel of Złoczów, of blessed memory, came to him in a dream during a Sabbath afternoon nap and said to him: "Did you know, my beloved son, the explanation of what is written [Gen: 38:11] 'And Judah said to Tamar his daughter-in-law, sit as a widow in your father's household until my son Shelah grows up'?"

He answered, "I did not know its meaning." And he explained it when he woke up: "**And Judah said**—He, the Holy One, blessed be He, has a name of four letters—**to Tamar his daughter-in-law**—she is the gathering of Israel—**sit as a widow in your father's household**—we were, being Israel in the Diaspora—**until my son Shelah grows up**—are the initials of *Hamachazir Shekhinati Letsion*, that which returns my Divine spirit to Zion, and the final letters of *yitgadaL veyitkadaSH shmayaH,* magnified and sanctified is His Name."*

The copier said: One day during the counting of the *omer* in 5725, I went through the gates of the Rambam Library in Tel Aviv to ask about R' Itsikel's teachings. I found the book *Ten Lights*, in which the author also included *From His Awesome Steps* by R' Itsikel, of blessed memory. After I copied the section presented above, written in the margin of the page, I

---

* *Translation editor's note:* In Hebrew, the first letters of the words in the phrases in boldface are H-Sh-L and L-Sh-H, the same as the letters highlighted in the final two Hebrew phrases.

found the date of the public celebration of his holy memory, 11 Iyar, may his soul be bound up in the bond of everlasting life.

Late that evening, when I sat down to copy the words onto a clean page, I was suddenly struck in a flash by the date 11 Iyar: indeed, that day was 11 Iyar! And all those Jews on whose behalf the author of *Ten Lights* wrote down the date of the public celebration of R' Itsikel's memory, as the observance of a commandment, where are they now? Suddenly I felt that the entire world was empty, and my soul was turbulent. I left the house and walked in the fields for a long time. Later, I returned home, and everyone was already sleeping. I put a skullcap on my head, stood in a corner of the wall facing east, and silently said Kaddish. Afterward, I even soiled my lips with two drops of brandy—for the ascent of his righteous soul with those who followed him, sleeping in eternal sleep. May God avenge their blood.
[page 33]

RYB"L in Radzivilov, 1807–1813[*]

The father of the Enlightenment in Russia, the scribe R' Yitschak Ber Levinzon (RYB"L, 1788-1860), was born in Kremenets and worked there for most of his life, apart from the years 1807–1823, which he spent away from the town, although he returned to the city and died there. From 1807 to1813, he lived in Radzivilov. The following is from a section in *A Short History of Modern Hebrew Literature,* by Y. Klausner, on RYB"L's years in Radzivilov.

In 1807, when RYB"L was 19, he married a woman from Radzivilov, which was near the Austrian border, and moved there. At the beginning, RYB"L loved his wife, but later there was discord, and he immediately divorced her against her wishes. It was heard that, out of anger, his wife tried to poison him before the divorce because he stopped loving her. But he did not marry again for the rest of his life (from this marriage, there was only one son, who died in infancy).

In Radzivilov, which was under Russian and Austrian control before the Polish liberation—and therefore was an educated city, and like every such

[*] Translated from Hebrew by Elizabeth Kessin Berman.

city had traffic, life, and great influence from the many who crossed the border—there was great opportunity for RYB"L, because he could learn not only Russian but also German. He also learned French, Latin, and a little Greek there. He worked as a private teacher, and in 1812, when the French were fighting in Russia, he was an official translator; that is, he was appointed to translate letters from Hebrew and Yiddish to Russian for the government and the army under the command of General Giers, then the commander of the local Radzivilov garrison. RYB"L excelled in his work as a translator, and Giers was very pleased. Also at that time, he began to write *First Fruits of the Pen*—poems and letters, a few of which appeared in the pamphlet *The Scribe's Topics*. At the end of 1812, he composed "Heroic Torment," a poem of praise for Russia's victory in the war against France. Giers sent the poem to the minister of internal affairs—and RYB"L was regarded favorably by the Russian government.

[page 34]

This was the first connection between RYB"L and the Russian government, a connection that was valuable to him for the rest of his life, and especially during his final days, when the government supported him with the sum of 3,000 rubles in memory of *Poems*, in which RYB"L praises the motherland's government in 1812.

But RYB"L's hard work in learning languages, reading widely, and translating led to a nervous breakdown, and to recover from his illness, he went to Brody, the center of the Enlightenment for the Jews in Galicia, in 1813, at the age of 25, after he had finished his work for the Franco-Russian War.

The Printing House in Radzivilov[*]

In the town of Radzivilov, which is in the Kremenets district, a printing house already existed in 5578 [1818], and in that same year *Charedim* [The Pious], *Yalkut Chadash* [New Anthology],[†] *Midrash Shmuel on Ethics of the Fathers,* and *Tikun Gadol* [Great Amendment] were published.

The printer's name was not specified on the title page of these books because he was hiding from the censor's dreaded wrath. However, there is no doubt that this mysterious printer was Rabbi Yehonatan, son of Rabbi Yakov, who previously worked in Dubno and later in Kremenets. Aside from the books' appearance, which proves that, I have other clues that validate

---

[*] Translated from Hebrew by Rivka Schiller with Judy Fixler. *Note in original:* From *History of Hebrew Printing* by Chayim Dov Fridberg, 1950.

[†] *Note in original:* Published by Rabbi Yosef, son of Mordekhay of Kremenets. They published it following the Lublin edition, omitting only the poem printed on the verso of the title page. And at the end of the book we find a "large announcement" concerning the few prayer books that had recently been printed, within which there were calendars for future years. It was printed that 5580 [1820] is a leap year, and they noted the appearances of the new moon for the two months of Adar. It is wrong; that year is a common year [i.e., with only one month of Adar]. Furthermore, bibles were found in which yearly calendars had been printed from 5573 [1813] to 5600 [1840]. And from 5580 [1820] onward, they changed the system of the years a great deal and made common years into leap years and leap years into common years; and heaven forbid that they would rely on this in the villages and small towns and encounter a major stumbling block. We saw from this that, therefore, to remove a stumbling block from the people's path and to publicize this, so as heaven forbid not to depend on the text in the bibles and prayer books in any of the calendar determinations; only on a calendar that is printed annually. And whoever possesses these bibles and prayer books mentioned above should erase and blot out the calendars or remove and cut them out with a razor, and fulfill 'and allow no evil to dwell in your tent'; and for those who heed, it will be pleasant for them, and they shall be blessed with the blessing of good and sweet years. Abundant peace (5578) [1818]."

The date 5578 [1818], which had been repeated in Efraim Zalman Margaliot's approbation, indicated clearly that the date 5575 [1815] on the title page is an error.

The researcher, Ringelblum, found in the archival documents (according to the statement in his book *Toward a History of the Jewish Book and Printing in Poland,* p. 62) the business transactions between the printer, Myantshinski, and the government, regarding the establishment of a Hebrew printing house in Radzivilov in 5548 [1788]; and apparently the plan was never carried out.

my supposition, such as the different pictures, as well as the mayor's sign at the end of *Yalkut Chadash,* which looks similar to the sign printed on the title pages of the books in Dubno, of which there is no other example in Poland.

In the beginning of 5579 [1819], the aforementioned Rabbi Yehonatan, the printer, left this town and bequeathed his position to "the exalted scholar, the famous wealthy man,"* our teacher and rabbi, Rabbi Pinchas, son of Asher Zelig Barats, a person who brings honor to the Torah and awe to the rabbis,† who acquired the typographic material from the printer in Poritzk.

[page 36]

And he enriched the printing house he received with various letters; and with the help of expert workers, he completed the printing of the five parts of *Chok Leyisrael [Law of Israel]* during the course of 5579 [1819], "Pinchas arose from within the middle of the assembly," and he applied himself to print these statute books ... on nice paper and with good ink and with precise proofreading .... In my opinion, it is not necessary to praise this superior printing production. However, the aforementioned exalted rabbi feared the emergence of an evil person who would want to undermine him and copy his work to profit from it himself and thus to cheat me. He begged me to support him and help seal the door in the face of these evildoers. I was glad to fulfill his request; and the printers in this country will not reprint *Chok Leyisrael* within 10 years from the day the printing was completed.‡

After the printing of the abovementioned book was completed, the printer also printed an expensive edition of *The Kuzari* and a second part of the *Sifri* with the commentary, *Zera Avraham* (5580) [1820].

---

* *Note in original:* He is referred to thus in the approbation of Rabbi Mordekhay, head of the rabbinic court of Kremenets.

† *Note in original:* Rabbi Moshe Likhtshteyn, who published his father's *Sifri* [Books] with *Zerah Avraham* [Seed of Avrahram] in Radzivilov, where he relates in his introduction that the printer took him home and fed him throughout the months of printing.

‡ *Note in original:* Words of Rabbi Efraim Zalman Margaliot with his approbation in the middle of Sivan 5579 [June 1819].

The printer stopped working because he could not contend with competition from the Slavist printers, and therefore he sold the publishing rights to *Chok Leyisrael* to Rabbi Aharon, son of Yone—as I have already mentioned above—but he sold the typographic equipment to Rabbi Yakov Finkelman, son of Rabbi Shmuel the printer, son of Rabbi Issakher Ber Segal of Berdichev. After he had given up everything he had, he printed many books in Berdichev while concealing the place of publication.

In one of the two printing houses in this town, a prayer book was printed with *Kavanat Hachasidim* [Devotions of the Pious] under the supervision of the righteous Rabbi Avraham Heshil of Opatów; and at this time, we know of no surviving copy.[*]

[page 37]

From "The Wanderings of a Melody"[†]

Y. L. Peretz

It was destined that Podotsur's wedding melody should be rehabilitated.

As the acrobats went from house to house and traveled from city to city, they dragged the poor girl along until (may it never happen to you!) she grew ill.

In the border town of Radzivil, they left the sick child behind a fence and crossed the border. Now they could no more be caught than the wind blowing across a field. The girl lay in a fever, half-naked, with black and blue marks all over her body.

Caring people lifted her up and carried her to the poorhouse. The child had typhus, and when she left its care, she was blind in both eyes.

And now the poor child begged. She went from house to house, from door to door, begging.

---

[*] *Note in original:* Compare *Kiryat Sefer,* year 9, p. 439, and year 11, p. 495.
[†] Translated from Hebrew by Yaacov David Shulman.

She barely said anything at all. She could not beg with words. She would stand somewhere and wait. If people didn't see her, she would sing her melody so that they would notice her—the melody from the hand-organ.

And what did the melody say now?

It asked for mercy—mercy for an unfortunate child.

"Bad people stole me from a good father, a loving mother, a warm and comfortable home. I was torn away from everything good; I was abused and thrown away like an empty shell. Mercy for a poor, poor child!"

And the melody also pleaded:

"It is cold, I am half-naked and hungry, I have nowhere to lay my head, and in addition, I am blind!"

[page 38]

That was what the melody pleaded. And that was its first ascent—because of it, people gave charity.

In Radzivil lived a learned Jew. He was not opposed to Hasidism, and certainly not hostile to it. He simply had no time to travel to righteous ones, because he never closed his Gemara. He was afraid to spend any time not learning.

In order not to be distracted in the study hall, he learned at home. His wife stayed in the store the entire day, and his children learned in cheder.

From time to time, the idea would flit through his mind that he should travel to a righteous one. No doubt this was what his good inclination whispered to him. What did his evil inclination do? It clothed itself in his good inclination and said: "Certainly, sometimes a person has to do that! But there is still time. First you have to finish the tractate." And in that way, months and years passed by.

But it appears that heaven wanted him to go to R' Duvid'l.

And this is how it happened.

One time, as the scholar was sitting and learning, he heard singing outside his door. He grew angry at himself: "When you are learning, you shouldn't hear anything in the street, anything happening on the other side of the door. You should be entirely absorbed in the Torah!"

Nevertheless, he heard. So he put his fingers in his ears. But the melody stole its way in through his fingers. He grew more upset. He angrily pulled his long beard into his mouth and, biting his beard, he kept learning. He forced himself to learn!

But the melody didn't stop. He heard it more clearly. Suddenly he realized that the voice was that of a girl. He yelled: "Shameless girl! Get away from my house!"

The melody left. But—and this was terrible—even though no one was singing, he still heard the melody.

[page 39]

The melody itself sang in his ears, in his soul. He made himself look in his book, he tried to force himself to study, but he couldn't. The scholar's soul swelled with the melody.

He closed the Gemara and stood up to recite the afternoon prayers.

But he couldn't—he couldn't learn, he couldn't pray—nothing! The melody rang like a silver bell. The man couldn't stand it. He was literally dying of suffering! A day passed, a second, a third—he grew depressed. He fasted, but it didn't help. He could not rid himself of the melody. At night, it would wake him up.

And this was a man who in his entire life had never acted as cantor, who had almost never sung! On the Sabbath, instead of singing at the table, he would learn a page of Gemara.

He understood that this was no simple matter. "This is the work of the devil!" he thought, and he felt himself falling to pieces.

Perhaps the time had in fact come to go to a righteous one.

But the evil inclination asked him: "Yes, but there are many righteous ones. Who is the true righteous one who can really help?" The scholar began to think about it.

He received another hint from above.

It happened that R' Duvid'l Talner[*] had to uproot himself, and in doing so he passed through Radzivil.

You certainly know the story about the libel that led to that. And I tell you that Talnoe deserved to be punished. They should not have stolen R' Duvid'l away from Vasilkov. They should not have shamed that town. Sadly, Vasilkov was left desolate. All of the guest houses were closed, all of the inns lay idle. People had nothing more than a loaf of bread (it shouldn't happen to you!).

But now he was again libeled, and this time Talnoe was left desolate.

What happened was that R' Duvid'l had a golden chair on which was carved the saying: "David, king of Israel, is alive and well!"

[page 40]

Informers gave this a political interpretation and their accusation found a hearing in Sankt Peterburg.

We know that this saying is in line with the Gemara's statement: "Who are the kings? The rabbis." But go explain that to the generals in Sankt Peterburg!

The upshot was that R' Duvid had to flee. On his way, he spent the Sabbath in Radzivil. And fortunately the Radzivil scholar went to the Sabbath third meal.

But his evil inclination still didn't give up. When he came in, he saw a small Jew, a tiny Jew, sitting at the head of the table. All that he could see was a large, a really large shtreimel and a face over which silver hair fell. People were sitting in silence. No one was saying any words of Torah. The scholar's heart fell. "Is that all there is?" he thought.

But R' Duvid'l saw him and said, "Sit down, scholar."

At that moment he was restored. Just setting his eyes on R' Duvid'l healed his soul.

---

[*] *Translation editor's note:* R' Duvid'l refers to David Twersky, known as Duvid'l, the Talner Rebbe, 1808–1882, who began his career in Vasilkov but in 1852 moved to Talnoe.

You have certainly heard of the Talner's eyes. His glance contained power, holiness, might; whatever you wanted was contained in his glance.

When R' Duvid'l said, "Sit down," people made room at the table for the scholar. He sat down and waited.

But when R' Duvid'l then said, "The scholar will please sing a melody!" his heart sank—him and a melody!

But someone slapped him on the back: when R' Duvid'l tells you, you sing! So he sang.

He began, the poor man, with a shiver, and he barely stammered out the beginning of a melody. And what did he intend to sing, the scholar? Of course, the orphan girl's melody—because he didn't know any other. And so he shivered and stammered, and sang. And the melody was again transformed! It now had a fragrance of the Torah, something of the holiness of the Sabbath, with a thought of repentance. And as the scholar sang, he felt the melody, and with every moment he began to sing better and more freely.

In the middle, R' Duvid'l, as was his custom, quietly began to sing along. Hearing this, the others joined in. Accompanied by the others, the scholar grew more enthusiastic. He burned. He was lifted out of himself—he was really singing!

[page 41]

The melody began to pour out like a river of flames, and its waves grew wider and higher, all fiery and flaming!

The room grew too narrow for the melody. It tore itself out of the window and into the street. Into the street poured an ocean of holiness, of fiery holiness. And confused and amazed, the people in the street called out, "The orphan girl's melody! The orphan girl's melody!"

Both the melody and the scholar received their rectification.

Before leaving, R' Duvid'l took him aside and said a few words. "Scholar," he told him, "you shamed a Jewish daughter. You didn't understand the root of her melody. You called her shameless!"

"Rebbe, help me repent," the scholar pleaded.

"Unnecessary," said the rebbe (may his memory be for a blessing). "Instead of repenting, better that you perform a commandment!"

"What sort of a commandment, rebbe?"

"Marry off the girl. Helping a girl get married is a great commandment!"

And now, hear the end of the story.

A few years later, the girl had long been married to a widower, a scribe. Only then did they learn where she came from.

It turned out that the girl was a grandchild of the old Katzner. And this is how it happened.

His son-in-law, the man from Kiev, once took his wife to the theater for the entire evening. That evening, his only child was stolen away.

It was no longer possible to return the daughter to her parents. The mother had not been alive for years, and the father had long since moved to America.

Rabbis Who Served in Radzivilov[*]

Rabbi Chayim, Son of the Gaon Rabbi Shmuel Rotenberg

He was born in 5624 (1863–1864). His father, the Gaon rabbi, head of the rabbinic court of the Varkovichi, Volhynia, community, was the son of R' Chayim, the righteous one of blessed memory, head of the Rovno community's rabbinic court, who was the son of the Gaon Rabbi Shmuel of Dubno, the righteous one of blessed memory, who was the son of the Gaon Rabbi Iser of Rovno, the righteous one of blessed memory, who published under the name Rabbi Spola, and over holy generation after generation of leading rabbis of Israel and Rabbi Moshe Isserles and the Maharsha, Rabbi Shmuel Eliezer Eydis, the righteous one of blessed memory. He was ordained by the Gaon Rabbi Avraham Binyamin Kluger, may he live a long and happy life, amen; the Gaon Rabbi Yitschak Chiyot, may he live a long and happy life, amen, of Brody; and the Gaon Rabbi Moshe Natan Rubinshteyn, may he live a long and happy life, amen, head of the Vinnitsa community's rabbinical court.

Brothers-in-law of the aforementioned Rabbi Chayim are Rabbi Aharon Liper, the righteous teacher in Rovno; Rabbi Meir Chayim of Varkovichi; Rabbi Eliezer Levin of Grodno; and Rabbi Mordekhay of Kozin.

He is related by marriage to the honorable Rabbi Shalom Levin, brother-in-law of the Gaon Rabbi Yisrael Iser Shapira, head of the Zbarazh community's rabbinic court, author of the responsa *Israel's Help,* based on *The Foundation and Root of Service.*

The son of Rabbi Chayim, the righteous one of blessed memory, is Moshe Eliezer, who served as rabbi in Rovno from the end of World War I to the Holocaust.

---

[*] Translated from Hebrew by Ellen Garshick. *Note in original:* From the book *Ohalei Shem.* [Translator's note: By Shmuel Noach Gottlieb, 1912, this book includes biographies of 1,500 rabbis who held rabbinical positions at the time of writing.]

His youngest son was R' Duvid'l, who served as rabbi of Radzivilov after the death of his father, of blessed memory.

His eldest daughter was married off to Varkovichi, and his second daughter, to a town near Kozin. Everyone, including the youngest son, Yosele; his daughter, Charne; and the rabbi's wife, were martyred, may their memory be a blessing.

Rabbi Avraham, Son of Rabbi Chayim Yehuda Pindros

He was born in 5637 (1876–1877), son and grandson of the Gaon author of the *Book of Generations,* the righteous one of blessed memory. He studied in Slutsk and Bobruisk as well as Kovno.

[page 43]

He was the teacher par excellence of the Gaon Rabbi Barukh Dov Libovits, may he live a long and happy life, amen, head of the rabbinical court and head Talmud teacher in Lutsk and now head Talmud teacher at the Slobodka yeshiva.

He was ordained by R' Chayim Halevi Soloveytsik, may he live a long and happy life, amen, head of the Brisk community's rabbinic court; the Gaon R' Tsvi Hirsh Rabinovits, the righteous one of blessed memory, head of the Kovno community's rabbinic court; the Gaon R' Moshe Danishevski, the righteous one of blessed memory, head of the Slobodka community's rabbinic court; the Gaon Yakov David Vilavski, may he live a long and happy life, amen; the Gaon R' Moshe Shmuel Shapira, may he live a long and happy life, amen, head of the Bobruisk community's rabbinic court; and the aforementioned Gaon R' Barukh Libovits, may he live a long and happy life, amen.

A Golden Chain*

My father, my teacher and rabbi, Rabbi Eliezer Yingerleyb, of blessed memory, was promoted to head of the Radzivilov Jewish community's religious court. At the age of 23, he received his rabbinic ordination (teaching permit) from the famous R' Shlome Kluger, of blessed memory, of the city of Brody, the author of the religious tome *Tuv Taam Vadaat* [Good Discernment and Knowledge] and many other religious tomes known within rabbinic literature. And at the time when my father, of blessed memory, received rabbinic ordination from him, the aforementioned Gaon, before those standing before him, he praised my father, of blessed memory, with these words: This young man is the offspring of Talmudic scholars and righteous people from the triple bond [i.e., the People of Israel, the Land of Israel, and the Faith of Israel]. And he knows the religious tome *Peri Megadim* [a commentary] on the *Shulchan Arukh* [Prepared Table], *Orach Chayim* [Manner of Life], and *Yoreh Deah* [Compiled Opinions] by heart just as a Jew who knows the prayer "Ashrei," which he is accustomed to saying three times a day; and therefore I ordained him with my whole heart and soul; may his merit protect us.

In 5633 [1873], he was appointed rabbinic head of the Radzivilov religious court, and his rabbinic writing spanned several years; and there is no way to describe the degree of esteem in this text; and there is no way to convey the love and affection from a written text. And what authority was given to him. And it was written there that he would adjudicate all matters of Jewish law and regulations in managing and administering the institutions; he would have the power and authority to add new regulations and abolish them as he saw fit, without any objections from anyone. As for salary, the rabbi would receive 10 Russian rubles per week, untaxed meat and alcoholic beverages; income from religious marriages and divorces would be divid-

---

* Translated from Hebrew by Rivka Schiller with Judy Fixler, and by Yaacov David Shulman. *Note in original:* From the religious tome *Golden Chain,* by Rabbi Shlome Gur-Arye (Yingerleyb).

ed—two parts to the rabbi and one part to the religious judges. I had this document in my possession, and it is a shame that I lost it in my itinerant movement; that I wandered from country to country, from the city of Akkerman, Bessarabia, to the city of Bucharest, the capital of Romania. In the first year after he was appointed head of the religious court, there was an incident during the Shavuot holiday. My father, of blessed memory, had a large, nice residence with a study hall in it, and the windows of his study hall faced the town's Great Synagogue. On Shavuot, it was raining during the morning prayers. From his window, my father, of blessed memory, saw three wealthy individuals who were some of the most well-known Enlightened of that generation—I do not wish to publicize their names, for two reasons.

[page 44]

(1) Because it is forbidden to speak ill of the dead and (2) so as not to embarrass their family members. When my father, of blessed memory, saw through the window that these people opened their umbrellas as they returned home from the synagogue, because of the rain and downpour, he opened the window and asked them to please throw them into the synagogue yard and not to violate the holiday in public and in his presence. He explained that he was responsible for their deeds, as stated in the Gemara, Tractate Sabbath, "Anyone who has in his capacity to admonish the residents of his city and does not admonish them is held accountable for his townsmen's sins." Right away, two of them threw the umbrellas into the synagogue yard. One was not willing to listen to the rabbi and died that same year, God help us, and did not live out the year. This was enough to show how my father, of blessed memory, fulfilled what is written in the Torah, "Do not fear man." It is written in the holy Torah in the portion of *Kedoshim*, "Do not defer to the great, but judge your fellow fairly." Thus it is written, "You shall rebuke your fellow man, and you shall not bear a sin because of him."

My father, of blessed memory, had inherited from his father, my forebear, the righteous, the head of the Radzivilov yeshiva, 18 pouches, each affixed with a piece of parchment bearing in Assyrian script which charity was placed within it. For example: "Needy Brides' Fund," "Redeeming Captives," "Rabbi Meir Baal Ha-Nes," "Education Tuition for Orphans and Needy," "Kin Support," "Charity for the Town's Poor," "Charity for the Poor of Other Towns," "Charity for Visiting the Sick," "Charity for Medications for Poor Patients," "Pouch for Needy Torah Scholars," "Yeshiva Support," "Purim Charity for Beggars," "Passover Charity for the Poor," "Pouch for Unforeseen Hardship That Might Befall the Town," "For Unforeseen Hardship That Might Befall Another Town," "Pouch for Jewish Soldiers in the Military," "Charity Dedicated to an Old Age Home," and "Funeral Expense for the Poor." There were 18 pouches. My father, of blessed memory, used these pouches and discreetly gave to the needy so they would not be embarrassed. He would pay a monthly salary to the orphans' teachers and those who supported the orphans and the poor. After his death, the teachers lamented, saying, "Who is going to pay the orphans' tuition?" Then my father's charitable deeds were revealed, because he had done it all as discreetly as possible.

My father, of blessed memory, was loved and adored by all his family members, all the rabbis of his generation, and all his kin and acquaintances from various Hasidic sects. And whenever he visited a different town, all the townspeople would come to greet him and get a blessing from him.

[page 45]

My great uncle, the *Magid* R' Avraham of Turiysk, author of *Magen Avraham* [Shield of Avraham], liked him very much, and when his followers from Poland and Lublin province would go by the town of Ustilug, by the Bug River, the Polish Bug, on their way to see him, he would ask them if they had visited the rabbi of Ustilug, saying that it should be known that he is a miracle worker like me. "And you could be helped by his blessings as you could by my blessings." He liked him that much. From here it is known and understood how his relatives and acquaintances and rabbis liked him;

all the more so the people surrounding him, his admirers and followers of various sects.

Two days before his death, he asked that a telegram be sent to his eldest son, my brother, Rabbi Yisrael Duvid Yingerleyb, of blessed memory, asking that he take his place as rabbi of Radzivilov, that he come to Hrubieszów. He calculated with precision that the following day he would certainly take the train from Radzivilov to the city of Chelm, and there was no additional train from Chelm to the town of Hrubieszów. And it was 60 kilometers from there to Hrubieszów, and according to his calculation, he said that he would arrive in two days at two o'clock in the afternoon. And that is precisely how it happened. He also instructed that his will not be opened until this son arrived. My father, of blessed memory, had a small box that at the time they called a pretty *shkatulka* [box] in his inheritance from his father, my forebear, may his memory be for a blessing in the next world, with closed double lids. And not a single person from his household approached this box to see what was in it. Before his passing, he said that he had a will inside this very box, the aforementioned *shkatulka*. When my brother, the aforementioned rabbi of blessed memory of Radzivilov, arrived, they opened up this box and found the will inside it. So it was that an ownership right was issued by the Hebron religious court of law and with the seal of the religious court of law saying that herein and with this certificate of approval that has been issued by the judges with the seal of the great religious court of law in Jerusalem how, one of the grandsons of the righteous R' Duvid Lelever, of blessed memory, who sold four ells of land that he had in Hebron as an inheritance from his grandfather, the aforementioned R' Duvid Lelever, of blessed memory, for 300 Russian rubles, which he sold to Rabbi Eliezer Yingerleyb, head of the Radzivilov Jewish community's religious court; and, with witnesses and their signatures, the religious court confirms that the seller received all the money and that the aforementioned four ells of land belong to the rabbi of Radzivilov. I remember the Hebron religious court's seal, which was green and bore the witnesses' signatures, and the

Jerusalem religious court's seal was red and had the witnesses' signatures. How awful, astonishing, and surprising it was to all the onlookers at that moment, and particularly for my righteous mother, may peace be upon her, who cried bitterly about this to an indescribable degree; and who, when she calmed down, related before us and everyone who was there at that moment how she remembered this man, the righteous rabbi from Lelev's grandson, coming to Radzivilov. For several days he was a guest in the home of my father, of blessed memory, and it is a given that he was a fitting guest for my father, of blessed memory. He would tell my father how it was that he had land in Hebron in his inheritance from his grandfather, and that if a buyer were to come upon him, he would sell it to him so that he would not need to travel overseas to collect money, as he needs money to marry off his daughter. This is what my mother, may peace be upon her, remembered.

[page 46]

But if my father, of blessed memory, was interested and bought it, my mother, may peace be upon her, did not know about this until that very moment. It was astounding: my father, of blessed memory, was then 25 and was interested in spending so much money on this. For 300 rubles was a large sum of money then, even for wealthy people. Especially for rabbis of the Jewish Nation. And then inside this box they also found a small linen sack attached to a letter in which my father wrote that in this sack was some soil from this land that he had received along with the ownership right from the aforementioned. And then they found a sash that he had in his inheritance from his forebear, the righteous Rabbi Barukh of Medzhibozh, of blessed memory, from his forebear, the Baal Shem Tov, may his memory be for a blessing in the next world. My father, of blessed memory, requested in his will that this soil be placed in his grave and that he be dipped in a kosher ritual bath three times and wrapped with this sash following the purification of his body, and then that several rubles be distributed to poor people around his bed. And also, as for all the money found in the aforementioned 18 pouches as an inheritance from his father, his forebear of blessed memory from Radzivilov, to distribute the money from every pouch according to what was written on it and not to switch from one charity to another charity, and to place the empty pouches in his grave. That was the entire content of the will. And thus they did everything written in the will. Before the funeral, an order was issued by the rabbi, the Gaon Henta of blessed memory, to assemble and participate in the funeral and to close the shops and workshops until after the funeral, indicating mourning and sorrow, and to pay last respects to the deceased. And thus all the townspeople participated; and thus people arrived from the entire vicinity, as did the important residents of Ustilug. And hundreds of thousands arrived, and it was not possible to walk in the street. Only with the [help of] police officers did they walk the deceased's coffin to the Great Synagogue. My brother, of blessed memory, eulogized him; and following him, the great chief rabbi of the town eulogized him, and throughout the eulogy the people bellowed in their great sobbing until the synagogue beadle was forced to pound several times with a hammer to calm and silence the cries and sobs so that it was possible to hear the final words of the aforementioned great rabbi of blessed memory's eulogy. And in his praise and eulogy, he mentioned the ownership right that was buried with him. And the eulogizer brought down a citation from one of the rabbinic commentaries that speaks in praiseworthy terms about the Land of Israel; that one who has four ells of land in the Land of Israel, "and He will appease His Land and His people," one who is placed and buried in the Land of Israel, even though he is buried outside Israel. I do not recall which commentary stated this or where in the Talmud this reference appears. The great rabbi, of blessed memory, concluded with these words: "Look and see the greatness of the deceased, who fulfilled the statement of our rabbinic sages, three types of blessings: If a contemptible person chances on you, drag him into the religious house of study. Should this gain him the victory [i.e., over his evil impulse], well and good; but if not, let him read the Shema. Should this gain him the victory, well and good; but if not, let him reflect upon the day of [his] death. And the deceased rabbi, when he was yet only 25 years old, reflected upon the day of [his] death and for 300 rubles purchased 4 ells of land for himself in the Land of Israel in Hebron, near the Cave of the Patriarchs, and secretly made a will. Now, the bill of ownership of the land and some of the soil from this land will be placed on him in his grave, and we will be able to say of him, happy is he who is virtuous and attains this point; and his righteousness, Torah, and virtue will stand him, his offspring, and all of us in good stead for eternity. Amen."

[page 47]

I heard from my brother-in-law, Rabbi Yitschak Lerner, of blessed memory, of Radzivilov that once my grandfather, of blessed memory, was asked to come to the city of Kremenets, I forget why. At that time, my great-uncle, the *magid* of Turiysk, Rabbi Avraham, of blessed memory, author of *Magen Avraham* on the Torah, had come to the city of Kremenets. And it was then the law of the land that the righteous were forbidden to travel from their place of residence to another city. In their place of residence, they were allowed to receive their followers, even by the thousands and tens of thousands, but not in another city. This law resulted from the dispute between the Hasidim and *mitnagdim*, as described in *Bet Rebbe*, the biography of the rabbi of Lyady, Rabbi Shneur Zalman, of blessed memory, author of the *Tanya* and *Shulchan Aruch Harav*. This law was instituted after he was freed from prison (see there). And this is not the place to expound on that matter. When my great-uncle, the *magid* of Turiysk, came to the city of Kremenets, the city official told him to go back home in accordance with the law. Therefore, when my grandfather was asked to this city, his relatives were afraid to allow him to travel to Kremenets lest he be treated disrespectfully, as the *magid* of Turiysk, of blessed memory, had been. When my grandfather, of blessed memory, received a second letter of introduction from Kremenets, the beadle and sexton sent back a letter saying that my grandfather, of blessed memory, did not want to travel there, for his own reasons. Meanwhile, the rumor spread among the Hasidim that the city official who had told the *magid*, of blessed memory, to return home had done so due to the influence of the rabbi, righteous one, and famous author, R' Yitschak Ber Levinson (RBY"L); peace be upon him), author of *Efes Damim*, *Zerubavel,* and *Bikurei* RBY"L. Therefore, Rabbi Y. of Radzivilov did not want to come to this city. At last, matters came to the attention of the pious Rabbi Yitschak Ber Levinson (peace be upon him). As the saying has it, "Your confidante has his own confidante." Then the pious RBY"L (peace be upon him) wrote a letter to my grandfather, of blessed memory, asking him not to believe this rumor, saying that it was not true and that he should come to the city of Kremenets, and that RBY"L and his colleagues would be responsible for upholding his honor. Of course, after receiving this letter from the wise RBY"L, of blessed memory, my grandfather, of blessed memory, traveled there. Then the wise rabbi (peace be upon him) came to him among the visitors, and my grandfather, of blessed memory, accorded him great honor. And the pious RBY"L would tell all the visitors standing there: "Everyone knows that I am not a Hasid and I do not pay any visits to the rabbis who come here. So why have I come to visit this rabbi? I have sufficient cause to do so." He then said, "When I was a young man, I married a woman from the city of Yampol"—which is close to our city. "At that time, this rabbi's grandfather, Rabbi Yosile Yampoler, of blessed memory— the present rabbi is named after him—was still alive. I will tell you what I remember. My father-in-law was a passionate, faithful follower of the rabbi, but I was far from all of Hasidism. And every time my father-in-law, peace be upon him, returned from the rabbi, he demanded that I accompany him to the rabbi. Once he came and told me that the rabbi had asked him, 'Where is your son-in-law? Why is he hiding from me?' I decided that I would not go and that it was better for me to learn Torah, because 'Torah learning is equal to [all other commandments].' [At the time,] some learned friends and I were studying Rambam's *Guide to the Perplexed* together.

[page 48]

We came to a very difficult passage. It was well known that the rabbi was an outstanding scholar. I told myself that I would test the rabbi with this passage. If he could explain it to me, then I would know that he was learned and [truly] a rabbi. I came to him with the *Guide to the Perplexed*. He put on his glasses, because he was already very old. He looked at the book and gave a satisfactory answer. A short while later, the rabbi passed on, and I regretted that I had not gone to him earlier, because I had been in Yampol for three years. And since I know that you are his grandson, I thought it right to pay you a visit. And as for why I wrote to you to come here and that I would be responsible to uphold your honor, there is another reason for that. It is because I heard an upsetting rumor in this city that my friends and students or I were involved in the fact that the *Magid* of Turiysk had to return home. That is a total falsehood. Maybe some foolish opponent was responsible for that. I am not guilty of such a terrible thing, heaven forbid. Maybe it was caused by jealousy and hatred. As to the question of how I can take on the responsibility of upholding your honor, the answer is that we all know that you do not have any opponents and enemies, and no one is jealous of you or hates you. Who among us cares if the poor of Kremenets give you money? What will this rabbi do with the money? He will not buy golden utensils and jewelry for himself and his family, but he will distribute it to his 18 charity funds. Then the money from the poor of Kremenets will be distributed to the poor of Radzivilov and Dubno and the surrounding area. And who would oppose that?" He turned to everyone standing there and asked, "Who can be opposed to this rabbi? And so I am capable of undertaking the responsibility of upholding his honor." And so my grandfather, of blessed memory, stayed in Kremenets for 10 days, and no one protested. And he returned home with great honor.

R' Yakov Ger, of Blessed Memory[*]

Tsvi Zagoroder

I remember the following: a little over 50 years ago, a Jew named Yakov Ger[†] lived in Brody. Every day, and sometimes twice a day, he would come in by train, stay about half an hour, and leave. He worked as a kind of mailman, bringing the mail from Brody to Radzivilov and vice versa. He would get home at 6:30 PM and go to a fixed location in town where people were waiting to retrieve letters, packages, money, and so forth. They would also give him valuable items—letters, packages, and so forth—to deliver to merchants in Radzivilov. He was highly trusted.

[page 49]

I was very surprised that the tax inspectors never questioned him. I never got an answer to why this was so, and I didn't know why Yakov Ger had the privilege of avoiding inspection by the tax authorities.

R' Yakov Ger was a very pious, upright man, and it never occurred to me to find out why he was called "Ger." And now, after so many years, I happened to get hold of a book written by Shlome Gur-Arye (Yingerleyb), now rabbi of Tel Aviv, the great-grandson of R' Itsikel (may the memory of a righteous one be for a blessing), who served as rabbi about a hundred years ago in Radzivilov. This book revealed the source of the name "Ger." Here is the story:[‡]

When I was 17 years old, I was a houseguest of my brother-in-law, Rabbi Y. Lerner, and my sister, the rabbi's wife, of blessed memory, in Radzivilov. One day, as I was learning Talmud, a 60-year-old man came to the door and asked me, "Are you the son of Rabbi Eliezer'l, of blessed memory?" When I answered that I was, he threw his arms around me and kissed me repeatedly. Who was this, and what was it all about? At that moment, my

---

[*] Translated from Hebrew by Yaacov David Shulman.

[†] *Translator's note: Ger* (literally, "stranger") means "convert" here.

[‡] *Note in original:* The story comes from the book *Golden Chain,* by Rabbi Shlome Gur-Arye (Yingerleyb).

sister, peace be upon her, came and said, "This is our good friend, Yakov Ger of Brody, whom our grandfather, of blessed memory, converted to Judaism." Afterward, my brother-in-law, of blessed memory, told me the story: When this person was six years old, orphaned of his father, he was kidnapped. At that time, during the reign of Czar Nicholas I, because of the terrible laws, small boys would be kidnapped. These Jewish children were handed over to non-Jews, who would raise them to be faithful Christians. And when they grew up, they would serve as soldiers in the army. When this boy was kidnapped, he was sent to a village near Moscow, where he grew up among Christians. It was then considered a good deed for a childless Christian to take such a Jewish boy and convert him to Christianity, to raise him, educate him, and give him a Christian name, and then send him to serve in the army. For this, the czar would give the man gifts and thanks. This is well known to knowledgeable people who have read Russia's history. As a boy, Yakov was talented. He could write and read Russian. After he graduated from public school, he became an officer among them. Afterward, he was appointed to work in their ministry of security. There he found the file that recorded the names of the children from the Zhitomir district. In it, he found himself described as Yakov, a native of Radzivilov, with the names of his father and mother and their family. He began to take an interest in this, and a spark of a Jewish spirit entered his heart. Although he knew that taking an interest in this was dangerous, completely forbidden by the law of the king and the land, he nevertheless felt impelled to send a letter from his office to the Radzivilov police, asking if there was such a family there.

[page 50]

He did this, and of course the police discovered that the head of the family (his father) was dead, but they found his widow's name and address. When he received this response from the police, he sent a letter in Russian directly to his mother, asking a few questions. She brought the letter to my grandfather, of blessed memory, understandably filled with fear and terror that this might be a trick by someone identifying himself as Yakov, her son—but who knew if this was truly her son or someone who knew her son's name, who wanted to do her some harm? My grandfather, of blessed memory, advised her to write back immediately that she was wealthy and that my grandfather, of blessed memory, was her brother-in-law and the town's rabbi and that she wanted him to come to Radzivilov, where he could live in comfort, and to ask that before he came, he should send her a telegram letting her know what day he would arrive at the address of her brother-in-law, Rabbi Yingerleyb. With the help of a professional, she wrote a literate letter in Russian, and my grandfather advised her and blessed her that she should soon see [Yakov] as a Jew. He told her that if she got another letter or telegram, she should immediately tell him about it. A month later, she received a telegram saying that on such-and-such a day of such-and-such a month, [Yakov] would come to see her. She brought this news to my grandfather, of blessed memory. He was glad to hear it. He told her to be at home on the day that [Yakov] came, and he told [my] grandmother, peace be upon her, to dress in her beautiful clothes, with golden rings on her fingers. And he also told [his] sons that on that day they should wear their Sabbath clothes and receive [Yakov] with warm kisses and treat him as though he were truly their flesh and blood. And in the house the table should be set with all sorts of good food, fruits, and good wine, as on a holiday. And the purpose of all of this was to persuade him to stay with them and convert. When [Yakov] arrived, the house was filled with joy and gladness, and they did everything as [my grandfather] had told them. When [Yakov] came to my grandfather's house, of blessed memory, a person who knew languages served as interpreter. The next day and the day after that, my grandfather asked [Yakov] some questions through the interpreter, which [Yakov] answered willingly. Afterward, among other questions, [my grandfather] asked him if he was married, and he answered, "No." Then my grandfather, of blessed memory, said that he had an attractive, educated young woman in his family, and tomorrow they would summon the girl to meet him to see if he liked her, and that she could speak Russian. But he said that he had two weeks' vacation and he must return to Moscow to arrange his affairs because he was afraid that otherwise he might be punished. Then my grandfather asked him why he needed to return. My grandfather said he intended to give him 500 rubles as a dowry and that through his acquaintances he could smuggle [Yakov] over the border whenever he wanted. [My grandfather said that] he would come to Brody to arrange the wedding and set [Yakov] up with some income. And with such words he persuaded him, until he agreed to everything. A few days later, they smuggled him, the bride, and his elderly mother over the border to the city of Brody. And my grandfather, of blessed memory, also traveled there and gave them the dowry.

[page 51]

They immersed him in a ritual bath, and [my grandfather] converted him in accordance with the words of the holy Torah, and he arranged the marriage for them and hired a teacher to teach him Torah and commandments. And he accepted the Torah and commandments with love. This was Yakov Ger. He attained great success in business, and he grew wealthy and rich and became an outstanding, wealthy merchant with sons and daughters. Afterward, whenever he came to Radzivilov on business, he would come to the house of my brother-in-law, the rabbi, of blessed memory, with gifts, and he gave an appropriate gift to each family member. And the next day he would come to receive a going-away blessing from my father-in-law, of blessed memory. He would hug and kiss me again with all his heart, and he would tell me that "there is no one as righteous as your grandfather." And he would say this with many tears on his face. And he was called Yakov Ger of Brody, peace be upon him.

Genealogy of Rabbi Yitschak Lerner, of Blessed Memory*

Pinchas Verthaym, R' Yitschak Lerner's Nephew

Father's Side:

Rabbi Mordekhay'le Lerner of Shumsk, son of

Rabbi Mikhele Lerner of Shumsk, son of

Rabbi Mordekhay of Lakhovtsy, of blessed memory, student of

R' Shlome of Karlin

Mother's Side:

Mrs. Reyzele, wife of R' Mordekhay'le of Shumsk, daughter of R' Yosele of Radzivilov, son of

R' Eliezer of Radzivilov,* son of

R' Yisrael of Teofipol, son of

R' Yosef of Yampol, son of

the *magid* of Złoczów

R' Yitschak of Radzivilov, son of the *magid* R' Yechiel Mikhel of Złoczów, was born in 1711 and died in 1826.

His son, R' Dan, was trained by the rabbi of Opatów, R' Avraham Yehoshue Heshel (author of *Ohev Yisrael*).

R' Dan's daughter married the son of R' Yosele of Ustilug, who was the son of R' Mordekhay of Nesukhoyezhe (the *magid* of Nesukhoyezhe).

This wedding is known in the Hasidic world as "the great Ustilug wedding." In attendance were the bride's grandfather, the righteous one of Opatów, and the groom's grandfather, the rabbi of Nesukhoyezhe. At this wedding, extensive discussions were held on the law of the Hasidism of Przysucha. According to tradition, hundreds of rabbis and righteous men and tens of thousands of Hasidim attended. Also known is the story of the "White Cossack."

---

* Translated from Hebrew by Ellen Garshick. *Note in original:* From the genealogy of the Baal Shem Tov, may the memory of the righteous be a blessing: R' Eliezer of Radzivilov's wife, Feyge Sosye, was the daughter of R' Berko Tulchiner and his wife, Reyzele, who was the daughter of R' Barukh of Medzhibozh; R' Barukh was the son of Hodele, the Baal Shem Tov's daughter.

Chane, granddaughter of R' Yosele of Ustilug and daughter of R' Pinchas of Ustilug, married R' Yosele of Radzivilov, son of R' Eliezer of Radzivilov, who was the son of R' Yisrael of Teofipol, son of R' Yosef of Yampol, son of the *magid* of Złoczów. Rabbi Eliezer of Radzivilov died in his prime, and R' Yosele, orphaned from his father at the age of four, was brought up by his grandfather, R' Yisrael of Teofipol.

R' Yosef of Radzivilov was the rabbi of Lanovtsy. He then moved to Radzivilov. He served time in prison under a sentence imposed by the Russians. When he was released, he fled to Galina, Galicia, where he died in 1875.

R' Yosef of Radzivilov had three children. His first son, R' Eliezer Yingerleyb (Gur Arye), was rabbi of Radzivilov and then of Ustilug; he died in 1898 in Hrubieszów. His daughter, Sore Treyne, was the wife of Rabbi Yitschak Verthaym of Bendery. R' Eliezer Yingerleyb of Ustilug's daughter married Rabbi Yitschak Lerner, who was the son of R' Mordekhay of Shumsk and, on his mother's (Mrs. Reyzel's) side, grandson of Rabbi Yosef of Radzivilov, who served as rabbi of Radzivilov until the Holocaust.

Radzivilov in Russia's First Hebrew Newspapers*

On the Fire in the City, Av 5642 (1882)
Pinchas Lerner

From Radzivilov comes the report that the fire that broke out there was catastrophic for our people and that many have been left with nothing, not even the basic necessities of life.—*HaMelits*, 1882, Vol. 29

On Sunday, 6 Menachem Av, a fire broke out in the city and consumed nearly 150 houses and another 150 shops, 6 study halls, and public bath-houses. An elderly woman was burned at her door. Yesterday, the leaders of the Nirenshteyn and Kalir families came from Brody and collected contribu-

---

* Translated from Hebrew by Elizabeth Kessin Berman.

tions to benefit the victims of the fire .... A few Christians also participated in the effort to help the victims.—*HaMelits,* 1882, Vol. 31

[page 53]

In 1991 in Radzivilov (Volhynia district), it was reported that a town resident sailed to America. He spent some time there, but life there did not suit him. So he managed to board a Russian ship sailing to Japan. There he went into business with an elite mercantile shipping company (Kutiki), which transported goods from Bahrain and hauled them to supply the Russian warships passing through Japanese waters to Vladivostok. After a few years, he became immensely wealthy and began to shower gifts on his relatives in our town.

After a time, he married a woman from our town—the daughter of one of our town's most honorable women—who traveled to Japan to be with him. It was known that there was no Jewish community in Japan, so the wedding had to be in Singapore, which is in India [sic]. But things did not go well, so it seems, because now there is a notice in every Hebrew newspaper that a certain rabbi from San Francisco in America was asked to come to Japan to arrange a divorce for a man named Gintsburg. Wasn't he born in our town? Now this Gintsburg comes from Yokohama, Japan, to visit his elderly mother and his relatives and to spread his "experience" in matters of charity in our town—10,000 rubles and more from his tainted hand.

In our little town, which is situated on the border, and where many inhabitants are so enlightened that they don't have to learn or forget anything, they have so far remained quite removed from the current nationalist movement. Neither of those two allegiances exist among us, nor is there anyone devoted to one particular movement, but none of the "elite" can be accounted for in our town. It is perfectly clear that no one pays any attention to national culture, but really, it is quite the opposite. In certain matters, we have reached great heights: in dressing luxuriously, playing cards, and having women ride bicycles. This last matter also was considered an insult to Israel's honor, because seeing these free-spirited women, including Jewish women, going around on bicycles was unheard of. However, on bicycles, the Jewish women gained better access to public places, even places in which Jewish women are forbidden to be …. Perhaps someone will provide an answer to this dilemma? Who knows? —*HaMelits*, 1899, Vol. 154; publisher: M. Sh. Geshuri

[page 54]

From "Motil, Son of Peysi the Cantor"*

Everyone is going now to America. That is what Yoyne, our nephew the bagel maker, wrote. And he is also going to America. He is on his way. He is, in fact. He's already at the border. It is not same border we ran. Ours had a bad reputation. They steal your linens there. They steal them in other places too, but they don't hold you at knifepoint. True, we've heard of borders where you're stripped naked and robbed of everything. You aren't killed though. That only almost happened to us. Except that we would have died of fright first. It was our luck that someone fired a gun. I must have told you about that. We can hardly remember it anymore.

Not that our women aren't still telling the world about the miracle that happened at the border. But Elye and Pinye never let them finish. They think they can tell it better. Pinye wants to write it up for the papers. He's even begun a poem about it. I've told you he writes poems. This one goes:

> The town of Radzivil's the size of a yawn
> with a border that has to be run before dawn—
> and while you are running it thieves run away
> with all that you have and leave you to say:
> "Thank God that it didn't turn out to be worse!
> We might have ended our days in a hearse
> with a slit in our throats and a slash in our purse!"

[page 55]

Pinye says that's just the first stanza. It will improve as it goes along. He has a poem about Brody, too. And about Lvov and Kraków, all in rhyme. He

---

* *Translation editor's note:* The English translation here differs slightly from the one in the yizkor book., which appears to come from a different edition of the story.

is the devil for rhymes, Pinye is. He's even written some about Taybl. I know them by heart.

The Synagogue in Radzivil and the Holy Ark That Was Hit by Lightning*

The synagogue in Radzivil was famous in all of Ukraine because of its original, unique architecture. Even though it was built completely of wood, it was still very tall, adorned with beautiful hand-carved cornices and carved balconies; curved steps led to the women's gallery and, from there, further on to a fenestrated, turret-like clerestory on the roof. From this clerestory, a large vault rose, looking like a velvet cap. On the ceiling inside were paintings of the 12 signs of the zodiac. The walls were decorated with wonderful drawings based on the subjects of Biblical verses, such as "The mountains skipped like rams, the hills like sheep, "Our hands were spread like the eagles of the heavens," "He made my feet like a doe's feet," "Horse and rider He has thrown into the sea," and others.

And like the paintings, the Biblical verses themselves were also painted in magnificent colors, with large, beautifully adorned letters, thought to have been done by an unknown graphic artist of exceptional quality; the intention was to write Biblical verses and verses from prayers in magnificent script because they decorated the four walls of the original synagogue.

In the register of the Radzivil community, there is a reference that in the days of R' Itsikel the righteous one, a Radzivil native, R' Velvele of Zbarazh, son of R' Yechiel Mikhel of Złoczów, came to spend the Sabbath in Radzivilov and pray in the Great Synagogue. He was so impressed with the synagogue that he could not stop praising it. Before leaving, he made a blessing as he departed the town, as is the custom, and in his blessing, he prayed

---

* Translated from Hebrew by Elizabeth Kessin Berman. *Note in original:* From the book *Jewish Ethnography and Folklore,* by Avraham Rekhtman. Memoirs of the ethnography delegation organized by Sh. Ansky, published by YIVO, Buenos Aires, 1958.

that the synagogue would never be destroyed and that fire would not overcome it.

As later became clear, his blessing was completely realized.

It was in 1883, 1 Shevat, Torah portion Va-etchanan, 10:00 AM, when the great fire broke out. It began in the butcher's house, where they were frying fat. It was a hot summer day, and the fire consumed almost the entire town.

[page 56]

The Old Great Synagogue

The New Great Synagogue

[page 57]

Numerous houses in Radzivil were built of wood, and quite a few had straw walls; these were the first to be consumed by the fire. And then even the stone houses, of which there were few, caught fire. The fire raged for two days. Residents of Radzivil, children and women, fled to the cemetery, which was far away from the city, with all the possessions they had managed to rescue from the fire. The whole town was completely obliterated, with the fire consuming everything—nothing survived except the old synagogue, even though it was made of wood. The fire didn't even touch it.

All the other holy places—such as the Husiatyn Hasidic *kloyz*, the Turiysk *kloyz*, the Rabbi's Study Hall, the Barani Study Hall, and all the houses of prayer near the Great Synagogue—were consumed by the fire. But the old, wooden Great Synagogue itself withstood the fire entirely. It would not let the fire overcome it.

Eyewitnesses later reported seeing a flock of white doves appear on all four sides when the fire raged there. The doves scattered onto the roof of the synagogue, flapped their wings, and didn't let the fire approach.

The old folks of Radzivil like to talk about another incredible thing that happened later in the same synagogue, 10 years after the Great Fire.[*] Radzivil had then already been rebuilt with the help of our people, the children of Israel, merciful sons of merciful fathers, and Radzivil's Jews returned to the routines of commerce and found contentment in earning their living. The congregation decided to honor the memory of the miracle that saved the synagogue from the fire, as well as Torah scrolls brought from other holy places that had been burnt by the fire, with a new, large ark with the appropriate degree of splendor. For this effort, the head of the Kremenets community procured a woodcarver who was famous throughout Ukraine.

---

[*] *Note in original:* After so many fires in the city, it became common to date events from a fire, for example, such and such after the second fire and the like.

For a full year, the woodcarver worked on the ark with delicate tools, creating wonderful drawings: engraved lions and tigers, gazelles and deer, eagles, doves, large and small beasts, and all sorts of different flowers.

Those who heard about the ark came from far away to see it, and they would pray for the construction and its progress.

After the artist had completed his work, he engraved his name on the lower edges of ark: Ozer son of Yechye—a magnificent work ....

[page 58]

After five months, when the ark was complete, at 2:00 in the afternoon on the first day of Shavuot, it suddenly started raining, and there was also thunder and lightning. A lightning bolt hit the synagogue, split the vault on the roof, penetrated the interior, and struck the edge of the ark with the name of the wood sculptor, specifically the words "a magnificent work."

Shortly, it was learned that this very same woodcarver had previously done similar engraving projects for a Catholic church. This was considered sacrilegious, and it was understood that the heavens would be angry because those words "a magnificent work" were engraved on the Holy Ark.

During the delegation's visit to Radzivil, no one recalled the former splendors of the Great Synagogue. The millionaire R' Moshe Ginzburg, known as the Baron of Port Arthur, who was born in Radzivil and was a supplier during the Russo-Japanese war, supported the town of his birth from afar and built many of its social institutions. At the same time, he also rebuilt the Great Synagogue in a modern style, both inside and out. He replaced the bronze candelabra and chandeliers hanging from the ceiling and installed electric lamps in their place. On the walls, there was no trace of any of the paintings that used to be there. Thus, in one stroke, the memory of the lightning strike and the beauty of Radzivil's beloved former Great Synagogue were erased.

A Note on the Great Synagogue and Its Holy Ark[*]

Mrs. Raçhel Gurman

At the request of Mr. Ts. Zagoroder, chairman of Radzivilov's Memorial Book Publication Committee, I copied the section on the damage to Radzivilov's Great Synagogue from A. Rekhtman's book on Jewish ethnography. There are a few things that should be pointed out:

1. Radzivil was not called "Radzivil" but rather Radzivilov-Volhynia until World War I. After that, during Polish rule, the town was called "Radzivilov near Brody," and the Jews simply called it "Radivil." The town was also mentioned in the story "Motel, Son of Peysi the Cantor," by Sholem Aleichem. There it said, among other things, that "Radzivil is big—because you can steal [across] a border."

2. The Great Synagogue was blown up with strategic precision by the Austrians during World War I. The synagogue stood in the way of the army's view of the machinery in the Brody forest. When I came to Radivil after World War I, they told me that during the war a particular young person had succeeded in photographing an Austrian officer giving the hand signal to blow up the synagogue.

[page 59]

I then sent the photograph to the YIVO Institute in Vilna, and Mr. Zagoroder also had a copy. It was clear from the beginning that after the synagogue was blown up, nothing was left but empty space, and nothing remained of the synagogue walls.

Accordingly, it is not correct that "they replaced the bronze candelabra and chandeliers that were hanging from the ceiling," as Mr. Rekhtman, the researcher, wrote. But he is not to be blamed. He received incorrect information. I must repeat that after the synagogue was blown up, the candelabra and hanging chandeliers did survive. In addition, Zeylig Fershtut told me that during the enirety of Austrian rule in Radivil, the Christians of

---

[*] Translated from Hebrew by Elizabeth Kessin Berman.

Radivil excavated the debris in the synagogue yard, believing that the Jews had hidden their precious possessions there. They apparently carried off the hanging chandeliers and other objects they found there.

3. Also, the story about the synagogue's reconstruction is somewhat distorted. The truth is completely different. When the first families returning to Radivil found the yard empty, they decided to temporarily reconstruct the synagogue. My father, Moshe Sheyn, of blessed memory, went to Antonovitsh, the mayor, who had been a major in the border guard corps before the war, and convinced him to allow the army hospital sheds, which were still in the town, to be used as a synagogue. Antonovitsh considered my father's request and, having full authority, gave my father and Zeylig Fershtut, of blessed memory, permission to renovate the sheds with their own hands to serve as a synagogue.

After some time, after daily life had returned to its regular rhythm, a committee was formed—if my memory is correct, Shmuel Fidel, of blessed memory, was the chairman—to collect donations from local residents. They also got $10,000 from Moshe Ginzburg, of blessed memory, and built a new synagogue. But unfortunately, they didn't raise enough for artistic decorations. No one wished, therefore, God forbid, "to erase the glory of the past."
[page 60]

Radzivilov, 1900–1916[*]

Menachem Goldgart

In 1905, after the pogroms in Russia, there was a massive immigration of Jews to America through the Brody/Radzivilov border. Apart from the carefully guarded border, the émigrés faced very serious hazards even before they reached it. Many émigrés traveled by train until they were about 50 kilometers from the border, and then they continued by wagon or on foot to the actual crossing. But one day something terrible happened to a large group of our children of Israel: when they were found crossing into a forest

---

[*] Translated from Hebrew by Elizabeth Kessin Berman.

in Belokrinitsa, about 3 kilometers from Radzivilov, the notorious thief Ivan Rodigody attacked them, and they were robbed. Destitute, the people reached the town and reported what had happened to them. Of course, it was impossible to go to the police, and the townspeople were not interested. But Ayzik Ayzvozchik (the wagoner) heard about the robbery, and it angered him. He collected a few of his friends, including Ozer Lobar and Moshe Munkhes, and they left town to protect the Jews who were there. They found Ivan Rodigody and fought him. Rodigody fell and never rose again. From that time on, the route to the border was open.

Close to the outbreak of World War I, Austrian-Russian defenses were fortified for readiness near Kremenets and along the banks of the Ikva River, but in the summer of 1915, General Brusilov, commander of the Galician forces, breached them, and in a very few days he crossed these defenses. His campaign completely destroyed numerous cities and towns near the battle, causing an exodus of Jewish refugees from Radzivilov and Pochayev to Kremenets. The wealthy families had already left Radzivilov, but now the iron door slammed shut on those setting out on foot to Kremenets, either openly or in secret. All their belongings had been burned. And they now found themselves fleeing for their lives behind the hordes who had marched into battle. Many wounded men were with them. By day, they would hide in villages along the way, and by night, they would continue on their way. It was a 35-kilometer march from Radzivilov to Kremenets, but it took the refugees weeks to make this journey. The plight of the refugees on the roads came to the attention of some of the town's "operators." An ad hoc committee was organized to help the refugees.

[page 61]

The first concern was to feed the refugees even before they reached the city, but it was soon a concern to help them as they continued on their way. If the refugees came to the city, they were to be housed in various public buildings: the Talmud Torah building, which had been used as a stable for the Russian army, became a place for refugees. A few wealthy young people from Zionist youth groups organized ways to help them. They opened a kitchen for refugees that fed three meals a day to more than 3,000 souls.

Youth Committee to Aid Refugees, 1916

Seated (from right): Vaser, ..., M. Goldgart, ..., Sonye Landsberg-Poltorak. Standing (first row): Belter, ..., ..., Zamberg, Sonye Poltorak, ... Standing (second row): Yitschak Eydelman, Dr. Binyamin Landsberg, Bezdieski ....

Our town was almost completely destroyed, but some unclaimed property remained buried in basements. After many lobbying efforts, the committee got permission from government officials to go around Radzivilov collecting whatever property could be retrieved. The committee rented 100 wagons from local farmers, and a large caravan left Radzivilov filled with the collected items, such as undergarments, clothing, dresses, and all sorts of basic necessities. Because the government suspected that the Jews would aid the enemy, they permitted only two Jews to accompany the caravan: the associate rabbi, Mr. Barats, of blessed memory, and the writer of these lines.

[page 62]

With great trepidation, we succeeded in rescuing undergarments, clothing, dresses, and everything related from the basements and bringing it all to Kremenets. There, it was all put into a warehouse and, from there, distributed among the refugees by a core group of young people who were also dedicated to the welfare of refugee children and had organized a temporary school for them.

Tarbut School Second Grade and Teacher

[page 63]

Radzivilov, 1914–1922*

Aleksander Balaban

For a long time, the town of Radzivilov was considered a small town. It was close to the free area that lay between the Russian and Austrian frontiers until the actual line of the border was finally determined to be between it and Brody. From then on, Radzivilov was a Russian border town. Following the expulsion of the Jews from the town of Krupets at the decree of the Russian government, refugees fled en masse to Radzivilov, which was about five versts from Krupets. Radzivilov suddenly grew. Another reason for Radzivilov's sudden growth was that it was close to the railroad crossings, so tax collection offices had been located there to supervise railroad affairs. During Russian rule, Jewish citizens prospered during the years leading up

---

* Translated from Hebrew by Elizabeth Kessin Berman.

to the outbreak of World War I. Border administration was important for the town, especially since the Russian army and Cossacks were stationed there, the latter being troublesome to the Jews.

With the declaration of war in July 1914, the Cossacks organized a security force to search Jews: they were looking for "hidden telephones." They looted and robbed in their wake, but finding none, they nevertheless arrested a few Jews. As a result of this, they exiled some Jewish families, whose sad fate it was to be sent far away to Siberia.

During the war years, Radzivilov changed hands many times, like night and day, between the Russians and the Austrians and back again. And because of this, many townspeople were completely bewildered. Life in town was paralyzed; many Jewish inhabitants dispersed, and only a few stayed. During the Austrian occupation, it was easy for the Jews. The occupying forces allowed them to govern themselves as they wished, and they elected Mr. Zaks as head of the community, but soon enough the Russians returned to town. In the meantime, the revolution broke out, and Radzivilov felt its far-reaching effects. Residents who had been exiled and dispersed returned to their town to cope with the new situation. Stores opened, businesses revived, and the town's life regained its rhythm. But the local Ukrainians saw that the Jews were returning and rebuilding the town, and plotted against the Jews. A Jewish home was set ablaze almost every night, so it became necessary to organize a nightly Jewish guard detail.
[page 64]

When it became clear that the Jews could defend themselves and their property, the Ukrainians stopped their harassment.

This first public effort to organize a security force in town did not result only in the protection of the town's weakest. It also resulted in the organization of a democratic community. This was not unlike current tendencies in the government of both Russia and Ukraine toward self-governing committees. Such a central committee was chosen, and its leader was R' Moshe Duvid Balaban, one of the town's most ardent Zionists and successful businessmen. The youth of the town volunteered to clean out a local school and prepare it for use, and there he established a special committee for social aid—its purpose was to collect and to distribute basic provisions, such as wood, money, and other supplies, in the town and its vicinity.

At the same time, there was a perceived overall demand in Russia for goods that were available in neighboring Galicia, such as kerosene, matches, etc. The Radzivilov Jews began to trade in these commodities, bringing them from Galicia to Russia. Ukrainians were involved in transporting these commodities, working for very high wages, and this strengthened relations between the Jews and their neighbors. No one could have predicted what would incite Ukrainians to rob the Jews, and even the Ukrainians themselves can't answer for their looting.

With the development of public life in town, the library was restored and organized to showcase plays and cultural activities. A few political parties also sprang up: Zionists, Labor Zionists, and Betar, which was well known in the community. And everyone went to poetry readings. But then came a period of uprising, a change of government, and then—attacks on Jews. This period of blood and tears for the Jews of Ukraine also gripped Radzivilov. People became aware of the suffering of Jews in the vicinity, and the danger was coming closer. The children of Radzivilov foresaw the danger and began to organize Jewish Haganah [self-defense] brigades to protect lives and property. The community was quite strong, composed of 12 men, as both security workers and guards, and the town's youth were at their disposal at a moment's notice.

The local governing authorities were aware of the existence of the Jewish Haganah, and there was even an open dialogue between them until they asked a few members of the Haganah to watch over a government storage warehouse when there was a lack of trained soldiers. And so one day, the army in town spread fear about a platoon of soldiers who had robbed Jewish stores in Rovno and were about to come to Radzivilov. Out of fear of the army and its soldiers, they fled the town, leaving the Jews, who were in a panic to gain control and set up a strong defense. At midnight, about 20 armed soldiers appeared and tried to open fire on the Jewish guards, but after it was explained to them that these civilian security guards had no authority—either political or military—they withdrew.

[page 65]

General Bank (In Honor of Esteemed Board Member Tsvi Zagoroder)

Standing (from right): Velye Rushteyn, Moshe Boym, Simche Plem, Psachye Viser, Shlome Marder, Shmuel Kufman, Yekel Shtinberg, Tsvi Landis. Standing: Eli Chomut, Zelig-Hirsh Fishman, Leyb Spektor, Tsvi Zagoroder, Leyzer Zinger, Yekutiel Cherniak, Arye Treybitsh.

[page 66]

The soldiers had wanted a pretext for robbery, but they contented themselves with the pressure of their presence. But in the minds of the town's Jews, awareness of their heavily armed guards caused the soldiers to back down and leave.

This situation caused a decline in the economy, because few commodities were exported from the town, and imports were curtailed. Also, the currencies of the various governments lost their value, and in addition, a shortage of basic foodstuffs grew. As a result, their prices went sky-high. A depression affected all aspects of life, but the community took charge of the situation.

The committee for social aid instituted a centralization policy and, in particular, the rationing of bread, tobacco, sugar, and other goods. Rioters came to the town to incite, rob, and complain that the Jews were hiding goods on speculation. They were disabused of this notion. But the rioters in their turn then demanded a lot of money, and therefore it was necessary to impose a heavy tax on local Jews to satisfy these rioters' needs. They came and went, they went and they returned, and the tax was collected frequently and in an orderly fashion; meanwhile, the situation worsened, and the town continued to decline.

Exchanging money was difficult. The peasants saw that the Ukrainian government was at death's door, and there was no solution for it. They depended on the Jews' kindness for small purchases. And this was no small matter, because against this background, the seeds of many conflicts and poisonous relationships were planted. Thus daily matters developed, each day had its share of hard times, and worries multiplied: the population was enveloped in fear, and no one knew what the next day would bring. And the community was standing in the breach.

In the last days of the raucous Ukrainian-Petliura government, it was learned that a few ministers had arrived at the Radzivilov railroad station. A distinguished delegate was sent to meet with a Jewish community leader. He listened to the delegate and then told him that the situation in the town was worse than it had ever been and that if he couldn't help, no one else could. And he added, "We're not sure whether there will soon be an uprising against the government." This was the situation—complete chaos.

During the one of the final days, the Ukrainian army commander ordered the community to send a man to his office a day after his departure. The order was carried out, and the man who was sent guarded the office, but the commander never returned; government rule had changed, and for some days the town remained without any government. All eyes turned to the community. Various rumors circulated, some good tidings and some bad and depressing. According to one rumor, the French army was advancing toward the town, enlisting recruits. However, one Friday morning, an army official did appear: someone who had once lived in the town had a commission from the Ukrainian army to announce in Polish that the Poles

had conquered the remnants of the Ukrainian army in the vicinity. If the town desired peace, the Polish army would advance and occupy the town.
[page 67]

Yisrael Balaban, son of the head of the community, was sent as a delegate to meet with the Poles with a white flag in his hand. He met with a few Polish officers and was received with honor. In the evening, the regular army occupied the town.

The town's Jews hoped that Polish rule would mean stability and liberalism. The day after the surrender, which was the Sabbath, the synagogues were filled with worshippers praising their conquerors. But the next day they were all disappointed: on Sunday, the head of the community, R' Moshe-Duvid Balaban, was summoned by the military commander, who was encamped at the railroad station, and ordered to find a decent quantity of flour for the army and barley for the horses, all to be brought at a specific time. In the meantime, as Polish soldiers under General Haller's command began sauntering around town, they attacked older Jews who got in their way. This caused great fear that the town had never experienced. In the space of the month that Haller's army camped in town, Jews were blackmailed and extorted, until the head of the community saw no other choice but to flee on foot to neighboring Brody.

But soon after the successful exchange of the town, the advance company left Radzivilov, and another army with a new Polish officer took its place, with the result that conditions quieted and tensions relaxed; equilibrium came to the Jewish residents. The Poles, who were suspicious of Jews and also of some Ukrainians who were thought to have aided the Bolsheviks, carried out an investigation, and after a few days they arrested six young Jews and six Ukrainians. They were brought to Brody and tortured there. Afterward, they were transferred to a jail in Lvov and there contracted typhus. The rabbi of Radzivilov, a Polish priest, and others from the town tried to plead with governing officials to free the prisoners. Eventually they were able to convince the government that the prisoners had no connection to the Bolsheviks. Once the prisoners were well again, they were freed and returned to Radzivilov

At the same time, with a sense of urgency, the town's youth organized a Pioneer chapter and began to discuss immigration to the Land of Israel. In Sivan 1921, the first four pioneers set out on foot from Radzivilov to Brody and made their way from there through Lvov, Warszawa, and Trieste. Three of them got to the Land of Israel: Dov Kemchi, Tsvi Saley, and Aleksander Balaban.

Eventually life in Radzivilov regained its course under Polish rule. Public institutions dedicated to public affairs and charity appeared; the group called Pioneer, comprising some 150 persons, began to be recognized for its work and continued its local inroads; the Hebrew school grew, Zionist youth organizations appeared, and the Labor Zionists expanded.

[page 68]

Memories of the Town*

Menachem Goldgart

The factory manager was Pini Liberman, a courageous man who didn't have an ounce of fear in him. Here is one of the many events that earned him his reputation.

Ivan "Roza-Guza," the well-known thief in the surrounding area in those days, was feared by all of the inhabitants and even more so by the Jews. One day, he appeared in our town and assaulted Shlome, Pini's young son. Shlome rushed home in tears and told his father about Ivan the Terrible's brutality. Without hesitation, but with empty hands, Pini headed out to the place where Ivan was known to be passing the time drinking. The Jewish bartender, who was totally terrified of the criminal, was serving him drinks on demand. And then here comes Pini Liberman with a stick in his hand that he grabbed from a gentile who by chance happened to come to the same place. And without saying a word, he began to beat the thief merci-

---

* Translated from Hebrew by Elizabeth Kessin Berman.

lessly. Ivan collapsed, powerless, falling off his chair and just managing to say, "Pini dobra baya" —Pini really knows how to land a punch.

After Pini's aggressive actions, Ivan the Terrible's retribution spread among those on the streets. But that didn't faze Pini at all. He walked out and went on his way.

I also remember another event connected to Pini that happened after World War I, when the town was already under Polish rule.

One of the Polish army "gun-butts" beat Pini's youngest, Mishka, a son of his old age. After confronting the man, Pini overpowered him, took his gun, struck him, and then went on his way, taking the man's gun with him. The soldier went back to his platoon and returned soon afterward with a few of his companions. Pini then returned his gun. But no one failed to recognize the courage involved in this event. Everyone throughout the region talked about it.

About Moshe Mendil Ginzburg

Moshe Mendil Ginzburg has certainly been mentioned many times in this memorial book. Therefore, I will describe only one incident connected with him.

[page 69]

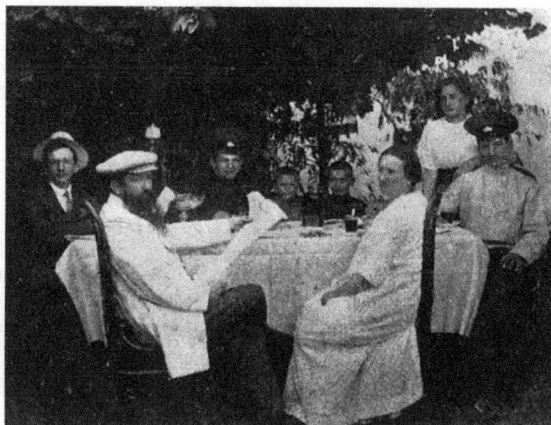

Moshe Goldgart and his family

Chana Goldgart

It is well known that Moshe Mendil Ginzburg contributed large sums of money to repair the Great Synagogue in our town, and, at his own expense, he also brought a painter from Lvov, who painted all the interior and exterior walls. When his work was done, the painter wrote on one of the walls that everything had been done through Moshe Mendil's contributions via the efforts of Chana and Moshe Goldgart and Velvel Zaks. A few groups in town believed this to be scandalous, because, in the opinion of many worshippers, writing anything like that in a holy place was forbidden. One Sabbath after the afternoon prayers, the people gathered to protest and threatened the elderly sexton; but the Eighteen Blessing prayers of grandfather Chana Goldgart calmed him down and soothed the other worshippers' anger.

[page 70]

But in the meantime, Yehoshue, the son of his old age, hurried to his elderly father's aid and leveled punches for the poor sexton ....

In the aftermath, this deed consequently raised by three rubles the price of the compensation for the teeth that suffered from the protruding arm of the son of his old age ....

The Life and Character of
Moshe Mendil Ginzburg (Mes)*

From the Russian: Duvid Zahavi

Moshe Mendil Mes was born in Radzivilov on December 19, 1851, to Akiva and Rosye Mes. The family was poor. Moshe Mendil was five when he started cheder, and he was also admitted to the town's Russian elementary school. There he excelled in his studies, and he was considered a promising student and suitable for further studies.

Even though he was hard at work at his studies, he still had time to work to help his parents, whose own situation was very dire. After Moshe Mendil had acquired a reputation for his German and Russian skills, he decided to try his luck in the greater world. He traveled to Odessa. There he found work as a junior clerk; but after two years of trying to get ahead and improve his position, he decided to go to America along with the many others who were seeking opportunities there. With no belongings, he traveled to Hamburg and from there sailed on to America in steerage. After 46 days of rough sailing, he arrived in the land of opportunity. There he worked at many jobs, gaining a command of English and changing his family name to Ginzburg, a name favored by his relatives, who were peddlers there. While dealing with a number of fellow workers who were Chinese, he suddenly got it into his head to travel to China. He believed that a wealth of trading opportunities were to be had there.

On his way to China, his boat stopped at the Japanese port of Yokohama. He was deeply impressed with the liveliness of this port city and swore in his heart that he would settle there. And so his trading career began.

He began working as a clerk in a trading house, and after a year and a half, after he had saved up 250 yen, he opened his own small trading company. Almost immediately, his business began to flourish and grow.

---

* Translated from Hebrew by Elizabeth Kessin Berman. *Note in original:* From the book published in 1933 in Paris by the Friends of M. Ginzburg.

[page 71]

Moshe Mendil Ginsburg

In the beginning, Ginzburg's trading contacts were the Russians who frequently came to Yokohama. But gradually, as the Russian language became more familiar in Japan and relations between Russians and Japanese became friendlier, Ginzburg succeeded in gaining confidence among the Japanese, and he thus began to cater to their needs.

The Russians were very impressed with Ginzburg's efforts, talent, and trustworthiness, and within a short time, Ginzburg was the man of choice for half the Russians of the Far East and in his town, Port Arthur.

[page 72]

Ginzburg was also instrumental in giving aid to the Russian fleet during the Boxer days in China, and for that he was given official thanks from the head of the czar's special staff in the Far East.

When the Russo-Japanese War broke out and the Russian fleet encountered hostility in the so-called neutral ports of the Far East, Ginzburg was able, merely on the strength of his talent and ingenuity, to acquire fuel and other equipment for the Russian fleet. This was a great moment for Ginzburg, and he became even greater. He received the title Actual State Councilor, a title that was unprecedented among the Jews of czarist Russia. All the Russian fleet officers, even the Russian fleet's highest officer in the Far East, Admiral Makarov, showered praise upon him.

It was said that when the minister of the naval fleet reported to the czar on supplying the Russian naval fleet on the open ocean, the czar answered him, "They don't have Ginzburg there!" But Ginzburg was not insulted.

It should be pointed out that Moshe Mendil never forgot his family, nor his town, Radzivilov, during all those years. He loved his mother very much and wrote her heartfelt letters even though he was so far away. He supported his brother, Shmuel, and his wife, Ratsi Mes, and their four children: Kostye, Yozye, Asye, Sonye, and Roze.* And in addition he supported these people: all elderly people (even if they were not connected specifically to the town of Radzivilov). If there was a money matter or a matter related to a license to live outside the Pale of Settlement, they would turn to him; his mother, who had a sympathetic Jewish heart; or his brother Shmuel. The matters would be sent on to Ginzburg, and they would be settled in the best possible way.

Ginzburg founded a hospital, a magnificent synagogue, a school, and much more in Radzivilov. When he came to visit Radzivilov many years after he had left the town, it was a holiday not only for his mother and his family but also for the entire town. Even the local authorities heaped praise on him, aware of his high stature. Also, while living in Port Arthur and Yokohama, Ginzburg supported the local Jewish communities and established magnificent institutions there.

However, the zenith of Ginzburg's charitable work for the public came when he settled in Sankt Peterburg. There he was very much influenced by Baron Gunzberg, and the pair spent much of their time working for the betterment of the local Jewish community. Accordingly, it should be recalled that Ginzburg achieved prominence by supporting Russian causes and giv-

---

* *Translator's note:* Although the author writes "four children," five names are given.

ing significant funds to non-Jewish Russian institutions and individuals, under the influence of Rabbi Ayzenshtadt, chief rabbi of Sankt Peterburg, and under the well-known lawyer Sliozberg. He founded a magnificent old-age home in Sankt Peterburg, and next to it a social hall and museum.

[page 73]

Moshe-Mendil Ginzburg, His Mother, and His Sister

For this museum, which abutted the old-age home, he hired the renowned folklorist, the writer Sh. An-sky, who brought to it his collections of antiquities, ritual objects, and other items that demonstrated Jewish life in Russia, which he had gathered during his ethnographic explorations in Russian towns and villages.*

When the revolution broke out, Ginzburg and his wife traveled from Argart to Paris. And even there in Paris, he continued to donate funds to help both Jews and non-Jews, although his fortune was greatly reduced. He supported yeshivas that had been transplanted from Russia and Poland to Paris. He founded a cultural institution in Paris called Yakov's Tent, at whose head were Rabbi Ayzenshtadt, Baron Gunzberg, lawyer Sliozberg,

---

* *Note in original:* I remember that during his investigations in Radzivilov, An-sky photographed old tombstones in the old Jewish cemetery and deposited these photographs in the museum in Sankt Peterburg.—Translator.

and other elite Russian Jews. But again it was Ginzburg who financed the work.

With Ginzburg's aid, an evening school was established. And he also gave money to support the Jewish student federation as well as non-Jewish students. At the same time, the Radzivilov community asked for his help in restoring the Great Synagogue, which had been destroyed during the war.

[page 74]

And he answered immediately, sending $5,000. When he was told that that sum was not enough, he sent another $2,500.

When Ginzburg reached the age of 80, the institutions he founded in Paris decided to celebrate this auspicious occasion. Non-Jewish organizations also participated in this event, among them the Russian navy officials, many of whom were generals and admirals who had fled the Bolshevik regime to Paris and, because of Ginzburg's help, were not idle there.

The party was held not in an auditorium, but in a home, as Ginzburg and his friends requested. Many toasts were offered by private citizens and those from the institutions he had founded, and there were many speeches by Jews and non-Jews alike. Everyone praised his dedication to helping the needy and the depth of his heart. The main speech was delivered by Rabbi Ayzenshtadt, who stressed among other things that Ginzburg, in spite of all that he did, was a man of extreme humility and modesty. Ginzburg received a letter from the town of Radzivilov, which announced that Ginzburg was named a distinguished citizen of the town and that one of the town's boulevards would be named for him.

So it was with this man called Ginzburg, and these were his good deeds.

Ginzburg's brother, Shmuel Mes, died in 1913, and his children and grandchildren[*] perished along with all of the Jews of Radzivilov, murdered by the Nazis and their Ukrainian collaborators.

---

[*] Translated from Hebrew by Rivka Schiller with Judy Fixler. *Note in original:* Among those who survived were his daughter Sonye in Paris and his daughter Roze in New York.

In Memory of
Teacher Avraham Yehuda Poliak,
of Blessed Memory

Aleksander Balaban

Avraham Yehuda Poliak

Avraham Yehuda was born in a village. He studied in yeshivas and in synagogues until he was taken to Berestechko, which is next to Radzivilov, and affianced to the daughter of one of the town's well-respected families.

The young prodigy was accepted enthusiastically by the Torah-oriented Hasidic family, which enabled him to continue to study even after the wedding. He devoted nights as well as days to the study of Talmud and the Gemara, Rashi commentary, and medieval commentaries; and his musical voice, solo at night and during the morning watch, when he would rise to do the Creator's work, is remembered by the townspeople.

That period—it was during the Enlightenment, which did not elude the town. Naturally, he was one of the first to be captured by it. And once he was captured, his special character stood out here, as well; he didn't know what compromise or adaptation was. And in his "apostatizing," he transferred all his piety to the new worlds being revealed to him. And from then on, that same tune that indicated his devotion while learning the words of

Abaye and Rava* began to remerge from the special room in his apartment. And chapters of Mapu, Yehuda Leyb Gordon, Manet, and issues of *Hamelits* and *Hatsefira* were heard. And years later, Bialik, Shneur, *Hashiloach*, and alongside them, philosophy, natural science, and social science: Nietzsche's *Thus Spake Zarathustra*, various articles on physiology, and the structure of elements. The daily and periodic press was bound by date, since the man knew how to collect and preserve every page of human and national contemplation. Beginning with issues of *Avigdor* and ending with *Hatekufah*, *Haolam*, etc., the bookshelves in the rooms filled up with every new item emerging in the Hebrew literature.

At home, people do not have enough to eat, but he does not skip one printed Hebrew letter, especially not the select ones.

[page 76]

He had a retentive memory like a cistern that does not lose a drop and is like an inexhaustible fountain. For he does not gather together only for himself; he brings together people and shares his knowledge and information with them.

From here on, he took the path to instructing adults and teaching children under all conditions: in the narrow living room in Berestechko and, later on, with the growth and expansion of the instruction, the establishment of the schools in the town and in Radzivilov.

This was before the orderly organization of various societies and associations. The entire burden fell on this man's shoulders, and, out of a sense of communal responsibility, he neglected matters of livelihood and normal family life for matters of society, the general community, and the nation over his personal affairs.

And another thing: In his new way of thinking, there was no room to continue with the idyllic traditional family life of the prodigal son-in-law supported by his father-in-law. This was also in contrast to his comprehension

---

* *Translator's note:* Abaye and Rava were two Talmudic scholars in Babylonia, friends who frequently debated one another.

of the social structure and the individual's obligations within it; and thus arose the question of material existence. He attempted trade, but soon gave up.

The first signs of Zionism appeared. It is a given that he was one of the first to be caught up in it, and again he was committed body and soul. For him, Zionism was not only an impulse for him to go to the Land of Israel; for him, Zionism was the emergence of a new Jew, proud of the nation's past and its future. And he devoted himself to the education of school-age children and instructed adolescents; and under his influence, the Second Immigration from Berestechko began a couple of years before it did in our town of Radzivilov.

He infected the youth within his family with his enthusiasm: his sisters-in-law absorbed the glory of the Enlightenment movement and Zionism and left with the Second Immigration to Israel, taking with them Bilhah, his 12-year-old eldest daughter (she died young and left behind one son in Israel).

However, social development in the town during that same period had not yet reached the height that it attained over time. Family members of those who immigrated saw themselves as negatively affected by the "inciter and distance," and there were episodes in which a mother or father of one of those who immigrated even attacked and took out all of his or her anger on Avraham Yehuda. The family's material troubles increased, and Avraham Yehuda was forced to leave town.

He came to Radzivilov and found a fertile field there. For Radzivilov was always Zionist, first on the list of monetary donors, even in comparison to larger towns.

His first act here was to open a school with the help of a group of Zionists in partnership with the teacher, Binyamin Finkelshteyn, of blessed memory. It was not easy to compete with the Russian government school, where you did not have to pay tuition.

[page 77]

Pioneer in 1923

Standing (right to left): Dore Balaban, M. Stirt, Frida Gershgorin, Keselman, Yehoshue Felman, Avraham Lindner, Tsvi Geler, Yehoshue Goldgart, Chave Halbershtet, ... Save Zaks.

Seated: Yoel Charap, Simche Ayzen, Ester Blekhman, Shimon Goldgart, Tsvi Kitayksher, Ester Margolis, Yozek Zaks, Brokhe Grobshteyn.

Below: Leyb Fik, R. Valigore, Munye Margolis, Geler, Bentsion Grobshteyn, Sore Mafshit, M. Geler.

Nevertheless, according to Avraham Yehuda, this was not at all a problem, as the essential thing was the goal; and for that he was prepared to be satisfied with the most meager of the meager: bread and tea and some potatoes. But even with this, there was no money to pay for the cleaning of the school—one does not mock such work; and in the evenings, when he finished his lessons, not for monetary compensation, naturally, he himself took care of the cleaning. The essential thing was for the school to exist, and indeed it existed until World War I broke out.

Before long, Avraham Yehuda's blessed influence with regard to the Second Immigration began to show its signs in Radzivilov as well. In this manner, the Shtofer brothers,* farmers in Be'er Tuvia; Tsvi Ben-Artsi (Luzman);*

---

* *Note in original:* One of the brothers, Binyamin, died several years ago.

Menachem Mendel Goldgart; Mordekhay Peker, member of Degania Alef; Bentsion Batlin (he did not stay); and others.

[page 78]

In 1918, when the refugees were returning after the war, Avraham Yehuda also appeared, and with the help of the Jewish community, he reopened the school. In 1919, he began to organize Pioneer. I recall that when Avraham Yehuda entered Yafe Broida's house and found 92 pioneers there who had come for the founding assembly—nearly every youth from Radzivilov—his face shone, and there was no limit to his joy and happiness.

Although he was open-minded in his views, disputes with him were most persistent, for he was resolute in his view that everything in Israel must be built in accordance with the local Jewish spirit.

In 1920, the minute it was possible to reach Warszawa, the first four pioneers took leave of him and set out on their way; and throughout the Third Immigration, dozens and dozens of his protégés, many of whom live on kibbutzim and moshavim today, streamed out. Indeed, unfortunately and shamefully, we must acknowledge that there is not a single individual, even from among his friends and protégés, those from the Second Immigration, who attempted to obtain a certificate for the teacher and educator who gave his soul for Zion, and it would have been only right to give him this small compensation for all his blessed work on behalf of Zionism. He was shattered and died at a young age in the Diaspora. May his memory be a blessing.

In Memory of the Teacher[†]

U. and R. Oren

If not for the destruction of the cemetery in Berestechko, a town near Radzivilov, the visitor's eye would have been drawn to the strange inscription on one of the headstones. It was written according to the deceased's

---

[*] *Note in original:* Tsvi Ben-Artsi died of yellow fever in Poriah during World War I.

[†] Translated from Hebrew by Rivka Schiller with Judy Fixler.

will, part of which is engraved in my memory: "Herein is buried a grain of eternity, foreign and strange to its surroundings, which once existed, and returned to its source." And a line from the written will that passed from the world along with its guard—the son: ... "Following my death, my remains should be cared for by people who are not my blood relatives, whose relationship is by chance and compulsion, but rather by kindred spirits whose relationship is likened to a hammer splitting a rock."

Indeed, the man was unusual within his surroundings, since he was one of the few who aspired to the wholeness that was imprinted in his character, woven into the fabric of the soul, as a foundational part of it. For this man was blessed with an extensive, strong intellectual capacity and much integrity. And so, from the religious study hall to the Enlightenment, to pedagogy and teaching. Teaching means "with all your resources,"* and not just for show. It also means a great desire to influence, instill faith in the hearts of those who waiver, to summon to the merciless struggle, without acquiescence, and compromise, for the great ideal of the nation's resurrection.

Such was the man who was totally devoted to the nation's resurrection, in its own land, which he himself never reached.

---

* *Translator's note:* From Deuteronomy 6:5, also uttered daily in the *Shema* (Hear, O Israel) prayer.

[page 79]

Memorial to Radzivilov*

A. A. Avtichi-Hadari

The name Radzivilov triggers many memories, some good and some sad. In Radzivilov, a typical Volhynia town, there were Jews who had been there for generations, and they made up most of the population of the town, even leaders of the town in the eyes of the both Jews and non-Jews, most of whom earned their livelihoods from Jewish businesses and their trade with them. Radzivilov Jews knew how to organize both their civic and their economic lives during the many different governments that changed hands frequently for many years. They were steadfast during the difficult changes from one ruling power to the next; they endured entanglements during the Polish uprising and conflicts with the Russians. And they suffered from the malicious exploits of border patrols—soldiers and Russian Cossacks—who were stationed about three kilometers from town. Radzivilov Jews drank from the cup of hardship as a result of the battles and conquests during World War I, when the town moved from the Russians to the Austrians a few times, but at the end of the war, they knew how to outrage the Russians, showing them up when they rehabilitated both their private and public lives.

Border trade, both legal and illegal, was very brisk for Jews and non-Jews, and generally you could say it was crucial for the town. However, incitement against Jews raged in those bitter enemies of Israel who lived in the famous monastery in neighboring Pochayev, and its priest, Ilyador Vitaly, who was known for sowing poison and hatred in the hearts of the many Christians who lived in the region and for spreading terror and fear among the Jews. At any rate, and in spite of the opposition of the "Black

---

* Translated from Hebrew by Elizabeth Kessin-Berman.

Hundred,"* Radzivilovers stocked their stores and even imported decorations from Austrian Brody for pilgrims to the Pochayev monastery. Monks would come for prayer and retreat in their most holy place, and on their way, they would buy basic goods and gifts in Jewish stores. Once, Ilyador the priest, with the help of an informer named Kolka, falsely accused two Jews, a brother and sister, saying that they intended to blow up the holy monastery. The informer, with Skorochodov, the police officer, sneaked out of Pochayev and went to Radzivilov, where the police officer hid the informer in a hotel. While the attack never happened and no one mentioned it among the Jews, the poison was nevertheless planted, and it bore much fruit in the coming days.

The road to the border passed close to Radzivilov, and on it, thousands of Jewish émigrés made their way to Austria and from there to America.

[page 80]

After leaving Russia, their way out was fraught with difficulty, and the passage was dangerous. And tears were many for mothers and children who set out in search of breadwinners who had gone ahead of them and who were soon discovered to be in different locations. Many times, the émigrés were captured and became part of a prisoners' transport, usually on foot. They eventually returned to their original homes, only to try their luck again later.

During Ukrainian rule, from 1918 to 1920, the Radzivilov Jews found themselves in the snares of paramilitary bands and many different types of fighters. The suffering was great, and the sword of Damocles hung over their heads every day. And once, when a delegation of Jews appealed to a Jewish Ukrainian government minister named Krasni, who was traveling by train near Radzivilov, asking him for protection, the minister said to them, "How is it possible to help the Jews? Even the government itself needs mer-

---

* *Translation editor's note:* The Black Hundred was an ultra-nationalist movement in Russia in the early 20th century.

cy from all the revolutionaries and soldiers. Who knows what will happen next?"

Then the Poles conquered the town, and a new atmosphere arose. Many businesses reopened, and the men of the Haganah [self-defense] that had operated during the days of terror returned. Gradually, community members who had left returned and got organized, and soon the economy improved. The destruction was repaired gradually, and soon the town flourished once again. Men of all types, men of the community who were there, lent a hand in organizing community and civic life and setting up educational and cultural institutions. Very quickly, Zionism took hold of many townspeople, causing many to start preparing for immigration to the Land of Israel.

At the same time, Radzivilov Jews also played an important role in the first Polish Sejm elections (after the founding Sejm), held in 1922. The Jewish politic declared itself a minority "bloc," organized by Yitschak Grinboym. There was a great victory, and 55 young Jews were elected to the Sejm and the senate in independent Poland. Young Avraham Levinson fondly recalls the vigor and energy of the Radzivilov politicians: Menashe Zagoroder, Moshe Duvid Balaban, Shmuel Fidel, Kalman Taykh, Shumker, Moshe Goldgart, and others from the young generation of Zionists, who proved their great dedication to Jewish and Zionist causes when a propaganda campaign arose in town against the "bloc."

Many people in Radzivilov prepared themselves, immigrated to Israel, put down roots there, and consequently brought about the reconstruction of the homeland. But thousands of Jews from the town fell under the Nazi enemy's plunder during the second Holocaust of the house of Israel throughout Europe, and especially in Poland.

The events in Radzivilov formed a link in the chain of the life of the Jews in Volhynia, one outcome uniting and connecting the circle of our generation's history. Radzivilov will forever have a place in the recounting of the days of the congregation of Israel on the soil of Volhynia and in Israel.

United Israel Appeal Committee—1923

Seated (right to left): Zilberman Zev, Tsvi Goldgart, Yehoshue Halbershtet, Moshe Duvid Balaban, Menashe Zagoroder, guest from the Land of Israel Gurzhelka, Ayzenberg of Rovno, Moshe Goldgart, Kalman Taykh, Shmuel Fidel. Standing: Shmuel Fershtut, Yisrael Reyf, Duvid Kagan, Duvid Shnayder.

From My Childhood Memories of Radzivilov*

Tsvi Saley

I was born in Radzivilov. But when I was very young, my parents moved to Kivertsy. We return to Radzivilov only in 1909. In 1914, World War I broke out. Our town, which was a border town, suffered badly from the fighting, and many residents fled. But in 1918, many of the inhabitants returned to their homes and began to rebuild what had been destroyed, and in 1920 I immigrated to Israel. Thus I spent very few years in Radzivilov. But even so, the town of Radzivilov is engraved in my memory, so I can offer a few descriptive lines for this book.

Sholem Aleichem once described Radzivilov in these words: "It isn't so big, but you can always steal [across] a border." But in actuality, Radzivilov was

---

* Translated from Hebrew by Elizabeth Kessin-Berman.

not so small that it would escape notice; it was a large town, nicely laid out in comparison with other neighboring towns like Pochayev, Varkovichi, Verba, Ozeryany, and others. Radzivilov was a major city compared to these.

From the edge of the railroad station, Pochayev Street ran to the flourmill, which was near the bridge that led to Brody Road and continued some two or three kilometers; and from the center ran a second street with gas streetlamps on both sides. On this street was the fire station, housed in a big garage, to take care of fires, with storage sheds for wagons and stables for the care of horses. On top of one of the sheds was a high tower with uninterrupted views for keeping watch, and in it hung the warning bell. In the center of the courtyard was a high column used for training exercises.

Our town had many large and small streets and numerous lanes. In the center were all kinds of stores with a variety of wares, including Efraim Rayzer's wine store.

The pride of the town was the Great Synagogue, which was magnificently decorated with paintings and woodcarvings. But it was destroyed during World War I.

[page 83]

There was also a government hospital on Pochayev Street, enclosed by a large gate, on which a large sign with golden letters identified it as "the government hospital donated by the government advisor, Moshe Mendil Gintsburg." This very large hospital, made of stone, contained many multistory wings. All of the city's residents received medical attention here, regardless of religion.

There was also a Talmud Torah in the town, housed in a modest building that served as a teaching facility for the poor. In 1911, the town elders decided to add another floor devoted to the oldest students, who were studying Talmud and commentary with R' Yitschak Leyb the Teacher. There were about 10 students in this class, the best students from the most respected families of Radzivilov and surrounding towns. A Hebrew teacher, Mr. Binyamin Finkelshteyn, was also invited to be part of the school; he taught us Bible and Hebrew literature. The year I spent at the Talmud Torah is etched deeply in my heart because of the great impressions the teachers made on us. R' Yitschak Leyb ushered us into the paradise of Talmud through his commentaries, and Mr. Finkelshteyn bestowed knowledge of Hebrew and Enlightenment literature on us.

Government Hospital Named for Moshe Mendil Gintsburg

[page 84]

R' Yitschak Leyb nicknamed two windows in our second-floor classroom "the town's eyes," and he was right because everyone could see them from the street.

Apart from the Talmud Torah, there were many respectable cheders, a government school, and a technical school for boys and for girls. Although most of the Jews were occupied with their work and their worries about making a living, they did not let these things stand in the way of getting an education for their children. Some sent their children abroad, to large cities and yeshivas.

There were many private teachers, and among them I recall Mr. Fershtut, a Russian language teacher, and his brother-in-law, who established a Hebrew kindergarten—the first one—for everyone in the area, and they all played energetically and sang Hebrew songs there.

Dad's House*

Yehudit Saleyt Luski (Grobshteyn)

Our house in Radzivilov was a one-story dwelling situated very close to a stream. On the other side was a long, narrow garden that stretched to a pool of water. A non-Jewish woman planted vegetables in it during the spring, although many others planted fruit trees. That was my father's private kingdom, where he took care of his plantings like a father caring for an infant. The tree trunks were neatly pruned, the paths were kept clear, the grass was nurtured, and the bushes sprouted like dew around the fence. Every morning before walking to morning prayers, Father would go out to the garden to view each and every flower that had bloomed and every bud that had opened, and he would take great pride in the flourishing garden.

As an ardent Zionist, Father saw his work in the garden as preparation for his future work in the Land of Israel. It was his intention to immigrate to Israel and farm there with his whole family.

Stories of our childhood are centered on our ancestors' old country: on life during the Bible's radiant period and the passage and transition to life in a new country. Our ears were eager to hear stories of this land of milk and honey in ruins, which those who were coming would surely rebuild. We never tired of hearing stories about the new settlements, the vineyard harvests, and the guards who stood watch, as well as the souls of the Jews who were there, their strength, and the courage of those who stood guard over the orchards, and so on and so on.

[page 85]

From earliest childhood, we learned Hebrew. I saw a film about the lives of Jews in the Land of Israel when I was three and a half. Everyone in our family saw this film, even babies in their mothers' arms.

---

* Translated from Hebrew by Elizabeth Kessin-Berman.

Tu Bishvat* was a cold and snowy day in Russia, but it was the new year for trees in Israel; and for us it was a joyous holiday when we ate the fruits of the vine, chewed dry carob—foods of the Land of Israel—and imagined the homeland's blue skies and sunshine and the trees blooming there.

Father had been planning intently to immigrate, but the war—World War I—broke out. Radzivilov, which was situated close to the border, was turned into a battlefield, and in 1915 the Austrians conquered the city. A year after that, in 1916, the Russians reconquered it, and the residents scattered to many faraway places.

I well remember the day we became war refugees. It was on Shavuot, which began on the Sabbath. The house was polished and decorated for a holiday, and the food had been prepared in an oven the day before; but not one person could touch the food. Dread of the future was in the air. Even we, the children, were anxious about what was in store for us. The Austrians withdrew, but the Russians immediately entered the town. The streets were empty and abandoned, there was complete silence all around, and an air of expectation was everywhere. At four in the afternoon, the Russian army entered the town, and the soldiers immediately began to go from house to house, commanding the residents to leave the town quickly for the surrounding forest because the fighting was about to begin. We speedily changed out of our holiday clothes into everyday clothes, gathered up bread and old blankets—old, certainly, in order to leave the best things we had safely in the house. This was quite naive, because my parents thought that everything they left behind would remain untouched. Thus they hid everything dear to us in the closets, including silver and expensive clothing. They locked the closets and the doors, and we set out on our way.

It is important to recall one small episode here. After we had gone a short way, my mother suddenly remembered that she hadn't locked the kitchen

---

* *Translation editor's note:* Tu Bishvat is a Jewish holiday occurring on the 15th day of the Hebrew month of Shevat (January/February). It is also called the "new year of trees."

door. We stopped walking, and Father went back to check the door. In the meantime, from afar, gunfire reverberated. But we still waited for and worried about Father. When he arrived, he was laughing and had a smile on his face. The door was locked, and the key was in his hand.

We all walked on, old people, women, and children with packs on their backs. Utterly fatigued, we distanced ourselves from the town. We rested at night, and in the morning, we were commanded to go even further from the town. We did this for three days, until we came to Kremenets.

[page 86]

As we arrived in the city, the residents came out to meet us, tea and fresh bread in their hands. Even to this day I remember the taste of this meal ... and especially the kindness of the people of Kremenets, who were so generous to us in our time of suffering.

From Kremenets, our family went on to Rovno, and there we began to restore our lives. We found a way to earn a living, the children attended school, and we made the best of our circumstances. But our concern for our town was never far from our minds, and after two years, in 1918, we returned to Radzivilov. Many others who were driven out from their homes on foot returned at the same time.

Where our house had been, we found ... an uprooted garden and huge weeds—we didn't know where the house was and where the garden was. But we still had the keys we had taken with us .... Not all of the town was destroyed; there were areas where the streets were not touched at all, but the houses that were left standing were in heaps that needed repair and reconstruction.

Even though we worried about how we would rebuild our lives from scratch, the children's education was not neglected. My parents took the initiative to open a school for Jewish students. Yehuda-Leyb Polak returned as a completely dedicated Hebrew and Bible teacher. He also gave instruction in Hebrew to adult groups. The Yiddish teacher, Mr. Marder, taught in the same school. But my father, who considered Yiddish inferior to the Hebrew language and considered Hebrew the language of the future, forbade us to participate in his classes. And so my sister Sore and I would get up and leave the class during the Yiddish lessons.

In the middle of winter of the same year, a class opened for boys who knew Torah. The lessons were held during the afternoon. I knew Hebrew and Bible, so I was accepted into this class, and as time passed, I was the only girl among 24 boys in that class. When it came time to dramatize one of the chapters of the Bible, I naturally was assigned all the women's roles.

We were all merely 9 and 10 years old. We heard about organizations called Young Zionists and Labor Zionists, but we didn't know the ideological difference between them. At any rate, we were dragged to all of the meetings of those who called themselves Young Zionists and those who saw themselves as Labor Zionists. Soon there was also a Zionist club.

During the same time, my brother Tsvi returned to Radzivilov with the intention of immigrating to Israel. He had been a Hebrew teacher in Rovno. Until then, he began to organize evening classes for young people who had grown up there and wanted to learn the language. But no textbooks could be found. Because of this, it was necessary to make lists, and the students would copy them into their notebooks.

[page 87]

Slowly the Zionist movement grew, developed, and took hold of the residents. I remember from that time two Zionist gatherings called "blue-and-white gatherings." The first began with the singing of the song from Psalms called "A Psalm for Dedicating the House of David," led by two soloists, Eydel Grobshteyn and Lize Goldberg.[*] But from the second gathering I recall a Yiddish song that caused an argument between a Zionist and a Hasidic Jew who thought Zionism was a sin:

> Listen Jews, oh the news that I have just heard;
> Somebody, of all people a doctor,
> he has countless transgressions,
> and he wishes, so he says,

---

[*] *Note in original:* Eydel Grobshteyn died in the Holocaust; Lize Goldberg lived in the Land.

Young Pioneer Chapter under the Direction of Bronye Balaban

[page 88]

to lead the Jews to the Land of Israel,
to lead them there,
before the coming of the Messiah.

After the argument, the Hasid was convinced of the righteousness of the Zionists, and the two concluded in a duet:

A boil on the Turk's hand,
and repossessed shall be the land.

During the same gathering, there was also a play about Hebrew guards in the Land of Israel.

In 1920, during the war between the Russians and the Poles, the first group from Radzivilov immigrated to Israel. Aleksander Balaban and my brother Tsvi were part of this first group. Their route was very complicated, and it took them about six months to reach the Land of Israel. When the first letter from my brother arrived telling us that he had already found work on the Haifa–Jeddah road, there was a great celebration in our house—"to him, it was a small thing": a group of Radzivilovers was paving roads for us in the Land of Israel!

The Balfour Declaration really motivated my father. He now believed that a state for Jewish people was now moving forward and getting organized. He became like a prophet in the synagogues, inspiring Jews to rise up and leave the Diaspora's "vale of tears" and "build the Land of Israel and be restored in it." "Jews, dear brothers!"—he said in the synagogues—"it is incumbent on us to leave this Diaspora without delay lest it be too late, because the Diaspora is like Sodom to us. As it is written in the Torah: 'And the men said to Lot (when he was advised to leave that place).' Today we can take everything we need and leave, but woe to those who linger." Many considered my father to be strange, a Jew possessed by a demon during the night. Just get up, leave everything, and travel to a desolate land? That was just a crazy man speaking! But when Father met people like these, he would open the Bible and read to them from the prophecies of redemption.

As we prepared to immigrate, Father bought a Torah scroll to take with him. In the meantime, it stayed with us in our house, a Zionist symbol, on the Sabbath and the rest of the holidays.

The second immigration group from Radzivilov left in 1921. This group included the Klomensky family, Sore Spektor, and my sister Rivke.

At the same time, the brothers Dudke and Shimon Goldgerd founded a Youth Guard branch. Those who were 13 and above were admitted as members. We were all students in the progynasium then, and teachers were forbidden to know that we were participating in a youth movement.
[page 89]

Naturally, this ban encouraged us to hold our meetings, which took place twice a week at the Gun family's house, as in the expression, "Stolen water will be sweeter."

Gradually the letters from Rivke and my brother Tsvi slackened off, and so the desire to immigrate grew. But mother, a "woman of valor" who relied on having all of her stores and wares available effortlessly in her cupboard, could not be persuaded to forsake her comforts and travel with five children, the smallest of whom was five years old, to a desolate desert. She asked that we wait a few years until the children had grown up. Father, however, ignored all her complaints and proved to her with tempting words that it would indeed be better to emigrate now. At their wits' end, our parents finally asked the children what they thought: who among you wants to remain here with Mother in the Diaspora, and who is willing to go with Father to the Land of Israel? All of us naturally declared that we wanted to go to the Land of Israel, and so we also convinced our mother. And so we began to pack our suitcases.

The day we left town was very moving. It was on a Monday, April 2, 1922. The train to Lvov was ready to leave at four in the afternoon, and at 1:30, all of the town's Zionists gathered at our house, so many relatives and friends helping as our parents packed our belongings into the wagon and participating in the loading as if they, too, were immigrating to Israel. We set out finally, and on the main road we encountered a parade of students from the Jewish school, led by their teachers, who were heading to the train station. Many others came with us, closing their shops to see us off. Another group gathered at the train station, and it seemed as though all of the town's residents had come out to bid us farewell. The well-respected R' Moshe-Duvid Balaban read a goodbye letter in Hebrew from the community. As the train approached, everyone sang "Hatikvah" and clapped, and in the end kissed us goodbye ....

The station manager was moved by the joy that he saw before him and the size of the assembly. Twice he held up the train from leaving on schedule in order to have the crowd gracefully separate themselves from us. In the end, the train began its route as the crowd clapped in its honor....

Allow me to say that the warm departure given to us by the town's residents will never be erased from our memories as long as we live.

[page 90]

[Blank]

[page 91]

A. Zionism

B. Culture and Education

C. Houses of Prayer and Study Halls

D. Welfare Institutions

[page 92]
[Blank]

Zionism

History of the
Zionist Organization in Radzivilov*

Menachem Goldgart

The Zionist Organization in our town languished until Avraham Yehuda, who before then had been active in Zionist life in his own town, Berestechko, came to us. He was devoted to this work for his entire life, and he helped many young people in Berestechko immigrate to Israel. When Avraham Yehuda came to us, he found that there was much to be done. Ben-Tsion Betlin helped him a lot. I remember how Ben-Tsion introduced me to his Zionist work, even though I was but a boy of 14. It was the Sabbath, during the Torah reading in the Great Synagogue, when Ben-Tsion suggested that I take a look at a Zionist library. He brought me to the elderly Mordekhay Betlin's house to show me the library. When we entered the house, he brought out from under the bed a crate that had a few pamphlets and books in Yiddish, Hebrew, and Russian. When it was obvious that I was surprised that the so-called library was concealed in a crate under a bed, he explained to me that because the Zionist Organization, and, of course also the library, were illegal, there was no choice but to keep the library hidden in the older man's house because the czarist police wouldn't suspect him.

Eventually the library wandered from house so that it would not fall into the hands of the police, heaven forbid. Finally, we decided that the safest place was at Shimon Rayzer's, whose father's house contained the *Fivnia Lovka,* that is to say, the beer pub, and this, of course, was because the policemen and the *pristov*—the police chief— themselves would come there to

---

* Translated from Hebrew by Elizabeth Kessin-Berman.

drink forcibly without paying for their drinks. Therefore, we were sure that even if suspicion were to fall on Shimon Rayzer, one glance at his father and a few bottles of beer would be enough to keep the peace.

After Avraham Yehuda got a sense of how things worked in the town and was convinced that this was a place to cultivate Zionism, he decided to begin by organizing free night classes in Hebrew in his apartment. He was decisive and energetic: he gathered a group of young people around him and began to instill the tenets of Zionism in them. Ben-Tsion Betlin, Tsvi Luzman, and the writer of these lines were in the first group, and they shortly became the advance party of pioneers from our town to the Land of Israel.

[page 94]

Ben-Tsion had little practical experience, so after a while he returned to the Diaspora. But Tsvi Luzman endured and found his vocation in farming in the Galilee. I'll relate my experiences later.

I recall that in 1904, at midnight, Velvel Zaks came to my father and reported Herzl's death to him. Heavy mourning descended on our house, and my father argued with Zaks until the dawning light; it seemed that they had decided that very night to join the World Zionist Organization. The Great Synagogue sexton did the same, as did the city's highly respected men and factory owners. These people were counted among the first Lovers of Zion, and my father was one of the first officials of the Odessa Committee founded by Ussishkin. The philanthropic Odessa Committee* did not fund my father, and then he brought me to request funding. I didn't succeed in getting funding, but I decided that it was very important to immigrate to Israel. So little by little, I found work in order to earn money for the Land of Israel.

---

* *Translation editor's note:* The Odessa Committee, officially known as the Society for the Support of Jewish Farmers and Artisans in Syria and Palestine, was a charitable, pre-Zionist organization in the Russian Empire that supported immigration to Israel.

After some time, the holiday of Sukkot arrived. I had the idea of doing something to promote *etrog** production in the Land of Israel. I brought some materials to the study hall beadles, but not one of the 15 study halls in the city agreed to give up using the Greek *etrog* for the preferred Land of Israel *etrog*. The Greek *etrog*, they claimed, was more "beautiful, more refined." Only those in the Great Synagogue agreed to acquire the Land of Israel *etrog*, and this only after long negotiations.

After R' Moshe, beadle of the Great Synagogue, brought the *etrogim* to the synagogue leaders to make a blessing over them, I explained to each one who was making the blessings that the Land of Israel *etrog* was preferable to Greek *etrog* because it was more "beautiful, more refined." But when my explanations failed to have much impact, the beadle gave the cantor both *etrogim*, the Land of Israel *etrog* and the Greek *etrog*, and asked him to choose. I got angry, and in my anger I broke the stem of the Greek *etrog* and fixed it by putting a pin in it. The cantor, of course, was shocked at the sight of what I had done, but the congregation did not notice anything, so I was saved from the hands of those who might "lynch" me, God forbid.

On Tisha B'Av, the day of the destruction of the Temple, I used to sell *shekalim* for the Zionist Organization members. The members sent me a list of the local bourgeoisie to canvas. I went to the Fayfel family. I found them all sitting around a set table, something you wouldn't expect on one of Israel's fast days. They greeted me, saying, "Blessed is he who comes," and said, "Here comes the Land of Israel Jew!" After all the family members left the dining room, only the elderly mother remained to talk with me. She posed a few questions to me, and I tried to answer them, while also trying to understand their relevance. Here are the questions that I remember.

---

* *Translation editor's note:* The *etrog* (plural: *etrogim*) is the yellow citron used by Jews on the weeklong holiday of Sukkot.

[page 95]

**Group of Zionists Hosted by Dr. Kopeyka and
His Wife for Immigration to the Land**

[page 96]

"Who will be the *gorodovoy,* that is to say the policemen, in the Land of Israel if all the Jews want to be officers?"

"I will be the *gorodovoy,*" I answered.

"And who will clean the sewer pits?"

"Indeed, I am willing to do this, too, in the Land of Israel."

At my words, the old woman nearly fainted with emotion and offense, and after she had composed herself, she said, "Is it possible that the honorable R' Chana Goldgart's grandson would do this sort of demeaning work?"

"That's right," I answered. "For the sake of the Land of Israel, you must be prepared to do anything."

After I had satisfied all the concerns expressed in Mrs. Fayfel's questions, she told me that she was ready to give a charitable donation to the Land of Israel. I explained that I wasn't collecting donations but, rather, raising money for members of the Zionist movement who were going to build the Land of Israel. And thus she agreed to buy a *shekel* with the explicit condition that doing so would not obligate her in any way.

With Poltorak, it was much more difficult. He didn't want to buy a *shekel*, and he didn't want to contribute to the Jewish National Fund or the Foundation Fund. He had an ideological problem with what he called "the gangsters"—what he called pioneers—because they played football on the Sabbath "in the brigade," that is, in the yard belonging to the firefighters, and also smoked on the Sabbath. It was difficult to change his opinion, and the Zionist Organization sent "their big guns" to influence him. They also asked me to go help with this, as a Jew from the Land of Israel, but not even I could do anything about this.

I used to go visit Rosye Mes, the mother of the Port Arthur millionaire Moshe Mendil Ginzburg, once a month on Saturday night on behalf of the Jewish National Fund. At first the elderly woman would criticize me, saying that the boys in the Land of Israel were accustomed to dancing with girls. After I convinced her to stop shouting and pointed out that there wasn't even a *pruta** in her Jewish National Fund can, the good lady gave me a whole ruble to benefit the Jewish National Fund. This was a large sum, and suffice it to say that all of the Jews of Radzivilov together would not have contributed a sum like this in a whole week ....

[page 97]

The Haganah in Radzivilov (1918–1919)[†]

Aleksander Balaban

With the end of World War I, Jews began to return to town to recreate a normal life in their homeland. This didn't sit well with the gentiles, as they still nursed their hatred of Jews, so they began systematically to set fire to still-unclaimed Jewish houses every night. It was obvious that these arson attacks were malicious, and the Jews therefore decided to protect themselves and their property. They organized a nightly watch, with two guards

---

* *Translation editor's note:* The *pruta* was an Israeli coin worth one thousandth of a pound.

[†] Translated from Hebrew by Elizabeth Kessin-Berman.

patrolling every street each evening. But this guard was not enough, because the agitators would watch for them in the gaps between the streets, hang a few burning kerosene-soaked rags on an abandoned house, and flee. Because of this, an incentive was issued: arson for arson—and so the arson stopped.

When the Community Council was established in the town, it also immediately set up a Haganah [self-defense], and two council members who were well suited to the role were appointed: Dr. Gredenshtin and A. Balaban. There was no lack of weapons then, because warehouses full of stockpiled weapons were located very close to the railroad station. The civilian government was there to collect taxes, and the army commander was not at all interested in civilian affairs (he was satisfied with occasional bribes from the council ...), so, for all intents and purposes, the Haganah found itself fulfilling the role of town militia. The Haganah kept the peace, collected taxes for the community, and took care of other matters. When stray soldiers wandering in Ukraine organized pogroms against the Jews, the Haganah summoned the Jewish youth in our town, organizing them into groups—commanded by a very courageous man, Maumon—to scare off the rioters. These groups demonstrated that agents of destruction would not be tolerated in our town, and they left town without harming a single Jew.

To our great delight, the gentiles in the area weren't interested in pogroms, because Ukraine was in complete chaos, and there was a severe lack of trade in many commodities available in nearby Galicia. The Jews would buy these goods in Galicia, and the gentiles would transport them, because the railroads were not available for civilian use. Hauling commodities allowed the gentiles to engage in currency-based transactions, so they weren't interested in disrupting this kind of order. They also took into account the Haganah's existence; it had become renowned in the area as a strong organization.

[page 98]

One reason for the disturbance of this peace that was bound to cause bloodshed was Ukrainian currency deflation. The rioters wanted nothing to do with currency at any cost. What did they do? They'd go into a Jewish shop, buy something, pay for it with a big 50-*karbovanets*[*] paper note, and then demand change in coins, something that Jewish shopkeeper could not abide. The Community Council, understanding the tenuous commercial situation, decided to do everything in its power to prevent a confrontation and not allow matters to evolve into a disturbance. The council collected a large sum of money in silver coins, and, when there was a conflict between a rioting gentile and a Jewish shopkeeper, the Haganah would intervene and hand out the requested sum to the gentile in coins.

Out of concern for maintaining peace and good relations between the Jews and their Ukrainian neighbors, the council also became involved in cultural affairs, because the Ukrainians had a cultural committee, although it did hardly anything. But to maintain good relations between the two cultural committees, the latter was invited to our plays from time to time for the purpose of being sociable.

Maccabee Soccer Team. Yosef Albert, Moshe Bespoyasnik, Avraham Fayfel, Beybik Shternberg, Shalom Fayfel, Yudke Chotiner, Duvid Lekhtman, Yakov Kletsel, Avraham Prochovnik. Seated: Dr. Veber.

---

[*] *Translation editor's note:* The *karbovanets* was a unit of currency in Ukraine.

[page 99]

It was also intended to give them an impression of our organization and make them aware of our abilities. In connection with our power, the following event must be recounted.

Once a revolt broke out in the region, and the Radzivilov commander sent forces to suppress a revolt in the Kremenets area. He came to us with a request for forces to join in suppressing the revolt. This did not appeal to us because we didn't want to interfere with matters involving them and others. We convinced the commander that it wasn't our role to interfere in political affairs; we were involved only in keeping the peace. After some time, the government forces returned, bearing with them the dead and wounded. In our desire to show our friendliness, we decided to participate in the funeral for their fallen. The funeral left from the hospital, which was on Railroad Street. Many Christian holy vessels led the procession. Then came the coffins of the dead attended by relatives, and at the end of the procession was a platoon of 120 Jewish Haganah boys with ceremonial rifles. The procession was solemn, and the band played songs of mourning from the start. In the cemetery, after the lamentations, the platoon fired a round of shots to honor the dead. This honor shown by the Jewish Haganah to the memory of the dead made a great impression on the residents, and their conversations were different during the following months.

The Haganah's reputation was so strong that the commander preferred to transfer the watch over the weapons warehouses near the train station to the Haganah boys because he could trust them more than he could trust his own soldiers. Furthermore, you might say that we had an interest in guarding the arsenals. But there were a few unpleasant events that caused us sorrow.

Once, one boy lost an eye while playing with a bomb that exploded. And another time, there was a more tragic event. One of the boys returned from guard duty believing that his rifle was unloaded, having taken out the magazine and emptied it of bullets. But he forgot to check the barrel chamber, and one bullet still remained, ready to be fired. He got home and was boasting to his bride that, he, a yeshiva boy, knew how to wield a weapon. Certain that the rifle wasn't loaded, he pointed it at his bride, and believing this to be only a joke, she raised her hands and said, "Fire!" He fired. The bullet inside pierced her heart. This was an unbearable tragedy ....

Hearing of the sad incident, the commander ordered the Haganah to disarm, but we succeeded in reversing his decree only after great negotiations, because worse incidents were to come for our townspeople.

[page 100]

Another incident happened to the wagoner's son. A rioter dressed in officer's clothing accosted him and asked him to help collect of a large tax in a neighboring village, Krupets, where his platoon was already located, so he said. The son agreed to his request and went with him. En route, the "officer" shot him in the back and killed him, and ran away with the wagon and horses. Afterward, we found out that the platoon of which the imposter spoke had never been there.

The Haganah continued to operate until the Polish army appeared. The fact that our town fared peacefully during that chaotic time and did not suffer from pogroms angered gentile rioters. So they brought accusations to the Polish military government against several Jews and Ukrainians who fought more, so it would seem, with the Bolsheviks. The Poles arrested and questioned six Jews, among them Tsvi Kuperman and the writer of these lines. We were all brought to a military prison in Lvov, and we returned in a week, only after great efforts by the town's businessmen and Rabbi Chayim the elder; none of us had any connection to the Bolsheviks, so we were freed.

With the First Ones*

Rachel Gurman

When he was lad of 14, Menachem Goldgart joined the Zionist Organization in our hometown, Radzivilov, and undertook a significant portion of the public Zionist work there. But he wasn't satisfied just working for Zionism; he aspired to immigrate to Israel himself, and in 1912 he set out for the Land of Israel in spite of all his parents' attempts to dissuade him. And so Menachem became "the first" from Radzivilov.

When he came to the Land of Israel, he found work as a laborer in the Rehovot orchards. For two years, his parents continued inundating him with letters, wanting to know what his "plans for the future" were, until finally he responded to them and told them that he had decided to become a pioneer in the development of industry in the Land of Israel. He ordered machines from Germany to make candles and soap, and also to make stearin, but for the factory to be set up and financed, he had to enlist partners, and because of this, he went to Russia to create a company that would take up the factory's organization and financing. Then World War I broke out, and his connection to the Land of Israel was severed.

Menachem remained in the Diaspora waiting for the fury to pass, and in the meantime, he did not to rest and was certainly not idle. When the town of Radzivilov was set on fire by enemy forces in 1915, Menachem went to Kremenets to represent an agency for refugees and became the head of the Relief Committee.

[page 101]

But he never forgot his plan to return to the Land of Israel, and when the first opportunity arose, he set out immediately.

He got to Harbin in Manchuria and settled there. What did he do? Not just sit with his arms folded! No. He started by taking part in civic life there as a member of the local Jewish community in 1918. He founded and

---

* Translated from Hebrew by Elizabeth Kessin-Berman.

chaired the Hebrew Legion, with the hope of uniting with the Jabotinsky Legion.* His friends from the Young Zionists had different opinions. Most of them were in favor of neutrality with Turkey. But not Menachem. Now was the time to act, in his mind! But in the meantime, the war came to an end, and the Legion dispersed.

Meanwhile, Menachem married Rive, and the two of them left for the Land of Israel. Theirs was a very long route, from Japan, China, and Indochina, then on a boat to Egypt, and from there to the Land of Israel. To Menachem's great disappointment, he did not find the machinery that he had brought to the Land of Israel before the war. Because of this, he had no choice but to work building roads and buildings. Meanwhile, his wife played in an orchestra and taught at Ron Shulamit, the first music school.

In 1928, the Goldgart family decided to live in a village. They settled in Ramat HaSharon, which was then in the middle of an Arab area, one of the first from this point of view. Bread was brought to them from Herzliya or from Tel Aviv. Water came on trucks from Herzliya. They had no electricity, certainly, but in spite of these conditions, they built a house and a small orchard. The difficulties were great. But they endured, believing that better days would come. And then World War II broke out, and it became difficult to maintain the orchard and harvest the fruit when it was ripe. The Goldgart family returned to Tel Aviv, and Menachem, who had once dreamed of establishing an industry in the Land of Israel, began working for others in a factory.

In 1947, Menachem became an active Haganah member, as a policeman and warehouseman. With the establishment of the state of Israel, Menachem was sent on border patrol. When the Israel Defense Forces were created, he was released from his position.

---

* *Translation editor's note:* The Jabotinsky Legion probably refers to the Jewish Legion of the British army in World War I, cofounded by Zev Jabotinsky.

Today, at the age of 75, Menachem Goldgart assesses his life with great satisfaction, very glad to have been able to come and see with his own eyes the restoration of Israel in its land.

[page 102]

Zionism and Pioneering in Our Town*

Duvid Zahavi

In our town, Radzivilov, as in many Volhynia towns, many diverse Zionist associations were organized after World War I. But before that, there were other clubs whose role was to influence our families' young people. Already from the earliest days of our childhood, our students' education in the government elementary school offered us a Hebrew Zionist education, and the Hebrew teacher, Hershel Katz, taught us and indoctrinated us. I recall that already during those days, there was a young Radzivilov man, Mendil (Menachem) Goldgart, a cousin, who left his respectable and wealthy parents' house and journeyed to the Land of Israel. We, the younger children, were then very much in favor of this. But not his parents. It wasn't easy for Mendil in the Land of Israel, because he'd had no experience of physical labor and, furthermore, in those days it wasn't easy for a Hebrew laborer to get work. But this did not alter his strong resolve, and he soon overcame the difficulties. After a number of years had passed, he came to visit Radzivilov, full of enthusiasm, and he began to enchant the young people with the tenets of Zionism. He finally convinced his father to advance him an amount of money in order to return to the Land of Israel to build a factory, not at all large, as a trial. But then World War I broke out.

As the military drew near, we, like others caught in the middle, fled from Radzivilov to Berdichev. There our parents continued in their business, and we children entered the gymnasium and continued to study. We dedicated all of our time to working for Zionist youth clubs. Youth in Russia were

---

* Translated from Hebrew by Elizabeth Kessin-Berman.

fired up by what Zev Jabotinsky was writing in his fiery articles. His articles were popular even among the gentiles.

When the revolution broke out in February 1917, and the Bolshevik revolution afterward, a number of things changed for us. I was the first in my family to cross the border into Poland, and I went to relatives in Lutsk. There in Poland, the Zionist movement was little by little gaining appeal, and many more were becoming interested in immigrating to the Land of Israel. Then, in Grochów, near Warszawa, there was a Pioneer training center, where a group of 10 girls and boys worked in agriculture to receive career training prior to immigrating. I participated with them.

[page 103]

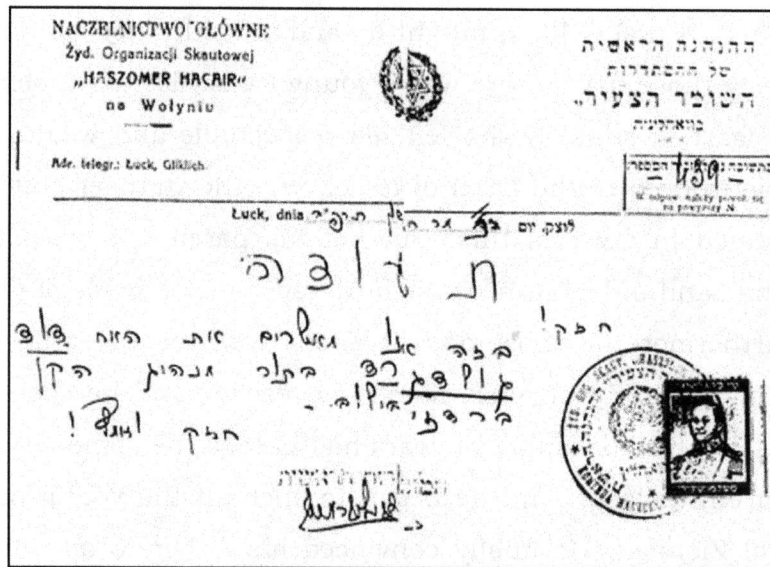

[The certificate reads, "Main Office, Jewish Scout Organization, Youth Guard of Volhynia, Lutsk, #439, 7 Heshvan 1922. Certificate. Congratulations! In this we certify this person, Duvid Goldgart, according to the nest's custom, in Radzivilov. Be strong and of good courage!"]

Young Lions of the Youth Guard, 1922

When my parents returned from Russia, I also returned to Radzivilov, and until I got my certificate, I devoted myself to work in the Youth Guard organization as a leader of the local "nest." Jewish youth began growing in stature, but the anti-Semites also raised their heads.

[page 104]

Youth Guard Graduates, 1922, Led by Duvid Zahavi

I remember one incident. It was on a Sabbath afternoon. A few Youth Guard platoons went out to check an announcement for a Zionist event that was supposed to take place on Saturday night. When the young people began to examine the announcement, a group of "settlers," Polish guard soldiers whom we knew were anti-Semitic killers, suddenly appeared and began to tear up the announcement. We shouted for the older members, the Liberman and Goldgart sons, who happened to be nearby. They appeared, and when they spoke roughly to the Polish rioters, one of the Poles snapped the whip that Shlome Liberman was holding. A fistfight broke out on both sides when Rivke Liberman, who didn't leave us a minute to spare, made booing sounds in the Poles' ears. Gradually more Poles appeared. We told ourselves to scatter, because we were worried about our relations with the Polish government, but they didn't back off. Shalom Goldgart, the youngest and smallest of his brothers, fell on one of the Polish brutes with raging fury, punching him, and the fight continued between them. But with difficulty, we came to an impasse, and then we quickly scattered.

But this incident raised awareness of the local youth in the eyes of both the gentiles and the authorities.

[page 105]

Young Lioness, Youth Guard

Because of this, the next day the government authorities met with the Jews and the "settlers," and the storm abated.

After a number of years, I finally received my certificate to immigrate to the Land of Israel.

The Pioneer Organization in Our Town[*]

Moshe Korin

Three years after the establishment of Polish rule in Volhynia, many Jewish residents of Radzivilov returned from the places to which they had scattered during World War I. At the same time, Zionist movements began working in earnest to organize Jewish young people, and Pioneer set out to train everyone who requested to leave the Diaspora and immigrate to the Land of Israel to take advantage of the conditions created when the British Mandate came into being in the Land of Israel.

Delegates from central Pioneer were sent to our town, and with their aid and advice, a local young workers' branch was organized in Radzivilov.
[page 106]

In 1923, the branch also acquired its own facility, even though it was an abandoned house recently vacated by the Zaks family, but there young people aged 17 and above engaged in listening to lectures on the movement, its teachings, and its political parties and their ideologies, and they discussed and planned their dreams of immigrating to the Land of Israel and the new life they would establish and advance there.

We mention here the first trainees to be ready to immigrate: Niuni Goldgart, Sabe Zaks Pontis, Kitayksher, Lindiner, Sirota, Yoel Charap, Simche Ayzen, Tsipore Gun, Ester Blekhman, and others. Working in cultural and social areas was Moshe Taykh, the oldest in the group, who it seems to me made great strides in establishing the local Pioneer chapter.

---

[*] Translated from Hebrew by Elizabeth Kessin Berman.

Pioneer. Standing, right to left: Chayim Kitayksher, Yehoshue Felman, Tsivye Zagoroder, Sore Kisis, Fayvish Lerner, Velvel Poltorak. Seated: Munye Margaliyot, Buntsye Vinshteyn, Dvore Taykh, Arye Vaynshteyn. Below: Akiva Vaserman, Teme Shif, Meir Vaynshteyn.

The first trainees left to work in 1923. The members of the first training group to be part of the agricultural collective were Beti Benderski, Aychis, Reshish, Berdichevski, and others.

[page 107]

The first group, which wrote one of the columns, left for the Radzivilov-Druzhkopol training kibbutz near Lvov, whose members worked in three large sections. These included Jews from the following villages: Michalow, Zvuche, and Volitsa Barylova. The kibbutz mentioned above had more than 150 boys and girls from all over Poland.

After working for four months in the summer, many gladly immigrated to the Land of Israel. And almost everyone from our town was able to acquire a certificate and immigrate, except for a few who remained for various reasons.

After the first group had immigrated (individuals had already immigrated on their own), the Pioneer branch rapidly developed, and many other cooperatives began the process of training and immigration. Among the Pioneer activists until the 1930s were Yakov Lerner and Avraham Vaysberg. Yakov

Lerner suddenly left the movement, and in the 1930s, there was also a crisis among the Pioneer leadership, and the movement almost dissolved. Buntsye and the Vaynshteyn brothers, as well as Yehoshue Felman, did everything they could to keep the movement intact, and Young Pioneer, which was organized in our town in the following years, came and strengthened its roots. Among the Young Pioneer members during the 1930s, I must mention B. Felman, Yosef Lerner, Duvid Vaynshteyn, Yakov Segal, Mordekhay Landis, Yosef Sigen, Yisrael Nudel, Avraham Korin, and others.

**Celebration in Honor of Radzivilov Trainees Who
Were Certified to Immigrate**

[page 108]

Yisrael Nudel did not get permission to immigrate, and it appears that he was a victim of the Holocaust that gripped our town.

All these activists that I have recalled above and, yes, many more after them, had years of training in different kibbutzim all over Poland. These were the days of great growth in of the youth pioneering movement, with branches and training kibbutzim in broad regions of Poland, but in terms of immigration, the results were almost insignificant. Many thousands of pioneers in training kibbutzim looked forward to immigration, and in our town, too, a substantially large training kibbutz was founded mainly to work in our town's flourmill, and the Jewish owners helped us operate it and establish a local cooperative. The cooperative itself served as a spiritual and cultural resource for the local branch.

Pioneers before Immigrating to the Land

And so it was that, in spite of the occasional crisis that befell the local Pioneer branch, they remained steady in their work until World War II broke out in September 1939. On the 17th, our town came under Soviet control, and then all Zionist operations halted, which thus confirmed the complete demise of the Radzivilov Pioneer branch.

[page 109]

More about Pioneer in Our Town*

Meir Vaynshteyn

With the end of World War I, many of the residents who had taken flight to different regions of Russia during the war returned to our town. Many of the returnees were enlightened individuals, sensing the need to organize young people and to teach them how to prepare for immigration to the Land

---

* Translated from Hebrew by Elizabeth Kessin Berman.

of Israel. Among the first initiators and organizers, who are remembered fondly, were comrades Shimon Goldgart, Yozik Zaks, and Shlome Libov.

These were days of national awakening, and the Pioneer movement in Poland was developing and taking hold. The objective was to try to immigrate to the Land of Israel. The abovementioned organizers unified many of the area's young people, made a connection to central Pioneer, and then established a local branch of Pioneer there. In the evenings and on the Sabbath, discussions and lectures were planned on the new life that was evolving and taking hold in the Land of Israel, life on the collective farm and commune, Zionism, and pioneering. The ideas that came like burning and raging flames to the young people aroused in them aspirations to immigrate. The realization of these ideas was a life of labor in the Land of Israel.

It wasn't long before a group of young people from our town began to go to the training kibbutzim organized by central Pioneer; and the Land-of-Israel spirit that enveloped our town gave them the impetus to learn Hebrew in evening classes, as well as to establish the Tarbut School. In the evening, we also occupied ourselves singing Hebrew folk songs, and this spirit so filled our parents' houses that they also received inspiration from the vision that new lives were rising from the dust in our Land of Israel. They began to realize how depressing it was for us to live in the Diaspora, how cruel the surroundings of our anti-Semitic town were, and compared with Zionism, how beautiful the dream of a new day in the future was for Jewish youth in the land of their fathers.

The Pioneer concept conquered all of us, and each day new members joined us and stopped pining for their home to join a life of training in preparation for immigrating to the Land of Israel. These were joyful days for us, for encouragement in an almost Land-of-Israel environment, and for the urge to be creative and organized. Zionist institutions and parties were founded and organized, as well as branches of Pioneer and Young Pioneer in our town. A local training "kibbutz" was also established, and pioneers from several cities came to us for training. Correspondingly, many from our town went for training in Grochów, near Warszawa; to Klosova; and to other points. The training program in our town centered on the flourmill, a monastery, the railroad station—in dismantled cars—and especially on chopping wood for the Jews of our town. It wasn't demeaning work for them—on the contrary, they asked for hard and menial labor in order to get used to and prepare for physical labor in the Land of Israel.

[page 110]

Life in the training programs followed a communal, cooperative structure, and for many, the wages were most meager and the standard of living very modest. Nevertheless, everyone greeted this difficult life with love, and the great reward was this—a certificate for immigration.

It should be pointed out that the Polish government did not restrict our progress, and the Pioneer organization acquired official government recognition all over Poland. The Pioneer branch in our town also acquired, certainly, legal status. And here I recall a delicate situation that happened to me one day. A Polish policeman came to collect information from me on our organization and its officers. He knew me in connection with various issues, and although I knew that the policeman was clearly an ardent anti-Semite, he related to me with great respect and tried to explain to me that even if I immigrated to the land of Israel, there would be a chance to return as a Polish citizen—if a war broke out—and fight here (in Poland) for the Polish homeland. I answered him immediately with the pride of a Jewish nationalist.

Our house was a haven for all Pioneer activities. It was open to everyone, and everyone who passed by felt an emotional need to enter, enjoy the camaraderie, and spend time in a pioneering Land-of-Israel atmosphere. On Sabbath eve and also on the Sabbath day, Pioneer and Young Pioneer members would gather in our house for discussion, a game of chess, sing-a-longs, and lectures on civic and Land of Israel subjects.

On Sabbath eve, our large table would be spread in the best Jewish tradition: covered with an immaculate tablecloth on which stood candlesticks with burning candles in them Everyone sat around the table with a good feeling of "sitting all together like brothers," singing hymns, Hasidic melodies, and songs of the Land of Israel that blended youthful dreams and aspirations. These were gatherings in a pleasant house to honor all of us, and even though we were removed from reality, in spirit we were still in the land of our fathers.

Neighbors, both Jewish and non-Jewish, knew that our house was filled with pioneers who were planning to immigrate to the Land of Israel. No one bothered us when we sang, sometimes by moonlight, even after the candles and streetlights had gone out. The policemen related to us with respect, and sometimes they even asked us to lower our voices so as to not disturb the serenity of the night.

With the rapid passing of years, 10 boys and girls immigrated to the Land of Israel, and they were accompanied to the train station by many of the town's Jews.

[page 111]

Zionist Activists[*]

Arye Ayzen

Radzivilov was a border town between Russia and Galicia, approximately nine kilometers from the well-known town, Brody.

This was a town like all towns in Volhynia, with Zionist organizations such as Pioneer, Youth Guard, Gordonia, Betar, General Zionism, and more. And then there were the philanthropic organizations, such as the poorhouse, the old-age home, the welcome committee, the committee for orphans, and more. It is important for me to call to memory at least a few of the people who worked, led, and prepared our town's young people in the spirit of Zionism with great personal talent.

Here are some of the leaders of the Zionist movement that were then in our town.

---

[*] Translated from Hebrew by Elizabeth Kessin Berman.

Chayim Kerman. They were already calling him the most enthusiastic Zionist in the days when many of our young people did not even understand what Zionism was. Enthusiastic, especially with those from religious groups who were opposed to it, who urged that we wait for a God who would surely come ... he would lecture at Zionist gatherings in our town, and his descriptions would illustrate life in the Land of Israel and how to build it, as if he were there building it. He was so accurate that many of his students could picture their own path and the work he was dreaming of.

Dudke Sheyn. He was at his best and strongest when educating and nurturing our Zionist youth. His life was already in the Land of Israel. No one could convince him otherwise—until his final departure from our town. He also created a memorial book for the community of Radzivilov and its martyrs. But their death did not prevent him from putting theory into practice.

The Zagoroder family. Everyone knew the first Zionist family in our town. R' Menashe Zagoroder's house was an open house offering hospitality to officials from the Land of Israel and delegates from the central Zionists in Warszawa, the largest and first Zionist organizations: the Jewish National Fund and United Israel Appeal. He would also appear at lectures, disseminating the concept of returning to Zion to the Jews of Radzivilov. He was also a representative to all the Yiddish and Hebrew newspapers in Poland and abroad. Totally devoted in heart and soul to Zionism, he educated his sons in the spirit of Zionism, and all of them immigrated to the Land of Israel.

His son, Tsvi Zagoroder, is to this very day a Zionist loyalist and leader of the descendants of Radzivilov in Israel.

[page 112]

He took upon himself the huge work of publishing this memorial book for the community of Radzivilov without losing any of the many connections he came upon.

Dudke Goldgart-Zahavi. I remember him as a leader and guide, the best of our pioneering youth. He was able to arouse in Zionist youth a sense of communalism and the desire to immigrate and lend a hand in building the Land of Israel.

The Herzliya Group Led by Tsvi Goldgart, 1925

To the best of my memory, these were the Zionist families who worked as leaders and heads of the Zionist institutions in our town:

Zagoroder, Goldgart (Moshe), Balaban, Korin, Tesler, Lerner, Gelman, Goldgart (Beyrish), Soybel, Zaks, Shumker, Kitayksher, Sigen, Kiperman, Kerman, Vaynshteyn, Grobshteyn (Saley), Margolit, Felman, Margolit, Sirota, Mikhel, Vayl, Chait, Stroyman, Grobshteyn (Yechiel-Duvid), Zats, Daniuk, Poltorak, Landis, Fishman.

Memories of Pioneering*

Yosef Spektor

I was 16 when I joined Pioneer in Radzivilov. My parents, who were very traditional, didn't approve of the Pioneers' work in the training center. They weren't used to seeing Jews doing the kind of work the gentiles did: chopping wood, sawing wood, doing the lowly work of the flourmill, and so on. They tried to convince me to give it up, but instead I decided to stand fast and continue on the path I had chosen and to fulfill the great dream of living as a Jew in the land of his ancestors.

In 1936 I went to the Brochów training kibbutz near Łódź. After training for more than two years, I was certified for immigration to the Land of Israel. I returned home to prepare for immigration. My parents didn't object to my immigrating to the Land of Israel, and my mother even wanted to equip me with all sorts of expensive items, although my family members weren't aware that I was immigrating in the second wave and there was no way to take anything with us but the most necessary things. Because of this, I didn't even take family photographs with me, and now I can only imagine them, the dear souls, as I have them fixed in my memory....

When my relatives came to bid me farewell, my father said he was comforted that his son was immigrating to the Land of Israel because he would live there as a Jew among Jews. During the last moments before my departure, he cried and said, "Who knows if I'll ever see you again, my son?" He didn't, not him or the rest of the family, who were torn from life at the Nazi murderers' hands.

---

* Translated from Hebrew by Elizabeth Kessin Berman.

[page 114]

Yafe Broida, the Female Tractor Driver*

Tsvi Zagoroder

Yafe Broida

Yafe Broida, daughter of R' Yehoshue Broida, of blessed memory, was among the first in Radzivilov to immigrate. She arrived in the Land of Israel in 1923 and entered the Immigrant House in Tel Aviv.

Roadways and Malaria

The Immigrant House in 1923 was nothing but a camp of tents set up in the middle of Tel Aviv, not far from the Robert Samuel Port of today. A huge wave of unemployment was then gripping the country. For three days, Yafe Broida rested in her tent doing nothing, along with an elderly Jewish woman who had come to the Land of Israel to die there. On the fourth day, she packed her belongings and left to search for work. She approached Avraham Hertsfeld, head of the agricultural agency, who was very sympathetic to youth from Poland, and explained to him in a decisive tone that "she had come to the Land of Israel to work, with God's help"—"the land calls to me; give me something to do." The head of the agricultural agency took her words seriously, and as a result, over the next 10 years Yafe Broida did the

---

* Translated from Hebrew by Elizabeth Kessin Berman. *Note in original:* Based on Eytan Mor, "The Female Tractor Driver from Makhtesh Ramon," in *LaMerhav*. [*Translation editor's note:* LaMerhav was a Hebrew language daily newspaper published in Israel between 1954 and 1971.]

following: she packed tobacco near Kfar Tabor; hauled goods and laid bricks with a team of workgroups near Kfar Yehezkel; laundered sheets at the Ein Harod hospital; participated in building Balfouria; paved the Afula road; caught malaria; and recovered, picked up an ax, and took part in the excavating the repair of drainage pipes for the Jezreel Valley.

[page 115]

In spite of the opposition of Dr. Krauze, manager of the agricultural school in Mikve Israel, to the excavation, she was the only girl to take a course on growing nursery plants intended only for boys; because she now found herself near Tel Aviv, she helped pave part of King George Street; she joined a team of road levelers and was a daily worker in the Kfar Saba orchards; during the day, she staked the trees and in the evenings, she utilized the course in nursery planting to establish the first nursery, giving Kibbutz Givat Haim a level surface for their current orchard; she left the country for two years as a movement delegate to the Volhynia region, her birthplace, and worked in Pioneer Kibbutz training centers; she returned to the Givat Haim orchards and began to work at sorting and wrapping. The "packaging guild," which opposed allowing a woman in the packing industry, found a worthy fighter in Yafe Broida; she learned the trade from a Givat Haim member in secret. The results of this were welcomed by many other members, and the trade was considered to have been conquered by the "weaker sex."

Left the Kibbutz Because of the Tractor

With the outbreak of the world war, life changed in Givat Haim because the weight of the economy fell on the women as the men left for the front. Yafe decided to take part in an accelerated course called "regional tractors." The members tried to dissuade Yafe, because how could she operate in a trade that was so masculine? When she returned from the course, the men grumbled and expressed their hostile opposition. But even so, they were compelled to accept her into the work, although it would not be tolerated for long. As Yafe recalled, "My life had no meaning. They talked behind my back, said that I broke parts, that I had impaired vision, and other slurs. This was unjust, but I had the feeling that it was only up to me to disprove to them and to myself ...."

When she realized that her hopes to join the Givat Haim tractor division of were shattered beyond repair, she left the workforce. For two and a half years, she was the secretary of a labor group in Ramat Gan. But her heart still beat for the earth and the tractor. When she finally met with the manager of the kibbutz, she asked if she could return to the workforce on fair terms and to take on a task that would not upset the male kibbutz members. The manager was very sympathetic, but he could not promise this. "I saw only one way before me: to take it upon myself to achieve my goal. I took 25 liras that I had received from my last salary and went to the Israeli ministry of civil tractors and equipment."

[page 116]

This was the first official payment for receipt of a tractor tendered by a girl. The manager told Yafe that 173 people, all men, were waiting, listed her as a girl, told her he didn't know how long it would take, and so on ....

Yafe's Turn Comes

Yafe became a cleaning woman and resigned herself to waiting. Five years later, the State of Israel was established, and she was finally rewarded. "Miss Broida," said the association official, "you can receive your tractor—but you must bring permission from the Ministry of Agriculture." In the Ministry of Agriculture, the clerks looked at her and laughed: "You have no prospects. The Ministry of Agriculture cancels the mechanical appointment and imposes a better method. You can fill out this form ...." The answer was negative.

[page 117]

Yafe wrote to an old acquaintance, Chayim Halperin, then manager of the Ministry of Agriculture, and told him of her struggles.

At the beginning of 1951, she received the long-awaited permission, and immediately afterward, she gathered a group of kibbutz members and older members in an effort to amass 1,800 lira—the amount needed to order a 4D-type "Caterpillar" from the association's warehouse. But there still was no respect for her.

There they asked her, "Who will operate the tractor, your husband?" "They recognized me well, they were polite, but they declined to allow me to come and go, they did not give me any work. I was a woman, and if I did this work—in their opinion—it might rattle every sector in the whole country."

The Arabs Were Not Surprised

Yafe Broida was stunned by the old-fashioned conservatism among the Hebrew farmers, while the Arabs couldn't have cared less who was driving the tractor. The idea arose to approach the Arabs and, indeed, she got her first work from them. The Arab guard of Ein Shemer returned to his village, Baqa, one day and told Knesset member Faras Hamdan of the signs and wonders of the woman with the tractor. For long weeks, she plowed triangulated borders until a letter arrived one day inviting her to come to the Negev to work on a deep plowing project. For two straight months, Yafe Broida plowed on the land of Ein Iron, which was wild with infiltrators. They would appear very frequently, coming down from the hills and stopping to hear the noise of the lonely tractor .... And Yafe was not one to let her guard down. But although there were frequent encounters, sometimes face to face, with those who were crossing the borders unseen, she did not fire even one bullet. She had a certain philosophy, and she literally used agriculture to express what was close to her heart: you should not let the Arabs who are close to you know that you fear them—because then they will become as quiet as water and as small as the chaff of the field.

A House on Wheels

Ever since her victory at the end of 1951, she could not tear herself away from conflicts. She still believed that she could join the tractor drivers' union. The wounds of the past had not yet healed. But agriculture would not suffer because of Yafe's determined independence. She set out to plow in the Negev, regions always far from the connections and opinions of the tractor drivers in the northern parts of the country.

[page 118]

Yafe Broida Tends Her Tractor

On her own, Yafe "conquered" thousands of dunams and many tens of kilometers, in which the Jewish National Fund sowed fields and planted trees—all in the Negev and along the Gaza strip.

When the American specialist who worked on the survey was about to return to his country, he left her the portable "trailer" that was used as a housing unit. And so she hauled it with her wherever she was sent and lived in it until she finished her work. Afterward, the "house on wheels" was turned into a small storage facility for field equipment, something she was very proud of, and when she went out on new jobs, Yafe would equip it with enough vegetarian food for a month and two tanks of water, using it as a mobile workshop trailing after her—everything in her world with her. She was full and complete. "How long, in your opinion, can you go on like this?"
[page 119]

"At my age (51), there are only single men in this industry to compare to. But I'm a woman, and it's hard to know."

In 1955, Yafe received an award at the Ministry of Labor celebration held in Beit Lessin for high performance and for her independent tractor service. Among those in the audience were Institute of Productivity and Industry and Labor Ministry officials, including Labor Minister Golda Meir.

To our questions about how many more years she thinks she will continue in this line of work, Yafe answers that she doesn't think about that at all. She will work until the last day.... We, the people of Radzivilov, wish her, a daughter of our city, a very long life.

M. Grinberg, Son of Our City, from Richmond in the United States, Founder of Nahala in Israel.

Culture and Education

The Tarbut School (1920–1924)[*]

Buntsye and Tsivye

After World War I, the Jews of the town began to gather again from the faraway places to which they had dispersed. The majority of the town was destroyed, and those who returned began to restore it and took it upon themselves to build new lives. The work was far-reaching and daunting, but even so, people still worried about the problems confronting their school-aged children.

The Girls' School before World War I

Although there had previously been a Ukrainian-Polish government school in town, a large number of Jews did not choose to study there, because Jews could in no way adapt to its strange, intimidating atmosphere.

---

[*] Translated from Hebrew by Elizabeth Kessin Berman.

The children were mostly Christians of various nationalities: Polish, Russian, Ukrainian, Czech, and even Gypsies, all residents of the town and its surroundings. Any-one who could secured a private education for his or her children; but there were still many children roaming the streets who were not being educated. What could be done about this situation?

One day, the news circulated in the Jewish streets that Zats, the teacher, and few young people were establishing a Jewish Hebrew school.

The Folk School Founded by Avraham Zats, 1921

People from all over town began to enroll their children in this school. Many of the children who were attending the government school left it for this school.

From the start, the Joint Distribution Committee gladly supported the school. The first problem was how to feed and clothe the many children who were suffering from the lack of nutrition and proper clothing. Eventually, we received a substantial pledge from the Joint to pay for enough food to feed more than 300 students.

Over time, the school intended to be tuition-based, but the funding situation was already quite difficult and caused a bit of a crisis.

The inflation that gripped the country in those days became worse and made things even more difficult for the school. It was possible to continue only because of its teachers' belief and volunteerism.

Elementary School Led by Avraham Zats, 1922

The school had seven classes. Russian was the primary language at first, but afterward, it was Yiddish, with more and more attention dedicated to Hebrew. Most of the teachers were local, and generally speaking, the course of studies was satisfactory.

After a time, a plan was formulated to teach in Hebrew as the major language and in Polish as the language of the country, and the school became part of the network of Tarbut schools.

Among the most distinguished teachers was Avraham Yehuda, of blessed memory, who came to us from Berestechko to broaden his horizons. He was brimming with charm and idealism. Before the school was established, he taught the poor children for practically no wages, for free, even though his situation was very bad. In our school, he served as teacher and janitor: he cleaned the schoolroom with his own hands when there were no funds to pay a janitor. His idealism had no limits.

Of the rest of the teachers, we must also mention the school's leader, Avraham Zats, teacher Yentele Sheyn, and beloved teacher Levitin, the authorities who established the school and managed the classes.

[page 123]

They carried all of the school's burdens and worries, small and large, and handled them with grace. Kind and gentle manners also prevailed between the teachers and students.

Under the leadership of Mr. Yechezkel Zats, father of our teacher Avraham Zats, we organized an orchestra and chorus that elevated and enriched the school's cultural life.

Officials of the central Tarbut organization in Rovno, to which the school belonged, arranged the teachers' and students' affairs and did everything they could to establish the school, especially with regard to lesson plans and curriculum. Among those who should be particularly mentioned is Mr. Shmuel Rozenhek.

On holidays, especially Hanukkah and Purim, parties and familiar plays were organized in the school. The plays were generally too popular for the tiny school, so they were offered to the public, and ticket sales helped support the school's budget. Many still remember the play "The Sale of Joseph," which was performed in the town's large theater and was very well received. On Lag BaOmer, we would set out from the town to the nearby forest, unfurling white and purple national flags above us, with our band playing nationalist songs. In the forest, we would organize various games, make bonfires, and enjoy ourselves in the fresh air. Our parades were the envy of even the Christians.

At first the Tarbut School had a good relationship with the Polish government. But as time went on and relations between the Polish government and the Jews worsened all over Poland, things changed for the worse, and these changes affected the school negatively. The government demanded a yearly renewal of the school's license, and each year we had three months to wonder anxiously if our license would be renewed. There was a celebra-

tion on the day our license renewal arrived: we would assemble and joyous-
ly sing in the chorus to celebrate.

Once the Polish Sejm representative, Avraham Levinson, of blessed
memory, visited us. His visit was a very special experience; we wore our
best holiday clothes to go out and greet him. He spoke to us in unblem-
ished, fluent Hebrew. He made a very strong impression on us. We felt that
the Hebrew language was alive and vibrant. He was very impressed with the
children of the school. Such a small town—but with such a large population
that would study Hebrew! He also worried about whether our license would
be renewed.

At the end of the third year of the school's operation, the government began to remove obstacles in its way. The sore spot for our school was that
because it was an independent Hebrew school, the government demanded
that the school employ only certified teachers. So began the school's downfall: a change in management.

[page 124]

In place of Avraham Zats came a manager from Lvov, a Mrs. Horvits.
Then Teacher Levitin fell sick and, after a time, died; and the smile that lit
up every student's face disappeared. The loss was difficult, and then Teacher Sheyn left. Another wind began to blow in the institution.

A parents' committee arose and worked well, being filled with parents who
were willing to work, but the possibilities were slim. The financial situation
continued to decline, and within a year of its establishment, the school
ceased to exist....

The heart greatly grieved for the loss of this public educational facility,
and it was especially hard on those whose studies were interrupted and
thus who could not complete their primary schooling. However, the school's
students did not lose their connection to the Zionist movement. After a
short while, they organized the Pioneer movement in our town. And many of
them immigrated to Israel and helped build the country.

After a few years, a new Hebrew primary "Tarbut" School was established, whose manager was Mr. Yosef Vayl.

The Tarbut School (1924–1939)[*]

Tsvi Zagoroder

During the early 1920s, when many Tarbut schools were opened in many Volhynia cities and towns under the direction of the Rovno center, and many children from various backgrounds and outlooks were drawn to them, the Zionists in our town were inspired to reopen the school out of a concern for teaching the younger generation the wonders of Hebrew language and culture. The local Zionist committee dedicated more and more discussions to the question of the school. They planned and planned, until finally, with the advice and approval of the Tarbut center in Rovno, they moved forward and opened the school in 1924.

At the same time, a two-year kindergarten in our town opened to prepare students for second grade.

We had some difficult issues to overcome before we could go forward with the school, such as a suitable space, good teachers, and a good and experienced principal to get the school started. Above all was the question of money and the resources to cover the school's budget. But we were not frightened by the difficulties ahead of us, and we geared up for the work.
[page 125]

The school was designated to be in Mrs. Boym's rental house, and we took it upon ourselves to refit the structure into a functioning school. Toward the beginning of the new school year, we opened our first classrooms, and just before studies began, we brought our library there and set it up there for the students' use. After a while, we also centralized our Zionist work there.

We invited Mr. Yosef Vayl to be the first principal of the school. The following women served as teachers: Eyda Vayl, the principal's wife; Mina

---

[*] Translated from Hebrew by Elizabeth Kessin Berman.

Fudlis; Lishtsinger; Henye Zeger; Tsivye Finkelshteyn; and Dvore Kitayk-sher-Kagan; as well as Mr. Dov Rechelski. After the Vayl family immigrated to the Land, Fave and his wife took their place.

Tarbut School Board. Standing (right to left): Lekhtman, Lerner, Sheyn, Fidel. Seated: Rechelski. Velkh, Vayl, Eyda Vayl, Gur-Arye, Fudlis, Zagoroder.

There were many girls in the school, and they did very well in their studies. It wasn't long before the sound of Hebrew was heard coming from our students in our town's houses and streets. The Zionists were very proud of this school, and the town's Jews of every type, even those who were not Zionists, chose to send their children to the Tarbut School and give them a Jewish education.

[page 126]

It is also worth noting that, without exaggeration, the school was the jewel in the crown of our town; and very quickly, word spread throughout the surrounding areas of the high standard of its studies in the primary and personal education its students were receiving.

Tarbut School Students and School Board, 1935

[page 127]

During its first year, the school counted its students by tens. In the following years, the number reached 300, studying in eight well-organized classes. At the same time, the Polish government school had seven classes and only about 50 Jewish students.

The local Zionist committee, along with the businessmen Duvid Sheyn, Chayim Kremen, and this writer, as well as the principals and teachers, invested their best talents in the institution, working with full harmony and familial concern to address its needs and development. Tarbut officials Messrs. Shmuel Rozenhek, Brakovski, Aynshteyn, and others who from time to time came from central Tarbut to visit the school, and other Zionist delegates who visited Radzivilov, were very impressed with the school. The Polish official who visited the school also praised the educational standard. What is particularly important to point out is that the pupils from our school were admitted to the government technical school in Brody.

Thus, we Zionists were filled with satisfaction at the sight of the students learning in an atmosphere of cultural Hebrew and Zionism and gaining talents to be used in the land of their ancestors.

[The certificate reads, in part, "Hebrew School Certificate for participation in seven grades of the Radzivilov Tarbut School. For Tsviye Sretbito, a girl, January, in the year … in the town of Radzivilov."]

[page 128]

Jewish Students from a Public Polish School Class with
Teacher of Jewish Religion Yitschak Grobshteyn.

When we arranged a celebration in school or when the students and teachers marched in the city streets, as they did on Lag BaOmer, for example, there was great joy in our hearts.

Over time, Tarbut School students constituted a large portion of the pioneers from Radzivilov. Sometimes they received specialized training, although many went to the Land of Israel at the beginning of the Fifth Immigration (1930–1939) and thereafter.

The Radzivilov Library[*]

Tsvi Zagoroder

The years 1918–1920 were the aftermath of World War I. Our townspeople began to return from their exile and their places of dispersion from east and west in order to rebuild the homesteads destroyed during the war and rebuild life in their birthplace.

I returned to Radzivilov from my exile in Czechoslovakia at the end of 1920. Terrible chaos raged in the city. The people were so desperate to earn a livelihood and meet their basic needs that I simply could hardly recognize the townspeople of the past.

[page 129]

I thought to myself: are these people really the same ones who escaped from here during the war? They're certainly similar, because they're striving by themselves to replace in one stroke everything they lost during war. Can anyone in these circumstances consider fundamentals such as institutions devoted to cultural life, schools, establishing public life, and welfare?

Nevertheless, several people like those I just described did come forward; they were "crazy about this one thing," such as Shimon Inspektor, Roze Lizek, Roze Sitner, Fronye Goldgart, and Manye Lebov, who took it upon themselves to establish a public library. They collected books wherever they could, in different languages, especially in Yiddish and Polish, and opened a library for one and all.

---

[*] Translated from Hebrew by Elizabeth Kessin Berman.

This was during the time when many communities were dominated by the Zionist movement and Zionists participated in all public institutions, so I joined the Library Committee in the Zionist Activist Group (the union of Zionist groups in our town).

Attention was then devoted to acquiring books in Hebrew. When I traveled to Warszawa in 1925 as the delegate from Radzivilov for the gathering of communities in Poland, one of my intentions was to purchase Hebrew books for a few hundred gold pieces.

Tarbut School Board
Fronye Goldgart-Korin, Manye Lebov, Tsvi Zagoroder,
Dore Lebov, Manye Fudlis

[page 130]

Eventually we expanded the Hebrew holdings of the library, so that later, with the development of the Tarbut School, the students were able to incorporate the books we obtained into the core of their studies. The library grew and developed, was transferred to a new setting in the Tarbut School, then housed in Mrs. Boym's house, and after some time was transferred to the Tarbut association.

When I left the city at the beginning of 1936, the library had grown to several thousand volumes, many of them in Hebrew.

The library existed until 1939. With the outbreak of World War II, it was cut down like all of the other town institutions—these and everything else that we built together.

Group of Tarbut School Students with Teacher Horenshteyn

Tarbut Teachers Rechelski, Velk, Groysman, Zagoroder

Tarbut Student Lag BaOmer Outing, 1931

[page 132]

Teachers in Radzivilov[*]

Arye Ayzen

Besides the teachers who educated Radzivilov's Jewish children in schools, there were also "instructors": teachers who taught very young children the Hebrew alphabet and then the Five Books with Rashi, and teachers of Gemara, who taught youngsters more Talmud at home. Among the former were these:

R' Moshe Roytman, R' Asher the Teacher, R. Mikhael the Teacher, R' Zalman-Hirsh the Teacher, R' Eli Brizgal, R' Shmuel Sinerekhes, R' Berel the Teacher, R' Tovye the Teacher, R' Motsel the Teacher.

And here are some of the latter, our Talmud teachers:

R' Shuel the Teacher, R' Itsik-Leyb the Teacher, R' Aba the Teacher, R' Marder, R' Dudye the Teacher, R' Moshe Tarnopoler, R' Avraham Sosover, R' Yoel Lerner, R' Yisrael the Teacher.

Members of the Radzivilov Drama Club before 1928

Shmuel Sher, Eli Chomut, Boske Brandvayn, Sluve Kremer, Boris Koltun, Chave Ayzen, Zeyde Fershtut, Feyge Grinboym, Leyeke Polem, Melekh Shtern, Nachman Nudel, Yankel Shrayer, Mikhel Shpizel, Rivkele Mandel, Moneke Stirt, Feyge Faktor, Matis Tsukerman, Tovye Yakire, Avraham Koyfman, Roze Ayzen.

Members of the New Drama Club

Shmuel Fershtut, Moshe Grinblat, Leyb Ayzen, Hirsh Poms, Avraham Grosman, Yitschak Furman, Shurtsel Zats, Itsikel Nudler, Rachele Fik, Yechezkel Royzman, Esterke Grosman, Neche Tsinayder, Yoske Stirt, Chane Polem, Leyzer Groysman, Serke Treybitsh, Yosel Karent, Boris Koltun.

---

[*] Translated from Hebrew by Ellen Garshick.

Houses of Prayer and Study Halls

Memories of the Great Synagogue*

Menachem Goldgart

The Great Synagogue in our town was very beautiful, but old, at least 150 years old. It rose high above the other buildings in our town even though it was built of wood. The wooden roof tiles were completely rotted, and green mildew was growing on the rafter beams and also spread increasingly on the windows. Rainwater would seep inside and the walls, and the floor was beginning to decay. So my grandfather and my father, and Velvel Zaks of blessed memory, approached Moshe Mendil Ginzburg, the millionaire from our town, who contributed a large sum to restore the synagogue, out of the kindness of his heart. The sextons took up the task quickly: they closed the fountain and got rid of the public toilet that stood in the front of the synagogue. But everyone who lived nearby was against this, especially the butchers, who never thought much at all of the clergy. And what is more, during market days, all the gentiles from the area used this toilet. The congregation complained and protested the sextons' work, and even more so when the sextons said they were going to take the roof off, including the ceiling with its holy decorations, to get rid of the mildew. And the anger of the congregation grew even more when they got together to take down the bronze candelabra and the chandeliers the people had donated over many generations in memory of holy souls. Even though the candelabra and chandeliers were crooked after so many years of use, and their candles were so distended that they dripped on the worshipers, the congregation refused to allow the sextons to remove them and replace them with new, modern candelabra. But the sextons reached a decision to carry on with the repairs and renovations in spite of the heated opposition. The city was in turmoil,

---

* Translated from Hebrew by Elizabeth Kessin Berman.

and the disagreement raged. On the Sabbath, the Torah reading was interrupted until finally, to prevent the desecration of God's Name, the sextons agreed to bring the entire matter to the local rabbi, Rabbi Chayim Brem. But Rabbi Chayim did not want to take the responsibility of deciding a matter this serious on himself alone, so he turned to the Gaon in Vilna. The Vilna Gaon decided accordingly to bring the tiles, the plans of the decorations, and all the decayed prayers and prayer books for burial in a Jewish grave. As for the bronze candelabra, if their weight is substantial, they should be sold, and the redeemed value should be used to purchase new and modern kerosene lamps. This they did.

[page 134]

Synagogues and Study Halls in Radzivilov*

Arye Ayzen

There were 12 synagogues and study halls in Radzivilov, each with its own congregation, united whether by a certain way of worshiping or by membership of a certain profession. First of all was the Great Synagogue, whose magnificent beauty stood out from all the rest. The following are listed by size and number of worshipers:

Rabbi Levi's Study Hall, known as the "Great Study Hall"

Rabbi Itsikel's Study Hall

Rabbi Chayim's Study Hall, known as the "Spanish Study Hall

Rabbi Duvid'l's Study Hall

The Uliki Study Hall, known as the "Turiysk *kloyz*"

The Barani Study Hall

The Zamd Study Hall, called the "Little Synagogue"

The *Magid*'s Study Hall

Zisye Kopf's Study Hall

The Tailors' Study Hall

R' Eli Vitels' Study Hall

---

* Translated from Hebrew by Ellen Garshick.

Religious Life in Radzivilov*

Tsvi Zagoroder

When I reflect on religious life in our town, I must point out that the existence of so many vibrant synagogues and study halls fostered not only religious life, but also economic, cultural, and political life.

Apart from the Great Synagogue, there were about 15 study halls in our town, which were named mostly after well-known rabbis from specific places, like the Ostra *kloyz,* the Trisk, Rabbi Itsikel's Study Hall, Rabbi Levi's Study Hall, and others. Rabbi Levi's (of blessed memory) Study Hall, which was once called "the Rabbi's Study Hall," was where my parents and I worshipped. I remember it from my childhood, and here are my memories of the place and those who worshiped there.

On the eastern wall, to the right of the Holy Ark, were seated R' Yitschak Bati, a hunchback, who made a living with the postal service; he owned many horses, and he used to deliver and haul the mail to the train station. Next to him sat Dov Bereles, the owner of a wholesale store, and next to him was Chayim Rimlober, a severe man who never had a smile on his face. He broke his leg once and had to have an artificial leg. Even though he lived far away from the study hall, very close to the train station, he would come to worship there every Sabbath. My father, now deceased, sat next to him, and next to my father was R' Noach Segal and four additional places for his four sons. He had an extremely long, white beard. He was a very progressive man, but he was still very observant. One of the four brothers was Nachum Segal, the firstborn, Duvid Sheyn's father-in-law, now deceased. The second brother was Itsi Segal, a very absentminded man who would smoke cigarette after cigarette, and when people said good morning to him, he would answer, "I don't have any, I don't have any ...." The third son was Yisrael Segal. The three brothers would come on the Sabbath and especially the

---

* Translated from Hebrew by Elizabeth Kessin Berman.

holidays, wearing top hats and making a great impression on us children. However, the fourth brother, Dov-Beril Segal, was not at all observant anymore, even though he would appear on the Sabbath for prayers. But he would disappear in the middle of the service. (By the way, they said of him, of Dov-Beril, that he survived the war, and I tried several times to find him when I was in Moscow.) And additionally, there was Nachum Segal's son-in-law, Yehoshue Gutman.

On the other side of the Holy Ark sat Herts Meirzun, a very observant, honorable man, and the Goldzberg family (Meir Goldzberg's sons are now in the Land of Israel, in Rishon Letsion, and his daughter, Leye, is in Tel Aviv). Next to them sat Shmuel-Leyb Matshteyn and his two sons; Dudye Magid; Kalman Taykh; and Dudye Magid's son Yisraelik, who was already, or almost, a heretic. I remember R' Leyb Magid (Leyb Zhov), Kalman Taykh's son-in-law, very vividly.

[page 136]

He had no permanent seat, so he used to walk around the study hall and plead with the Master of the Universe, gesticulating like a pious Hasid.

I also remember Mendil the Sexton, a pious, God-fearing man who would get up each night at midnight, put on his shoes, dress, and recite Psalms and Lamentations on the destruction of the Temple and the expulsion of the presence of God, raising his cries to the heavens, and he remained like that until dawn, when he would begin to pray the morning service. There was a grand beggar who lived on the "*perutas*" that he collected from the important people, "the rich."

There was also a man called Akiva Nose because of the length of his nose. He had a terrible temper, and we children would tease and torture him until

....

I said at the beginning of this piece that religious matters were not the only affairs conducted there—the study hall was also the center of economic and political life. Business? Yes, for sure, business in the study hall. There were men meeting and conducting negotiations, trading, and closing deals. And certainly! Everyone participated in political matters, especially between the afternoon and evening prayers in the war years. There were two opposing groups: those who sided with Russia, and those on Germany's side, prophesying victory over Russia. There is no doubt that the reason for hating Russia was the Russians' hatred of the Jews and the pogroms they organized against them. But in those days, how could the Jews know what would happen to them under those "cultured" Germans, those who loved them would learn in the coming days ....

In those days, the study hall served as a kind of club for Jews, who were there frequently during the day. In addition to coming there three times a day for public prayers, men used to sit and study Mishna and Gemara. And there were also those who were running away from trouble at home to the study hall.... They hoped the Holy One, blessed be He, would create some treasure for them that would in include something to make their home life bearable. Also, craftsmen, shopkeepers, and artisans would drop by the study hall to "catch" the afternoon or evening prayers and at the same time catch us up on the news. Having them there was like having a living newspaper in our midst.

Generally, you can say that all the Jews would come to the study hall with their wives and children on the Sabbath and on the intermediate days of the festivals. Early on Sabbath morning, they would begin the order of the service, the Torah portion of the week, with two readings and one in translation, and they would study until nine in the morning. After that they would drink a cup of coffee (and many would drink coffee without sugar, because sugar was considered food, and who would permit himself to eat before prayers?) and go to the study hall. The prayers would continue until 11:00 or 12:00, and then they would go home to eat *cholent*[*] and take an afternoon nap, which was the so-called "enjoyment of Sabbath rest" ....

---

[*] *Translation editor's note: Cholent* is a stew that is usually simmered overnight for 12 hours or more.

[page 137]

After that, they would return to the study hall to study—in the summer, *Ethics of the Fathers,* and in the winter, *Bless My Soul*—before adjourning to the third Sabbath meal. Each of the participants would receive a small challah with which he could say a blessing, some brandy (schnapps) to sip, and some fish or gefilte fish. The main part of the third meal was the reading of the Torah by the rabbi or another Torah reader and the melody that accompanied the chanting of the Torah. Then they would sit and hum Sabbath hymns to accompany the passage of the day, creating what is called "the preparation for the departure of the Sabbath" ... and finally they would recite the grace after meals and stand to pray the evening service. There was an overall impression that no one wanted to leave the Sabbath's peace and rest, when there were no worries about having to make a living. So many struggling, and no one overcoming .... They returned to their homes to do Havdalah* with a lighted candle and sit down to a dairy meal with songs and hymns and words of Torah—until the mundane took over ....

My description of the study hall in which I worshipped with my now-deceased father is typical of most of the houses of study and prayer in our town of Radzivilov. Thus our life went on in those days in the complete belief in the Rock of Israel and the coming of the redeemer, a belief our fathers were right to put their faith in ... and also gave us. May their memory be a blessing forever.

---

* *Translation editor's note:* Havdalah is the ceremony performed at the end of the Sabbath to separate it from the return to the work week.

The Zionist Minyan[*]

Tsvi Zagoroder

A long time ago, at the beginning of the current century, Zionists would gather together for public prayer services during the Sabbath, holy days, and festivals. This gathering was known as "the Zionist minyan." The participants were mainly young people who were strongly influenced by the spirit of Zionism. These minyans were also served as a place to meet with Zionists in a stimulating and uplifting setting, giving hope and meaning to the Jews' dismal life during that period.

Radzivilov had such a Zionist minyan, and quite a lot of people were proud to be part of it, because so many who participated were the town's enlightened of the town.

As the years passed, curious people came and went, but the Zionist minyan continued to grow. At various times, the participants would collect money for the Jewish National Fund, and revenues collected for holy Torah honors were also collected for the Jewish National Fund.

Zionist minyans didn't have synagogue management or sextons; anyone who felt worthy of the task could approach the ark, and it was the same with the other roles, such as Torah reader, shofar blower or other responsibilities.

Visiting Zionists who occasionally came to town on the Sabbath would come to worship at the Zionist minyan, and many would discuss the Zionist movement and talk about its activities and about the impression Zionism was making in different areas.

The Zionist minyan continued to exist until the days of Petliura. Even during the final years, when the numbers were drastically reduced, the minyan still endured, until the Jewish community of Radzivilov was completely cut down.

---

[*] Translated from Hebrew by Elizabeth Kessin Berman.

[page 139]

Welfare Institutions*

The Orphans Committee

Tsvi Zagoroder

An Orphans Committee existed in our town long before the outbreak of World War I. Its objective was to support orphans and widows and give them a foundation and the ability to function on their own.

The Orphans Committee and the Orphans

[page 140]

From the beginning, these women were in leadership roles: Rachel Vaynshteyn, Sashe Boym, Sore Balaban, Gitel Vaser, Batye Berndoyn, Es-ter Landis, Tsilye Bedeker, and Roze Lizek; and with them were the men A. Balaban and Shmuel Inspektor.

On Sabbath afternoons, the committee members would gather and divide up the next week's responsibilities among themselves. The many tasks were

---

* Translated from Hebrew by Elizabeth Kessin Berman.

organizing the kitchen that distributed lunches to the orphans; strategizing for the summer dormitory where the orphans spent two to three months of the year, which freed their mothers from worrying about them; and making sure the orphans were settled in school and their fees were paid, particularly in the vocational and ORT schools.

Revenues came from membership fees collected monthly from individuals, couples, and so forth. In addition, they received basic goods from the town shopkeepers. Thus they managed the institution's meager budget, trying their best to do the best for the children, who had such a desperate fate.

The group of men and women who took care of this institution did their work with great devotion and are worthy of praise.

Mutual Aid

Tsvi Zagoroder

According to its constitution, the purpose of the Mutual Aid Society was to assist and support the sick and destitute, to send members to their bedsides and watch over them. The society's leaders believed that they were doing holy work, as people ought to care for those who could not take care of themselves.

In actuality, the society didn't limit itself to caring for the sick: members also took on the burden of easing the suffering of anyone who needed help. Thus, they were concerned with aiding the disadvantaged without hesitation, distributing charitable donations to buy flour, matzo, and other Passover needs to those occupied with preparing the holiday, including lessening the daily burdens and hunger that resulted from their poverty and depressed situation. Also, the society's care for the residents of the old-age home involved sheltering the elderly who lacked their own homes.

The society's leaders weren't merely philanthropists whose role was simply to distribute funds to help and aid the needy. They were people with an intense sense of social responsibility, and no social or public issue repulsed them. They were the superheroes of the community—the ones who founded other institutions in our town.

[page 141]

Heading the Mutual Aid Society were Yechezkel Zherker, Berel-Volf Yuger, Binyamin Sirota, Moshe Zukenmakher, Yitschak Kripes, Manish Shrayer, and Duvid Shnayder. The secretary was Esterke Groysman.

Flower Day for the Benefit of the Mutual Aid Society. Standing (right to left): Yashke Treyger, Sonye Balaban, Avraham Royzman, Chayim Kitayksher, Leyb Fik, Rachel Sirota, Yakov Shrayer, Eliezer Chait. Seated: Grine Bernshteyn, Moshe Zukenmakher, Yechezkel Zherker, Binyamin Sirota, Rive Kroyt. On the floor: Buntsye Vinshteyn, Munke Margoliot, Dvore Kagan, Avraham Groysman.

[page 142]

[Blank]

[page 143]

Out of the Woe

[page 144]

[Blank]

Town Characters*

Arye Ayzen

Boris Yefimovitsh Koltun

Everyone in Radzivilov knew Boris Yefimovitch Koltun, who owned a library of various theater scripts. It was not easy to get a script from him for a performance. First of all, you had to make a down payment, such as a watch and two *zlotys*.† And afterward, you had to count all the pages of the script to make sure that not even one was missing after you'd used it. And you had to sign that you were responsible for returning it.

Each booklet was stamped and had the owner's [name and] address in Russian doggerel that read:

This book is mine, God is my witness together with me;
Whoever steals this book, may his hand dry up;
If you do not know me, read the following:
Boris Yefimovitsh Koltun, Ogrodova Street 22.

Yosele Pesi-Rudes

Not everyone remembers him. He was a political activist, and not everyone understood what he said. While he was living in the Lodging for the Poor charity's old-age home, Yosele asked the management of the old-age home to send him to a health resort. He received the reply that they only sent weak and crippled people there. Yosele thought and thought and came up with a wonderful idea: he ordered a pair of shoes, one of which had a tall heel. When he got the shoes, he practiced limping on one foot like a lame person, until he appeared to be a true cripple, and the management sent him to the health resort.

---

* Translated from Hebrew by Yaacov David Shulman.
† *Note in original:* A Polish coin: two *zehuvim* ("gold coins").

[page 146]

Pinya the Tailor

He was a small craftsman but a big miser—a man with many children, one younger than the other, a man whose every thought was focused on eating. His wife, Chane Keyle, helped him earn a living. She worked hard to make a living. She brought a sad loaf of bread into their house, which was grabbed and swallowed like the first fruit before the summer.

Chane Keyle constantly visited her neighbor Rachel Milder, who supported her as much as she could afford. And Chane Keyle poured her bitter heart out to her.

In the midst of this grinding poverty that she lived in with her family, Chane Keyle brought a new child into the world every year. When Rachel Milder tried to persuade her that in their sad state of affairs she should stop having children, Chane Keyle replied naively, "But what other pleasure does my Pinya have with me?"

The Woman from Kazimierz

She had four sons and one daughter, each bigger than the next, clever and shrewd grain merchants, all of whom lisped. They were crazy about exotic romantic love, and matchmakers enjoyed proposing what they called solid matches. But the person in charge in the house was their mother, and when the matchmaker Yekele Shteynberg proposed a match for which she would have to pay a $1,000 dowry, the mother said, "For that amount of money, he can rot for another few years."

No one could battle the income tax officer as this woman from Kazimierz could. Every time the officer came to carry out an inspection and the house was filled with grain, the woman from Kazimierz would seal the chimney and fill the house with so much smoke that it was impossible to breathe, and the officer had to stand outside and take down the details that she dictated to him.

Malkele Yuntsikhes

She was a maiden, no longer young, over 30. She always used to say, "Whoever wants to marry me should come to me." If my memory doesn't deceive me, by the time of World War II, no one had come to marry her.

When the Russians entered in 1939, Malkele was selling all kinds of forbidden items, such as liquor, soap, and so on. She would look out the window, and when she saw the police coming to search her property, she would quickly put the soap into her bed mattress and hang it outside as for an airing, and she would put the liquor bottles in a tub, cover them with dirty laundry and stand crouched over the tub covered with sweat and launder with all her might, while singing some song to herself.
[page 147]

After an hour's search, the police left as they had come, without having discovered a thing.

Binyamin the Water Carrier

Not everyone knew him. He lived with his wife Dvorele in the Kitas's basement. They did not have children. Binyamin was blessed with a mother-in-law named Chakentekhe, who was a woman not to be underestimated, a dedicated mother ... who always slept with her daughter. Binyamin was by nature quiet and shy. When Devorele went out on the Sabbath for a walk with her husband and met old friends on her way, she would present her husband and tell him: "Introduce yourself. Put your hand out and say: Binyamin."

This saying was often repeated by the people of Radzivilov.

Motele Savory

He was an orphan, a messenger-boy. Goodhearted people took an interest in him and decided that it would be a good deed to marry him off to Rachele, after the two had fallen in love at first sight at Shintsiuk's wedding, when they were standing behind the window. The wedding was arranged, and the writer of these lines participated in the preparations for the wedding, and after a while for the circumcision as well, which many people attended.

At the circumcision, R' Yosef the ritual slaughterer noticed that they needed "circumciser's powder" and told Motele to bring it. Motele "did" before he "heard." He raced like a deer and came back immediately—but instead of "circumciser's powder," he brought fine flour.

R' Yeshaye Fishkes

He was always a happy person, rejoicing in his portion, loving to perform a commandment. When Motele Savory was preparing to get married, Yeshaye was in charge of supplying everything with a royal hand. He went in his horse-drawn wagon to gather all of the necessary items that goodhearted people had donated.

And when R' Yeshaye was ready to marry off his daughter to one Zanvele of Brody, there was no end to his joy. He lost all restraint for seven days and could not separate himself from the bottle. When people saw him two weeks later, his head was bandaged, and he had two black eyes. They asked him, "Yeshaye, what happened to you?" He replied: "I was the Sabbath guest of my son-in-law [to be]."

[page 148]

R' Moshe Chadash

He served as sexton at the Barani Study Hall. He also kept the Burial Society's charity box. Radzivilov householders also hired him to distribute invitations to weddings and circumcisions.

The same week that Leybish Porochovnik arranged his daughter's wedding, Leybish Kozultsik's mother passed away. As R' Moshe was going about with the charity box, he remembered the wedding invitations in his pocket. When he saw Fayvish Norban passing by in the street, he began jingling his box and told him to go to the funeral, and incidentally told him that Leybish Porokhovnik and his wife were inviting him and his entire family to the wedding that would take place on Friday.

Moshe Aharon the Gravedigger

He also served as sexton, at the Magid's Study Hall. He was an upright Jew in all ways. He suffered a great deal at the hands of his beadle, R' Binyamin, who always argued with him and could not speak with him peaceably. R' Moshe Aharon would stand on the pulpit, a pinch of snuff in his hand, and listen with a tranquil spirit to the insults without answering. When a group of clowns would provoke him and say, "Moshe Aharon, why do you stay quiet?" he would answer them, "Bring me a note from Beril Volf, and then I will speak with him."

Beril Volf was the person who distributed the Burial Society notices.

Yankele the Sexton

He served as sexton in Zisye Kopf's Study Hall. He was always seen singing happily, with a smile on his lips, and his mouth spoke words of wisdom. He headed the food-for-the-poor institution, on whose behalf he raised money to help the needy.

He was a regular visitor to Dubtshak's house. When Dubtshak told him of the difficulties he was facing in bringing his wife and son from Russia, Yankele the Sexton undertook to carry out this mission. He disappeared from Radzivilov for two weeks. He supposedly traveled to Truskawiec, but in fact he had a border smuggler take him across the border; and after many tries he succeeded in bringing Dubtshak's wife and son.

In those days, this was a great sensation in our town of Radzivilov.

[page 149]

Sore Beyle the Butcher Woman

Not everyone knew her. She was literally a saintly woman: she worked during the day in a butcher shop, and at night she repaired overshoes. She knew nothing of this world, and she considered performing kind deeds in secret a commandment of the first rank. Those who buy animals for the butchers who did not have a cent in their pockets knew that Sore Beyle would take care of them, so that they would have the money to travel to the fair to buy a few heads. And if it happened that she herself did not have the money to lend them, she would take her silver candlesticks and go to Gitel Vaser and give them as a deposit in order to engage in the great commandment of performing kind deeds. And every Friday, you could see Sore Beyle carrying a large apron in which she gathered loaves of challah for the poor and for needy families.

Tsile Badaker

All possible praise and appreciation would not suffice for this refined woman, Tsile Badaker, who was totally dedicated to the impoverished class of people of our town. Not everyone knew this. The writer of these lines turned to her more than once when there was an urgent need to increase funds for a very needy person. Tsile did not even ask for whom, but would give generously and rush her help to the needy. And she treated everyone who turned to her pleasantly and generously.

Tsile Badaker participated in all of the philanthropic institutions of our town and helped with a generous heart.

Beyle-Rive Vaynshteyn

This woman was the mother to the Pioneer youth in our town. They would meet in her tiny home on Pochayev Street and talk about various problems, arrange lectures, and argue about different Zionist topics. The atmosphere there was warm. She was unreservedly dedicated to the youth, whom other mothers could not comprehend and understand. She was always happy, always with a smile on her face, until she herself immigrated with her family to the Land of Israel.

[page 150]

In Contrast*

Moshe Korin

Our town—one of many in Volhynia—was very much like all of them: in character, appearance, and also population, being situated on the typical

---

* Translated from Hebrew by Elizabeth Kessin Berman.

Ukraine plains, surrounded by vast pine forests and green fields, and with a river flowing along its edge, streaming as if it were the border between it and all the encroaching villages. Apart from a relatively small area that encompassed the market and mercantile center, the town was completely shaded with trees and filled with vegetable gardens and fruit orchards. If you could view the town from an airplane, you would see it engulfed in green trees with roads winding their way between them. There were no mansions in town, but there were a few flourmills poking out from among the houses.

Even though the majority of the inhabitants in every city and town in Ukraine were gentiles, their numbers were insignificant because the economic energy in each town center and the neighboring streets was dominated by the Jewish population, and they, in turn, gave the town its own special character. On the Sabbath and holidays, you never saw anyone but Jews, and no one disturbed the days of rest and celebrations except to visit acquaintances. But the rest of the time, gentiles from the surrounding areas would come to shop in Jewish stores and then return to their villages. So there was an impression that the city was completely the Jews' domain.

So it was in Radzivilov. There were Jews of every type: rabbis and kosher butchers, enlightened people and simple folk, rich ones and poor ones, merchants and artisans, good-for-nothings and do-nothings, thieves and lunatics, and on top of it all, converts to Christianity and converts to Judaism. The last two types are important to note here.

Once, before World War I, a Jew by the name of Shvartsapel, son of a well-respected, devout family, converted to Christianity and changed his name to Pavlov—a distinguished Russian name. He married the daughter of a well-respected gentile in town and became a rich farmer. He tried to raise his stature among the gentiles, and he succeeded—he was a village elder and head of the local church. His children were farmers and merchants, and his daughter traveled to fairs in the area to sell fabrics. He himself related to Jews with complete indifference, but he didn't harass them as the other converts had done in the past. More than that, a longing for his roots probably took hold of him in the depths of his heart, but he would never, ever speak about this to a Jew. But the following incident occurred.

When he traveled to fairs with his daughter to sell fabrics, he took other travelers for a fee. The travelers were generally Jews. Once it happened that an inquisitive Jew was traveling with him, or perhaps this fellow was really provocative, and he asked him, "Tell me, sir, what caused you to change your religion?"

[page 151]

Pavlov jumped up from his seat. "Because of damn Jews like you! Take your things and get off of my wagon right now." The Jew started to back-pedal: "I didn't mean to insult your honor, heaven forbid. You don't have need to answer me, sir, no, not at all." But he spoke in vain. Pavlov would not be moved by his apologies. The Jew had to get off the wagon in the middle of nowhere, walk in in the mud and rain, and beg a ride to his destination.

But during the Nazi regime, Pavlov was also forced to find shelter in a well-known monastery near the village of Pochayev.

The second character was a Polish policeman in our town who was drawn to the Jewish people and then converted to Judaism. As is the case in every town, there was a Polish police force in which every policeman was a devout Catholic. It happened, however, that one of the policemen, a father of four children, Semeneyvich was his name, fell in love with a Jewish girl. And he was so in love that he divorced his wife and abandoned his children. No one could reason with him, not even his family or the Poles—so the policeman embraced the faith of Moses and Israel and married the Jewish girl. In spite of the Poles' animosity, the couple remained in town and lived among the Jewish residents, as if to demonstrate their contempt for gentiles and further provoke them. One Sunday, however, at a large gathering in the Catholic church, the priest preached and stirred up sentiments against the Jews, and especially against the convert, who passed by the church daily with his prayer shawl and phylacteries on his way to the study hall. The priest called for his excommunication, for revenge on him, and even for a pogrom as punishment for this shameful matter. The younger Poles were aroused by the opportunity to riot against the Jews, but the police chief, who used to receive an "anonymous donation" each month from our community, maintained peace and order and prevented a pogrom.

In 1939, when the Soviets came and upset our lives, knocking them off their very foundations, the convert did not change sides: he kept going to the study hall every day to pray as a devout Jew. And when the Nazis entered our town, Avraham son of Avraham did not run away; he suffered along with all of the Jews and stayed with them all until the end. During the first "action," he went on his last march to the killing pit and sacrificed himself with all of the people of our town as a martyr for the sanctification of God's name.

[page 152]

Episodes*

Arye Ayzen

Selling the World to Come for a Sack of Flour

Anything can happen in this world, including in our town of Radzivilov. The following incident took place in the 20th century, when our culture had already reached a very high level.

One Sunday, a cold day that froze the blood in the veins, at the time of day when all the storekeepers and merchants used to get together in the Barani Study Hall not to pray but to discuss politics and hear what was going on in our Jewish world, they were sitting and talking about this and that, and arguing about problems that had no connection at all to the Jewish people. As usual, the conversation rolled around to the world-to-come. Those people participating in the debate, Jews whose bread was assured and whose water was dependable and whose minds were settled, could allow themselves to sit and debate this topic. R' B.T., a grain merchant, said that he could prove that there is a world-to-come and that a person can merit to go there after 120 years. Similarly, there is a supernal providence that recompenses the righteous for his righteousness and the wicked for his wickedness. R' H.K. the storekeeper didn't agree with R' B.T., and he proposed that B.T. buy H.K.'s portion in the world-to-come in exchange for a sack of grain. R' B.T. accepted the proposal. The two sides sealed the deal with a handshake, and R' B.T. weighed 33 *zlotys*—the price of a sack of flour—into R' H.K.'s hand.

People were having a good time, joking and laughing at the big deal. R' H.K. boasted of his great cleverness as he told his mother about his "deal." Hearing his story, his mother was understandably shocked. She almost

---

* Translated from Hebrew by Yaacov David Shulman.

fainted out of fear of what might happen to him, heaven forbid, and she demanded that he go immediately to R' B.T. and cancel the deal. But R' B.T. didn't easily agree to give up his double portion of the world-to-come. Other people got involved.

[page 153]

They began to persuade R' B.T. to give in, and after much coaxing, he agreed to cancel the handshake in exchange for two flour sacks, which would be distributed to the poor of the town.

This "deal" was the talk of the town, and people discussed it for a long time.

Funeral for the Living Dead

This didn't happen in Radzivilov but in the city of Brody, in 1928. Posters announcing the sudden death of the great merchant, the wealthy Mr. D., appeared in the streets of Brody, saying that the funeral would take place at 3:00 that afternoon.

The beginning of the story was connected to an impoverished, destitute Jewish tinsmith who lived in a cellar with his wife and five children, who didn't have enough money to pay rent to the landlord, Mr. D. In those days, the Professional Association for the Well-Being of Workers took an interest in the tinsmith's situation, intervened in the matter, and attempted to persuade Mr. D. not to evict the poor family from the cellar—but in vain. One fine morning, the poor Jew and his family, with their few meager possessions, were in the street without a roof over their heads.

In protest at the honorable magnate's behavior, it was decided to arrange his funeral: [a funeral] of the living dead. The bier was brought from the cemetery, and many people gathered and began to move down the length of Leshnev Street, Market Street, Gold Street, and Lemberg Street until [they reached] the house of the "man of the hour." The farther they went, the greater the number of participants. People who knew about the matter joined in, and people who didn't know came in their innocence to pay their final respects to Mr. D. Photographers took many photos of the funeral procession, for it was known that a great many people would want to buy photographs of this "funeral."

As the funeral procession approached Mr. D.'s house, a special cantor from the worker's movement sang [the mourner's dirge] *El Malei Rachamim.*

A delegation of three members of the Professional Association entered into negotiations with Mr. D. and received 1,000 *zlotys* from him, a decidedly large amount of money in those days, to help the family. There was also a large income from the sale of the photographs. With this money, the tinsmith's poor family was set up in an apartment, and work was also found for him.

The story became a great sensation in Brody and the entire area.

Anything Can Happen

Among all the few men of our town of Radzivilov, Leybish Prochobnik, of blessed memory, had an honored place. It goes without saying that he moved worlds so that his only son, Mikhael, wouldn't fall into the hands of strangers but would be freed from army service.

[page 154]

When the time came for him to go to the army, an "arrangement" was reached with the military physician, Rabtshenko of Dubno, that in exchange for $100 he would write one word in his report: *nyazkalni,* i.e., "unfit."

Everything appeared fine, but the work of the devil [interfered, and] a terrible error occurred: there was a gentile in the town with the same name, Mikhael Prochobnik, who was also summoned to the army at that time, and he was freed first. When the mistake was discovered, it was already too late.

Having no choice, Leybish Prochobnik was forced to secretly add another $100 to free the gentile, on the condition that the matter would not be made known to anyone. But the news spread immediately, as quick as lightning across the entire town.

A few days later, the gentile came to Leybish, his hat in his hand, and said: "Thank you, Mr. Prochobnik, for your kindness."

The people of Radzivilov certainly remember this story.

A Pauper with a Starched Collar

That was the appearance of a Jew, someone from Lvov, who made his way to us, to [our] town—not, heaven forbid, to seek alms but to raise money to support a bride: to marry off his daughter.

When he arrived in Radzivilov, he arranged his first visit with me, with Berel Lober's recommendation. He greeted me very politely, mentioned his family name with a smile, and said to me, "I haven't come to you for a donation, but to ask you to give me a few addresses of grain mill owners, because I'm connected to that profession. I worked my entire life as an accountant in Frenkel's grain mill. I believe you know that the grain mill in Przemyśl burned down, and I remained without work. Now I must marry off my daughter, and I'm forced to turn to people of my profession to stand by my side in my hour of difficulty."

This was the introduction of a poor, intelligent Jew with a starched collar. He had aristocratic features and used Germanized expressions. Of course, making the list took only a short time, and he left to visit the flourmills, where he called each mill owner on the list by his family name to make an impression. The men of our town showed their generosity and gave magnanimously.

After he returned and ate a satisfying lunch that he had ordered earlier, my guest lay down to rest for a while.

[page 155]

After he got up, he asked if there was a study hall nearby and whether wealthy people prayed there. He went there and stood and prayed with great feeling, almost like a rabbi, without taking his eye off the congregation. He spoke with no one but replied to those who greeted him, peace be with you! He kissed the *mezuzah* and went back to the house. Supper was already prepared according to his orders. After he ate, he struck up a conversation with me about the years before and after World War I. He said, spicing up his conversation with German expressions:

"In 1914, as a young man, I began to deal in livestock, although by profession I was a tailor. I saw a blessing in my business, but the war frustrated my plans. During the war, I supplied meat to the army and created a good business. I believe that in your town there are many butchers. Won't you in your goodness give me their addresses?"

The next day, after eating a tasty breakfast, my guest went to visit the butchers. He spoke with them as a professional colleague, and again he returned with money in his hands. In the evening, we continued our conversation on that topic. He told me:

"When the revolution broke out in 1917, I was very devoted to the workers' situation. But as time passed, I changed my mind and I lost my love for Marx-Engels' plans, because I myself come from a religious family. Then I returned to my old profession, tailoring, until 1922. I believe that there is no lack of tailors in your city. If it's not difficult for you, give me the addresses of my former professional colleagues. I'd like to visit them."

On the third night as well, we talked about the time after the war and the present situation in Poland (he was also conversant in politics). Although I knew that all this was connected to his money collecting, I enjoyed hearing his made-up stories, as he continued telling me with a serious expression on his face:

"I saw that there was no blessing in tailoring. Also, my departed wife was against this. I therefore began little by little to deal in furs. As an expert in this profession, I made a great deal in the business, and I did very well. To my great sorrow, my wife passed away after a difficult illness, leaving me with two daughters and a son. Are there furriers Here? Won't you do me a favor and give me their addresses?"

I again made a list of addresses, as I took pleasure in his made-up stories, which were arranged with great expertise.

After he "arranged" his business with the small hide dealers, he rested for a few hours. After that, he proposed that I go with him on a short walk. He again began to tell about his past, about his work as an accountant in Frenkel's grain mill, and that after the fire he was left without bread.

[page 156]

"Since I didn't know what to do, I became a cantor in a small synagogue. The beadles weren't happy with my Hebrew, and I soon had to leave my post. In the meantime, my daughter got engaged to a very fine young man, an expert in the lumber profession. Maybe I'll succeed in getting back on my feet through him, because before the war my departed father owned a sawmill, and I'm an expert in this profession as well. The border regions are famous for their large forests. Do you also have sawmills? Maybe it's worth visiting their owners? I promised a dowry for my daughter and also clothes, and as a result I have to travel through the world and raise money. I believe that after the Sabbath I will, with God's help, leave town. To you, sir, I have one more request; perhaps you can arrange a few people to go out in pairs and collect some *zlotys*. This will be a good deed for you, because it's not pleasant for me to go door to door. I don't have any money, but I do have my self-respect. I am, after all is said and done, a merchant who's had bad times."

I asked him if it had been worth his while to come to our town. To that he replied comfortably that he had raised 250 *zlotys* in a few days in this town—a very respectable amount. And he wanted to laud all those who had helped him—most of all, myself, of course, because I was the "man of the hour" as he arranged the wedding. "Yes," he said, "I want to speak with your householders from the Barani Study Hall. I believe that they'll deal with me and help me in my difficult position. On Sunday I'm going to Dubno. Perhaps you have acquaintances who know the city well?"

On Sunday morning, our guest left town as he shook my hand. "*Auf wiedersehen*—we'll meet again!" And he thanked me as he promised to invite me to the wedding.

Of course, Berel Lober came to receive his "broker's fee" on behalf of the guest whom he had sent me. Whether or not I was pleased, I had to pay. He also promised to send other guests.

The incident remains in my memory, and it taught me not to look at a person's outer appearance, but to judge him in accordance with his words and stories.

[page 157]

Personalities and Figures

[page 158]

[Blank]

Moshe Taykh*

He was born in Radizivilov in 1904 to Kalman and Alte Taykh, his parents. His father was a clever man, very well educated in Torah, who was a rabbinical lawyer in our town. Moshe studied in a cheder until World War I, when the Taykh family fled to Russia and lived there until 1920. After their return to Radizivilov, Moshe was a Pioneer Youth leader, belonging to the Freedom section of the movement.

R' Kalman Taykh and Family Members

R' Kalman was a Zionist, and as an honest man, he immigrated to the Land of Israel with his wife and settled with his wife near his children, Moshe and Dvore, on the Ein Harod farm. There, too, the parents died at an old age.†

---

* Translated from Hebrew by Rosalind Romem.
† *Note in original:* Three daughters, Chaye, Peye, and Sore, were killed by the Nazis.

[page 160]

The Modest One[*]

D. Melts

Moshe Taykh

Moshe Taykh was one of the first of the lines of "movers and shakers." He was a founder of Kibbutz Vohlyn in Hadera and one of the first people of Givat Brenner; he came to Ein Harod from Givat Brenner. He worked there in the vineyards for many years and gave his strength and tenacity to developing industry. Here he organized work in general and worked in the kibbutz secretariat.

Moshe, who was a Talmud scholar steeped in Torah and culture, was eventually called to educate and direct the groups of youth immigrating to Israel. He knew how to instill this simply into youth—the primary, basic, internal values of the Labor Movement in the Land of Israel—in his own humble, modest way.

He was, as stated, a Torah scholar, who drew from the wells of both our ancient and our new cultures. It was pleasant to sit with him at the table in the noisy dining room and listen to the topics he raised that day, whether

---

[*] Translated from Hebrew by Rosalind Romem. *Note in original:* Articles taken from a booklet in his memory produced in Ein Harod.

from a chapter of *Duties of the Heart* by Our Teacher Bachya[*] or from works by writers and poets of our new literature. He knew how to combine the past and the present, knew how to recognize the links of the dynasty of the continuing....

There was a connection between what he learned and his modest lifestyle. He lived a life of spirituality, searching in sources to satisfy his soul's hunger to know, the "oil to light." Within our generation's divided and confused world, he belonged to those who still believed in the value of ideas and the strength of the spirit and soul. And in the strength of these he also knew, apparently, how to do his work with modest simplicity.

The Loyal Pioneer[†]

Sh. Broida

Grochów was a Pioneer agricultural farm near Warszawa. To visit Grochów was the desire of every pioneer and the pride of everyone who was preparing to immigrate to the Land.

[page 161]

In the spring of 1926, on my way to the Land, I visited there. For half a day I walked around every corner of the farm, and everything I saw was not enough for me: starting with the beautiful plant nursery, the henhouse, and ending with a wagon that appeared in the yard, full of tall sheaves and with a young man on top driving the horses with a sure hand. Something sang around me—and in my heart. From then on, a correction was made in Bialik's "field"—"our hands formed your sheaves, the Jewish pioneer hand, made the sheaves taller" .... But most of the surprise awaited me beyond the farm's fence, where the cows were roaming in the nearby dust. A sun-tanned shepherd with curly hair, wearing a white farmer's shirt, occasional-

---

[*] *Translation editor's note: Duties of the Heart* (*Chovot HaLevavot*) was the primary work of the Jewish philosopher Bachya ibn Paquda (called Our Teacher Bachya), who lived in Saragossa, Spain, in the first half of the 11th century.

[†] Translated from Hebrew by Rosalind Romem.

ly pushed his flock toward the pastures while carefully watching that the cows did not cross the border. I approached him. Smiling eyes met me with "Shalom," and the shepherd spoke to me in Hebrew.... For several moments it was as if I were in Wonderland. I quickly left him so as not to disturb him and let him do his "holy work."

That was my first meeting with Taykh. And this meeting remains in my memory whenever I see "I made you a shepherd."...

A year passed, and again—in Hadera. Hadera—the center of malaria and parties in Israel: Labor Unity and Young Worker and Conquest of Labor and stormy debates. On the dunes outside the settlement, two kibbutz tent camps were set up, one called Brotherhood and the other, Vohlyn. Good neighborliness and the unity of labor brought them closer together. From the leaky tents, our members and the Kibbutz Volhyn members went to get work in the fields every day. On one such day, as we worked with hoes in the field, happy and sweaty, I recognized to my pleasant surprise the pioneer shepherd from Grochów. Since then, we have connected many threads: Grochów; the image of Hadera; and the hoe, which we conquered and played with our hands like a musical instrument. We dealt in depth not only with the fields but also with all the problems of society, settlement, kibbutz, and party. "Injil"—couch grass, which is the blessed earth's parasite—was a symbol for us, and together we attacked it to destroy it at the root. "Look, I removed it completely, not even the 'eye' is left," Taykh would say, showing me the flourishing injil, his eyes smiling with happiness.

In the evenings, after the meal of olives and soup, the tents were full of debates: the way of the kibbutz and settlement. The battle of status, and the Arab question, on which many "experts" could be found among the settlement workers. Taykh was aware of all these questions, on many occasions attending public meetings in the settlement, and his comments were greatly valued. Later there was a crisis in the immigration settlements, and we were scattered throughout the land. Only two years later, when one of us came from the south and one from the north, did we meet again, very happily, in Ein Harod.

"If a person thought while meeting his friend that this was possibly their last meeting—who knows, perhaps life would appear differently"—
[page 162]

Who knows?

Many decades would pass, and there would be no one who knew his friend, even his good friend whom he met daily for many years in one branch.... And when the time comes, after "the last meeting," you stand with regret and pain when you discover that you know almost nothing about your friend, you stand and regret how it happened that you can't describe his life, his youth, his past until his immigration to the Land of Israel. It becomes clear to you that you didn't know the man who was your friend for years at all ... the heart breaks. And it's important to think about it a great deal.

I met with Taykh many times, and we would talk for many hours. We thought deeply about the movement, society, the individual, and the kibbutz. The world and the institute. And Taykh, in his way, delved deep and searched, sometimes cruelly toward himself and his friends, while searching for the basis of these matters, to their roots, delving, in his period of roots of "the tip of the sting," to the very end. We had very interesting periods, but there was no shortage of low periods while striving toward equality in the kibbutz and sorting out the "minor matters" and conversations about "current questions" at the pinnacle of our world, and what is a commune? And "living according to these principles"—for all the people, or "you have chosen us." And so it was until we were together "at the side of the railway tracks, which pass us noisily." ...

Taykh never gave up. He spoke sarcastically about unrealistic people. This was because he believed in human beings and the truth of life, which ends in victory. He knew how to overcome internal depression and encourage others. He would frequently use his slogan, which was known only to a few: "Take care of yourself," meaning, do not allow weakness around you to overcome you. In later years he added "and your close friend" to this slogan ….

The man was modest and full of humility. And if in regard to movement or labor he knew how to demand a lot from himself and others, and not to give up—in his private and personal matters, he knew how to rise above it and forgive, sometimes to the point of neglect. Also in health matters. He was very careful not to bother other people about himself—"not to bother, God forbid." And so he modestly avoided things, passed on, and left us.[*]

A dear friend has been taken from us, a good friend, an expert in Jewish studies, to whom you could always turn and share what was in your heart and receive encouragement. His many students could relate his fatherly and sincere approach to their most intimate and personal distress; they always left him encouraged and self-confident. His task in educating youth was to inspire them to be loyal to the Labor Movement and the state. It was very important to him, holy, although it was difficult for him to be completely cut off from the fields, the plants, to which he was attached with all his heart. Indeed, he returned to it, to the earth, the mother of all living creatures that he loved—too soon.

[page 163]

The memory of Taykh, the friend, the loyal member of the movement, dear and holy, will remain in his friends' hearts. They will forever mourn his absence.

About His Image[†]

Menachem Goldberg

A scholar, steeped in the spirit of the generations of the people of Israel, eager to know—this is part of his image.

---

[*] *Note in original:* He died on 26 Av 1950 in Ein Harod.
[†] Translated from Hebrew by Rosalind Romem.

Five or six years ago, we guarded together. At night, he drew my little knowledge of chemistry and physics from me. During the day, he would read and study these subjects, and at night he would have me clarify this information. He was very thorough, delving into the basis and roots of these questions until he could find the unknown—and then he would look at me victoriously. He did not accept that the obvious assumption was the entire matter. With the determination and diligence of a yeshiva student, he continued to deal with these scientific problems for a long time.

When, on behalf of the education committee, it was suggested to him that he prepare himself to teach science, he said, "Although the laws of nature are of great interest to me, my existence is—the spirit of our people." And he did that.

Originality and independent thought were the second part of his image. He did not accept routine matters even if based on life experience. He would consider and analyze every problem and only then come to conclusions.

Initiative—that characteristic was part of his personality. When he worked in the vineyard, he used to bring us, "the work organizers," various inventions: to remove branches, organize the vintage, remove the fruit from the vineyard, and more. In that year he succeeded in reducing the workdays required for a dunam of vineyard by an extremely large percentage.

Primary pioneering. The "scholar" and "man of thought" always saw the main content of a man's life to be physical labor. When I suggested to him five years earlier that he prepare himself to instruct youth, he did not agree, because he did not want to abandon physical labor. And after a great deal of persuasion, telling him of the importance of the matter even for himself by giving him the opportunity to study, he looked at me with an eye that penetrated heart and soul and with a laugh—which took away one's confidence in the truth of one's words and thoughts. And finally, when he accepted the verdict, he did so on the condition that the preparation would require him to teach only one group, maximum two, and that after that he would return to physical labor.

[page 164]

Recently, when group 7 was about to complete its course, he talked about having fulfilled his duty and that he now wished to return to work in the vineyard.

He educated youth group 7. He invested himself and all his abilities in this, and it was the final task of his life. He did not live to enjoy this work.

In the final days, when he realized that the majority of the group members were going to be pioneers and even build a new settlement, even before they had concluded the youth group period, he used to say, "I'm very busy. Now is my 'harvest season.'"

His memory will be part of Nir Eliyahu—the kibbutz built by his students, among others.

Defining Character*

The defining character has very great value in the education of man and the formation of society's image. This character might be concrete, realistic—a person who lives and functions in a specific period and place, acting as an example and symbol to the members of his generation and his environment: or else it is imaginary, mythical, historic—an imaginary creation adjusted to the passion of the generation, its observations and ideas.

According to this, this character fulfills a double role: it illustrates the image of the generation within which it functions and it also ennobles through its spirit and educates the young generation.

When life is stable, when the generation is static, and the character is perfect and has no duality, then parents and educators know what image of a person they want to present as a symbol and powerful attraction for their students.

This is not so with a revolutionary generation in a period of transition. The image of the desired character looks misty to them and suffers from

---

* Translated from Hebrew by Rosalind Romem. *Note in original: Cogitation on Our Spirit*—from the same booklet.

lack of backbone. This deficiency grows and becomes obvious in the revolution's second period, when construction replaces destruction, the positive replaces the negative, and a clear and complete image is needed.

This deficiency is also discovered in our own society. From here stems the tragedy of our situation and the embarrassment that often overcomes us. We know how to use terms for a negative character: "Diaspora type," "homeowner," petit bourgeoisie," etc. But when we are asked about the positive person's characteristics, desirable in our society, about his qualities and spiritual image—it is very difficult for us to respond, if we want to be honest and genuine about ourselves and not use empty phrases.

Our debate presents us with two tasks:

[page 165]

a) To establish an independent Jewish agricultural economy, to establish it, expand it, and improve it. A mandatory condition for this—maximal effort, physical and cognitive. The concentration of all our spiritual strength, the best of our skills and abilities.

We are still in our beginning stages, without an important economic tradition and with a lack of experience. Technical Improvements and inventions cannot replace a person's dedication to his livelihood.

And when I want to describe to myself, in my imagination, the image of the complete person, who fulfills his duty, in other words, what kind of a person might be educated in a society that places this specific task at the center of its affairs, I view him along these lines:

A person tries to do the duties of his work and economy from early in the morning until sunset. In the evenings and when he has a few hours of leisure, he is busy organizing and preparing for the next day's work. His brain has no time to read a book. With difficulty, dozing off, he glances through the newspaper. When he wants to read a textbook that he badly needs for his work, he has to make a special effort. And so he continues for days and years, until he becomes unable to absorb material, exhausted, closed, shrunk. But sometimes a desire awakens for literature, art, the wide world, rest, and easy thinking. However, his awareness of his responsibility and the seriousness of his task help him get over this mood and continue in his usual way.

Our second task is education and the development of the movement. And to concentrate a lot of Jews around us, educate youth in our country and overseas, prepare them for a life of work, and instill in them the ideology of our movement and ease their absorption into the land and the economy. This task also demands concentrated thought and enthusiasm, training in public activities, political awareness, and a talent for fighting and for expressing oneself. The central character that defines is the person who has all these qualities.

In daily life, when these two roles demand their perfect fulfillment, you discover contradictions and friction. When contradictions arise concerning the individual, they cause imperfection and dissatisfaction. And in society, these cause social division and lower its image.

The most suitable and preferred way for our period of time is the combined method, which we should adopt, but as yet we have not begun to do this. The problem would not have been so critical if we could have split the tasks between two different types of people among us so that integrity would not be damaged. But the crux of the matter is that the character that defines the fulfillment of the second task is attractive and charming and influences the surroundings and youth. They want to be like that.

[page 166]

Yosef (Yozik) Zaks*

From the *Galilee Bulletin*

He was born in Radzivilov in 1904 to Zindel and Viktoria Zaks, a wealthy and respected family. He attended school there. When his family went to Odessa during World War I, he attended the Russian gymnasium. After the war, his

---

* Translated from Hebrew by Elizabeth Kessin Berman.

family returned to Radzivilov. As a result of the influence of nationalism at the war's end and the growing movement to rebuild and settle the Land of Israel, he joined Pioneer. He was part of the group of pioneers who immigrated in 1924.

The group went to the Kineret settlement, and Yozik worked with the tobacco crop. There he was first exposed to Kibbutz Kineret members and kibbutz life in general. There also, an awareness of kibbutz ideals and communal life crystallized for him. After working in the settlement for a year, and after his group quickly dispersed, Yozik became a member of Kibbutz Kineret. At first, he held various jobs at the Rutenberg power plant in Naharayim and elsewhere. Every position he held revealed his determination and talent. In Kineret, he started a family and had three children.

When he went to work permanently in the dairy barn, he worked with an extraordinary effort and efficiency that impressed everyone. For 25 years—until the year he died—he worked diligently to improve and promote the dairy industry. When he needed information, he did research and took courses and even taught himself from books. His work in this area was not limited to the kibbutz sector. He shared his work with the Dairy Association.

[page 167]

His knowledge, experience, and work with dairy livestock earned him respect, and his colleagues were all eager to hear his ideas.

He died on 4 Tammuz 1954 (July 5, 1954).

Yozik[*]

Miryam Barats

"Yozik" is how we—his Jordan Valley friends—knew him.

There are three ways to describe Yozik: pioneer, achiever, and trusted friend. He was a pioneer from the day he entered the country until the day he died. He managed the dairy for 25 years, exactly half his life. This is no

---

[*] Translated from Hebrew by Elizabeth Kessin Berman.

small thing. He knew how to overcome numerous difficulties and get results.

He was a good friend to everyone, personally and professionally. He was not a great prophet, but he had the ear of all his fellow dairy association members, who loved and listened to him because he spoke from experience and knowledge of life.

This is how we knew Yozik, and this is how we will preserve his blessed memory.

A Youthful Soul[*]

It appears that only in a situation like this, death, can one comprehend him. He had a youthful vitality, and he didn't slow down until old age. In recent years, he spoke out in a meeting with the thin voice of youth and exploded even though the matter was not simple—just as a young person would. He had no lack of experience, and the things he did know, he was a master at. He had a youthful manner, but this did not mean he lacked maturity. Just the opposite: this is a natural gift. Everything that happened to him and around him, he considered and reacted to as if he were a boy of 18. There is little difference between what he was then and when he grew older.

Was this easy for him? Not at all.

So it seems that being young is not just a phase; it is part of one's character.

Happy is the man whose soul is young although he himself has reached his seniority.

And so take note of youthfulness like this, for it not only surely guides your years well, but also preserves your youth.

Mid-July 1954

---

[*] Translated from Hebrew by Elizabeth Kessin Berman. *Note in original:* From the papers of Ben-Tsion Yisraeli of Kineret—it appears to be a summary of sorts of the eulogy he gave for Yozik.

Avraham Aychis[*]

From the *Givah Bulletin*

Avraham Aychis was born in Radzivilov in 1896 to a family of wealthy merchants. His earliest education was a traditional Jewish one. In 1912, he went to the technical school for trade in Kiev. The same year, he joined the Young Zionists, and shortly thereafter he distinguished himself. He was a quiet, polite, genteel young man, a good listener, and there was always a song on his lips.

Unlike many of his friends, who increased their knowledge by reading books on politics and sociology, he preferred philosophy. He would always engage in discussions with his friends, but he would never attend meetings. He distanced himself from the tedium of instruction and information, although he busied himself with lowly day-to-day work, and he did it with polished and talented execution. In 1914, Aychis disappeared from the inner circles of the movement. We found out that he had decided to study the fundamentals of the Hebrew language. His teacher was Cantor Glants, and in return, Aychis taught him musical notation.

When discussions became heated and divisive, prior to the formation of *Et Livnot* [A Season to Build] (at the beginning of 1915), Aychis returned to us. He heard, he listened, and he weighed. With the increase in activity after the February Revolution, Aychis devoted himself to the Organization, becoming involved in a variety of movement committees. He led the organization of youth groups, set up conditions for a Hebrew sports team, and devoted much time and effort to the revival tax)[†]—all with amazing dedication and meticulousness for the party, without taking any credit.

---

[*] Translated from Hebrew by Elizabeth Kessin Berman.

[†] *Note in original:* On behalf of the Dror federation in Kiev, the revival tax was divided up as follows: 70% for the Jewish National Fund, 20% for the cooperative fund, 10% for the cultural fund.

In 1921, Aychis went from Russia to Poland with many Dror members, and there he worked on the Pioneer movement in Volhynia.

He immigrated in July 1930 and joined his family at Givat Hashlosha. There he was always found working in different kibbutz administration jobs: secretary of education, teacher in the kibbutz school and the regional school, treasurer, or active member of many different committees. As the years passed, he nurtured musical enterprises as director of the school choir and conductor of the kibbutz orchestra.

[page 169]

From Testimonials by Kibbutz and Movement Members[*]

I met Avraham Aychis, of blessed memory, for the first time during the stormy period of the 1917 Russian Revolution. This was, I believe, at a Jewish student meeting in Kiev, where there was an ongoing discussion on this question: do we need to join the general militia to keep the peace, or should we set up a separate, independent organization? They told me he had already been connected to an underground group associated with the Zionist group *Et Livnot* for a long time.[†]

From our first meeting, I remember that he was always involved in in all arenas of Zionist work and, after that, in the ranks of Dror. Mainly I remember, with pleasure, his work for the Jewish National Fund.

Following the cessation of immigration in 1925–1927, Aychis had to stay in the Polish diaspora for an additional year. When the gates to the Land of Israel opened, he was among the first to immigrate. He went with his family to Kibbutz Givat Hashlosha, and there he remained for the rest of his life ....—*Y. Bereginski*

---

[*] Translated from Hebrew by Elizabeth Kessin Berman.

[†] *Note in original:* In those days, *Et Livnot,* the precursor of the Dror federation, developed and organized the Independent Defense, and its leader, Mr. Yeshayahu Fisrovsky, emerged from the community in Kiev. In a Hebrew speech, he urged the community to prepare to defend itself—The Editor.

A man of the Dror movement.—This movement was an amalgam, and in its amalgamation it resembled the aspirations of all of the pioneer movements in Poland. Aychis was levelheaded and acted deliberately, but he actually accomplished many things; but when he had to take credit for what he accomplished, he was captivated by dedication and devotion, which were his primary characteristics.

I first met him in the stormy days of the Pioneer movement, during the days of Klosova—in 1827 [sic] in Rovno. Everything was wildly exciting, but Aychis was moderate and self-restrained.

He cultivated in himself the most sincere quality a man like him could possess—unlimited and unflinching trust of all of his comrades—and only because of his complete honesty. He was always honest, even when it was painful, and he was always convincing.

In the midst of all of his dedicated work, Aychis, along with Yehuda Sharat, may he have a long life, led our chorus. Many parties were enhanced by his pleasant voice. He knew many special traditional Passover seder songs. Now we will no longer hear his special songs ....—*B. Marshak*

[page 170]

Batye Aychis (Benderska)[*]

Batye was born in 1903 in Zhitomir to enlightened parents. Her father was a Hebrew teacher, and her love of the people and homeland came from him. She was educated in a Russian gymnasium and, like many others who were joining youth movements, she joined Dror.

When the more senior members of the movement decided to move to Poland on their way to the Land of Israel, the local members, including Batye, decided to follow, and thus they set off on the difficult routes to the borders traveled by the senior members.

In October 1921, Batye and her female comrades crossed the Polish-Russian border near Austria and reached Rovno in Volhynia. There, on her

---

[*] Translated from Hebrew by Elizabeth Kessin Berman.

own, she organized Hebrew language lessons for both young people and adults. Also at that time, she embarked on married life when she met Avraham Aychis.

Afterward came her work for Pioneer, which was then being spread in Polish regions by Dror members from Russia. With Pioneer's encroachment into the Volhynia region, many training centers were established to teach the basics of kibbutz life, mostly in Klosova, where the first years were the most difficult.

In 1929, she finally fulfilled her personal aspirations, immigrating to Israel with the first immigrants of the Fifth Aliyah, and along with the first immigrants from Klosova, she joined Kibbutz Givat Hashlosha. Shortly after her arrival, her daughter Yael was born. Batye soon put her heart and soul into the kibbutz.

Batye's primary responsibility was to care for the younger generation. She was the administration's secretary of education, organizing the curriculum in all grades, and she did this for many years. Similarly, she dedicated a significant amount of time to the absorption of new immigrants to Israel, and most of them were successfully integrated.

In 1937–1938, she was a kibbutz ambassador for immigration in Poland.

While immigration was banned and the immigrants were concentrated in Cyprus, she struggled to represent the immigrants there.

She died on 33 Tishrei (October) 1952.

Notes on Batye*

It was enough just to meet her once and be convinced—here is motherhood, here is family closeness. Closeness that is certain to last even if many years pass without seeing her.

[page 171]

When we worked together in Pioneer in Poland, I saw her as a person of the movement and as a good and devoted mother. Then, the pioneers were

---

* Translated from Hebrew by Elizabeth Kessin Berman.

rotting away by themselves in Poland with no hope of ever immigrating. And her job was to encourage, comfort, and inspire them to go on living.

She was living a life absolutely without comforts, but she was deeply satisfied anyway. If she asked you something, you felt as though your mother were asking you, your sister was worrying about you. Batye was from a large and accomplished family: labor movements without which the kibbutz movement would never have arisen or given rise to the many famous labor parties in this land of ours.

Batye was completely identified with the movement, and it gave her internal happiness.—*Rachel Katsnelson-Shezer*

There in the miserable villages of Volhynia, you were so happy to go with this group and believe in the strength of the great Jewish revolution. You always went along paths with no roads, passing the crooked byways with the common people, and if you were not at the head of the march, you were marching with them in their midst. You knew how to exist in the movement as one of them and as one caring for them. You needed to give—to put yourself last, to be the work in progress. Batye was completely of Volhynia. Every child and young person knew Batye. She was awakened by pioneering, and it brought her inspiration for a new life.—*Chuma Chayot*

[page 172]

Shimon Zahavi*

Y. Amir

Shimon Zahavi (Goldhart) was born in 1903 to an affluent, educated merchant family in Radzivilov. After wandering during World War I, he immigrated to the Land of Israel in 1924. During his first years there, he worked at a number of menial jobs: in the port, in agriculture (in the Galilee and Beit Shemen), and in construction.

---

* Translated from Hebrew by Elizabeth Kessin Berman.

In 1927, he went to Jerusalem to further his education, and from that time on his future was linked to Hebrew University. He was accepted into the Institute of Mathematics. Due to his impoverished circumstances, he had to work—first in the university building on Har HaSofim and then, during the days of unrest, as a watchman at the university.

In 1933, he received a humanities degree in both philosophy and mathematics. He continued to work at the university, first as a guide for those touring the university and later as a clerk in the bursar's office. He was thus able to continue studying in the Mandate government's law school and was awarded a law degree. In 1956, he was appointed secretary of the university treasury, and he distinguished himself in this role. Among his great accomplishments was the creation of a new university campus. In this role he was very modest and served as a model of diligence and gentility.

In his own research, Zahavi studied the issues of pensions in Israel and abroad and became the foremost specialist in this area. And many other institutions sought his aid, advice, and guidance. His work brought him great personal satisfaction, because he could advocate for the weak, for aid to the handicapped and elderly, for orphans and widows, and for all who were needy.

[page 173]

For time he was a labor union member, and he especially involved himself in the affairs of people in the lowest stratum of the society that he had thoroughly researched.

In 1959, he was 56 years old, and after 32 years of work at the university, he retired, intending to devote himself to research, but a terrible illness took hold of him. After a year and a half of suffering and torment, he passed away in Jerusalem on 16 Heshvan 1961.

The Soul of Shimon Zahavi, of Blessed Memory*

I met him almost 17 years ago. From the very beginning, I knew that I was encountering a person with deep conviction, spirit, and compassion. I immediately perceived him as a special man, a unique person who takes it upon himself to serve with integrity and goodness. I was not mistaken. Year after year, my esteem of him grew as I enjoyed meeting him from time to time and always viewed him as someone who simply loved to serve with integrity and fairness.

He had a good heart, a heart of gold. One among a thousand or tens of thousands. Often, I would stand in front of him in astonishment, and my heart would beat quickly and with intensity when he was speaking passionately about suffering and the need for relief. He himself was not deterred by any hindrance, nuisance, or annoyance that prevented him from helping someone in need. So many good deeds were done because of his love and dedication, in his own right or through funding—and even beyond his limitations as an employee who received his salary once a month. And so it was for him: day in and day out, he did not distinguish between people who were important and those who were not especially important, between a laborer and a student, between an illiterate person and a learned person. Everyone had his or her own measure of worth.

He gave more than half of his life to Hebrew University, working first as a laborer and guard, then as a student and a guide for visitors to the university. After that, he was a clerk in the bursar's office until he became the secretary of the treasurer's office, and with just a degree in philosophy, he managed to bring stability to the university's financial affairs during the years of its development and construction projects on its new campus.

Then, a new flame was lit in his soul—he discovered a new light in the tradition of Israel, in its prayer. Zahavi embraced the timeliness of prayer—

---

* Translated from Hebrew by Elizabeth Kessin Berman. *Note in original:* From a memorial service at Hebrew University, Jerusalem.

and driven by a love for the Land of Israel, nationhood, and its people, he became religious and came to a love of God, the Eternal of Israel, and the customs of Israel that were sanctified over the generations of the Nation of Israel. He absorbed the tenets of Judaism completely.—*Aleksander Elyash*
[page 174]

In Memory of Duvid Sheyn, of Blessed Memory*

It was a double, even a triple, loss: a loss of a man who was in the prime of life, enjoying his best years, at the height of his profession, and suddenly, bizarrely and very cruelly, he was severed from life's tide. A loss to his family—an unheard of, unfathomable loss—a loss that unleashed limitless sorrow; a loss for all of us, the Cooperative agency, the Cooperative management, and the Cooperative members who all loved him, everyone who was associated with him, and he to them.

He was one of our best assessors, but he was not satisfied with the task of evaluation alone, because even if he had lived his whole life devoted completely to the concept of cooperativism, and even if his life had been the entire Cooperative, he would still have risen above debate for the most advantage to the Cooperative.

He was one of the few who were people qualified to concern himself diligently, passionately, and with love to the proliferation and completion of Cooperative projects. For so many, he served as a hub who carried out his tasks with affability and affection.—*Y. Ritov*

He immigrated from Poland in 1934 and brought with him a vibrant Zionist ideology and Jewish initiative. He worked in many different places and was hindered by the challenges of absorption until he found his place in central branch of the Cooperative in Haifa in 1945.

He despised laissez-faire attitudes and struggled with the negative aspects of the Cooperative: but even so, he gained a good measure of trust be-

---

* Translated from Hebrew by Elizabeth Kessin Berman. *Note in original:* By his work colleagues at Cooperative headquarters and the supervisory unit.

cause he lived up to his principles. He achieved much with very little, he was happy with his lot, and he was very humble, man, a man of the people in the full sense of the word, incorruptible and guileless. He had an innate sense of proportion, of moderation when dealing with people, a deep awareness of the ways operations functioned—all these traits informed his advice and actions during times of crisis. He was never reprimanded even once during his 20 years of work with the Cooperative.—*M. Livai*

He was happy with his lot, a man who had so many aspirations and a completely unique way of life.

He had a constant, heartfelt smile always on his face and was ever-ready with timely jokes on his lips—making his philosophy of life transparent and not shirking death. So a deep sadness was felt among his colleagues and friends when his death was announced.

[page 175]

He was a well-rounded, very well-read man, and was very genial and amiable. Every conversation with him was like a lively folktale, a comedy routine, or a rich and spirited anecdote.

It seems that underneath his calm exterior was a very sensitive interior. This is reinforced A. L's. words on Sheyn's tenure at the Central Cooperative in Haifa, a post he held for almost 20 years: "In remembering his accomplishments, we must mention the following: in every matter in which he participated, he searched for the positive. He was not quick to disqualify a person or discount an idea. On the contrary, he tried hard to find a way to either defend the person or protect the idea." These words are very appropriate and very worthy of Sheyn because he was dedicated to the good apart from the rest and to seeking the most appropriate way of dealing with every matter.—*A. Sh. Tal*

Duvid Sheyn, of Blessed Memory*

There is no heart that can cope with so great a loss, for death so cruelly uprooted him in his prime—a friend and companion, a Cooperative activist, a moral leader, whose spirit inspired everyone around him.

Our comrade emigrated from Russia in 1934. He worked at various jobs. He had a difficult time adjusting until he found his place with us in 1945.

It did not take long for him to go from the back room to the front office. Word spread of his extraordinary and personable qualities, his enthusiasm, serving to establish his collegiality with everyone he came in contact with. He was friendly by nature and excelled in listening to his fellow man, and, with his ability to help, Duvid Sheyn's heart was wide open to any comrade or friend, especially those from the Cooperative who turned to him for guidance and advice. He was involved in all the Cooperative meetings in Haifa and the surrounding area, despite the great effort required, and he knew how to fight for the essentials of cooperation and also to mollify negative elements.

Everyone grew to love him because of his energy to be endearing and his goodwill, which was full of humor. It didn't take much to make him content; he was satisfied with his lot—a man of the people in every sense and a man with limitless gratitude. He loved life; he recognized its breadth and knew its goodness, although he was humble, shy, and modest. He adhered to the great commandment "you shall love your neighbor as yourself," which embodies the underlying creed of the Cooperative.

And so, the man and our dear comrade has departed. Even after many months, his passing is still very much felt, as is the absence of his powerful stature, his moderation, his deliberation, his wise counsel, his competence in considerately managing those in his sphere, and his wisdom that his words would be calmly heeded

---

* Translated from Hebrew by Elizabeth Kessin Berman.

His deeds will be preserved in the book of Cooperative acts and accomplishments, and his contributions will be sealed in our hearts like a precious prize.

In his death, we lost a friend, a public representative, and a devoted worker, who will never be duplicated.

Yosef Oheli (Vayl)*

Ida

Yosef Oheli

Yosef Oheli was born in November 1887. His father was liberal minded, but he nevertheless gave his son an enlightened education as well as a traditional one. So Yosef received a basic traditional education until he was 14, and those years instilled a great love of Israel in him. After his finishing his certificate of studies with honors at the Tikhon school, he studied at the technical school for a year and a half, but his studies were interrupted by the outbreak of World War I. He enlisted in the Austrian army and was injured while serving.

During his entire career as a student, he did not abandon his study of the Hebrew language. Having learned the fundamentals, he sought to supplement and expand on his knowledge of the language and, in particular, He-

---

* Translated from Hebrew by Elizabeth Kessin Berman.

brew grammar, which he loved, even as he had excelled in his studies of the natural sciences and mathematics.

After World War I, Yosef devoted himself zealously to Hebrew education and instruction. His first job was in the Czech Republic. He taught there for three years. After returning to Poland, he was invited to serve as the principal of the school in Berestechko, a village in Volhynia, whose Hebrew school predates the foundation of the Tarbut School movement in Poland. Yosef introduced Sephardic pronunciation to his school and created a Land-of-Israel-like atmosphere into a foreign environment. He was not only imparting the Hebrew language to his students, but also immersing them in its culture and in Judaism.

[page 177]

The second place where Yosef advanced his work in education was Radzivilov. The first year the school was open, he and I worked with some 70 students, and until we immigrated to the Land of Israel, we taught nearly 300 students and the teacher roster was always full.

Yosef was completely devoted to educating children. He had a natural ability for instruction and extraordinary patience, answering every question or problem put to him. He was a quiet man, and he adhered to the saying of R' Yehoshue son of Perachia, "Give everyone the benefit of the doubt." He often said with a smile, "I don't care if someone insults me, but I'm extremely sorry if I learn that I've insulted someone." He had a good temperament and was always content with his lot, especially after we immigrated and he was able to continue his pedagogical work.

At first, after immigration, we were in the Merhavia settlement, but after that we went to Beit She'arim, where he lived for 22 years, until his death.

Yosef was very involved with the Esperanto club, and he loved to investigate the international language because he believed that it encouraged a greater understanding among nations. He could read this language and spoke fluently with other club members.

He was very sociable and always participated in all the parties and meetings thrown by the veteran teachers and village residents. On March 22, before he left for a party organized by veteran teachers at the Teachers House in Haifa, I asked him, "Maybe you shouldn't go?" He laughed and answered, "Don't you known how much I love to be around people?" He left the party happy—but suddenly fell down on the street and died.

He used to say, "I'd like to die in good health." He achieved this and made the proverb come true.—*Ida*

From "small things great glory emerges," for just 50 years ago there was no comprehensive lesson plan for teaching Hebrew throughout the Diaspora. So, for those of us whose hopes were bound up in the redemption of bringing Hebrew education out of its fog, we will always think of and remember Yosef. In Berestechko, a town in Volhynia, which is known for its pioneering in the Second and Third Immigration, Yosef Oheli-Vayl set himself up less as a prophet, but more as a representative of the yet-to-be-established Hebrew state. There the people withdrew from the reality that surrounded them and sowed the belief and their yearnings to journey to this longed-for land, even though they had been speaking another language from their infancy. With every fear that I entertained on my way to this town on a peasant wagon from the train station, I was drawn into a deep darkness, but in my first meeting with the principal of the Hebrew school (which predates the foundation of the Tarbut Association in Poland), a brilliant light was illuminated, and so it was in every hour that I was there.
[page 178]

Ah, how the questions multiplied as I was challenged to answer them, and how the number of words grew and grew in a place that was insulated from the affecting currents of the outside world, particularly during the many changes of regime after World War I. He was one of the very first who were forced to create teaching materials almost by himself, with whatever he had and whatever he didn't have. And so there he was, a Hebrew teacher in Berestechko, between Lutsk and Brody. With his fundamentals and broad knowledge, Oheli was perceived as the supreme leader of the effort, and al-though he participated in everything related to pioneering in the town as an educator unlike any we had ever seen before, that was not his goal. It was to enrich and oversee; those were his guiding intentions, to spread his consistent philosophies.

He immigrated after having gone from a one-room house of his own, having only a well-packed knapsack and sanctity in his heart. It wasn't long before he joined a settlement and saw rewards in spreading his talents until his retirement. Even in his retirement, he did not stop delivering his teachings and his vigilance until his sudden death.

The funeral procession drew near the valley, was saddened for a moment, and then stood in silence near Beit She'arim, where Yosef Vayl, also known as Oheli, may his name be blessed, lived, worked, and is buried.—*Sh. Rozenhek*

How do we account for a man from Berestechko in Radzivilov? The truth of the matter is that it is due to the character of Yosef Oheli, who first worked as an educator after he came from Poland to Berestechko, a town in Volhynia that was once considered the "Jerusalem of Volhynia." During the same era, at least 40 years earlier, it was a remote town without even a passable road or a train station, and to go there, you had to drive dozens of kilometers in a horse and wagon. It had about 5,000 inhabitants, half of whom were Jews. And I must note that Berestechko didn't even have a modern school until a few "crazies" decided that the town needed a Tarbut school. This school is described in the Berestechko yizkor book:

"We saw results immediately, as many children came to the school when it was established because there was no other school teaching Hebrew in town. Most of the children had attended a Russian school. A committee was elected to run it, but it was not easy for them, and there were many doubts whether they could rise to the task. So we turned to the central Tarbut organization in Rovno and told them we were planning to open a school. We requested financial support, especially the authority to hire teachers.

[page 179]

Tarbut School with Teacher Vayl and His Wife

We received an affirmative answer: although the funds available were minuscule, that was no reason give up or despair. And so we persevered, and we finally established the school. The teachers' agency sent us teachers that matched our ambitions, and they all had connections to the pioneering movement."

One of the first teachers to come to the town was Mr. Perech Tsvi, who in the same yizkor book describes the conditions he found when he arrived:

"Finally, we reached Berestechko just before sunrise, covered with mud, but that very day my companion and I met with the committee and we were briefed on the work. At first, I assumed that everything was organized and ready to go, but immediately it became clear that nothing at all had been done. There was no building, no furniture, no teaching materials, and not a cent to begin to do anything. But I did find one important thing—a strong desire to work toward and sustain the ideal of education and our redemption through it. These good Jews were imbued with this lofty ideal in their souls, their deeds, and their great ambitions."

Their perseverance was great because of their determination to complete the work.

[page 180]

In the meantime, more teachers came: Yosef Vayl, of blessed memory, who shared his long life with Ida Chereg (Oheli), and others. They all began working like ants, full of equal strength to create a Hebrew school that was beautiful in form and full of content with the aim of establishing strong foundations. There was an effort to have the Poles recognize it and a great desire to change the Berestechko school into an example of learning for the whole area. This handful of teachers from the Berestechko Tarbut school, under the direction and leadership of Yosef Vayl, made the effort into a celebration. Yosef Vayl was a teacher, a trainer, and a miracle worker, and when he came to town, he brought a wellspring of positivity with him that made an impression on the students. With his explanations, his way of interpretation, and his easy temperament, he had a great impact on the children. And furthermore, we must add that Yosef Vayl changed the lives of not only those children who were already students in the school that he was developing, but also others as he put a stamp on their lives.

We would go for tours outside the town to get a break from the close quarters and congestion of our daily lives. We would breathe the fresh air of the wide-open spaces. There we would also hear our teacher Yosef lecture on his passion for the future of a Jewish world, Zionism, pioneering, working with our hands, the development of agriculture in the Land of Israel, and the farming life of pioneering, this new type of Hebrew man who implants his vision to revive a newly awakened homeland, and the joys of the creativity that accompanied him and in his work.

Tarbut School of [illegible] Sukkot 1936

[page 181]

These were exciting lectures that implanted in us the strong feeling that we ourselves could experience everything going on in the land of our ancestors. And so it developed in us the desire to go out to work, to make something out of nothing, to make an effort to get pioneer training in order to prepare for immigration to the rebuilt Land of Israel. Under our teachers' inspiration and Yosef Vayl's leadership, we believed that "a new song will make us joyous," and we did not see any alternative other than to go up to the Land of Israel and to participate in rebuilding the homeland.

His uprightness, frankness, love of man, and devotion to his educational and behavioral work with the students made such an impression on us that many from our town who are in Israel now are members of kibbutzim or settlements or members of the Labor Movement.

Yosef Vayl the teacher was a friend and good mentor to all of his students. His gracious humility and love of peace will never fade from our hearts, and his memory will forever be preserved in us.—*Aharon Kahana*

In Memory of Our Teacher[*]

Chave Zilberman

On the day of the commemoration of our town's martyrs, I went to the café in which the descendants of Radzivilov were going to meet. I knew I was late right away, because I saw a long procession moving slowly and people talking with one another, using every possible moment of their yearly meeting .... They had just returned from the cemetery, honoring the stone monument dedicated to the martyrs of the Holocaust who fell for the Jewish people, ...

I went into the crowd in the large hall and a found myself a place a near a long table so I could see the faces of the people from my birthplace, my people, who had shared a large part of my life... Someone was drinking a cup of tea next to me and reminded me of someone.... Everyone had changed since then; like me, they had matured, and I felt as though I had not been separated from them for all these years, until I started to ask a friend of mine from school, and behold! None remained except for a few who could be counted on the fingers of my hands....

I sat and listened to the traditional speeches, and suddenly I raised my eyes and I saw two people I recognized sitting in the corner. I immediately got their attention and signaled my greetings and deep respect, and they reciprocated with deep affection. Who were those two people?

In a second, memories of my childhood in Radzivilov appeared before my eyes. The person sitting in the corner with his wife was Mr. Vayl, the principal of the school, and I knew both of them for their strength and dedication, their focus, and their devotion to this school.

[page 182]

They did not just teach their students, but rather they also instilled a new sense of awareness in them, very different from what one can acquire in the Diaspora: an awareness of Israeli nationhood and a love of our ancestors'

---

[*] Translated from Hebrew by Elizabeth Kessin Berman.

homeland and the Jewish life to rise from within it. Mrs. Vayl was my teacher. She knew how to make an impact on children's hearts. And everyone listened intently to her.

I recalled the time when we celebrated Purim, my first at the school, when I saw Mr. Vayl and his wife standing near their house, their eyes filling with tears. All the schoolchildren, in costume, were heading toward their house, me proud in my long white dress and golden crown shining on my head. I was Pharaoh's daughter; my brother Sunye, next to me, was dressed as Ahashueros, holding my hand with noise and a bright stream of colors surrounding us. The Vayls were overjoyed to welcome their students in costume to their home. And they seemed well satisfied with their work.

And then came their departure. If I am not mistaken, it was in 1936 when the Vayls decided to immigrate in order to do themselves what they had been preaching to others—to participate in the building. It was difficult to part from these beloved teachers, and all the people in our town were saddened to learn of their departure, but they very much supported their decision and their courage in making such a move. Everyone knew that love of the homeland was what drew them to decide to leave the Diaspora and join those builders. I stood among the hundreds of people who went to the train station to accompany the teachers as they made their ascent to the Land of Israel. It was a day laden with heavy rain; clouds hid the sky, and only from time to time did rays of sunshine appear between the clouds and darkness. I had the feeling that this was some sort of sign—light emerging from darkness ....

This was no time for thoughts, for reflections—the solemn sound of "Hatikvah" broke into our thoughts, and then we heard Mr. Vayl's slightly hoarse and emotion-filled voice giving his parting speech....

Slowly, the train left the station, as if it were accompanying the hands that were waving and hats heralding—shalom, goodbye....

And then years passed, and so we met once again at a memorial service for our townsfolk in mutual respect, with deep acknowledgment in our hearts for their influence on us.

[page 183]

R' Moshe Duvid Balaban*

Aleksander Balaban

My father's house was used as a meeting place for civic gatherings, but most of all for Zionist activism. I remember when about a dozen Zionists gathered in our house and decided to improve the Talmud Torah because the educational standards were low. A committee of three men was elected to immediately begin hiring teachers, including a teacher for the young children, and of course Hebrew, Russian, and mathematics teachers. This angered many members of the religious leadership, and they put pressure on R' Shmuel Mes, the famous Moshe-Mendil Mes-Ginzburg's brother, so that he withdrew his support of the institution. This caused a difficult financial crisis, so the committee decided to attract students from the affluent classes to the Talmud Torah and charge tuition. The committee members set an example by sending their children to the Talmud Torah. Among the first to do so was my father, of blessed memory, who sent his sons Avraham, Shimon Diniuk, and others. After a while, a teacher named Avraham Yehuda appeared in our town; he was recruited because of his Zionist activism. He recommended the founding of a Hebrew school, and father helped him toward that end. After a while, there was a push to create a Hebrew kindergarten, and again our father's influence was essential to its establishment.

I also remember well the town's Zionist meetings, in which they debated the possibility of a cooperative to acquire land in the Land of Israel to plant vineyards. After these vineyards indeed began to give fruit, members of the cooperative immigrated to Israel in their respective abilities.

---

* Translated from Hebrew by Elizabeth Kessin Berman.

But many could not go.

Moshe Duvid Balaban and His Family

It was already customary in our time to sell shekels to collect funds for the Land of Israel and place containers for them in the synagogues on Yom Kippur eve. There were still towns in which the rabbis were opposed to this practice. Kozin was one of the last of these towns. But father was able to convince the town's rabbi to agree to allow the containers to be placed to collect funds for the Land of Israel.

Although my father was a "progressive Zionist," he continued to observe his father's traditions of hosting the Ostrog rabbi and his disciples in our house.

With the outbreak of World War I, most of the Jews of the town tried to leave and began to return only in 1918. When we came back, we found many of the houses destroyed and blown up, and the few Jews who remained were mostly poor.

[page 185]

A few families were living in the fire department stables. Some were living in the school or in some of the synagogues. They had no beds or bedding. They wrapped themselves in whatever they had carried with them.

Then a community committee formed that included representatives of all the parties of those days. My father was its chairman. The committee's major activity was to organize social aid and administer support to the many who were in need.

During the change of regimes, when the Petliura government broke up and the Poles were advancing on the town, the gangs disappeared, and the town was left with no governing body. The Poles began to bomb the town. Suddenly, a Pole appeared in our house and announced that if we didn't immediately tell the Polish army that the town was undefended and that there would be no opposition to its entry, the Polish army would blow up the entire town. So my brother Yisrael, who was a member of the town council, volunteered to go with the Pole to the Brody forest waving a white kerchief. The Polish guard apprehended him and ushered him to the command unit. After it was verified that that no army remained in the city, the bombing ceased, and the Poles entered the town.

A Polish commander entered our house and demanded that our father give him a large amount of flour and barley without any promise of payment. During those early days, it was still possible to gather the amount he demanded. But afterward it was difficult for my father to do so. Even so, the commander threatened my father with death if he failed to gather enough. My father tried to escape to Brody on foot in the dark of night. But luckily the commander was soon replaced, and Father was able to return home.

As the flourmill manager, Father tried to engage in pioneer training. And so a unit of the pioneer training program was created in the mill. He also exposed his sons to the spirit of Zionism. It was also so for my sister Sore, who founded a committee for orphans and worked to found an institution to teach sewing, called ORT; and also my sister Bronye, who was a certified kindergarten teacher, having trained in the Alperin School in Odessa. After the war, a Hebrew kindergarten was established in Radzivilov, and she was its headmistress.

With the beginning of the Third Immigration during the 1920s, three members of our family immigrated to the Land of Israel. In the ensuing years, Father visited the Land of Israel three times, and the third time, he brought Mother. He bought agricultural land with the hope of returning and settling as a farmer. In the interim, he helped establish his children there.

When Father returned to Radzivilov from the Land of Israel, he was accused of transferring a large sum of money from Poland to the Land of Israel.

[page 186]

To bring him to trial when they couldn't prove this, they plotted and schemed against him: near the outside porch of his house, they planted a few counterfeit coins. The police appeared and began to search for a coin-minting machine in our house. They found the counterfeit coins and accused Father. To our great relief, several respected Poles, including the Polish priest, argued on his behalf. It was clear that he couldn't have done this, and they succeeded in freeing him even before he was brought to a judge.

Of our scattered family, only those who immigrated to Israel during the 1920s, settling and raising families there, survived World War I. My oldest brother, Yisrael, the firstborn, was exiled to Siberia by the Russians at the beginning of the war and vanished there. His wife and children, who survived the Holocaust, immigrated to Israel and settled there.

It is written: "The righteous are taken away from the evil to come" (Isaiah 57:1).

So this can be said of Father when he died of natural causes. But he died without a penny, because Soviet rule had taken everything he owned. Mother and the rest of the family were consumed in the flames of the great Holocaust. May their memory be a blessing.

R' Shmuel-Zev Vaynshteyn[*]

Yitschak Vaynshteyn

R' Shmuel-Zev Vaynshteyn was born in Kremenets, a district in Volhynia, in 1879, at the same time that his mother departed from this world.

Shmuel-Zev grew up in the home of his deceased mother's parents, the Nagid R' Avraham Moshe Rozenfeld, where he and his friend Noach Prilutski were ordained as rabbis at the age of 16. But neither of them was to take advantage of their training. R' Avraham Moshe Rozenfeld soon died, and at age 17, Shmuel-Zev began managing the affairs of a lumber-trading company.

In 1900, when he was 21, he married Rachel, daughter of R' Chaykel and Chane Bernshteyn of Kremenets. From then, on he began to work on his own in the lumber trade, exporting timber to build ships in Germany. Gradually, his family grew: in 1901 his first son, Avraham Moshe, was born; in 1902, his second son, Yitschak; and in 1910, the third son, Eliezer (Siunye).

R' Shmuel worked away from home eight to nine months out of each year.

[page 187]

He spent summers in Kremenets. But with the outbreak of World War I, all of his capital was drained because the Germans did not pay for the timbers he had sent to them. Instead, they sent him bills like IOUs instead of bank drafts. He would give them to his wife, Rachel, who could turn them into cash with Ayzik Kranz, nicknamed "the key," and she would deposit the money in the Russian-Asiatic Bank.

In 1914, the Russian army became fully entrenched in Galicia and conquered the Przemyśl stronghold. At that point, R' Shmuel took up a commercial endeavor, in which R' Yitschak Vakman partially participated, as well as Matus Chazan and others, with the intention of trading with the defeated Galicia.

---

[*] Translated from Hebrew by Elizabeth Kessin Berman.

In 1916, R' Shmuel was drafted into the army, and with the turning in 1917, he was in a military hospital in Moscow. When he returned home, R' Shmuel again went into partnership with his brother-in-law, R' Shalom Krivan, to trade in hides that were stripped off horses that had been killed during the war. These hides were sent to Radziechów for processing at the tannery there.

In 1919, R' Shmuel organized a cooperative to the salvage machinery from the flourmill in the village of Sapanuv near Kremenets, much of which had been badly burned. Among the participants in this cooperative were R' Moshe-Duvid Balaban and R' Shlome Vaser, both from Radzivilov. They salvaged the machinery from the middle of the Ikva River and sent it for repair. They sold part of the wheels and the sawing mechanisms, but then it occurred to one of the participants to bring the machines from a large factory to Radzivilov and set up a flourmill there. In Radzivilov, they bought an old furniture factory on Lipobov Street and a spacious house next to it. They set up the machinery they had brought from Sapanuv. They acquired a millstone and then a filter to strain the crushed flour. The peasants from the surrounding area would come to have their wheat ground. The work was carried out in two stages. Because the peasants had no cash, they paid with goods, that is to say, they paid for the grinding with a portion of their wheat. As production grew, they acquired an additional grinding wheel and produced bran and semolina from the shaft. At that time, there weren't many other mills, and the flourmill on Lipobov Street flourished. It employed a large number of people in many different positions that were essential to its development. The partners divided up the various management tasks. R' Moshe-Duvid Balaban was associated with technical affairs, R' Shmuel Vaynshteyn was involved in administration, and R' Shlome Vaser was devoted to commercial affairs.

The production grew to two and two and a half wagons of grain per each working day, which had three shifts.

In 1921, R' Shmuel moved his family to Radzivilov, where they settled in a large house near the mill.

[page 188]

In 1925, he married off his oldest son, Avraham Moshe, while his second son, Yitschak, finished high school in Kremenets and was accepted at the university in Lvov, but then transferred to the university in Krakow. But his father called him back to help him work at the mill.

Even though he was busy with his own affairs, R' Shmuel always found time to be involved with community affairs and in communal conflicts that required arbitration, serving in the arbitration hearing as the guarantor between the opposing sides.

The Vaynshteyn Family

[page 189]

In this capacity over the years, R' Shmuel represented the General Zionists in the town and the local community during the appropriation for the administration of the Talmud Torah. His help was also enlisted whenever a resolution was necessary—whether acting aboveboard or "under the table." His wife, Rachel, was his helpmate in all of these endeavors.

With the Russian conquest of Radzivilov in 1939, the mill was confiscated. Everyone who was living in the large house or the capacious buildings attached to the mill was evicted and had to find other living quarters. R' Shmuel and his family moved into one room across from the Great Synagogue. As the mill owner and a past employer, R' Shmuel now became a second-class citizen, namely, a citizen who had liabilities, and was prohibited from leaving the town, finding suitable work, and the like. His family members were also reduced to the same status, except for his son Avraham, who found work as an electrician. Because of this, R' Shmuel was not deported to prison in Siberia. Others, including Yisrael Balaban, Shlome Viser, Bukshteyn, Yakov Boym, and Yehoshue Halbershtadt, were deported to Siberia and Kazakhstan. They vanished, and nothing has been heard of them to this day. Only their family members returned.

With the German conquest in 1941, all of R' Shmuel's family members were in Radzivilov. Siunye, the youngest son, was sent for a few months beforehand to work far away from the city, but as the Germans were entering the town, he returned to share his fate with all the other victims. When the ghetto was divided between the useful and the not-useful, R' Shmuel and his wife fell into the latter group. Their sons Yitschak and Siunye worked in the sawmill, so they were counted among those in the first ghetto.

When the "not-useful" were marched to their deaths, R' Shmuel Vaynshteyn was seen marching with Rabbi Itsikel and Fishel Margulis in the first row .... May his memory be a blessing!

[page 190]

A Portrait of My Father*

Tsvi Saley

R' Yosef-Mendil Saley (Grobshteyn) was the youngest of three pairs of kosher butchers in Radzivilov: R' Hershil and his brother, Yosef; R' Bentsion and his brother-in-law, Yosef Tsurf; and my father and his older brother, Yechiel-Duvid. My father was

---

* Translated from Hebrew by Elizabeth Kessin Berman.

younger than they were, but he was nevertheless mature, perceptive, and dedicated to public service. Our house was always open to any foreign visitor, whether a preacher, an interpreter, a representative of a yeshiva or some institution, or even a delegate from the Holy Land—they all received a warm welcome and were offered enough money to support their cause by R' Yosef-Mendil the butcher. And even more so, the young Zionists regarded him as one of them. He helped them collect Jewish National Fund donations on Yom Kippur in the Great Synagogue, placing the Jewish National Fund collection box among the other charity boxes, even though many Hasidim were opposed to Zionism. He was committed to trying to persuade them that they were wrong and to convince them of the wisdom of Zionism and the restoration of the Land of Israel. He praised the quality of the *etrogim* from the Land of Israel; even if the *etrogim* from Corfu were more perfect, father stressed, we should use the ones from the Land of Israel because they came from the Holy Land, for they were certainly preferable to other *etrogim*.

As a Zionist, Father concerned himself with giving us, his children, a Hebrew education. In Kivertsy, where we once lived, he brought a Hebrew teacher from Lutsk to teach Bible and literature to a group of children, thus supplementing their Talmud studies. Afterward, he sent me to the yeshiva in Kremenets even though I had dreamed that he would send me to Mikve Israel to train in agriculture so I could join one the collective farms in the Land of Israel. My yeshiva studies did not inspire me as did the creativity of Bialik, Mapu, Smolenskin, and other Enlightenment writers.

[page 191]

It is important to note how my father related to the socialist movements that flourished among Jews in those days. As a man with incredible foresight and understanding, my father approved of the labor unions, and at that time no one dared to speak against the rich and powerful, who thought, habitually, that because they were the lords of the era, they were the protectors of knowledge. Oh no, not even a butcher or one single Jew whose livelihood was so dependent dared to challenge the powers that were.

Once, a Zionist film about Jews' life of in the Land of Israel was shown in Radzivilov. Father brought the entire family to see it. It was an extraordinary event because no Jew there had ever gone to see a film. However, this event was seen as a threat to traditional life in the town. And, certainly, in regard to a kosher butcher! Father put his livelihood at risk, because he could have been rendered "unqualified" as a butcher. But Father did not give any credence to this belief, and the community understood his foresight and his Zionism.

After the World War I, and after I decided to immigrate to Israel, Father spoke to me of the difficulties that awaited me: "Transportation was not yet organized, railroads were not laid out, war was still smoldering in parts of the world. How would I ever get there?"

R' Yosef-Mendil Saley (Grobshteyn) and his family

[page 192]

Nevertheless, because he believed I was right and knew I would go anyway, he added, "My son, here are 300 rubles for the journey. You should know that you've burned all the bridges behind you, and ahead of you lies only your determination to achieve your goals." By the way, this money was all that he had. He blessed me in the belief and hope that he would follow me. After a year, he also sent my sister Rivke to the Land of Israel, as in the prophesy "he prepared the way." And a year later, he immigrated with Mother and the rest of the family. It was a daring thing to do in those days, to uproot a large family and commit them to a journey to a country where acclimatization would be endless.

He didn't leave his optimism behind when the difficulties of adjusting to life in the Land of Israel exhausted him. To build his home, he had to overcome every obstacle. He built a beautiful house in Hadar HaCarmel, Haifa; raised and educated all his children; and fully believed that he was living in the "days of the Messiah." He went to his eternal rest two years before the establishment of the State of Israel. May his memory be blessed.

[page 193]

Profile of Dvore Likhtman*

Tsvi Saley

Dvore Likhtman's father and I were childhood friends. We attended primary school together, and after we came home from exile after World War I, we renewed our friendship. We went into business together and continued for 15 years until I immigrated to Israel in 1935.

Dvore's mother, Leye Beynish, was also her father's childhood friend, and around town they were considered destined to be together, Mr. and Mrs. Right. So, in 1924, they married, and a year later, Dvore was born. She was the most beautiful and sweet-tempered child. She was very much a part of my family, having a strong, loving connection that was common among Jews. When she was in kindergarten, she would come to our house instead of going home. Once she got lost, and when asked where she was going, she said that she was going to her uncle Menashele's house.

---

* Translated from Hebrew by Elizabeth Kessin Berman.

When I set out for the Land, the entire Likhtman family accompanied me to Lvov. At my departure, I saw tears in their eyes. I knew they were not crying because I was leaving them. These were tears of worry for me, for my journey to a faraway, desolate place where life would be difficult—all the good food they were blessed to have was to be found in the Polish heavenly "garden of Eden" on earth.

How can we remember what we understood as the Polish "garden of Eden" before the war with Nazi Germany? The new laws imposed on the Jews, forbidding the Jewish rite of slaughtering animals, the "quotas" in the high schools, and many, many more ... that changed the "garden of Eden" into hell for the Jews.

[page 194]

Thus, through the conquest of Poland by the Nazis, it became a place for the fundamental annihilation of Jews throughout Europe.

In 1947, I received a letter from Dvore, who was in Italy, telling me that she and her sister Yafe had survived and that they intended to come to Israel. When I found out that Dora (as we had called her for so many years) was coming to Israel with her husband and baby, I hurried to prepare a separate room for them so they could stay with me. I didn't want them to be sent to a resettlement camp. After a month, her husband managed to get them an apartment in Jaffa. And so they settled there. He worked in the military. But this work caused him a lot of suffering because he contracted a serious illness. In the meantime, another child, Shmuel, was born. They decided to buy an apartment with a store in Ramat HaHayal, and they moved there. Everything seemed fine, but suddenly Dora became gravely ill, and after a short time, she died.

You could write an entire book about her ordeals in the ghetto. But I relate only a very tiny version here. Her father, Binyamin, died in Brody during the first year of the German occupation. And her mother was shot by a peasant in an open field as she carried her daughter Yafe. How the two girls, Yafe and Dvore, survived is a miracle. They were finally able to immigrate to Israel after wandering around for a long time, but even here in Israel there was no rest for Dvore and no time when she was granted a reprieve. May her memory be a blessing!

In Memory of the Shif Family*

Buntsye

When World War I ended, the Yosef Shif family made its way back to the town from exile. Life there was very difficult; it was hard for the family to earn a living, and a serious illness claimed the life of the head of the family after much suffering, leaving a wife, a son, and three daughters.

Yosef Shif's house was a Zionist household, and it housed one of the largest nationalism and Zionism libraries in Russian and Yiddish in the town. The son was very intelligent and was constantly reading. But he was very sickly, and there was no cure for him. And he also passed away.

The mother and her three daughters toiled in poverty. They got meager aid from time to time from their relatives in America. But they somehow got along.

When the Pioneer movement and Young Pioneer were established in our town, the family got a breath of life.

[page 195]

They envisioned the sparks of future new beginnings through immigration to the Land of Israel—for their renewal and also to rebuild the land there! Sore, the middle child, went first for training, immigrated, joined the labor movement, and was very content as she reached her goals.

---

* Translated from Hebrew by Elizabeth Kessin Berman.

Pesye, Sore, and Teme Shif

The youngest daughter, Teme, went the route of a training camp organized by Pioneer in Grochów, near Warszawa, and then immigrated to Israel. After she, too, was settled in her work, her mother's two sisters immigrated, along with the oldest daughter, Pesye, and they all lived together, working and hoping for better days.

But a bitter fate befell this family. It wasn't long after the mother set out that Teme married, found work, and was content .... But suddenly she became ill, and she did not rise from her bed. Sore married a man who was also a Holocaust survivor. He lived in bitterness. Finally, he succumbed to despair: one night he took his own life ....

And the oldest daughter, Pesye, who never married, had a lonely, miserable life, laboring in sorrow in difficult jobs. She fell out of bed and, after suffering and great pain, also died.

This is the story of one of the finest, humblest families of our town, who yearned for a life of work and honesty. They suffered all their lives and never found peace. May they all be remembered as a blessing.

[page 196]

Mikhael Prochobnik*

Ch. F.

As the news spread in Radzivilov that the Germans were advancing to Brody and many local young people began to flee toward Russia and Romania, Leybish said to his only son that in spite of his family's wishes, it was the right time for the family to scatter and divide to avoid the imminent danger. He knew that his son, Mikhael, did not want to wander alone and leave his family, but regardless, he fled to Shumsk with his youth group friends. When the Russians captured the town, Mikhael came home, but he was immediately conscripted into the Red Army. He was sent to Siberia and lived there under extremely difficult conditions—work, hunger, and cold, without proper clothing. It was an inhuman existence. But while he was there, Radzivilov was conquered by the Germans, and his entire family was destroyed along with the other Jews of the town.

Mikhael survived his sufferings and the torments he endured, and in 1948 he came to Israel. There he planned to begin a new life: technical school for the future. But suddenly he grew ill, and on April 12, 1961, he died.

---

* Translated from Hebrew by Elizabeth Kessin Berman.

Bat-Sheve Nir (Strumin)*

Sh. N.

Humble in her ways, delicate in her features, and refined in her spirit, she was a person who adopted her parents' Jewish traditions and their love of mankind. She was a dedicated and beloved teacher who strove to impart the fundamentals of Judaism to the children of Israel. This was our Bat-Sheve, who was plucked from us prematurely. She dedicated her talents and charm to the public benefit, and she did this without help or assistance, secretly or openly.

Her greatest success was her organization of a club to teach Bible each week, and through this she supported those who were thirsty for spiritual learning.

In satisfying work, in her enlightened work, she was our friend, and so she will ever be remembered.

[page 198]

[Blank]

---

* Translated from Hebrew by Elizabeth Kessin Berman.

[page 199]

The Holocaust

[page 200]

Map of Radzivilov during the Holocaust
Translated from Hebrew by Yaacov David Shulman

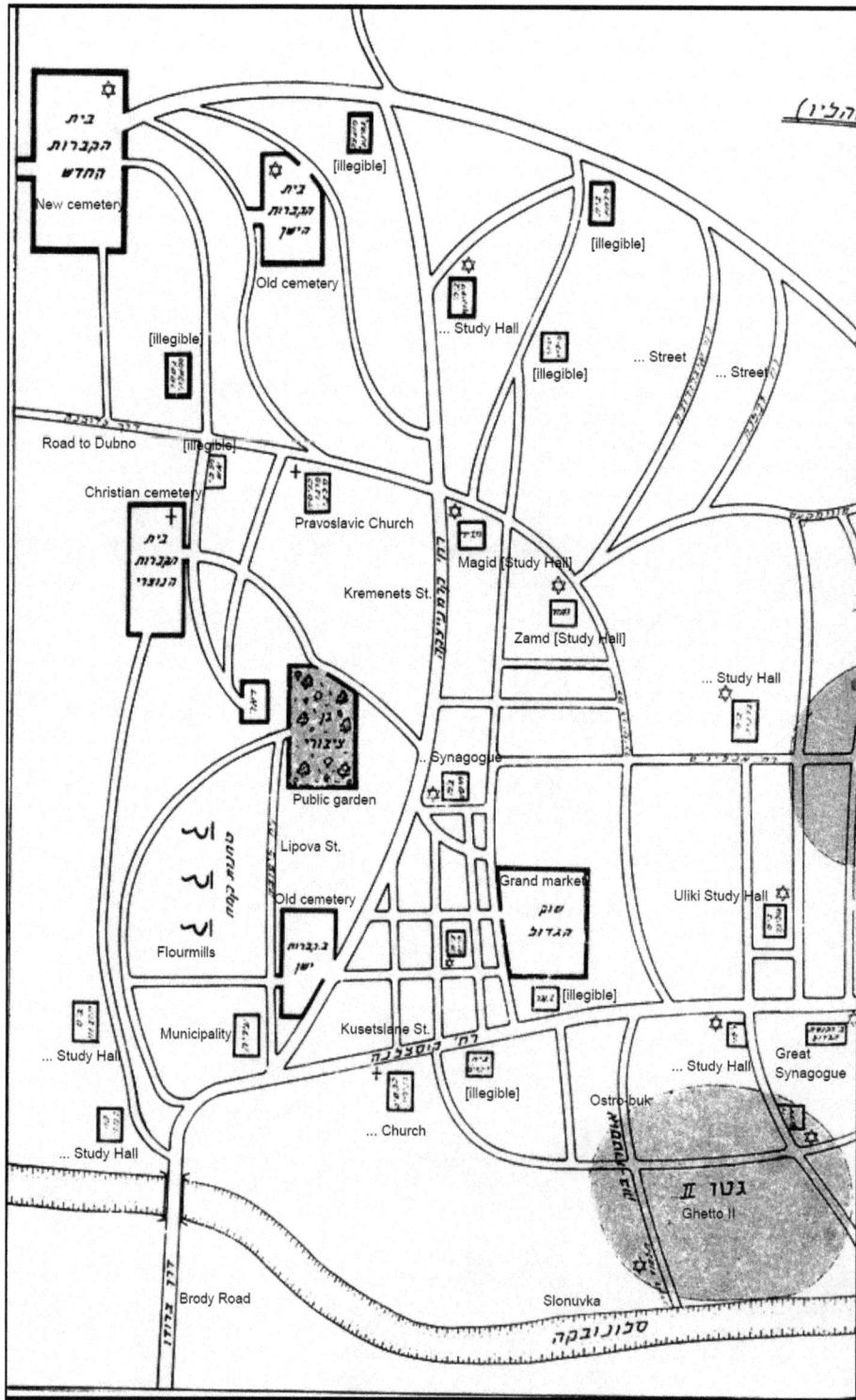

בית הקברות החדש
New cemetery

[illegible]

בית הקברות הישן
Old cemetery

[illegible]

[illegible]

... Study Hall

[illegible]

... Street

... Street

[illegible]

Road to Dubno   [illegible]

Christian cemetery

Pravoslavic Church

בית הקברות הנוצרי

Kremenets St.

Magid [Study Hall]

Zamd [Study Hall]

... Study Hall

גן עירוני
Public garden

עיר שטעטל

Flourmills

Lipova St.

Old cemetery

בקברות ישן

Synagogue

Grand market
שוק הגדול

Uliki Study Hall

Municipality

Kusetslane St.

[illegible]

... Study Hall

... Study Hall

... Church

[illegible]

... Study Hall

Great Synagogue

Ostro-buk

גטו II
Ghetto II

Brody Road

Slonuvka

סלונובקה

[page 201]

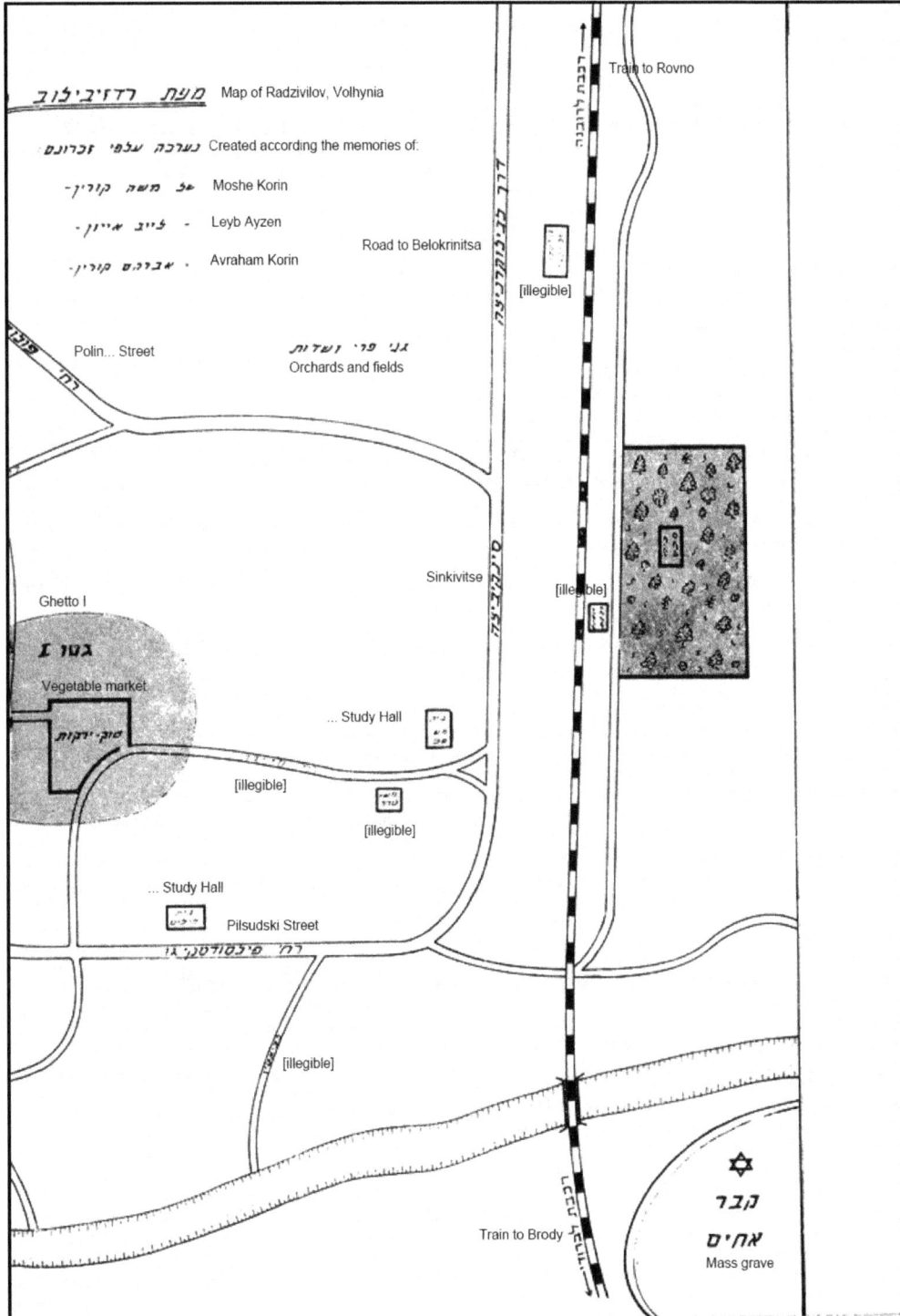

Map of Radzivilov, Volhynia

Created according the memories of:

Moshe Korin

Leyb Ayzen

Avraham Korin

Road to Belokrinitsa

Train to Rovno

[illegible]

Polin... Street

Orchards and fields

Sinkivitse

[illegible]

Ghetto I

Vegetable market

... Study Hall

[illegible]

[illegible]

... Study Hall

Pilsudski Street

[illegible]

Train to Brody

Mass grave

[page 202]

[Blank]

[page 203]

The Soul of Yosi, My Sister Bronya's Son[*]

Amir Gilboa

The entire night, stars fell onto my lap
And weary beyond words, I laughed alone into the night, happy.
Thus sleepy and fantasizing, firmaments painted my eyes and eagles
plunged to the depths.
Then I opened my eyes to the dream. Little Yosi came and redeemed the
song, and he soared and sang.

The voice of the turtledove is heard in the land, and upon the buds of the
morning, the rain streams, blue.
At the foot of the predawn mountain, I bow and remember, and remember
and remember.
My head is in water that falls from the heights in green tones of the soaked,
heavy dream.
I hear all of your songs, Yosi, small, radiant Yosi, Yosi who was truly killed.
Your deer that wander upon every path capture the echo of your laughing
voice.

God, God, all of the valleys were then filled with water,
And after the rain the green poured over us and made our steps drunk,
And with filled hands, mushrooms grew white, like a legend that hints at
the pupils of a thousand eyes,
And all of the trees set fire to the windowpanes with their words in our hon-
or.

Oh Yosi, oh Yosi! I sent my whisper with the end of the night upon the face
of the pond
And your white ducks turned over and over to raise a crown to the ripples.
But with the rising sun I too rise up entirely ... and burn with a fire of
yearning
To kiss the dust of the choicest of loves.

[page 204]

[Blank]

---

[*] Translated from Hebrew by Yaacov David Shulman.

[page 205]

Testimony[*]

Yitschak Vaynshteyn was the author of the account *The Destruction of Radzivilov,* the only documentation of the annihilation of the community of Radzivilov.

When transmitting his testimony, Vaynshteyn repeated events that were already written in *The Destruction of Radzivilov,* but in it, he enhanced and expanded on his earlier account, particularly in the last section of his eyewitness account, which deals with the period that will be now presented—the events after liberation.

Before the war, he was a merchant who managed large ventures and was a respected resident of the town of Radzivilov. He was well educated even though he did not finish his higher education. During the years of Russian occupation, he did manual labor.

He was astute and practical, which served him well during the catastrophic days because then his only ambition was to survive in spirit and help his family survive. In his testimony, he recounts in detail how he was able to save his life and those of his wife and children from the flames of death.

During the entire Nazi occupation, he did not seek a comfortable position on the *Judenrat* or with the police, even though he was offered such positions many times. His response was characteristic when Viderhorn, the first *Judenrat* chairman, asked him to become chairman in his place: "All my life I have been a giver, not a taker. I don't want to be a tool of the Gestapo; I can't take the last slice of bread from the Jewish people." As an example of his character—something Vaynshteyn did not want published—he told me that when his younger brother Sunye came to him and confided that he

---

[*] Translated from Hebrew by Elizabeth Kessin Berman. *Note in original:* From the Yad Vashem archives, transcribed by Mr. V. Alperovich, May 1962.]

wanted to join the Jewish police to make his life easier, "I gave him three solid slaps and said to him, "Don't cast your lot with this snot-nosed gang, and don't ruin your yourself or stain our family name." In retelling this incident, he was overcome with emotion and began to cry, and it was some time until he recovered. During the Russian occupation, he worked as a purser, so he was familiar with the rules of taking liberties with their rules and he knew of the bitter penalties—being deported to Siberia with his family as "white bears," saboteurs.

[page 206]

But thanks to the war that broke out between Russia and Germany, he remained in Radzivilov.

Vaynshteyn was one of the distinct and rare persons who survived the Radzivilov ghetto. Fortunately, he wrote everything he could about the life and destruction of the Radzivilov community in 1948. Now he can hardly remember anything at all. Recording his testimony was a tremendous effort. During my many meetings with him, I could only catch a glimpse of the polite man who had generated such fervor.

In taking down his testimony, he asked me to read back everything that had been written down, and he checked everything carefully to see if it was as he had stated.

The last time we met, we lingered on matters that involved the liberation of the Radzivilov ghetto. He had come from England, where he has a son, and he has a son in Israel. Should I ask him his plans for the future? He said, "Right now, I am planning to attend *ulpan*, and after that I will think of a plan."

Yitschak Vaynshteyn's Testimony

In *The Destruction of Radzivilov*, I have already written down at length my life and my memories of life in the Radzivilov ghetto during World War II, so I will now only briefly touch on this subject.

I was born in Kremenets in 1907. In 1922, my family moved to Radzivilov. My father was a well-respected Jew who managed large businesses. Between the two wars, we had a flourmill and a good income. My father was progressive, and he gave his children an enlightened education. During my childhood, I attended cheder, and after that, until World War I began in 1914, I studied at the primary school in Kremenets, and after that at the High School of Commerce. I completed high school at the Ukrainian school, and I continued at the universities of Lvov and Kraków, studying mathematics and law. I greatly regret that I was unable to complete my studies because I had to return to help my father in his business. In 1926, I opened a writing equipment and haberdashery store in Radzivilov. The business developed until World War II broke out in 1939. In 1933, I married Batye Goldenshteyn of Brody. In 1936, my son Yosef (the one in Israel) was born, and in 1938, my second son, Shimon (now in England). During Polish rule, until 1936, the Jews in Radzivilov made their living, as they did in all the towns in our region, in trade, as artisans, everyone according to his profession. After 1936, there was a wave of anti-Semitism throughout Poland, and our situation changed for the worse. The Polish government opened stores and pitted the Poles and the Ukrainians against the Jews. But there were no outward excesses.

[page 207]

When the war between Poland and Germany broke out on September 1, 1939, we knew Poland could not hold out against the German army. Waves of refugees began to stream to Radzivilov from western and central Poland. Daily, we feared the appearance of the Germans. To our great relief, the Russian army entered Radzivilov on September 19, and the Jews breathed a sigh of relief.

Life under the Russians

When the Russians took charge, they immediately began nationalizing all the large businesses, mills, factories, and more. Immediately, I assessed the situation, and I proceeded to hand over the store without waiting for it to be confiscated. I went to work in the Soviet cooperative as a purser and later as an accountant. My store was taken over by the Soviets and managed by a Ukrainian by the name of Tushakovski, who was a black marketeer, and he sold a lot of my merchandise, from which he profited greatly.

Before the war, a woman by the name of Manye Vaynshteyn worked for me as a clerk. During the Soviet era, she was an activist, and she was appointed to the committee of the professional union. She was aware of both the extent of his black-market dealings and how much merchandise was in my store. She tried to expose his actions, but he did not stop what he was doing, and eventually my entire stock was sold off.

In all the Soviet institutions, only certified leftist proletariats, Jews and Christians alike, worked. Immediately, there was a severe shortage of food and clothing, and there were long lines everywhere. The community was naturally not very pleased with this arrangement, but it was clear that this situation was much better than life under the Nazis. At least we were alive.

When the Soviets issued identity cards, they did not neglect to classify people according to their class, and those classified as bourgeois were in danger of being deported to Siberia at any time. My father and I were classified as bourgeois, so we were fired from our jobs. With no choice but to try to become a proletarian, I went to work at the mill as a laborer. I worked there with my brother Sunye until the war between Russia and Germany began.

Life under the Nazis

On June 22, 1941, war broke out between Germany and the Soviet Union. The German army advanced and drew close to Radzivilov. The Red Army panicked and fled, and terror descended on the Jewish population. Everyone began to flee by horse, car, and bicycle. But the Germans were already blocking the roads.

[page 208]

On the July 19, the Germans conquered Radzivilov. The Ukrainians welcomed the Germans with great joy. They were immediately allowed to govern the local town administration, and at its head was Mateyko, who claimed that he himself was an "ethnic German." The Ukrainians became lawless, confiscating property from the Jews and showing the Germans which houses had goods to steal. They also handed over names of Jews who had aided the Soviets. And so began the reign of terror. Among the first victims was Manye Vaynshteyn, whom I mentioned previously.

The First Decrees

The Germans set up a local government administered by the Ukrainians and gave them far-reaching authority. At the beginning of July, representatives from the Dubno region came to structure the local authority in Radzivilov, and they immediately began to issue anti-Semitic decrees. All Jews were ordered to wear a white strip of cloth with a blue star on their arms. All Jews were forbidden to leave Radzivilov without permission. Failure to observe these laws was punishable by death.[*]

The Russians advanced and captured the village where my family and those of Semigran and Kiperman were hiding. The village changed hands seven times. There were many casualties on both sides. When we heard Russian being spoken, we ran out. The Russians enlisted me to bury the bodies, but the young Christian who was working with me fled. Afterward, I got word that my family was looking for me. I asked the Russians to let me return to my family, and they let me go, but it was very difficult to reach my family because the Germans were still holding their defenses, and they were firing on anyone who was in the area. I asked the Russians if I could ride with them in a wagon, because I had no strength left in me to walk. But they refused. Stricken with fatigue and hunger, but calling on my last measure of strength, I reached the place where my family had been. But there was no one left. Instead I found partisans, who were waiting to see who would succeed in the final battles. They wouldn't let me stand outside to call attention to them, so they made me come inside. I learned that my entire family and everyone else had gone on to Radzivilov. Although I was exhausted, I finally reached Radzivilov, which was already in Russian

[*] *Note in original:* Here, refer to the events described in "The Destruction of Radzivilov."—The editor

hands. Near the Great Synagogue, in an abandoned apartment, all the survivors of Radzivilov were gathered: Semigran and his family, Kiperman and
his family, Treybitsh, Sheyndel Zats, Oks, and a niece, Feldman. Each day
someone else returned.

[page 209]

The same management that had been in place before the war returned to
Radzivilov. They enlisted all the men as firefighters. They were also deporting Ukrainians and Jews to Siberia. I was afraid of deportation, so I met up
with a young Ukrainian who had been a friend of my brother's before the
war and was now the head of the finance department to ask him if he would
hire me, but he put me off, saying, "I can't hire anyone who was a 'bourgeois' to work with me in a Soviet department." I went to the party secretary, who overruled him. With this, I started working in that office. After a
few days, they wanted to send me for training in Kraków. I agreed only on
the condition that my family be moved to Rovno, and they agreed. After I
passed the course, which lasted three months, I returned to my family in
Rovno, and there I began to work in the regional income tax department.
We were moved into an apartment that had once belonged to a Jewish family. I lived there until the "repatriation." I was in Poland until 1945, and then
I moved to Germany. There I worked in a camp in which there were 2,500
refugees. I was elected to a committee of five judges tasked with mediating
conflicts among the refugees and other administrative tasks. We had no
connection with the Germans.

Court at the Hofgeismar Camp, Germany (with Yitschak Vaynshteyn)

In 1947, I went with my family to England. We settled in Nottingham, where I worked as a miller. After that, I opened a business. In 1953, my wife died at the age of 50. My oldest son went to Israel in 1956. My younger son remained in England. In 1961, I immigrated to Israel.

[page 210]

The Destruction of Radzivilov[*]

Yitschak Vaynshteyn

Radzivilov was situated between Lvov and Rovno. It once belonged to the Kremenets district, but during Polish rule, it belonged to Dubno. Its population was 6,000, of which 3,300 were Jews. Most Jews were involved in commerce. Peasants from the surrounding areas would come to sell their produce and at the same time return home having bought their basic necessities. Jews also owned the flourmill and sawmill, and employed Jews as their workers. In addition, many different kinds of craftsmen sold their products at the markets or fairs in addition to the usual daily sales.

Cultural and social life focused mainly on the Zionist movement and its various factions and parties. The main groups were Pioneer, Youth Guard, and the Revisionists. The children were educated either at the Tarbut School or the Polish national school. There was also a Talmud Torah in which many children received a religious education. There were many synagogues and study halls, and of these one must mention the Great Synagogue.[†] It had two rabbis who served the congregation, three ritual slaughterers, and other "clergy."

Until 1935, the economic situation was generally stable, although that year it began to change for the worse because of the Polish government's economic policies—"*realpolitik*"—whose goal was to wrest the bulk of commerce from Jewish ownership and transfer it to Poles. The Poles opened stores that could be used to boycott Jewish stores and merchandise, offer-

---

[*] Translated from Hebrew by Elizabeth Kessin Berman.
[†] *Note in original:* See the article on the Great Synagogue on page 58.

ing deferred payment terms of up to 15 years (!) for any account. In this way, the Poles could destroy the Jews' way of life in the town and its vicinity and prevent them from enjoying influential positions. About all this, the Jews could only say that it was not so bad—that is, until the war between Poland and Germany broke out.

[page 211]

On September 1, 1939, Germany began its blitzkrieg of Poland, and Poland's defenses were immediately broken. The Germans swiftly cut off all transportation routes in the country. Thus, the multitudes fleeing the terrors of the assault were trapped on the roads and highways with no chance to get to safety. Actually, there was no point in fleeing because the Germans were steadily advancing everywhere.

The Red Army entered the war on September 19, after the Germans had reached the outer parts of eastern Poland. On the same day, the Red Army reached Radzivilov with little opposition from the Poles. The Jews there breathed a sigh of relief—they had been saved from the Nazis' claws.

With the entrance of the Soviet government, the order of life in town immediately began to change—"new times, new songs"—and naturally the first to suffer under this new era were the Jews. First, they banned all shops, and in their place, they imposed a central cooperative with 10 branches and another 30 in the surrounding villages. Thus they "nationalized" the flour-mill, the sawmill, and the rest of the factories, whose Jewish owners were "classified" as bourgeois by their special office for identify permits—so they had "the mark of Cain" as far as any government office or workplace was concerned.

Every school in town was closed, and only one school with 10 grades was opened in their place. All the children attended. They also established a library and a debate club.

The town they created was administered by a central Ukrainian authority in Kiev, although the civil authorities were stationed in Rovno.

Here it is noteworthy to relate the following event: when the Red Army entered, the Ukrainians followed them in proudly, waving their national flags when the Soviets recognized *samostayne Ukraine*—"independent Ukraine." But how disappointed they were when the army took the flags from their hands and dissolved their community!

In early 1940, the Soviets began to construct a road from Kiev to Lvov, and a large portion of the population worked on it. Ironically, at the beginning of the German attack on Russia, the Germans used this road to their great advantage.

In the meantime, the Russians had begun to deport the area's Polish residents to Siberia and the regions bordering Finland. The Polish government had been aiding the settlement of Poles there after World War I in order to expand its influence. Thus the Soviets began to deport these "undesirables," and among them were 12 Jewish families: Balaban, Vas, the Milder brothers, and others. In 1946, these families returned from their exile in Siberia.
[page 212]

But almost all the women returned without their husbands. According to one exile, Dr. Zayontshkovsky, the husbands were sent to jails in Dubno and Kiev, but their fates are unknown.

On June 22, 1941, everyone began to feel that the situation was about to change. Molotov's speech on the radio, airplanes flying above the town's skies—everything heralded ill. It was quite clear: the Germans were frustrated in their attempts to defeat their enemy, the British, so they turned their forces against Russia.

The Germans advanced on two fronts: Czernowitz and Sokal near Lvov—the intention was clear: seal off the advancing pincers of the huge army in Galicia. The Soviets fought resolutely near Kremenets-Brody, and they were able to extract the army and its weapons piece by piece. Part of the army also retreated near Radzivilov. All the routes had been blown up by enemy fire, and there was no way for the residents to escape. Only the party officers and their clerks fled with the retreating Soviet army. Some tried to escape on horses and wagons, but they were forced to turn back because the advancing enemy armies were so swift. Only a few government agency workers succeeded in taking shelter with the fleeing armies, but they had to leave their families behind, and they alone were saved from death. Of the hundreds of young people who were sent to labor camps by the Soviet government, only a few (among them Siunye Vaynshteyn) returned from the camps, which were more than 250 kilometers from their home. But they returned only to share in the bitter fate that later took everyone.

On the June 29, we heard Nazi boots marching on the roads to Radzivilov. And we were filled with terror....

Forgetting what they had pledged the day before, most of the Ukrainians changed sides immediately and created a triumphal arch for the holy procession. They welcomed the Germans with shouts of joy, calling them "our redeemers." They showed all the platoons of soldiers occupying the town where the Jewish homes were and encouraged them to take whatever they wanted.

To prevent rioting and general lawlessness, a committee was put together, with Mr. Viderhorn as the leader. The committee contacted the governing authorities and discussed how best to handle the situation; all requests were filtered through this committee, which would judge how best to execute what was required, because there was no reason for random looting and robbery. This committee eventually became the *Judenrat.*

Already at the beginning of July, the Commissioner of Labor in Dubno appointed a commander in Radzivilov along with a few SS officers. The Jews immediately sensed how cruel the governing officials would be to them. The first anti-Semitic orders were proclaimed:

1. All Jews are commanded to wear a strip of white cloth with a Jewish star on their arms.

[page 213]

2. All Jews are required to give up their radios.

3. All Jews are forbidden to leave the town without permission.

4. Anyone found transgressing these orders will be punished by death.

It was abundantly clear that the Jews were to be dealt with separately from and more severely than the rest of the residents, and that they had no protection.

On July 15, a group of Gestapo officers approached the Ukrainian committee and asked them to prepare a list "dangerous Jews." The Ukrainians immediately drew up a list of a few Jews who fit that description and also provided an additional list of a few wealthy Jews. For some reason, they later reduced the first list to approximately 18 persons. These were the ones the Ukrainians wanted to destroy because of personal vendettas. These Jews hid money and various precious personal objects because they saw this as a pretext for confiscating and stealing their property. Zalman Levitin, Shimon Marder, Manye Vaynshteyn, Duvid Vaser, Ester Groysman, the Chomut brothers, and others were included on this list.

That same morning, the Gestapo unit marched these Jews out with shovels and ordered them to dig a large pit in the Brody forest not far from the Brody–Radzivilov railroad. When the pit was dug, they ordered the Jews to run forward quickly .... From afar the shots and the cries of despair rang out ....

These details were reported by Leyb Rakhentses, who was one of the diggers.

The next day, a group of Ukrainians entered the Great Synagogue. They grabbed the Torah scrolls, threw them outside, and set them on fire. They then dragged out Rabbi Yitschak Lerner, of blessed memory, and forced him to prance around the flames. At the head of this group of Ukrainians was a 19-year-old named Kashuba.

From that day on, they began to round up Jews for slave labor, mainly to dig trenches to lay the Lvov–Kiev telephone cable. Germans commanded these brigades.

On August 15, the Jewish committee was reorganized, and it was now called the *Judenrat.* Viderhorn resigned his position on the grounds of conscience, because he could not fulfill such a heavy responsibility. In his place, Yakov Furman, a man without any conscience, a sadist who in cold blood cared only for his own skin and his relatives without a thought for anyone else, was appointed the new *Judenrat* chairman.

On August 27, the Gestapo unit undertook the second "review" of us. The order—all orders were accompanied by a threat of death—was issued to everyone, young or old, healthy or sick, without distinction. All were to assemble in the market square within two hours. Everyone was compressed into Valdman's courtyard, which was 10 by 60 meters in size, none of us knowing why we were gathered there. Before we gathered, we were ordered to leave our houses open.

[page 214]

The gates closed, and soldiers with machineguns sprang out as if from out of the earth. Terrible panic erupted; crying and wailing was heard from all sides as people began to prepare themselves to be separated from each other and murdered.

Valdman's courtyard was situated near the Kiev–Lvov road. Just then a caravan of soldiers was passing by on the road. A vehicle suddenly pulled up, and a high-ranking officer got out. He called the head of the Gestapo unit to him, spoke to him for a few minutes, and then drove on. The situation immediately changed for the better: the gates opened, and we were marched out in rows to the marketplace and handed over to the Ukrainian militia, led by Misha Zaleski, and from there to work details.

When we returned to our homes after the work detail, we found them empty. Platoons of Ukrainians rounded up local peasants—with the city council's agreement—and these peasants loaded up wagons with whatever they wanted. It was robbery carried out in broad daylight.

A few days later, it was announced that the Jews were to bring all silver, gold, and other precious objects they owned to the city council. Because of Viderhorn's efforts (he was the translator), the Germans agreed to allow people to keep their wedding rings. The Jews stood in organized rows in front of Kitas's house with the rest of their property and handed it over with trembling hands: candelabra that had been in their families for generations, silver forks and spoons, golden boxes, gold earrings, and all kinds of ornaments and jewelry, all the while telling themselves that doing this would save their souls from their slayers.

However, open robbery did not end there. Each day different groups of soldiers would freely enter Jewish houses and take whatever leftovers appealed to them, whether pots, household items, laundry equipment, or even clothing. Nor did the Ukrainians go empty-handed, because they were good at imitating the Nazi thieves.

Unfortunately, we have to report that our *Judenrat* served us Jews badly. It organized its own police force, which not only carried out the Germans' terrible decrees but also extorted whatever they could from the Jews on behalf of the Germans, the Ukrainians, the labor brigades—and also for themselves. Truth be told, the *Judenrat* and its police force were all too ready to sell their people for execution if doing so would save themselves. But in the end, their fate was no different from that of their brothers whom they extorted and sold into their murderers' hands.

In October 1941, the Ukrainian committee issued a decree forbidding Jews to own any animals, horses, or sheep, under penalty of death; but they could sell their animals to the Ukrainians, although it was perfectly clear from the start that the exchange would be at half the price.

[page 215]

On December 20, an order was issued from Dubno to switch from wearing armbands to wearing a round yellow patch on the left side of the chest and the right side of the back.

The aim of the Nazi conquest was clear: destroy the Jews economically, suppress them, and humiliate them morally and spiritually. And after that, liquidate them physically. Once there was nothing left to take from the Jews, they were ordered to hand over their wedding rings. The distress grew even greater. Hunger began in the Jews' homes. Only then did we organize a committee to help ourselves, without telling the *Judenrat*.

The commander of the work brigades from Dubno, Hamershteyn, was concerned because no Jew ever opted out of the compulsory slave labor brigades. These brigades included skilled workers, whom he sent to labor camps in Vinnitsa. Thousands of Jewish tradesmen from all over Ukraine were there. Hamershteyn imposed the responsibility of selecting the men on the *Judenrat*.

Forced Laborers in 1942

And this last matter was just a cruel act for those who were sent: they were promised that they would be replaced with others after six weeks. If only they knew what a lie this was. Among those who were sent were Avraham Vaynshteyn the electrician, Volf the tinsmith, and others.

[page 216]

At first, no one heard from them at all, and no one even knew where they were or whether they were still alive. After a while, we managed to connect with them through a man from Vinnitsa, so letters and a bit of food were sent with him. One letter that came back reported that there had been a large fire and that only the camp remained intact. It was clear that the "great fire" meant that the all the Jews there had been exterminated and that only the Jews in the camp survived. This was in June 1942. Porochovnik, who was there and survived, reported that the camp existed until 1943. One day, in the early morning, everyone in the camp was marched out and organized into rows. They told every tenth person to step aside, and the rest were murdered.

On March 5, 1942, about 80 peasant wagons from the surrounding area appeared. The Dubno district governor was also there, accompanied by the local police and police from other areas. Fear gripped the Jews, because they thought there would be another selection of men to send to the labor camps, and they began to hide if they could. Later that day, it quickly became clear that this was not going to be just an organized robbery ... the police began going house to house confiscating anything that was still valuable to them. In this "action," the head of the Ukrainian committee, Mateyko, also took part. He was a sadistic man who discovered that he had some German grandmother in his family and proudly adopted the identity of an "ethnic German."

The Radzivilov Jews were extremely depressed. There was the news of the Germans advancing into Russia and also the murder of most of the Rovno Jews, "a city that could be in Israel," as well as most of the Jewish communities in western Ukraine. There no longer remained one shred of doubt about their future .... This was the situation after the first 10 months of the Nazi conquest.

My brother Siunye and I, along with seven other Jews, worked in the sawmill that had once belonged to Yakov Boym. We suffered many hardships there at the Ukrainians' hands, led by Yurchenko and Filip.

On the second day of Passover, we learned that the Dubno Jews had been concentrated in a ghetto. This information made the already tense situation even more strained. Many believed that we also would be transferred to the Dubno ghetto. But when we saw paths created and fences being erected and topped with barbed wire on streets where Jews lived, we perceived that they were preparing a local ghetto for us. The Great Synagogue was in the fenced-off area.

On April 9, the order came for all Jews to go into the fenced-off area within two days. The Jews began to drag their worthless belongings, as if the household junk and rags they still held on to were like refugees, too, after all the looting.

[page 217]

Our neighbors, the Ukrainians, saw the Jews being imprisoned in the ghetto and took great interest, taking account of everything that remained, which would eventually come into their hands.

The division of the ghetto from the rest of the surrounding area was very narrow, and the houses nearby were small and desolate. The Great Synagogue was used as a warehouse for the army, and Jews were forbidden to take care of it. It wasn't only Radzivilov Jews who were forced into the ghetto—all the Jews from the surrounding villages were squeezed into it, so the number of Jews in the ghetto reached 2,600. The *Judenrat* assigned the living quarters to the detainees after reserving a few buildings for itself. Gardis's and Dubtshak's large buildings were excluded from the ghetto, as if they wanted to make the ghetto even more crowded. We were forced to organize bunks, one on top of the other, to allow space for everyone to sleep. Many slept in attics, sheds, storage areas, and the like, and for the sick and little ones, there were small houses. For each person, a space of 1.8 meters, including toilet facilities, was allotted.

The ghetto was divided into two parts. Two gates on opposite sides led from Railroad Street between the two parts of the ghetto. The first part ran the length of Railroad Street to the Grebli near the Slonuvka [River] and ended at the Ikva River, and its width was from the old Brody Road to Hospital Street. The Ukrainians who were evicted from this area got to move into good houses that had belonged to Jews.

The second part of the ghetto had a peculiar shape. It ran the entire length of Railroad Street and continued to the Dubno Pozhumkis route; crosswise, it ran from the Dubno road to Hospital Alley.

There were also a few gardens in the ghetto. There was no water shortage, so we started to organize gardens, sowing and planting vegetables in the hope that we would reap them when they grew.

Early on, we were not starving because there were all sorts of ways to smuggle bread and other basic goods into the ghetto. For example, Betsalel Tishelman, whose job was to hand out the meager portions of bread that the murders "threw" at the Jews—I think about 200 grams per person—was able to bribe the Ukrainian bakers to throw in a few more loaves so that there was a little more to eat. Also, the Jewish guards got involved in "business" with Ukrainian guards, and as a result there were a few more basics to eat. Also, with government approval, we sawmill workers would bring a wagon with wood shavings into the ghetto—and we would hide food in it.

At first, anyone could live wherever they wanted in the ghetto, but soon enough, at least a week later, an order was issued that those Jews who were "useful" would have to live in the second ghetto, and the "not-useful" ones would remain in the section near the river.

[page 219]

The "useful" workers received a permit signed by the labor commandant from Dubno, Hamershteyn, and also by the Ukrainian committee, headed by Mateyko, who took care of handing these out. Very soon we learned that any Jew in Rovno and other cities who was not a permit holder was put to death, so those who did have these permits were relieved, because they and their families could hope to survive. Riots erupted as people became more desperate about getting a permit from the *Judenrat* and Mateyko, who drew up the lists according to his own greed and who was himself responsible for delivering them to the Labor Ministry in Dubno. The *Judenrat* demanded a lot of money as a bribe for dredging up each permit and assigning it—a bribe that certainly went to Mateyko. And so it was that many laborers who worked in significant places did not get work permits, and people who worked in completely unimportant places did get work permits. Nothing could be done about this state of affairs, in which Jews were stealing other Jews' professions. There were only 400 permits for some 2,600 souls!

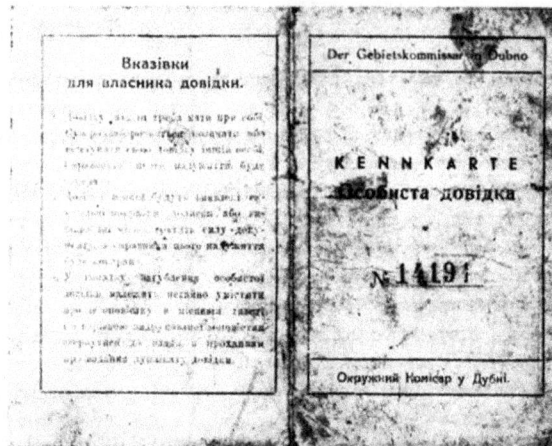

Identity Work Permit

After the last "distribution," it was much more crowded in the second ghetto, and there was more space in the first ghetto. Residents near the river felt that their days were numbered, but the *Judenrat* kept them close so none of them would ever go over to the "useful" side ....

On May 27, 1942, we heard rumors that all the Dubno Jews had been killed and that not one had a work permit. That is, all the "worthless" workers were killed.

Not far from the city, there was a Russian prisoner-of-war camp. The prisoners were put to work at all sorts of jobs. When they marched past the town, they looked starved, eager for cigarette butts that they collected from the ground they walked on and taking the murderous lashes they received for doing this from their Nazi guards. We discovered that these prisoners had been brought here to dig large pits about two kilometers from Radzivilov.

The Nazis liquidated the Jews in the lands they conquered with various methods. For example, in the Russian lands, where the Jews could not flee with the Red Army, Germans would slaughter them right then and there, using all available means. So it was in Kiev, Kharkov, and other cities. In western Ukraine, the murderers first exterminated them without bothering to leave any records. After that, they began to concentrate them in ghettos and destroy them "officially" in "actions," meaning taking them out of the city and slaughtering them in huge pits prepared beforehand. But in the general government in the Polish area, which before the war included Galicia and its capital, Kraków, they mainly transported Jews to killing centers with gas chambers.

[page 220]

Nevertheless, the situation was perfectly clear, and there was no room for delusion. Anyone who was able tried immediately to find a place outside the ghetto, mainly in work camps, where they thought they would be safer. It was awful during the nights because everyone was forced to return to his or her home. Certainly no one could sleep peacefully, listening for any noise from the outside.

And then came the evening of May 29, 1942.

The day before, my brother Siunye and I had obtained a work permit with the help of the sawmill manager, Tushakovski. We were living with our parents on the side of the ghetto near the river. When we got the work permit, we asked to move to the second ghetto with my wife and two children, but this put me in jeopardy because of the intervention of the Jewish police. Finally, I got to move to the "good" side of the ghetto, the side where everyone was "content," or such as it was. I found the people very nervous, preparing hiding places, and some succeeded in not returning from their workplaces to their houses so they could sleep outside the ghetto.

At four in the morning, we heard the rumblings of soldiers marching on Railroad Street. We saw nearly 30 SS troopers approaching the ghetto gates, and beyond them marched the Ukrainian local police and other out-of-town units. They surrounded the ghetto, and we immediately heard echoes of shots and wild shouts calling "*Juden raus!*", "Jews outside!" The storm troopers ran from house to house and with terrible beatings dragged out the wretched souls, who cried and howled in terror. The murderers herded everyone into the Great Synagogue courtyard. As they were force-marching people, they separated the men from the women and children. The elderly and sick who could not walk were shot right then and there and hauled into wagons. This was the fate of Yisrael Genzelman, Viktoria Zakhs, and others. Afterward, they moved the men out in packed rows toward the railroad station. In the first row were Rabbi Yitschak Lerner, Fishel Margaliot, Shmuel Vaynshteyn, Yisrael Reyf, and Hirsh Linder. The Ukrainian police utilized every brutal means to speed up the marching of those condemned to death. Many were bleeding from being struck, and many were weakened along the way. Among them were Leyb Kozulchik and others. These last ones were shot immediately and thrown into wagons that were following behind.

At first the men thought they were being marched to the railroad, and they mustered some hope .... But when they began crossing the tracks, they saw that they were being led to the right, to the west of the city, near the village of Radzivilov Gais. There, large, deep pits about 50 by 20 meters had already been prepared for them.

All the "nobles" of the town and its vicinity—powerful government officials—came to this killing operation: the government representative in Dubno, High Commander Hauptman; Hamershteyn, commandant of labor; SS Commander Kramoda; SS Sergeants Bandler and Lubling; Chairman of the Ukrainian Committee Mateyko; Head of the Ukrainian Police Gritsishen; Representative of the Ukrainian Command Volyniuk, also called Ohida; and others.

[page 221]

The circle around the wretched victims grew smaller as the killers drew closer to begin their slaughter, shouting viciously and lashing out with whips. They forced the wretched people to take off their clothes and stand naked. Then they prodded them toward the open pits, where more SS troopers fired on them with a storm of machinegun fire. The victims fell directly into the open pits like bundles of grain after harvest.... Many of those who fell into the pits were not shot or were shot but not killed. The earth then covered them all, and those who were still alive were smothered. Only one Jewish boy managed to lift himself out of the valley of death; he hid naked among the tree branches.

Meanwhile, the women and children were still being held in the Great Synagogue courtyard by the Ukrainian police. Cries and moaning tore their hearts. Among them was a young unmarried woman named Liuba Tishelman, who had a permit. But she didn't want to be separated from her parents, so she joined her fate with theirs. They sat on the ground like sheep near their butchers, waiting to be slaughtered....

At eight in the morning, their doom was sealed, their fate the same as that of their husbands, sons, and brothers an hour before. They saw signs of blood as they trudged along the same route that their loved ones had taken earlier. When they got to the killing site, they saw two pits, one covered over and the other empty, lined with lime. They had no doubt about what this was—it was only too clear to them. Shouts and wails went up to the heavens, but the gates of mercy did not open.... The half-naked women wailed horribly and cried bitterly. A few went mad, such as Mrs. Krips, who clutched her children in her arms.

The armed and cruel beasts masquerading as men easily dominated their victims, killing them in cold blood, filling the empty pit with their bodies, and then covering them with dirt. After they carried out their mission of murdering helpless women and children, the killers went off to eat, well pleased and congratulating themselves heartily. While eating and feasting, they made an accounting of their killing, and they all attested to it. The account was of the death of 1,549 Jews from Radzivilov and Brody, all accomplished by noon. After that, the SS leader entered the second ghetto and ordered the *Judenrat* to hand over 1,000 cigarettes to the murderers. The *Judenrat* immediately set out to carry out the order and fulfilled the demand for cigarettes.

After that, peasant wagons came to the ghetto with the victims' clothing. On Mateyko's order, the clothes were put into Rabbi Yitschak Lerner's house and locked up there.

[page 222]

Even though not a soul remained in this section, the first ghetto, it was still under guard. A group of people from the second ghetto was sent to clean up the blood and erase all traces of infamous slaughter, especially in the streets and courtyards. I was among those sent to clean up. At the first opportunity, I went to the place where my parents had been living. I looked for them in the hiding place I had prepared, which was covered with shavings I had brought from the sawmill—it was in vain; I did not find them .... The thread of their life had been cut just a few hours before, and they found themselves in the vast common grave on the west side of the forest near the village of Gai Leviatinski.

Among other things, I should say that during the liquidation of the first ghetto, two Jews were in the hospital. One was Zelig Vitser. The hospital manager, a Ukrainian woman, hid them and didn't hand them over to the Gestapo.

Peasants said that even on the third day after the mass killing, the earth shook, blood seeped from the common grave, and a river of blood flowed into the cavity of the forest.

Some 40 people managed to escape from the mass murder, a few because they hadn't returned to the ghetto from work. Among these were Gelman Rudman, Binyamin Geler, and Yakov-Moshe Goldenberg, who worked with me in the sawmill, and Sore Karsh. The last two were saved and survived.

The situation in the ghetto worsened day by day. Despair and depression shadowed those who went out on the work brigades in crowded rows under the Jewish police's or the Ukrainian guards' watch. They would march in the middle of the road because Jews were forbidden to walk on the sidewalks.

A tailors' cooperative had been founded well before the "action" in order to increase the ranks of "useful" people so more work permits could be received. They occupied the Kitas house outside the ghetto. Yakov Shtern and Yosef Stirt managed the work there. According to an order issued by Mateyko, the cooperative was supposed to produce work only for non-Jews. Women also took part in the work there, and in this way, they could get permission to leave the ghetto.

My wife was able to get work as a Ukrainian-German translator with a Christian lawyer named Gorski. He would also send her to the post office with messages. Once, the translator from the SS office saw her and recognized her from her yellow patch. He brought her to the SS office, and there Officer Krauze gave her a vicious beating as punishment for walking outside the ghetto.

Rumors were circulating about the organization of another "action" for children who were still alive. So people began hiding children. Secretly, I took my son, aged six, to the sawmill and hid him between the boards. My wife took our younger son, aged four, with her. Often, I had to escape with my son by climbing a fence out of the city.

[page 223]

Our nerves were very tense and our spirits extremely thin until a voice rose, floating on the wind, that seemed to push us onward.

On June 5, 1942, the labor minister of Dubno, High Commander Hamershteyn, came to the ghetto to take workers to a labor camp in Rovno. About 40 people were sent there, but only one, Chalivki-Salop, survived. He said that they'd stayed in the closed camp near Rovno the whole time. One day, they were guarded by the Ukrainians and SS. They were marched out of the camp and murdered. Afterward, we found out that a few miraculously survived.

On June 25, the SS killers, the same ones who had participated in the "action," returned to Radzivilov. They entered Valdman's restaurant, sent for the *Judenrat,* and demanded a "handout" from them in exchange for "protection" over the next three to four months. These murderers also spoke fluent Russian.

Thus far, the victims' clothing had been kept in secret. Mateyko ordered the *Judenrat* to sort the clothing left from when the victims had been forced to undress and to select the best to be handed over to non-Jews. The *Judenrat* dealt with this over a period of a few weeks, checking all the sewing. I recognized my father's trousers on one of Mateyko's deputies.

At the same time, there was an epidemic of many illnesses. On the one hand, there were shortages and overcrowding, and on the other, unsanitary conditions that caused the outbreak. Water was also lacking, because the main pump operated by Kuperman had broken a while back, and in addition there was a large break in the line that brought water there.

The destruction of Volhynia's Jews quickly accelerated on all sides. We have already recounted the "actions," that is to say, the partial liquidation of the Jewish population at various times. But now people were beginning to speak of a total liquidation. The cities and villages of Volhynia, which had once bubbled over with Jewish life, were about to become *Judenrein,* that is, swept clean of Jews.

Mrs. Veber reports that on July 14, 1942, she traveled on an Aryan permit to Kremenets to see her sister Fafi. They were both married to doctors. There, she saw 11,000 Kremenets Jews being moved toward the Dubno suburb to a killing field, where they were exterminated.

At the same time, a group of SS troopers entered our town and entered the ghetto with a local SS trooper unit and the local Ukrainian police. They conducted a search and loaded up wagons with any remaining foodstuffs. Now it was clear that we no longer had any hope, because they were behaving exactly as they had everywhere there had been a complete liquidation. We started to look for places to hide in our time of trouble.

[page 224]

We found many hiding places with the peasants who had already amassed a great deal of Jewish property when the Jews were ghettoized. Our concern was to acquire enough food to last for a few days. A few people sent their families to these types of hiding places first, and then they themselves planned to flee there at the last possible moment. I must say that the market for these "places" was very brisk, and those who had a trusted peasant also had to be tough and strong enough to settle the "business." Some were also involved in forging false permits: changing signatures, copying various passes, and forging identities—and so it was a very courageous person who could get these kinds of things into the ghetto and use them to pass to the Aryan side and "fit in" there.

My family and I got such an Aryan identity card in the name of Ivan and Marye Ivaniuk. But many people couldn't bring themselves to leave the ghetto. Many didn't know how to secure a hiding place for themselves. And many were selling "places" just to give them over to the Germans. The vile, miserable Kashuba, who had forced Rabbi Yitschak Lerner to dance around the pyre of Torah scrolls, also informed on his friend Mazye Fudim when he recognized him in Lvov. So not all holders of false Aryan papers survived, but there were nevertheless a few men and women, such as Tsiril Karmer, Sluve Karmer, Finkelshteyn-Batlin, Bele Boym, Yehoshue Goldgart and his wife, Frume Feldman and her family, Chane Kozulchik, and others.

At the same time, the young people got word of an organization that was rebelling against the murderers so that people would not be led like sheep to the slaughter. They argued, among other things, that we had nothing left to lose; it was better to die bravely, with honor. Some called on us to take revenge on the murderers, to become partisans, escape to the forest, and take up arms against both the Germans and the Ukrainians. The biggest advocates of this movement were in the tailors' cooperative. They would gather in Cholianka's house after work in the evenings and argue among themselves about the concept and how to make it work. The distance from the city was far, opposition among the population of the surrounding area was great, but greater still was opposition of the *Judenrat* and the Jewish police, as well as Viderhorn, who all still believed that we would remain alive. They argued that bloodshed would only cause the complete devastation of the ghetto. But the most difficult hurdle was the need to leave behind those family members who couldn't be taken to the forest.

Out of hatred of the *Judenrat* led by Yakov Furman, Motel Valdman, and Yakov Sherer, and their Jewish police, with Muntag and Sirota, the Jews crowded into young Rabbi Duvid Rotenberg's hall, which was located in Chardinik's house. Both the observant and the nonobservant would come to pour out the bitterness in their hearts in prayer during the Days of Awe. The prayers were cried out with such bitterness when the *unetaneh tokef*[*] was recited and they turned with a broken heart to the One who sits in the Heavens: "... Master of the universe, pour out Your anger on them so that they will be banished from your world by the hands of the mortal king of the distressed.

[page 225]

"If we have sinned, forgive us now according to our ancestors, do not forsake the surviving remnants of this generation and the congregation who says Kaddish to remember the holy ones who suffered and were murdered. Who will say Kaddish for all of them if you will not rescue and save us?" These reflections, openly expressed or said without moving the lips, were in the mind of everyone who came to the synagogue.

During Sukkot, two lists were put together and written on parchment: the first, the victims of the liquidation of the first ghetto, and the second, those who remained in the ghetto but whose lives were very tenuous. They were placed in hermetically sealed glass jars and buried near the synagogue for

---

[*] *Translation editor's note: Unetaneh tokef* ("Let us speak of the awesomeness") is an important liturgical poem in the Rosh Hashanah and Yom Kippur liturgy.

eternal memory, that there once was a Jewish community annihilated by the Nazi German government, may its name be erased, in 1942.

At the end of September, we learned that the Russian prisoners of war were again digging pits in the same place, the western forest. Again, despair and deep anguish took hold. Many people did not wish to undergo the terrible suffering that the prior victims had endured, and they decided to determine their own fate. They began searching for poison, whether arsenic or cyanide, and to leave the accursed land of the living as quickly as possible. The Nazis shored up the guard around the ghetto, and it was now impossible for anyone to leave, because they knew that many were trying to escape. Just a few hours before the awful closing of the ghetto, I managed to escape with my child, and after me, so did my wife with our second child. We ran to the ruins of the first ghetto and hid in the attic of a shack whose door was locked.

The pursuit of fleeing Jews began. The Ukrainian police exercised beastly cruelty on everyone they caught and returned them to the ghetto beaten and bleeding. However, a few managed to shelter in Brody, an area considered to be in the General Government, where there were still Jews. Just a month before, they had conducted the first "action," in which 3,000 Jews were transported in closed train cars to the gas chambers in Belzec. In the same "action," my wife's parents and her brother, Dr. Mikhael Goldenshteyn, perished. Those who escaped from the ghetto and managed to hide from the Ukrainian murderers' eyes during the day crossed the forest at night and reached Brody at dawn. Many were felled along the way by the murderers' shots, and that is how the Kostye Mes-Burshteyn, Inspektor-Marder, and other families died. Dr. Chaset and his wife made it to Brody carrying their dead children in their arms. The way to Brody was terrible.

After we came down from the attic where we were hiding, we went to a peasant we knew, who was living in the first ghetto. I have already said that when this part of the ghetto was liquidated, the property was given over to peasants to live in. The peasant wouldn't let us enter his house. But he showed us how to cross the ford so we could get to Brody, because the bridge was guarded by the Ukrainians and border guards.

[page 226]

Near the ford, I encountered Rabbi Duvid Rotenberg and R' Yochanen, Rabbi Y. Lerner's son-in-law, and his family, about 15 people in all. I explained to them that they were endangering themselves by staying there, because they could fall into the murderers' hands at any moment. But they decided to stay there, hiding among the trees. So I went on, wading into the water first to determine its depth. The water was up to my neck. I returned, lifted the children in my arms, and crossed over. Then I returned for my wife and did the same. We could not continue on foot because our clothes were soaked, so we courted danger by staying in the village of Leviatin, which we had to travel through. At that moment a Ukrainian woman came upon us, saw our desperate situation, brought us into her shed, and covered us with clothes and straw. A day of dreadful fear passed for this kindly Christian woman, because Gritsishen the murderer was in the village looking for Jews trying to escape. We were lucky, as he did not find us. The woman asked us to leave immediately because she was so frightened; but her husband, a railroad worker who had returned from his work, convinced us to stay until the evening, and then he would guide us through the fields to the place where we would have to cross the ford again. He also gave us half a loaf of bread for the way.

We crossed the ford again, but this time it was narrow and not deep, and although we were wet, we continued to make our way in the dark toward Brody. We saw a Hungarian soldier standing guard on the railroad tracks, but we managed to evade him by hiding among the trees. Toward dawn, we got to Brody safely.

My older brother Avraham, whom the *Judenrat* had sent to the Vinnitsa labor camp as an electrician, had left his wife and his two children, Ronye, aged 15, and Yitschak, aged 13, in our care. He even sent me a letter from the camp begging me to look after them. But I was quite unable to do very much for them. Of course, I did as much as I possibly could. I managed to place them as family members whose father had been sent to work in a peat mine eight kilometers from our town, near the Brody-Radzivilov border and not far from the village of Sestratin. I warned them to flee to Brody the instant they heard bad news from the ghetto, which was some six kilometers from their work. When the Holocaust drew near, my brother's wife Ester ran toward the ghetto to her house, which she had left only a few days before. It was clear that no one could leave the ghetto any longer. My younger brother had trusted a school friend, Homera, from the village of Batkov. He sent him everything he had left and then went to him with his wife and in-laws. I warned him, telling him that it seemed to me that this gentile didn't want him, just his possessions, but my brother trusted him and didn't listen to me. We parted in the rainy night. After the liquidation of the ghetto, the friend's uncle reported him to the Ukrainian police in the village of Berezhtsy in the Kremenets district.

[page 227]

We found Jews living in their own houses in Brody, along with other families who had been evicted from their houses, which were on the city's main streets. We, that is, my wife and children and I, decided for safety's sake to set ourselves up in different places. We wouldn't go outside so as not be apprehended by the Radzivilov police, who were certainly looking for Jews from Radzivilov. That is what happened when the police recognized Rozenblum, and they dragged him through the streets back to the ghetto and smothered him with anti-Jewish posters until he died. Afterward, it became clear that this was an act of revenge against the anti-Hitler posters that were found the grain warehouses, written by the Jewish workers there. Rozenblum was in charge of the work there. Workers in his group were not found during the destruction of the ghetto; they were hiding in the warehouses. Afterward, they were discovered and killed there.

Six days after our escape from the ghetto, the bitter end came; the ghetto's complete destruction occurred on June 10, 1942.

During the ensuing days, solitary refuges began to come to Brody, and they described the final days of life there. There were also Christian messengers who brought us details of the liquidation. We learned that days before the destruction, the manager of accounts in the tailors' cooperative, Yosef Stirt, committed suicide, but not before burning all the money and receipts.

On October 5, we in the ghetto learned that the murderers of the first ghetto were again gathered in Valdman's restaurant drinking schnapps and planning the operation. It was well known that schnapps was a great aid for those who were planning slaughter and murder. In this restaurant, the murderers welcomed everyone who was eager for this moment: the police, ethnic Germans from the surrounding area, and everyone else who wanted to ass-lick the Germans and to prove their devotion to the Nazis by beating up Jews and murdering them. All of them now received rubber clubs, guns, and gas ....

The situation in the ghetto was now completely different. This time, there was no distinction between the *Judenrat* or the Jewish police and the "plain" Jews. All the illusions of those who had hoped they would overcome the wickedness and bypass the final liquidation intact and healthy were dissolved. There was not one person left who did not search for a place to hide in attics and basements, running like mice from pursuing cats. The only contented person was Zalman Goldshmid, who hanged himself in his own house .... People organized into groups to commit suicide by injecting poison into their bodies. The leader of this group was Dr. Veber, who injected poison first into Rokeach Dubtshak and his wife; Sashe Boym and her son; Duvid Margulis and his wife; and finally his only son, his wife, and himself. The sick people died immediately, after an hour. But many suffered greatly.

Peasants reported that as in the earlier "action," the men and then the women and children were forced along the same route.

[page 228]

Many were killed on their way to the pits, hauled into wagons, and then thrown into the open pits. Also, as before, there were two pits. But for some reason, the killers decided to bury everyone, some 900 souls, in one pit. Apparently about 300 people somehow managed to escape during the final days. But about half of those who did were caught and then murdered, and their bodies were transported to Vasil the shoemaker, who buried them. He also brought additional bodies of escapees for burial, such as the body of Rive Goldshmid, Libov Zamberg, and others.

There were also reports that the Germans brought the translator Vider-horn and his family in a special vehicle and offered him the opportunity to escape. But he refused and told them that he preferred to die with all the Jews. A former Austrian officer stood with his family and all the rest of the Jews beside the open pit and, in an act of defiance, said Kaddish in a thundering voice and recited the *Shema,* and the mothers held their children tightly to their heart and howled bitterly. The killers ordered everyone to undress and then immediately began to push everyone into the open pits as they shot them with machineguns. The victims fell one on top of the other, pressing those who had already fallen deeper, and anyone who was still breathing would surely be suffocated by someone who had been murdered and fell on top.

Having completed their work, the murders again returned to Valdman's restaurant to drink and stuff themselves. Again they made an accounting— 900 murdered Jews, the last remaining Jews of the Radzivilov ghetto. The town of Radzivilov was now *Judenrein,* free of Jews.

Thus was the Jewish community of Radzivilov destroyed by the Nazi murderers in 5702–5703 (1942).

Rabbi Itsikel Lerner's Last Journey

Avraham Blum (New York)

Recorded by Yitschak Rudman

(13 Sivan 1942—the Destruction of the First Ghetto)

Rabbi Itsikel

"I go and you will go with me—everything according to the heavenly will." These were Rabbi Itsikel's last words as he was led by his Gestapo killers to the slaughtering site along with 1,200 women, children, and elderly people.

To this bloody spectacle, where wild beasts preyed at every turn, as he was forced to wear his ceremonial garments, clad in a long silk coat with a fur hat on his head and wrapped in a prayer shawl, he marched silently with measured steps on his way as if to perform a blessing ceremony, and near him were Fishel and Duvid Margulis and the brothers Itsik and Nechemye Grin, who were also on their way to the Eternal.

The rabbi marched proudly, his face solemn as he walked to welcome the Divine Presence, and his lips were filled with prayers—probably "even as I walk in the shadow of death, I will see no evil because You are with me." Or perhaps an objection was on his lips, because he and his flock were being led to slaughter, and the One who sits on high was silent: "The Judge of the world will not do justice."

---

* Translated from Hebrew by Elizabeth Kessin Berman.

When they arrived at Leviatin, there were already two huge, wide-open pits ready to engulf them. The Ukrainian killers ordered them to undress and go down into the pits. There was a spray of machinegun fire and death screams, as all the shouted orders of the killers' commanders blended with cries of the *Shema*. And the bodies of our dear ones, breathing and still choking, became dust.

These 1,200 souls had been brought from the first ghetto, whose walls were in Starvak. The second ghetto was located on Butcher Street.
[page 230]

It lasted another six months after that; miraculously, a very few took shelter when the second ghetto was destroyed. Some of the very few who escaped were able to report these words.

Four Jewish families are now in Radzivilov (1951), which is now under Soviet rule. Perhaps we may still hear of their circumstances one of these days, but for now these are the final regards from the city of our birth.

Testimony[*]

Yechiel Porochovnik was 17 in June 1941, when the Germans conquered parts of the Soviet Union. A son of a family of laborers, he helped his father, who was a wagon driver, support his family from an early age. He was a member of Young Pioneer in Radzivilov. He yearned to be sent for pioneer training and then to immigrate to Israel. The war interfered with his plans.

In the early years of the German occupation, his brother Avraham suffered terribly at the Ukrainian fascists' hands because he had been a Soviet operative. On his brother's grave, Yechiel swore to avenge his brother's spilled blood. Afterward, when his entire family was exterminated by the Germans, he saw only one goal ahead of him: vengeance.

During the Nazi occupation, Yechiel endured many agonies of the war against the Germans: hiding in bunkers, fighting with the partisans, surviving as a Jew alone in the forest and, after that, as a soldier in the Red Army. He never once laid down his weapons for any battle until he lost his right leg.

He was one of the first young people in the ghetto to try to organize armed resistance to the enemy. After the liquidation of the city's Jews, and after he had lost his family, he fled to Brody, and while hiding out in a bunker, he made connections with the partisans, recruited young people in the Brody ghetto, and then led them from the ghetto to the forest. He never went into battle alone; he always had followers who were armed and ready to defend the honor of the Jewish people and their redemption.

He was among the first young Jews to serve with the partisans in the area around Brody, and he took part in dangerous assaults on German and Ukrainian legions. Even when he was injured and laid up for six weeks with

---

[*] *Note in original:* From the Yad Vashem archives, transcribed by Mr. Y. Alperovich from the oral history of Mr. Yechiel Porochovnik.

bullet wounds in his leg, he continued to send out communications to his comrades.

He was a member of a three-person partisan delegation sent to negotiate with Ukrainian Nationalist Division officers for a ceasefire so they wouldn't engage with each other.

Both the Germans and the Ukrainians were hindered significantly by him. In one successful operation he organized, he got food and supplies to 40 Jews who were dying from starvation as they hid in a bunker in Brody.

[page 232]

In their despair, they turned to him, and they saw their salvation in him. Afterward, when the bunker was uncovered by the Germans, he led some of them to the forest. On their way, they killed a few Germans.

It was his fate, so it seems, to suffer alone after his group of partisans was lost. He was armed, but he wandered in the forest by himself. The local murderous Ukrainians and Germans hunted him, and he killed one German who pursued him.

After he fell into the hands of the Soviet Red Army, he joined a Red Army division and fought with them as they liberated the region. For his courageous actions in the Red Army, he was awarded medals three times, all medals of the highest order: Red Banner, Red Star, and the order Slava First Class, as well as many other medals. He volunteered to lead a group of soldiers, all whom volunteered for a very difficult battle, and found himself face to face with the enemy. In the battle, he lost his right leg. Only then did he stop fighting, knowing that he had fulfilled his vow.

After the war concluded and he was decorated, he returned to Radzivilov. He waived his right to go to Poland under the repatriation law in order to track down the murderers of his family and of the city's Jews. After a diligent search, he found some and made accusations against them. A list of their names was sent to the NKVD, and only after they were sent for judgment did he move on.

In 1957, he acted on his second opportunity to leave Russia. He left with his Russian wife and two daughters, first for Poland and then for Israel.

Yechiel Porochovnik mentioned many of his comrades' names during his testimony. He shared many details of his wartime confrontation with the vicious enemy. He transmitted very important information on the Jews' role in the partisan movement and also on the Ukrainians' collaboration in the Radzivilov Jews' murder and on their liquidation.

From the Memories of Yechiel Porochovnik

In my earliest years, I was taught first at cheder, then at the Tarbut School, and later at the Polish public school until the Polish-German war broke out in 1939.

My father, Yakov-Moshe Porochovnik, of blessed memory, worked at the flourmill in Radzivilov. He had a huge wagon and four or five horses. He used to haul sacks of flour from the mill to the warehouses owned by the merchants. My brother and I used to help my father with his work.

The young people of Radzivilov used to frequent Zionist youth clubs.
[page 233]

I was a member of Young Pioneer. During our meetings, we would talk about the Land of Israel, and we would dream about our connection to the Land and about immigrating there. But the war put an end to all of our plans.

When the Germans occupied Poland, the Russians entered our region. I went to work as a common laborer at the sawmill. I worked there until the war between the Germans and the Russians broke out in June 1941.

During Russian rule in Radzivilov, great changes took place in the large work facilities: the flourmills, sawmills, bakeries, shops, and factories were nationalized. They organized all sorts of cooperatives. The government put many people to work in these various organizations, especially those from the ranks of workers and those who were Soviet operatives. They also brought many Ukrainians into their ranks, and all but a few were blatant anti-Semites who showed their hatred of Jews at every opportunity.

At the same time, many refugees from Poland came to Radzivilov. From their family members who had stayed in areas conquered by the Germans, they received reports of assaults against Jews. Despite this, many wished to return to their families, but the Soviet militia prevented them from returning and sent them to Russia. But this bitter fate worked out for the best for them and actually saved their lives.

When the war between Russia and Germany broke out on June 22, 1941, great alarm spread among the refugees—and rightly so—that Germany would ghettoize all the Jews and that their fate would be terrible. Young people looked for ways to escape, in particular Jews who had been operatives under Russian rule. The Soviets couldn't mobilize quickly enough, and the Red Army hastily retreated. Jews fled to Kremenets, toward the Russian border, but the Russian border guards sealed the crossing, and those in flight were forced to return to the town, left behind without any way to cross the border.

Early Days of German Rule

My brother Avraham and I were among those who had tried to escape from Radzivilov. I returned home, but my brother stayed in Kremenets because he had been a Soviet activist; it was entirely clear that he couldn't go back.

The Ukrainians put together a list of Jews who had been Russian sympathizers, and my brother Avraham was on their list. Although the Ukrainians had cooperated with the Soviets, they immediately switched their allegiance, changing their red color to serve the Germans. They organized their own militias, got special permission from the Germans, and began to consider what to do with Jews, in particular with the Communists, Communist Youth members, and activists during Soviet rule.

[page 234]

Under this pretext, they launched an assault on the Jews and their property.

The Death of My Brother Abraham

As I have already mentioned, my brother Avraham stayed in Kremenets. A rumor broke out among the Ukrainians that the Jews had killed a Ukrainian in the prison, so they called for vengeance on the Jews. My brother was among the Jews in the Kremenets prison. More than 100 incensed and wild peasants armed with pickaxes, knives, and clubs descended on the prison and organized a bloody uprising. At least 10 Jews were killed. My brother escaped from the jail and went home to Radzivilov.

Two German officers were living in our home. We thought it was better for us to host them, and safer, too. But one night, when my brother and I were asleep in the same room, the Ukrainians appeared, banged on a window, and demanded that we open it. My brother and I dressed, preparing to run away through the back door. My father opened the door as my brother, running, first sprang out of the house. But the house was surrounded by guards, and they immediately opened fire on him. He was killed instantly. I was running just behind him, following him, but when I saw him fall, I stopped and stayed where I was.

My brother's corpse was left sprawled on the steps of our house. The German officers wouldn't let us bring the body inside, making the excuse that an investigation would have to be done because the police, according to them, didn't have permission, in their opinion, to fire on a man who hadn't crossed the threshold of his house. But the next evening, the police came and dragged my brother's body outside the city. In the morning, we found his grave. My father went to the police and begged to be allowed to bring the body to the Jewish cemetery. But the Ukrainian police commander, Zalewski, who knew my father well, ignored his request. Taking it on ourselves, we dug up the body in great terror and brought it to the Jewish cemetery ourselves. To do the burial, we convinced a few other men to help, and as we were finishing, the police appeared and stopped us. They released everyone except me. No one heard from me for days. They accused me of being a

Communist Youth member, but I didn't break. I told myself that they couldn't keep me forever and that they would let me go.

My brother's murder drove us into despair. The news spread throughout the town that he was the first one martyred by the Nazis in Radzivilov.

On my brother's grave I swore to take revenge on his Fascist murderers, the Germans and the Ukrainians.

[page 235]

I also want to add that on the night of my brother's murder, the Ukrainian police murdered 30 to 40 more Jews who had been operatives during Russian rule, including Yitschak Vaynshteyn's brother-in-law (his wife's brother) and Yakira, who was a government rabbi during Polish rule.

The Germans Show Their Teeth

During the first weeks of the German occupation, there were signs that the Ukrainian police would unleash unrestrained terror. But soon afterward, a Gestapo platoon arrived. They set up headquarters. But a new wave of robbery, destruction, and murder then began. The first order was that all Jews had to wear a white armband with a Star of David painted in blue on their arm. It was forbidden for Jews to walk on the sidewalks. It was also forbidden for them to mingle with the Christian population.

Two or three weeks after that, they published another decree that all Jewish residents, from young to old, must gather in the market square. There the Germans would identify all those who had professions and those who were unskilled. The square was enclosed on all sides, and soldiers and guards patrolled every exit. Meanwhille, they swarmed like flies on the Jews' houses and hauled away anything they found. When they let the Jews go back, the Jews found their homes burgled and empty.

The Jewish organization that was established at the Germans' behest was tasked with collecting a penalty tax in the form of gold and silver vessels and jewelry. Or else people would be sent for forced labor. Dozens of professional men were sent to Vinnitsa to work in a camp. Among those sent to the camp were my uncle Nechemye Porochovnik (who died January 27,

1961, in Israel); the two Barash brothers, who were carpenters; two of the Beregovski brothers; Volf Kaplan (now in Chelyabinsk, Russia); and others whose names I can no longer remember. Most of them died there.

Two Ghettos: For the "Useful" and the "Not-Useful"

The Germans concentrated the Jews into a ghetto. They carved out the area of punishment for the Jewish population and fenced it in with barbed wire and guarded it with both Ukrainian and Jewish police. After they set up the ghetto, they divided the Jews into two groups, those who were "useful" and those who were "not-useful," that is, workers with a trade and those who had no plausible skills. Skilled workers and tradesmen got special permits and were allowed to live with their families in the area called "Korea," and those without skills—the elderly, women, children, and the ill—didn't get permits and were concentrated in a separate area "by the river." I don't know how many people were in the ghetto.*

[page 236]

My brother and I received skilled-worker permits because I had worked in the sawmill and then with my brother Gershon in the flourmill. So our families were guaranteed flour and groats. With our whole family, we moved to the "useful" ghetto. No one had permission to leave the ghetto, but I could because I worked in the flourmill, which was on the "Aryan" side. Life was extremely hard, but somehow it was possible to exist.

The Destruction of the "Not-Useful" Ghetto

Months passed after the establishment of the "not-useful" ghetto. One day at the end of June, in the early morning, while people were still asleep, the ghetto was suddenly surrounded by Germans and guardsmen, and anyone who didn't have a work permit had to take their most essential belongings with them. They were all arranged in rows, and the sick, who couldn't walk, were brought in wagons and vehicles. Leybush Kaziultshik and Chayim, his

---

* *Note in original:* On this action, Mr. Yitschak Vaynshteyn reports that it was organized on August 28, not a few weeks after the Germans entered the town, as Mr. Porochovnik reports—the Editor

son, revolted and refused to go, and they were shot on the spot. A few other Jews who refused to leave were immediately shot, and the Germans removed their bodies. Everyone was moved under heavily armed guard to the grove near the old village of Leviatin. There they shot everyone in pits that had been prepared for them.

The same day, that is, the day the ghetto was destroyed, I was working with the horses in the flourmill. The gentiles told me about the atrocity in detail. Toward evening, I went out to the site on horseback with one of the gentiles, Pietro Kostiuk. Those who had been shot in the pits were still twitching, while the earth that covered them rose and fell. Blood was pooled everywhere. I don't know if I helped anyone escape from there, but it seems to me that there was one boy, Ruven Zeyger (now in the Soviet Union), who managed to flee from the pits. It was said that the victims were forced to take off their clothes and lie down naked on the ground. Then a murderous shower of machinegun fire fell on them. Afterward, a second group of people were forced to lie down on the backs of the murdered people, and thus it went, one on top of the other, until they were all killed. This was how a large number of the Radzivilov Jews were wiped out.

The Young People Try to Organize

After the Germans liquidated the "not-useful" ghetto, the remaining Jews knew that time was running out and that the Germans would also destroy the "skilled" ghetto. We were getting reports from various places in Volhynia that the Germans intended to kill all the Jews eventually and without distinction.

A group of young people in the Radzivilov ghetto decided to organize: the Fayfel brothers, Shalom and Pinchas (Pipa) (Shalom was killed after the second action, and Pinchas lives in Vienna); Chayim Royzen (now in America); Simche Yakira (Siunye), and others.

[page 237]

The leader of the group was Asher Cherkovski. I was also a member.

We were trying to figure out how to get weapons, arguing about how to fight. We were all of the same mind—if the Germans destroyed the ghetto, we'd stand up to them with force and weapons. We also decided to organize the escape of the remaining young people to the forests to join the partisans' flight against the Germans.

The Liquidation of the Second Ghetto

No more than five months after the destruction of the first ghetto, we heard rumors that the Germans were preparing to destroy all the Radzivilov Jews, down to the very last one. We had heard that the life was easier for of Jews in Brody than in other places, so when fear of the ultimate liquidation spread and everyone believed the days of the ghetto were numbered, many began to flee to Brody. Many who fled had no family connections. It didn't take long—it seems to me that it was in October 1942—for all the Germans and the guards to surround the ghetto and, as in the previous "action," force everyone into the same place. There, against the backdrop of their brothers' graves, where pits had already been made ready, into their depths, the last of Radzivilov's Jews were thrown. The Germans had prepared two pits, but they filled only one. The second remained empty.

It was said that the Germans specified that Viderhorn the translator stay alive, but he chose to die with his family. In this catastrophic slaughter, my parents and sister also perished.

The night before the second "action," I ran away with my friend Genye Rayzman, and we crossed the border into Brody. The Germans had established the border between Radzivilov and Brody that divided Volhynia from Galicia, as it had before World War I. Many Jews were caught crossing the border and were shot on the spot, but my friend Genye Rayzman and I crossed safely and reached Brody. I want to point out that the *Judenrat* in Brody didn't receive Jews fleeing from Radzivilov kindly. Every Gestapo demand to the *Judenrat* for workers was filled by those from Radzivilov. Tsverling, the *Judenrat* deputy chairman, and a *Judenrat* policeman named Rubin would roam the ghetto and harass Jews from Radzivilov.

Once when the Germans demanded that the *Judenrat* send a specific number of Jews (we didn't know if it was for work or extermination), my name was added to the list, and so was the name of my friend Chayim Feldman. Mendel Tsverling was in the same transport wagon. They both spoke of escaping during the journey, because they had a saw with which they cut a hole near the door, and eventually they were able to open the door; in this way, many people managed to jump from the train and return to Brody.

[page 238]

When my friend and I returned to Brody, we decided not to go back to the ghetto. We met up with our friend Henekh Tishker. Under his former home was a bunker. In the bunker, nearly 30 people were taking shelter, many of them young people, and among them were five from Radzivilov: Chayim Feldman, Leyb Kripitser (who was murdered), Yakov Paritski (who now lives in England), Simche Zats (who lives in America), and me.

The Bunker in Brody

The bunker was well built and equipped with everything we needed. There were two exits, both camouflaged. From these, we stayed in constant contact with friends in the ghetto and with other concealed places in the city.

As I have already said, the bunker was built below the former apartment of our friend Henekh Tishker. A Christian woman lived there now, and she took care of providing food for us. We were there for almost half a year. We knew we couldn't stay there forever and that we couldn't be leisurely about leaving, so we began to plan to leave the bunker and go to the forest. I knew that there were partisans about 30 kilometers from Brody, in the Leshniov forest. We decided that I would leave for the Leshniov forest to make a connection with the partisans.

I Meet the Partisans

I left the bunker and after a few days arrived safely in the Leshniov forest. I connected with a group of armed partisans. Many had been prisoners of war—Russians, Poles, Jews, and others. At first, they didn't trust me, and they interrogated me. After a few weeks, however, they gave me a gun and trusted me to go back to the Brody ghetto and get other young people. In the end, the group decided that they could absorb about 20 men and that there was a need for good people, because they were helping to develop the partisan movement that was fighting against two enemies: the Germans and the Ukrainian nationalists.

I Take a Group of Jews from Brody to the Forest

Another boy from Lvov, who was a novice (I don't remember his name), and I operated together. Armed, we went to Brody to bring a group of Jews to the forest. The boy from Lvov headed toward the ghetto, and I, to the bunker. We were supposed to meet up at a predetermined place with two groups of Jews.

[page 239]

I was already in the bunker when we suddenly heard shouts in German: "Jews, out!" I have already said that there was a second, secret exit from the bunker. The people in the bunker immediately started toward this exit to escape. At the same time, the Germans began to destroy the other entrance to the bunker. I yelled, "Don't leave," and then I fired three shots at the camouflaged exit that the Germans were now beginning to destroy. The Germans were surprised to hear shots, and they thought there was a well-armed group of partisans inside, so they left. I was the first to run outside, and I fired shots in the direction of the fleeing soldiers. I gave an order for everyone to run after me. I was able to avoid the panic that ensued among the retreating Germans and to lead the young people, 28 Jews in all, through the alleys toward the way out of the city to the road to the forest. We left the city safely and eventually got to the forest.

But the comrade from Lvov was caught during the night in the ghetto when police began a sudden search, and he was apprehended.

The Heroic Deed of a Boy from Radzivilov

I want to mention an event that occurred at the beginning of 1943. While we were in the bunker in Brody, Hersh Marder, a boy from Radzivilov who had recently escaped from the Radzivilov ghetto and who had fought like an armed partisan, was captured by the Germans. They brought him to Brody and put him in the prison, which was located below the fire station. But he still had his gun hidden, and when they brought him to the police inspector, he fired directly at the guard who was accompanying him and fled to the ghetto.

When the Germans found out about this, they came to the ghetto to search for him. They allowed the Ukrainian police and the fire brigade to take revenge for Marder's actions. For a half an hour, the murderers rampaged through the Brody ghetto and killed many Jews.

The Death of a Polish informer

When we were in the bunker and heard the Germans crying, "Jews, out!", Comrade Tishker recognized the voice of his neighbor, a Pole named Yantshin, among the German voices. After we had safely exited the bunker, we decided to kill Yantshin, the Polish informer. Before we left the city, Tishker, Chayim Feldman, Simche Zats, Leyb Kripitser, and I returned to Brody and went to Yantshin's house. Tishker, who was his neighbor, called him outside. When he came out and saw not only Tishker but four other men, he became frightened.

[page 240]

Tishker turned to him and said, "Now that the Germans have uncovered the bunker and everyone has run away to the forest, we need food. I'm asking you to bring us food for the people who were in the bunker." Yantshin said, "In my house I have only pork and other such things. But maybe my neighbor has just now baked some bread. Why don't you guys go to my neighbor now and get it from him. In the meantime, I'll go and get the pork for you."

We already knew that many Germans were at the neighbor's house where Yantshin was telling us to go and that they were there drinking whisky. We said, "You go and get some bread for us." We were sure he'd do this and tell the Germans about us. He then turned as if to urinate, and I shot him. And the bastard dropped on his ass. We cleared out of there quickly. When the Germans heard the shots, they sprang into action and began firing at us, but we were already scattered and were beginning to run to the group that was waiting for us in the forest. We brought them to the partisans.

Sakovitsh, the Jews' Friend

I want to take this opportunity to say a few words about Sakovitsh, a real friend of the Jews.

During our days in the bunker, our connection Tishker was connected to a Lithuanian named Sakovitsh. He was a communist, and he loved Jews. It was he who looked out for the needs of the 28 Jews in the bunker. He organized a network of peasants who were sympathetic to Jews. They'd bring him provisions for the Jews regularly. Sakovitsh would send the provisions to Tishker's neighbor, and she would deliver them to us. I'll have more to say about Sakovitsh later.

We Take 20 Jews out of the Brody Ghetto

While we were in the city, during spring 1943, we were hearing rumors that the Germans were planning to liquidate the ghetto in Brody. There were no other ghettos remaining in all of Volhynia in those days. Cities and town were all *Judenrein* (free of Jews). A friend and I entered the Brody ghetto and succeeded in bringing 20 Jews out before the destruction of the ghetto. We brought them to the partisans.

When the ghetto was destroyed, more Jews managed to escape, and they joined us. Our platoon grew to almost 100 people, most of them Jews. Among them were five from Radzivilov: myself, Feldman, Leyb Kripitser, Yakov Paritski, and Simche Zats.

Partisan Activities

Our partisan unit was the only one operating in the Brody area. We worked against the Germans and the Ukrainian nationalists.

[page 241]

We had no contact whatsoever with the partisans' central command, and we operated independently, according to our own choices and interest. The head of the unit was someone who had been a Russian captain and who had fled from the fort at Brisk. I don't remember his name, but we called him "Comrade D."

Our unit was divided into four groups, 25 men in each. Each group had a commander. I was the commander of the one that included the five Radzivilov men. Sonderkommandos patrolled its perimeter. We attacked small groups of Germans, but we didn't go near the larger groups. We were a local unit, making raids on food, ammunition. The main partisan forces were concentrated some 100 kilometers from us, in the Polesia region. As I said, we had no connection with them.

The Ukrainian Nationalist Division

In the surrounding area, the Ukrainian national division organized by the Germans was operating. It was called the Ukrainian Volunteer Division. This division fought against the Red Army and Russian partisans. This division, as a separate army unit, was under the German SD's command, and the Germans threatened to send them to the front, but they refused to go. They wanted to form an independent Ukraine, so they scattered in the forests and fought the against the Germans there.

We had people in this division with whom we could cooperate. At the head of the division was a Ukrainian named Zaluzshny, who, for all intents and purposes, was a friend of the partisans. We got reconnaissance from him about operations planned against the partisans. This division commander didn't exactly know our strengths, but he never once asked us for a review; he knew we were fighting the Germans—our common enemy. Our commander sent a three-man delegation to division headquarters to negotiate to prevent us from fighting each other. I was a member of the delegation.

The division headquarters was camped some 10 kilometers from the town of Leshniov, 30 kilometers from Brody.

The results of the negotiations were good. We agreed not to fight each other. Our units and theirs would operate independently in the entire area. But we also learned that the purpose of our talks, according to Commander

Zaluzshny, was to impress on us the need to be vigilant and to warn each other in written reports that would be transmitted to each of our headquarters.

[page 242]

When we returned after the two-day negotiations, we couldn't ignore Zaluzshny's warning that this Ukrainian division had agreed to suspend hostilities between us with the intention using our fighting force and then disarming and destroying us.

Therefore, this warning revealed something very essential, and thanks to it, we knew enough to be ready for any sudden attack by the Ukrainians.

Getting food for the unit was very difficult. We didn't want to take food from the peasants by force. We didn't want them to think we were a robber gang, and we didn't want to provoke them. Doing this would likely inspire the peasants to help the Ukrainians destroy us. So we had to get food from farther away, which meant that we had to diversify and split up, and in doing so we diluted our already weakened forces. We trained a band of scouts who came in contact with a few Poles in the area, and they gave us information on the local population's mood.

Despite our intensive efforts, some successful, some not so successful, the unit suffered from severe starvation.

In September 1943, we were surrounded by a platoon of German soldiers, who numbered some 2,500. There was no way for us to break through their circle. Someone apparently turned us in. We fought to our last drop of strength and suffered many casualties. Our commander was also killed. Only 11 men from our entire unit, 8 Jews and 3 Russians, were still alive. I was the commander of this small group.

When the Ukrainian nationalists heard of our losses, they decided to destroy us down to the very last one. They began to organize ambushes, and they forced us to move from place to place in order to weaken us. During one battle with the Ukrainians, I was severely injured in my leg, which was hit by four bullets. I was forced to lie on my back for six weeks until I recovered. I stayed with a Pole that I knew. My dear friend Chayim Feldman watched over me and didn't leave me for even a minute.

Meanwhile, our group implemented different operations in the Poniekowice region, where Zaluzshny's sister lived, whom I have already mentioned. She was a friend to the Jews and a helper of the partisans. She told us about two Ukrainian leaders who were in the area and identified where they were living.

The Death of Leyb Kripitser

We planned to kill the two Ukrainian leaders. At the head of our group—sent instead of me because my wound hadn't healed—was Mikolay Martshenko, a peasant from Zhitomir.

[page 243]

When the men from the group arrived at the site, they surrounded the house. They burst inside and shot the two Ukrainian leaders. They escaped in the dead of night from there to Zaluzshny's sister's home. This was a stupid thing to do, because the Ukrainians, who understood this as an act of murder, searched for our men and immediately found them hiding in the woman's house. They told this to the German soldier in charge in Brody. And so they appeared immediately to surround the Zaluzshny woman's house. In a difficult battle, four of our men fell, two Jews and two Russians, among them Commander Martshenko. Leyb Kripitser was hurt badly. Under heavy fire lobbed furiously by the Germans, comrades carried him to the place where Chayim Feldman and I were. But when they got to us, Kripitser was no longer alive; he died on the way. We buried him in the forest. And so this was the end of one of the best men of Radzivilov.

We were down to just six. Afterward, three from our group fell in a few other battles, and then there were only Chayim Feldman, Eliahu Valakh from Brody, and me.

We Return to Brody

When we were reduced to only three, we had no desire to stay in the forest. We were pursued on every side with no means of survival. Eliahu had a sister in Brody who was hiding with 40 Jews in a bunker. We decided to return to Brody and go to this bunker. Eliahu knew its location, but its entrance was heavily camouflaged. The bunker was in the city center, in a four-story building, and there were many Poles and Ukrainians living in it. For some time, the Germans had suspected that there were Jews hiding in a bunker beneath the building, but they couldn't tell where the entrance was. And they didn't want to blow up the entire building. The bunker had been built by a Jewish engineer as a two-floor living unit, and it was equipped with electricity and plumbing.

When we got there, we immediately figured out the entrance from our partisan experience: we saw a number of Jews coming out to get food. We stopped them. They were frightened and at once went back to the bunker. We followed them and went inside with them. A horrible sight appeared before my eyes: 40 or more Jews were lying rotting and swollen from starvation without any ability to move. Eliahu Valakh's sister immediately recognized us and was glad that we had come. In the bunker we also found a Jew from Radzivilov, Itshe Lerner. We brought our weapons to the bunker.

After a few days, we began to plan our survival.

[page 244]

I made an attempt to get in contact with our friend Sakovitsh, the peasant with whom we had connected when we were in Tishker's bunker, and also Yanek Stakhovski, Tishker's school friend. I was able to get in touch with them, and they promised to help get food if possible. But the food they got for us wasn't enough for more than 40 people. After a stormy meeting, we decided that a group of 12 young people in the bunker would carry out a partisan-like operation. The Jewish residents of Brody in the bunker told us that a rich Ukrainian who had two grocery stores lived on Railroad Street.

A Successful Operation

On Christmas Eve 1943–1944, I, as the head of the group, went to the Ukrainian's house. We knocked on the door and went inside. I spoke to him in fluent Ukrainian (I had learned to speak Ukrainian really well when I was in the forest), saying, "We come to you in the name of the Ukrainian underground to acquire a quantity of this and that including medicine, food, and clothing. I give you a timeline to get all this to us. Because of the hour, we'll take what we need now, and then we'll come for the medicine. If you tell anyone about anything that's happened here, you and your entire household will go up in smoke." The Ukrainian and his household members were frightened, and we took everything there was to take. The Ukrainian didn't resist, and he didn't seem disturbed. We also took his radio and bundles packed with food and returned to the bunker, our operation having succeeded. When the Jews saw how many supplies we had brought, they began to hug and kiss us, happy that we could break their starvation.

The same evening, we heard on the same radio that we brought with us that the underground was coming close to Sarny. Our joy was great. But not for long.

The Germans Discover the Bunker

Chayim Feldman and Eliahu Valakh's sister left the bunker to take care of something or other. When they went out, they noticed a group of armed German soldiers. The Germans leaped to stop them, and they both became confused and didn't know what to do—return to the bunker, but in doing so, reveal the whereabouts of the entrance, or fall into the Germans' hands. They decided to run back to the bunker. The Germans immediately opened fire and shot Chayim Feldman in the leg. He hurried to me and quickly told me about the incident, saying that the entrance to the bunker had been revealed to the Germans. It didn't take long for the situation to deteriorate, so I shouted loudly, "Everyone leave immediately through the secondary exit." I carried Chayim, whose leg was injured, in my arms.

[page 245]

Everyone managed to get out safely, and luckily we saw two peasants hauling a snow sleigh. I grabbed the sleigh and then dragged Chayim, putting him in it, and then brought him to Sakovitsh's house. There he got first aid. I must point out that when we broke out of the bunker, we went in many different directions, but a group of about 15 followed me to Sakovitsh's home. When Sakovitsh saw so large a group of Jews, he said that there was no way to hide everyone, because he was worried about the neighbors talking and about his life and the lives of his family members. Indeed, this was the truth, so I decided to take the injured and the entire group of Jews out of Brody.

The Death of Chayim Feldman

I led the group out by night through the former Brody ghetto. In those days, the front was getting closer to Brody, and German columns were on the outskirts of the city. Not far from the Brody ghetto, we encountered a group of armed Germans, who spotted us and started firing on us heavily. We withdrew to the ruins of the ghetto, and even there we were surprised by Germans who opened fire on us. I was still hauling Chayim Feldman in the snow sleigh, but still I returned the Germans' gunfire. Suddenly Chayim rose from the sleigh and sprang from it and, jumping on one foot, disappeared from sight. We hid among the ruins. After that, we looked for Chayim for an hour. But we didn't find him. The Germans were on a rampage and fired constantly. No doubt, they were looking for Chayim. It wasn't conceivable that he could go far in his condition. I didn't hear from him again. I assumed that he had died. The loss of my best friend was a very great blow for me. We had been devoted friends since childhood. When I was laid up with an injury, he stayed by my bedside for six weeks. I tried to carry him, but in an instant, he was lost to me forever.

The Death of Lize Kober

When the Germans opened fire on us in the ruins of the ghetto, we all scattered. Only Eliahu and his sister, I, and one other young single girl from Brody, named Lize Kober, regrouped. That same night, we stayed together in one of the basements, and we decided to stay there the next day and to leave Brody on the following day and go back to the Leshniov forest. We decided that Eliahu's sister would go to the peasants she knew and bring us something to eat. We would wait for her in the basement.

A few gentiles who spotted us reported us to the Germans.

[page 246]

In the basement, we heard someone describing our hiding place in Ukrainian. We decided there was no point in lingering, so we left the basement. Lize and I ran in one direction and Eliahu in another. The German opened fire on us, and Lize fell to the ground. A bullet hit her, and she was covered in blood. She said to me, "Run, save yourself. I'm lost." This happened in January 1944.

The Germans Pursue Me

I ran on by myself, leaving behind the wounded Lize Kober. The Germans shot at me constantly. After running some 10 meters, I slipped into a ruined house, and the Germans followed me. I hid behind a column. When the first German burst in, I shot him, and he fell on the spot. I went up to the second floor, shooting behind me as I went, and the Germans followed in my footsteps. Then I jumped from the second floor to the street and from there blended into the crowd. As I walked, I tried to figure out what to do. I decided to go to Sakovitsh. I tapped on his door, and he came outside. I told him I was alone. He told me that a partisan had killed a German in the city. And I told him everything that had happened. And he advised me to leave his house and not to linger because the Germans and Ukrainians were searching for the person who did it, and they were tracking him.

The Death of Zaluzshny, the Jews' Friend

I had no choice but to return to the Leshniov forest, on whose outskirts Zaluzshny lived. When I got to his house, I was shocked to see the door wide open. There wasn't a living soul inside, and everything inside was destroyed and broken. I went to other Polish neighbors, but I didn't find them either. I learned afterward that the Poles were afraid to sleep in their homes because gangs of Ukrainians were organizing attacks on Poles and killing them. One Polish guy told me that a few days ago the Ukrainians had killed Zaluzshny and his entire family because of his partisan connections.

Alone in the forest, I became a man of the forest: alone, without family, without comrades or friends. My situation was terrible. Hunger hunted me like death. For many months I wandered from place to place, banging on peasants' doors, begging for something to eat. Eventually the Ukrainians caught on to my trail, but I was quiet and stayed hidden, and I managed to evade them.

[page 247]

Salvation

This occurred between March 15 and 20, 1944. I was hanging around by myself in the forest, and suddenly I heard men speaking Russian. Thinking that they were Ukrainian nationalists, I ran to hide, but they spotted me. I decided that what would be would be; I would approach, my gun in my hand. The Russians trained their rifles on me, ready to fire. I started speaking to them in Russian. At first, they were suspicious that I was spying for the Germans. They roughed me up and dragged me to their headquarters. This was the vanguard of the Red Army.

After a thorough investigation, and after I proved to them who I was, I asked to join them because I wanted to fight the Germans and take my revenge for my family's blood, which they had shed. They wanted to send me to the rear lines, to the home front, but I convinced them that I was determined to stay at the front. In the end, they put me in a platoon that was connected to the 192nd Tashkent Division.

I Fight in the Flanks of the Red Army

The Red Army advanced as it pursued the Germans westward and liberated cities and towns. The Germans showed great resistance in their withdrawal. In April 1944, we reestablished the offensive front line, and our forces drew close to Brody as they liberated Gorokhov and Radziechów. In the battle to free Brody, thousands were sacrificed on both sides. The Germans defended Brody strongly with tanks. For an entire month there were heavy battles, until the main divisions fell.

About six kilometers from Brody, the village of Konyushkov spread out over a hill, and Germans were firing on our forces from there. Our unit was ordered to take them out and regain the village. The village exchanged hands five times. On the sixth attempt, our unit commander was killed, and our entire unit was destroyed except for four soldiers with two machineguns. We decided to not to leave our position and to hold it no matter what. The Germans tried numerous times to attack us, but they weren't successful. We resisted their assault for 14 hours until new forces arrived. Thanks to our brave actions, we were rewarded. The four of us received the Slava Order First Class. We fought in other battles until the winter offensive was called off.

Before the summer offensive in July 1944, we were involved in several battles in the Brody region. I participated in many of them, and twice I was highly commended.

[page 248]

The Soviet command recommended that I be sent to officers' training school. This was on July 13. But on the same day, we learned that the summer offensive would be launched the next day. So I requested that they not send me back to officers' training school but let me stay at the front. I wanted to fulfill my vow to avenge my perished family. I didn't want to take myself out of battles as long as I could fight.

In July 1944, the summer offensive started to push our front line forward. In the early morning, when all the roads were scouted and there was no patience for delaying our longed-for ambitions, we set out for battle. The artillery forces and the armored and airborne divisions rained fire for an hour and a half and blew up the German positions. After "the weakening," we swept down on the German lines. The Germans fired an inferno from machineguns and mortars toward our regulars' line. Our battalion couldn't advance. I could tell where the heavy fire was coming from, and I went to the battalion's commanding officer for permission to take out the German mortar positions. He agreed, and together with my aide, Arlov, I opened heavy fire from behind. This was a surprise to the Germans, and it finished them off. We destroyed their mortar position, and our battalion was now ready to advance without difficulty. For this action I received a medal, the Red Star. Our division, the 192nd Tashkent, liberated Brody. And after Brody, many cities and town in the region. We continued on to Lvov (Lemberg).

I Lose My Right Leg

Between July 14 and 17, we met with little resistance, but when we got close to Lvov, we encountered strong German forces defending the city. In order to withstand the enemy forces, our commander, Gretshko, asked the soldiers to volunteer to go out on a scouting mission. Not many volunteered, but I myself did.

The commander put me in charge of a group of soldiers. Our orders were to pinpoint the enemy's firing site. I went out to scout as the head of the group. The Germans were firing at everything. When we approached, we found ourselves face to face with the Germans, and a horrible battle raged. Many of our group fell, and many were injured. Suddenly I felt a strong blow to my right leg as though fire were shooting through me, and I was covered with blood. I lay bleeding on the battlefield for three hours because the field medics couldn't rescue me under the heavy fire that was being launched close to me. Finally, our men were able to repel the Germans. I was brought to the closest first aid field station in very grave condition.
[page 249]

My right leg was punctured with bullets, and my left leg was also injured, but less so. The station medic immediately amputated my leg below the knee. This was on July 7, 1944.

I was brought to the army hospital in Rovno, and I stayed there for two weeks. The Germans bombed Rovno, and all those who were injured badly were sent in a special medical train to the Caucasus. I was in terrible condition the entire way. I suffered from terrible pain and high fever. Because of this, the health services' chief physician transferred me from the train to army hospital 4656 in Rostov.

I was put into a private room. No one from the staff believed that I would pull through and stay alive. I stayed in this hospital for nearly a year. During that time, I was able to recover and regain my strength. There I met another soldier from my same battalion who was injured near the Vistula River. He told me that after I had been injured on the battlefield, many spoke highly of me and praised my efforts, and also that I had been recommended for the highest award, the Red Banner.

News from Radzivilov

In the hospital I met a fellow from Radzivilov, Mendel Vaynshteyn (now in Russia). He got out of the hospital before me and went back to Radzivilov. Then he returned to the hospital and told me that a few survivors had returned to the city, and that my uncle Nechemye Porochovnik was among them. He also told me that all the Jews of Radzivilov, which was now in Russia, intended to go to Poland. Hearing this, I decided to leave the hospital and return to Radzivilov, but my injury hadn't yet healed and the doctor refused to discharge me, so I appealed to the hospital administrator, a Jew, Major Yakov Kelman, and told him why I wanted to leave the hospital. He understood my distress and let me leave.

While I was in the hospital, I married Gertrude Kalishnikova.

Return to Radzivilov

On April 28, I reached Radzivilov. I found my uncle Nechemye and other Jews who had survived. They were all preparing to go to Poland. My uncle and I decided not to go to Poland. I still wanted to take revenge on the Ukrainian murderers who had killed our family and caused such agony to the Jews. We decided to trace the Ukrainian murderers and report them to the NKVD. After much difficulty and dreadful searches, I found a few of the murderers, in particular Mikhal Zalewski, the town police commander in Radzivilov; Jefimczuk, his deputy; Tushakovski, who worked for the SD; and Zudanowski, the civilian police commander.

All of them had a hand in the killing of the Radzivilov Jews. They were sentenced to 25 years' hard labor by the Soviet army court, each and every one of them. In addition to the "big ones, "the "lesser ones" from the police, like Demko and others, were also sentenced. After they had been brought to punishment, I felt that I had fulfilled my vow and my duty to humanity.

After the war's end, I worked in Rovno for a few more years, until 1949. In 1946 my daughter Irit was born, and in 1949 my second daughter, Tova, was born.

In 1949 I was recommended to be named a manager of a factory in Radzivilov. I worked in this capacity for two and a half years. But it was difficult to continue to live in the city where my family and all the Jews had been slaughtered. I requested a transfer, and I was sent to Zdolbunov. I worked there from 1951 to 1954. In 1954 we decided, my wife and I, to go to the Urals, and we settled in Chelyabinsk. We lived there until 1956. I received a letter giving me permission to return to Poland, and I decided to go to Poland with my family in order to immigrate to Israel, where my uncle Nechemye had been since 1948.

We were in Breslau, which is in Poland, for seven weeks, and at the end of April 1957, we immigrated to Israel.

We stayed with my family in Shaar HaAliya. And after 10 months, the Jewish Agency moved us the Holon. Now I work in the Globus factory in Tel Aviv.

Finally, I want to add this important information, that the chief gendarme in Radzivilov was Krauser.

[page 251]

Review[*]

Ite Gun was 55 when war broke out between Germany and the Soviet Union. During the German conquest, she faced danger many times and survived only through perseverance, especially during the final days before liberation.

She came from a wealthy family. Her father was a merchant who owned large, successful enterprises. During her childhood, she attended high school, and after her marriage in 1905, she ran her own businesses—a matzo factory and home supply stores. After her husband's death, she continued to run the businesses until 1939, when the Russians came.

Her businesses were very successful, and she became wealthy. She attended very well to her two daughters. Radzivilov Jews remember her as a wealthy, respectable woman, very clever and determined, a woman who succeeded in everything she did. Thanks to her talents, she was able to survive the dark period of German occupation until she was liberated.

Actually, to her the German occupation was just the continuation of the troubles and sufferings brought by the preceding Russian occupation.

When the Soviets began their rule, her stores and the matzo factory were taken from her. The matzo factory was turned into a bakery. She worked in it as a lowly worker in the "bourgeoisie." The Soviets treated her badly. She received identity papers stamped with *"seif,"* that is, someone assigned a lower rank among the citizenry and likely to be exiled to Siberia with her family. Many nights she lay sleepless, because every knock on the door aroused fear of the NKVD.

Many wealthy women were sent to Siberia, but she was tried once for leaving work a half-hour earlier than usual without permission. When the

---

*Translated from Hebrew by Elizabeth Kessin Berman. *Note in original:* From an oral history taken at Yad Vashem; the summary and transcription of the testimony were written in Yiddish by Mr. Alperovich and translated by Mr. Tsvi Sley.

Germans occupied the town, she already was broken in body and spirit. Because she was well known as a once-wealthy woman, the Ukrainians did not overlook this, and they paid her visits quite often and stole anything they wanted.

[page 252]

Nor did the Germans leave her alone. The *Judenrat* and the Jewish police made her life miserable, especially the head of the *Judenrat,* Yakov Furman. He frequently demanded money, as well as gold and other precious objects, for himself and the Germans.

She escaped from the roundups twice, once during the destruction of the Radzivilov ghetto and once during the destruction of the Brody ghetto. In these two episodes, she was helped by a peasant named Pietro Moroz. The period from her flight from the Brody ghetto until liberation was the most difficult for her: 17 months without a roof over her head, wandering from place to place in fields, wetlands, forests, frost, and snow, clothed in rags and starved for bread. She was content if she could lie down in a pen with pigs, eating the food in their trough. For several months she hid in a hollow tree with her nine-year-old nephew. At every turn and every step, there was something to haunt a Jewish soul, whether it was the Ukrainians, Germans, police, or peasants. It required a great deal of effort, caution, and vigilance not to fall into these pursuers' hands. And she was not only concerned for herself—she was responsible for her nephew, the her only remaining family member. Not once did she succumb to despair or become indifferent to her existence; it was enough for her to look at her nephew and think of his possibilities, and she got the strength to overcome her desperation.

Now she is 76 years old and lives in Tel Aviv with her daughter, who immigrated to Israel in 1925. For her, memories of her terrible trials elicit sorrow, but also a strong desire to transmit this testimony. With my questions, I tried to arouse her memories and thoughts. A year ago, she received a picture from the nephew whom she saved. He is now in the Soviet Union studying in a conservatory in Rovno. She keeps this picture as if it were a holy relic.

Testimony: Ite Gun Recalls

Date and place of birth: Radzivilov, 1886

Residence: Tel Aviv, 6 King David Blvd.

Relatives who died during World War II: Her daughter, Sheyntse Norban, born in 1908, and her husband and child, aged 7; and many other family members.

Ite Gun reports:

I was born in Radzivilov. My father was a merchant. He owned a haberdashery store.

[page 253]

I was educated at the Russian high school. I was married in 1905 to Aharon Gun. He died in 1920. I had two daughters, one named Tsipore Yenai, with whom I now live; she immigrated to Israel in 1925. My second daughter married Chayim Norban. We lived together until they were killed. During the Russian period and after that under Polish rule, I had a store selling housewares and also a large factory that made matzo. I supplied matzo to every region in Volhynia. After my husband died and my daughter got married, we continued to run the businesses until the Bolsheviks occupied the town. I was a wealthy woman, running a large, well-appointed home and educating my children well. We lived well until war broke out between Germany and Poland. A few weeks later, the Russians came upon us.

Life under the Soviets

As the Russians took over, we wealthy people were filled with fear, knowing that many would be sent to Siberia. I feared that they would send my family and me. When the Russians started handing out identity cards to the citizens, they stamped the merchants' forms with *"seif."* My daughter, my son-in-law, and I naturally got these stamps.... I believed that it would be better if I voluntarily handed over all of my businesses to them, including the matzo factory and flour warehouse. I only asked them to allow me to continue working there, and they agreed. The matzo factory was transformed to bake bread for the residents. Because the flour warehouse was at my house, I was put in charge of the flour.

Once I left work a half-hour early without receiving prior permission from the labor manager. One of their "big shots," a Jew like me, accosted me and asked me where I was going during work hours. I told him, and he answered, "You're on work time. You must be a saboteur. I'm reporting you to the authorities." The judge turned to be the chairman, who declared that I was a "*borozeka*," that is, a bourgeoise, and that I was committing sabotage. So he deducted 120 rubles from my wages, 25% of my monthly salary, for 6 months. I was warned that if I did this again, I would be put in jail.

They wanted to confiscate my house. But it remained mine because my son-in-law was a member of the proletariat.

There was a complete shortage of everything, and long lines for bread and other basics formed in front of the shops. Because I worked in the bakery, I was assured a supply of bread, and I could also give some to others. There were Jews who worked for the Soviets and they became wealthy. They took out their anger on the Christians, and this caused an increase in antisemitism.

[page 254]

During the German occupation, the Christians took revenge for this on the Jews.

As I said previously, I was constantly in fear of being exiled. Even though the Soviets were for now occupied with expelling Polish officials, I thought they'd soon turn to us. In the meantime, during the Russian occupation I gave shelter in my house to two boys from Stanislau who had escaped from a German camp. One was named Suretski, and the other, Zelzinger. They were both well educated: one was a German teacher, and the other studied mathematics. Both helped me afterward, when the Germans came. We lived in fear until the German-Soviet war. At the end of June 1941, the Germans entered. From the outset, the Ukrainians celebrated the Germans' takeover, being anxious to avenge themselves on those who had collaborated with the Soviets, communists, and Komsomol members.[*]

Before the Germans entered, the "members" tried to flee, but they couldn't because the Germans were already advancing on the main roads, and they were forced to return. The Ukrainians started to go from house to house stealing anything they wanted. The Germans ordered all Jews to wear a strip of white cloth on their arms with a blue Star of David. Later, it was a yellow patch on the front and back.

The First Jewish Victims

The Germans gathered 30 Jews and ordered them to dig pits in the forest. Then they shot them. Among them was Zalman Leviten, the account manager at the station; the rabbi Yakira; and a young man, Sunye Zilberman.

The Germans Persecute the Jews

Once, the Gestapo entered our house, opened the closets, and chose the best clothing. After that, they went into the flour warehouse that the Russians had abandoned and ordered my son-in-law to load a sack of flour on their vehicle. After he had loaded it, they told him to wash and clean up, especially his chest region, because they intended to shoot him in the heart. But this all was to frighten us, because they left the house without shooting him.

Once a German entered my house, went upstairs, broke a desk, stole all sorts of things, and then fled. The situation was terrible. For entire nights I didn't close my eyes, and every noise outside caused me to panic about being robbed.

Once two Ukrainians were passing our house and saw my son-in-law standing outside without his yellow patch. They dragged him to headquar-

---

[*] *Note in original:* Abbreviation for *Kommunisticheskii Soyuz Molodyozhi,* the Union of Communist Youth.

ters, beat him hard, and sent him into the basement. I saw everything, and I asked a policeman, someone I knew, to help me free him.

[page 255]

He promised to take care of the matter, and I believed him because within a short while, they released my son-in-law. Again, everything ended just in fear.

It seems to me that it was in February 1942 that the Germans ordered all the Jews to move into the ghetto within just a day. We thought maybe it would be better if we were all together. The terror would not be that great. Everyone took what he or she could. I took a lot of basic food to eat, enough to last for at least two years. The Germans came into the ghetto only infrequently. My son-in-law worked outside the ghetto; he delivered German messages, so he had permission to walk freely around the city. But at night, he had to sleep in the ghetto. Before the war, a young Christian girl, Hanye Shaykovski, worked for me for 13 years, and she was very devoted to us. Every day she would come to the ghetto fence and bring us packages of food. On Thursday she would bring a hen for the Sabbath. Once a Ukrainian policeman stopped her, beat her, and dragged her to headquarters. She begged them to forgive her. He threatened her that if she were found again anywhere near the fence, she would pay with her life. I gave him 50 gold coins, and he released her. She never came again.

In the ghetto, I was in a room with 11 other people. It was very crowded. We managed somehow with the food, and I helped others. As I have already said, I was fully provisioned, and my son-in-law would also bring something every day.

The *Judenrat* and the Police

We suffered a lot at the hands of the *Judenrat* and the police. The *Judenrat* chairman was Yakov Furman. He was crude and very evil. They exploited us, especially those who had once been wealthy. They demanded money, gold, and all the rest for themselves and the Germans. Yakov Furman wanted my son-in-law to work for the *Judenrat*. But he refused. I would never have believed that Jews could be so evil, harsh, and without conscience, ready to take the last piece of bread from your mouth. It's true that the Germans demanded money and gold and gold wares daily, and the police were charged with collecting it all. I gave everything I had, but they divided the ghetto into the "useful" and the "not-useful." The "useful" were given passes, and the others were not. My son-in-law was given a pass that included his family. I was not given a pass, but I continued to live with them. When the news came of the extermination of the "not-useful" Jews in Dubno, we knew what awaited us ....

Before the extermination, Yakov Furman said to me, you can't live in the ghetto. You must go with the "not-usefuls." He knew that in a few days the ghetto would be destroyed, and he wanted me to go there. But I knew that going there would mean my death.

[page 256]

The "not-usefuls" lived in constant fear. Even those who were in the part of the ghetto sanctioned for the "usefuls" but did not have passes shook with terror. As I have said, I didn't have a pass, so what was I to do? I said earlier that during Soviet rule, I hid two boys, and now both were working for the Germans. One was a translator, and the other worked in an office. They very much wanted to help me, but they couldn't. When the Germans surrounded the part of the ghetto for the "not-usefuls," Suretski came to me and said, "Don't be afraid. I'll stay with you, and you'll hide in the closet. When they see me, they won't search any more." And that's how it was. The Germans forced all the Jews out to a place beyond the forest and killed them, but I stayed alive. A few who escaped told of how the Germans and Ukrainians dragged the elderly and sick from their homes and loaded them into wagons and trucks and brought them to their deaths. Those who rebelled were shot on the spot. The Germans promised not to harm the "usefuls." The rabbis also clung to a vain hope. But everyone knew that you could not depend on the Germans' promises, and they began to look for ways to escape. Peasants came to negotiate hiding places in exchange for a lot of money. Happy was the one who had good acquaintance with a peasant. The owner of the house in which I lived went to Mateyko (the mayor) and asked him how long we would be in the ghetto. He answered that we would still eat the summer fruit, but not the winter fruit. We understood what he meant well enough.

We Flee from the Ghetto

Peasants came and told us they were digging pits again. We didn't want to believe it. We thought the peasants wanted to plant fear among us so we would go ahead and stash our gold and money with them. No, the pits were for storing potatoes during the winter. They were creating distractions because in Brody, the Jews weren't suffering so much, and there was still no ghetto there. So why would they want to kill the Radzivilov Jews?

I had an acquaintance with a peasant whose name was Pietro Moroz. He said to me, "Don't be afraid. When the time comes, I'll hide you and your family with me." My son-in-law said, "How long can we hide with a gentile? Who knows how long the war will last? He can't hide us for long." But there was no other choice.

And the time certainly came. The Germans and police surrounded the ghetto—the "action" had begun. We decided to flee one after another to one of the peasants whom Moroz had told us about. At night, Moroz would come and take us to his home. When we were fleeing from the ghetto, Itshi Treybitsh's family saw us—he, his wife, and two of his children. They said to us, "Wherever you're going, we're going with you. We won't leave you."

[page 257]

When Moroz saw them, he said he couldn't take them, only my family. He wouldn't let them enter his home, and he left us all of us in the forest. He was too afraid to hide so many people. While we were in the forest, the German killed the Jews in the ghetto.

In the surrounding area, a rumor was spreading that about 20 Jews from Brody who had a lot of money were hiding in the forest. Suddenly a peasant appeared holding an axe and asked, "What are you doing here in the forest?" We answered, "We're resting for a while before we continue to Brody."

We didn't want him to think we were staying in the forest. I gave him 100 marks, and he went off, but afterward two others came with the same tune, so the whole business began again.

When Moroz returned, we told him that peasants were coming all the time. He agreed to take us to another place. The Treybitsh family stayed with us. The second place was not far from Brody. He said, "No one will harm you here." He also promised to bring food. The new place was a pig-slaughtering field owned by a wealthy peasant. The following day, workers came to turn the pork. We afraid they would see us and turn us over us to the Germans. When Moroz came again, we told him we couldn't stay there: it would be better for us to go to Brody, where Jews were still living. Moroz brought us food, and then another peasant came and, for money, took us to the border. We got to Brody safely.

The situation in Brody was very bad. There was nothing to eat. The Germans were choking everything out of the Jews under threat of death, everything they had. But there was still no ghetto. A few Jews made hiding places for themselves. My brother's sister-in-law, Selki Potashnik, was in Brody. I stayed with her. After that, we moved to another flat. After five weeks, the Jews were concentrated into a ghetto. This was during Passover 1943, and our house was in the ghetto. Conditions in the ghetto were very bad: there wasn't anything to eat, it was impossible to leave the ghetto to get any food, and I knew nobody. Someone told the *Judenrat* I had once been a wealthy woman, and they demanded that I hand over my money and gold. They didn't believe I had nothing left, and when they heard I had nothing to give them, they threatened to throw my son-in-law in prison. But he hid. What did they do? They took my daughter and held her in jail for six days, all the while threatening not to release her until I handed over my money. The chairman of the *Judenrat*, Barash, was an acquaintance of mine. I went to him, begging him to release my daughter, and he answered, "When her husband comes, we'll release your daughter." There was no other way. My son-in-law went to them, and they released my daughter. After some time, they also released him.

The Germans demanded young men for labor brigades from the *Judenrat*. They gathered more than 300 young men, including my son-in-law. They sent them to a camp in Olevsk. There they killed everyone. This was at the beginning of 1943.

[page 258]

After my son-in-law's death, I stayed with my daughter and two grandsons. Suddenly, the Germans surrounded the ghetto. My daughter, the two grandsons, and I hid between two fences. There were 19 Jews there. From there, we saw the Germans going through all the houses and dragging Jews out of their hiding places, throwing them into the fire, and shooting them. We hid there for a few days. At every moment, we saw death before us. One of Barash's deputies, Shmuel Sherer, told us that it would be best for us to flee. At night, we left and returned to Moroz. When he saw so many people with us, he refused to let us inside and left us in the forest. We were eight people. Suddenly the Germans and police surrounded the forest and began to approach us. My daughter and the children turned to run away, but the Germans ran after them. I was weak and fell to the ground. The Germans paid no attention to me and continued to pursue them. They caught my relatives and family and killed them. After that, they also killed my daughter and grandson. The other grandson, Siunye, aged nine, hid, and the Germans never saw him. I lay there until evening; the death of my dear ones broke me completely. I longed for my death, because nothing in my life had value. After a few days, Moroz found me and told me he had found my grandson Siunye. I was happy that at least my grandson had survived.

Moroz could not keep us at his house because his wife objected, so he hid us in a hollow tree in the forest, and he would bring us food. It was difficult to approach the tree. It was surrounded by water, and only with great effort could he get close enough to give us the food.

It is difficult to recall everything that happened to us. I am already tired, so I'll cut my story short.

Once, some peasants killed six Germans. The Germans raided and took their revenge on them. They also went into Moroz's house because, it seems, he had been accused. They killed his wife and burned his house, but he himself managed to escape. But we were left without anyone to help us and without food. I had to go from house to house to beg for food. The gentiles were anti-Semites, but I was surprised that no one turned us over to the Germans and that they didn't kill us themselves. My grandson and I wandered like this, sleeping outside in the snow, starving and clothed in rags. Days passed when we ate nothing at all. I felt that my strength was leaving me. Many times, my grandson and I slept in the feeding trough of the pigsty. More than once I told my nephew, "My child, I'm already lost, I can't go on any longer. But you're still young. Go on and save yourself." But he didn't want to leave me. He said his fate was linked to mine. At one point, my strength completely gave out. I crawled on my knees for almost four kilometers until I got to a village, and I stayed there lying in a field, begging for death. So it was for me for about 17 months. The most difficult were the last three to four months.

[page 259]

Meanwhile, the battlefront was coming close to Radzivilov. This was in spring 1944. I went to a peasant woman's house and asked for food. At first, she wouldn't let me in. But when she heard the Soviets were approaching, she changed her mind. She gave us food and also a place to lie down. She even suggested that we stay. A peasant came and told us that the Russians were in the village, but in withdrawing, the Germans had set fire to the village. My grandson and I started walking to the forest. One peasant allowed my grandson to ride on a wagon filled with pork, and I walked. the Russians were coming along the way. The boy caught their eye, and they gave him food and clothing. He stayed with them. I was very happy because they loved him; they called him "the wandering boy."

I went to Radzivilov. My house was destroyed and burned. There were a few Jews wandering alone. After a few days, I went on to Dubno. There I found Shmuel Gun, my brother-in-law's son, who is now in Tel Aviv. I stayed with him until 1946, and then I went to Poland, to Beuthen. From there I traveled to Austria. I was in a refugee camp until 1948. From there I went to Israel, to my daughter, Tsipore Yenai.

A year ago, I received notification that my grandson was still alive. I later received a letter from him with a picture of his wife and son. He is in Vladimir, a student at the Rovno Conservatory. I cherish his picture like the pupils in my eyes.

A Daughter of Radzivilov on Her Town*

Shifra Poltorak

Jewish Radzivilov, which established and supported a large Hebrew day school dedicated to Zionist education; the town that fostered a pioneering kibbutz with about 150 people and supported its members with different employment and cultural institutions; its community, which encouraged public and charitable institutions—this Radzivilov, which was so much like other towns in Volhynia, suffered under the pressure of the Nazi boot and endured, and then disappeared completely from the world. Its Jews suffered until they were herded out to their slaughter and killed in places of carnage. The final resting place of the Jews of Radzivilov was in vast graves outside town.

The downfall began before the end of 1939, when the Russian Red Army entered the town and expelled the Poles. From then on, the character of life changed. Private enterprise was forbidden by the new government. Businesses were closed, or banned, or forfeited to the government. The rich of yesterday were debased, and those suspected of private commerce were deported to the interior of Russia. The Hebrew school became a Yiddish

---

* Translated from Hebrew by Elizabeth Kessin Berman.

school, and its teachers were sent away. Everyone was forced to do compulsory work, and 15% of their salary went to the government.

[page 260]

Many also worked outside the town. The Jews of the town found it difficult to adjust to the new order. But these days didn't last long, and soon enough the Russians also evacuated Radzivilov as the Germans advanced. When they entered the town, the terror began immediately.

The first thing the Nazis did when they occupied the town was to gather 25 young Jewish men and women accused of being Bolsheviks, according to a list—which apparently was supplied by the local Ukrainians. They were taken to the forest close to town, commanded to dig a grave for themselves, and shot right there. This act alone was just the first act of terror for the Jews. After that came one decree after another, orders, announcements, and extortions, in order to abuse the Jews until one day they made a selection of Jewish professionals from among those who had no trade and forced them into a ghetto.

Communiques from different sources on the Nazis' acts of murder against the Jews made the hair stand on end. The situation worsened day by day. What were the Jews of Radzivilov to do? Escaping from the ghetto was very difficult, because there were not only Germans to contend with, but also Ukrainians out for the Jews' blood, willing to catch any Jew trying to escape and deliver him into the murderers' hands. For those professionals, the Germans forced them into different kinds of tasks. They endured their suffering only in the hope that they would one day escape from this desolation.

And finally, the time came for the destruction of the children of Radzivilov. One day, 13 Sivan 1942, Nazi storm troopers rounded up 1,500 non-professionals from the ghetto—old folks and children—and marched them, men and women separately—to the train station. There they were surrounded by uniformed Ukrainian security guards. That same day, they were cruelly killed. Some of the poor souls tried to flee. But the Ukrainian guards shot them, and almost all of them were killed (these events were described by those who miraculously escaped).

The fate of the professionals was not much better. After the slaughter, they continued to live in severe pain and suffering for the better part of a year, until 5 Tishrei 1943, until the bitter day came for them, too, and they all were taken out and killed.

The Jews who had previously been deported by the Russians to work details outside Radzivilov fared better, spending their time in Russia and escaping the Nazi slaughter. Some Jews managed to hide or take temporary shelter in Brody or neighboring villages. Some of them were rounded up and killed.

Some Jews found refuge among evangelical sects in a few Volhynian villages. But the Ukrainians searched for and found them. It should be pointed out that the evangelicals showed respect to the Jews who were hiding with them, but not one of them endangered himself on behalf of the Jews.
[page 261]

Those who survived in this way were R' Yosil Hoyzman, an elderly 75-year-old; Roze Fik, aged 30; Sore, Yitschak-Leyb Karsh's daughter, and his brother and sister; Moshe, Bilhah, and Shifra Poltorak; and others. The latter three found refuge with the Baptists in the village of Kopilovka in 1942, staying until the Germans were defeated in 1944. In one village, Yanivka, almost 50 Jews were hidden.

There were few left among the remnants of Radzivilov, but they turned their backs on their homeland and went to the Land of Israel.

Fate*

Bela Finkelshteyn-Rashin

On that dark day, I set out for the ghetto gate. My father was already gone. The Germans took him and didn't bring him back. My brother, Munye, was also gone. He fled the ghetto and disappeared, and to this day we have not seen him.

---

* Translated from Hebrew by Elizabeth Kessin Berman.

At the ghetto gate, a guard was posted, and he didn't allow anyone to pass. I stood on the opposite side gazing outward. Where to go? There was a wide expanse before me.

Suddenly a vehicle stopped, and an ethnic German got out. He addressed me in Polish and told me he could bring me to a safer place, where perhaps he might save my life. Such a decision to make, quickly and measured.

But how? And I was so young. I lacked courage and experience. I was worried. I didn't know him at all! I hesitated—how could I leave my mother alone? In one moment, thousands of confusing thoughts filled my mind. I was sick with panic. I longed for freedom, to cast off of the chains of the ghetto. But thoughts of my mother kept me from fleeing. I stood for a few seconds, dumbfounded. I didn't know what to do. And then I ran to tell my mother.

She didn't waver for a second; she didn't ask me who, and who the man was. Out of motherly instinct, she felt that saying "yes" could save my life, and she said—I will never ever forget her words—"Run to him and go. God will watch over you!"

I ran to the gate and was seized by so many different questions. Will he wait for me, will he already be gone? But he was there. He had waited for me.

We drove without exchanging a word. I didn't dare ask him who he was or what he was doing. I didn't know where he was taking me or what my future would be. Who among us could think of a future? Our life was living from day to day. Only the bitter present agonized us more.

[page 262]

We traveled to Rovno. There he began to speak in measured words: I am Yuzhek, and you are my sister. We arrived at a house belonging to a Polish family, and he introduced me to them as his sister. It was clear that he was very dear to this family.

I was fortunate that they didn't ask me any details. Where did I come from? Why? And, naively, nor did I prepare any responses for myself in case I were to be besieged by many confusing questions from all sides.

Sunday came. The girls of the family were going to church, and they invited me to come along. I managed to evade going, telling them that because my coat was torn, it was unpleasant for me to go out. Yuzhek was certainly going to bring me one. I don't know if they believed me, but in any event, I got out of going.

Yuzhek was like a meteor. He would appear with some necessary things, and then he would vanish just as he had come.

One day, we heard that Yuzhek had been apprehended by the Gestapo and jailed. I fled the house with nothing, not even a walking stick. I wandered into many mishaps and dangers. But the hand of fate led me and saved me from the Nazis.

Today, from great hindsight, when I ask myself who this Yuzhek was, I cannot answer. But I believe without any doubt that he was a Jew who had disguised himself as a Pole to save himself and others.

[page 263]

The Evils and Hardships I Endured[*]

Sheyndil Oks

Editor: Arye Ayzen

The Germany-Poland War

In 1939, a war breaks out that sends fire throughout the entire world.

Hitler's army swiftly advances and conquers portions of Poland. The Soviet army mobilizes "to aid Poland" and consequently "liberates" Ukraine, agreeing to the new borders between them. My husband, Leyb Zats, and others are called to enlist by the Russian governors. I receive letters from him without ever knowing where he's stationed. After a time, I eventually learn that my husband and other men from Radzivilov are near Lutsk-Kivertsy. A few other women and I, anxious to visit our husbands, pay a

---

[*] Translated from Hebrew by Elizabeth Kessin Berman.

surprise visit, but it's too late—they've been sent to a faraway place in Russia.

Radzivilov, our town, is filled with refugees from many different places that have already been conquered by the Germans. They speak of the atrocities during the first days of the Hitler regime in their localities. Although no one wants to believe the murderers' hand will also come to us, this day does indeed come.

In 1941, on June 22, war breaks out between Russia and Germany. Cities and towns are conquered, one after the other. The refugees' warnings aren't just empty words anymore, but still no one wants to believe that the most evil of evils is upon us. Everyone comforts himself and even deludes himself, thinking, America and England won't allow this aggression. But in the meantime, the Jews have bigger problems: protecting their property, the property that the "good" gentiles will inherit afterward.

Our town is conquered by the Germans. The gentiles are incited, and they side firmly with Hitler. With each day come new proclamations, and the Jews begin to look for ways to escape, looking for "good gentiles" among their acquaintances, and these are rare. My sister, Sime Oks (Rishnivker), gets lucky: she gets the best situation, bringing her belongings to Langin Taranovski, the well-known priest, who is a good acquaintance. Gentiles from the town and its vicinity indulge themselves: they come every day with empty sacks and, with no interference, fill them with the best that the Jews have. And thus begins the stormy period, full of the evil and suffering of World War II.

[page 264]

The Jewish way of life is declared heretical. The city's governing body passes to the Ukrainian nationalists, who align themselves with the Germans and leave control in the SS officers' hands. Taranovski the priest is chosen as mayor; "ethnic German" Mateyko, the city manager; and good-for-nothing Ukrainians.

The First Command

All residents are commanded to black out their windows, allowing no ray of light to penetrate. Any noncompliance with the order means death. The first martyr is Avraham Yitschak Chomut, who unwittingly shifts the window covering. The German who sees this kills him right on the spot. After a few days, the Germans gather a group of innocent men and murder them in the Brody forest. Anguish falls on the town. It's clear that danger is ahead for everyone. The German commander and the Ukrainians are beginning to take vengeance on the Jews.

Another severe command: all Jews are to put a white strip with a Jewish star embroidered on it on their arms. After a time, they replace the strip with yellow patches so that the Jew can be seen from afar.

And again: every Jewish person, man and woman, is ordered to give up his or her gold, furs, and fancy-dress clothes.

After we are "liberated" from our belongings, making us, in effect, empty vessels, they begin to assault our souls. They set up a ghetto for us that is divided into two sections, surrounded by wire, I recall, and daily they start to take people out for work brigades under the guards' supervision. After some time, we find out that the Rovno ghetto has been destroyed and no Jew left alive. Not everyone believes these evil tidings. Many visit Sime Oks to hear what happened from her own lips because of her friendship with Taranovski the priest, who is now our "community leader." His good, well-known wife, Burotski the priest's daughter, steals into the ghetto to sneak a conversation with my sister. All the Jews believe my sister will live because the priest and his wife, with Dr. Burotski's help, promise to rescue her. My sister also sometimes sneaks out of the ghetto to the priest's house to hear new reports, because no newspaper that Jews can read can be found and no one can listen to the radio; thus her efforts become the Jews' news source. The ghetto Jews ask her to go out to collect news and wait anxiously for her return.

[page 265]

As the suffering grows, she returns one day from the priest's home with awful tidings for us, innocent Jews, that our fate is sealed and we are destined to die.

This is just before Shavuot, a holiday for us that coincides with their terror. We cower in despair, our spirits distraught, and the one thought, the one we have in our minds is, where will help come from? We peer outside— everything is alive and flourishing, the gentiles walking about wearing the Jews' fine clothing, which they stole, and their faces merry. Our hearts ache and our flesh crawls at this sight, but we are helpless .... On the street that divides the two sections of the ghetto, they stroll around like little devils, throwing stones and sticks, spitting in our direction, and taunting us, crying, "Look at yourselves, you Jews, you've lived too long!" We raise our eyes to the heavens as if to hope our salvation will come from the sky. Perhaps a miracle will happen, as has sometimes happened for Jews during times of woe, as in the prayer, "Our Lord of the world, give us the strength to stand fast against troubles that seek to destroy us." The sun rises, the night falls, and darkness engulfs the houses, because lamps are forbidden, and the windows have to be entirely covered so the starlight won't seep into our minds....

We cower in the darkness, but our hearts are aware that none of us knows what will happen to us. We then see searchlights illuminating the second section of the ghetto, and shortly after, we see bloodthirsty killers approaching with rubber clubs in their hands, shouting, hitting, and pushing the Jews from the ghetto—the sick, the old, decrepit folks who can hardly walk are shot in place. Infants, little children, become like sports balls in their hands. Young people and those of age are forcefully thrown and organized six in a row, under the armed German and Ukrainian guards' command, and herded like sheep to their slaughter. At the edge of the city of Suchodol, they find freshly dug pits, and they murder everyone in the pits there; the wounded and still living alike are buried with the dead....

So it is for our mothers, brothers, sisters, and children, ignorant of their slaughter, with no hope and no rescue for the Jews.

After the destruction of the first section of the ghetto, the area has all manner of things left behind by the victims: clothing, shoes, children's shoes, various books, prayer books that Jews used for praying and appealing to the heavens for a miracle. But the miracle never comes, it never comes.... The surviving Jews begin searching for gentiles they know who are willing to build bunkers for them.

[page 266]

Among those who are still alive after the first section of the ghetto is destroyed are the two sisters, Leyeke and Zelde Charash, and their mother, Dobe. They hid in the attic. Then the order comes: completely clear the space where the destroyed ghetto stood. Under the guards' watchful eyes, people from the second section of the ghetto are sent to work on the desolation. The two sisters and their mother leave their hiding place, blend into a workgroup, and join the work. Heartbroken and choking back tears, the people work to bring order to the belongings and clothing shed by the martyrs, their murdered brothers and sisters, doing their work under the Germans' excessive pettiness. The earth rumbles beneath us, the heavens cry out, and ominous blackness hangs over our heads. Who knows what awaits us, who knows if the future of those who have survived is to envy their lost ones, whose suffering and torment is already behind them!

Each day, Jews are taken out for different types of work brigades. They leave, and there is one prayer in their hearts: just let us return in peace!

One day, the German judge's uncle, Volodka Kobit, comes to the ghetto (I must point out that Sasha Kobit was a German judge in our town). He visits with us and offers help in rescuing us. Since I know Sasha Kobit from a happier time when he was a teacher and used to visit our house, I'm delighted with his offer and ready to go with him. But my brother doesn't trust him; he cautions me and tells me, "Sasha Kobit is no longer a teacher. He's a German judge, and Volodka Kobit is certainly the most notorious thief in town. He'll be the first to hand you over to the Germans. You're so naive, and you think you can trust everyone. We'd better go with Yashke Gopman. Many gentiles know him, and they've set up a large bunker for him and his whole family. They love him, he spent many years with Vladek the forester and another gentile, Vasil, in the Chotin forest. Gopman says that this is an 'iron bridge.' It's the only place where we can find salvation and get revenge for our murdered brothers and sisters."

Night falls, and we set out. I walk with Yakov Oks, his wife, and his little girl Zore. Yakov Gopman and his family are also with us. He's our guide, because he's familiar with the area. After walking for several hours, we come to the designated place. We crawl on our hands and knees through the thick branches, and we enter the bunker.... Gopman invites the owner to toast our safe and successful journey with brandy. After a while, we are content. The bunker is comfortable; we can talk with each other and go for walks in the forest. The bunker is well equipped, the gentile Vasil relates to us very nicely, and we don't want for food. He brings us good news every day.

[page 267]

The Germans will lose the war, the Russians are advancing, and it won't be long before we're free. However, one day he comes and tells us, don't leave the bunker because a small group of evil gangsters is gathering in the area, and they're likely to detect us and our shelter. In the meantime, he himself disappears. The Jews in the bunker maintain that he is no gentile—he is an angel. I'm the only one who doubts his words, and I try to leave the bunker. Gopman becomes very angry and orders me to come back. When I emerge from the bunker, my eyes are unaccustomed to the darkness: I see in the distance that we are surrounded by SS and Ukrainians holding weapons. I can still scream, "Jews, save yourselves!" My brother, who has gone out to call me back, is able to flee, but he wants to save his wife and his child. I hear shouting behind me, "Halt"—"Stop!" But I run on, panting and breathing with great difficulty. In the distance I hear my brother cry, "Zarumya, my daughter, run!" Alone, on my own in the dark night, I run in the dense forest. There's no one else with me. Where am I? Who am I? What use is it to prolong my life? What benefit can I bring? Alone, on my own, what awaits me? Who needs me? Everything is lost, lost without memory....

No, I have to go on and get to where I can see my dear, lost ones with my own eyes. Yes, Sheyndele—I am filled completely with confusion.—Yes, you go on in spite of your madness.... But Vasil will be there, Gopman's "angel," the murderer, who gave us all up to the SS. I now know everything, but what supernatural strength I have to propel me forward; I must go. I go blindly, with cautious steps; I fall soundlessly in the forest, and I fall asleep.

My Terrible Personal Tragedy

I'm awakened from a deep sleep by the steady howling of dogs. My first thought is that certainly something has happened, and immediately after, the murderers are certainly close by with their dogs, already looking for more victims. But I don't fear death anymore; I have no one left to live for. I continue.... Avoiding the howling dogs and the killers' boots, I come to the killing place and see my great tragedy: everyone who was in the bunker lies dead. Among them are my brother and his wife. My heart is broken. I tear my hair—but where is my brother's daughter? She isn't there among the dead.

[page 268]

I go to the forest and shout, Hear O Israel, God of gods, can this be possible? No one but the girl is alive? To fall into the murderers' hands and still be alive? Can it be that the girl knew to fall down with those who were killed and then run to safety? No, no, it can't be.

The day turns into evening. I'm alone in the middle of the murderers. I don't close my eyes, and I wander alone with a troubled soul and a bloodless heart. No tears and no end to my suffering—daylight comes .... I rise to face the turmoil of another day of existence. Alone, I am beset with an unnatural thought, and everything around me points to one idea: the girl. Where's the girl? Without knowing the danger that awaited her, wouldn't she, having no choice, run straight to the gentile murderer? I must run fast so that I won't waste any time. I wander the forest and the fields; I convince myself that maybe I can find the child? I comfort myself with this belief. It's very hard for me to find the killer's house, but finally I spot the house from afar. And in the yard, I see what looks like a child wandering around. I weigh carefully what I see. What kind of courage do I possess to push me forward? A miracle for me and the opening of the heavenly gates .... I hear the child's voice: "Sheyndele, you're alive?" "Yes, my dear one, I'm alive. And now I have someone to live and fight for."

Our joy has no limit. We laugh and cry and for a moment forget the events that brought us to this. I thank God that my lost treasure is restored to me. My child caresses my face with her small, shaking hands. Now there's someone who will comfort me. And then I see the killer on the side looking at me with his savage eyes and a smile of ridicule at the tragic reunion. No doubt he's telling himself, "Your happiness won't last long...." I know that I really must talk to him, so I tell him he was right to warn us not to leave the bunker. If we'd listened to him, everyone would have lived. The killer is pleased with my understanding.... He says they're not looking for Jews anymore. You can stay with him, the war is ending, and rescue is sure to come. He prepares some food for us, and drinks, and takes us to the woodshed. Then he tells us he has to go to Radzivilov, and tonight, when he comes back, he'll let us into the house to wash up a little. I eye the "angel" through murderous tears. I understand instantly that he's going to town to report us.

After he leaves, we decide to run away. We run away to the fields, far from his house, and we find a haystack along our way. We don't close our eyes, and we listen for any noise near us. Suddenly, we hear dogs barking insistently. We listen more closely, and in the dim night, we hear the murderer Vasil calling my name in Russian: "Sonye! Sonye!" We're completely covered, glued to one another, hardly breathing, our hearts beating wildly. We hear the guards cursing wildly like beasts after their prey.

They shoot at everything in their way. We crouch in terror and say a prayer, wondering if this is enough for our rescue. This time, we aren't discovered. We don't become their prey. Even after the terrible fright, the shots, and the barking dogs have passed, we still crouch in terror without moving or exchanging a word. After several hours, when peace has settled in our surroundings and normalcy returned, we know that dawn will come soon, and it will be impossible to remain there. We'll have to run. But where? All roads are dangerous for us, death surrounds us on every side and with every step, but even so, we have to fight for our lives and run as far as our feet can carry us. We want to approach one of the peasants to beg for a piece of bread. But the danger is still great. We walk slowly, bypassing the villages so we won't be recognized among the peasants, and so the day passes. In the evening, we enter the gentiles' cemetery, and there we remain for the entire night, frightened of both the dead and the sign of any living killers.

The light of day shines. We walk onward. We see a hut from afar and turn toward it. The peasant walks toward us, a murderous spark in his eyes. He doesn't even give me a chance to beg bread from him, but shouts, "You're still alive!" and raises his ax above our heads. I shout at him, "Just a minute! I want to tell you something. If I haven't found favor in your eyes, do what you want with me, but listen to me, my dear peasant.... We've been wandering along the edges of villages looking for shelter. We're staying in Baranye with a peasant. We have a lot of gold. If you agree, we'll stay with you until after the war. We'll give you all of it. We'll take it all from there and bring it to you here." The murderous gentile considers this. This suggestion appeals to him. He goes and brings us bread, water. He also agrees also to go to Baranye with us. We approach the river. He lifts up the girl and carries her, then me, across the water, and he shows us which way to walk. He himself is to wait by the river, and he warns us not to be too long. We walk on, our hearts trembling, and so we come to Baranye. The gentiles we knew before the war greet us with tears of joy. They tell us to hurry up to the attic before we're discovered. They bring us food and comfort us with kind words that better times will come, but we feel their fear. They tell us that Radzivilov is swept clean of Jews. Only in Brody is there still no ghetto, and many Jews from Radzivilov are there. We decide to go to Brody and decide our fate with all the Jews there. We have no more strength to freeze or struggle. The gentile knows this, and I ask him to be our guide on the way. I see that the gentile is afraid, but he has a compassionate heart. He wants to help us.

[page 270]

He tells us that the border is well guarded by German patrols. We completely understand, but we're determined to go. We have no choice. The good gentile goes to a neighbor, who knows the routes well, and asks him to haul some "banned goods." The girl and I change into gentile peasants' clothes. Our heads veiled and carrying baskets, we set out on the road with the two good gentiles, one walking ahead of us, the other behind us, hauling large jars for buying kerosene in Brody. Not far from the border, we stop near a tree. They walk on by themselves to inspect the area. When we approach the Germans stationed there, we cross the border without any incident, and we arrive in Brody safely. We reach the city—to our great shock, Jews are milling around looking for places available in the forests, the fields, the bunkers. Each day "actions," mass murders of Jews, take place before my very eyes, a well-known sight that I've already seen in this wave of terror.

We find our relatives, and they receive us graciously, but again we feel the household's pain. Radzivilovers come and tell me the news that my sister's son, Izi Viser, is still alive. I become so anxious for my family, and in my heart I think, who knows how long we'll live? My friends who live in Brody have already made themselves a bunker, and they're secure in the thought that they'll live.

One day, I meet a few gentiles from Radzivilov who have come to Brody to buy kerosene. I try to find out about Volodka Kobit from them. I say that he visited us before, when we were living in the ghetto in Radzivilov, and offered to arrange for our rescue. But my brother didn't believe him. But because Sasha Kobit had been a good friend of mine for some time and had often visited us, I see an opportunity regardless of my brother and send a letter to him through his uncle. In it, I ask for his help, saying that he's the only one with the power to save us from death. My letter must convey a heartfelt message, because immediately afterward, Volodka Kobit comes to get us, as he promised Sasha Kobit. People simply envy me. In these hellish days, this is great happiness.

Reye Kestler from Kremenets comes to ask how she can join us, and then my sister's son, Izi Viser. Volodka Kobit waits each day. They say we'll be going any day. I suggest to my friends from Brody that they come with us, but to our regret, they don't trust our guide. They just wish us well on the way to cross the border safely in peace. We cross the border without incident in the dead of night. Volodka Kobit takes us straight to his house and settles us in the attic. But we can't stay there because it's not safe. We have to find another place.

[page 271]

"Good gentiles" have apparently told the Germans that Volodka Kobit is hiding Jews at his house. One night, the house is surrounded by Germans, searching in every corner, torturing and beating Volodka Kobit, but they can't prove him guilty, and he doesn't give us up, because, to our great luck, we're in a temporary bunker not far from the house. Apparently, Volodka was already worried, and he tried to arrange another place for us until he found a bunker. It's no small thing to describe what Volodka does to save us, because in trying to rescue us, he puts his life in danger. Volodka pays no attention to this. He has one goal: to save our lives. He also helps other Radzivilov Jews find other bunkers.

The danger grows worse from day to day as the Germans continue to post their terrible orders: any gentiles caught offering help to a Jew will get the death penalty. But even so, Volodka Kobit goes from village to village looking for a secure place for us. With his knowledge of all the bunkers to which Jews have already been brought, he takes us to the village of Gai Leviatinski. There we meet Yitschak Treybitsh and his family, and we find refuge with them until liberation. Volodka, along with other gentiles, prepares a new bunker for us, even though it's still not completely safe. The Ukrainian police patrol from time to time looking for Jews. But we don't lose hope because every day Volodka comes with news: the day of our redemption is coming closer. He also announces to other gentiles that those who help the Jews now will be blessed, and a reward will come for their courageous help.

The time passes. Volodka Kobit often comes bearing good news, that the Russians are advancing and the Germans are beginning to withdraw. One morning, Volodka comes and tells me that in Radzivilov there are two young women wandering around who have been brought from different places. They're in grave danger from both the Germans and the *banaronim.*[*]

He doesn't know who they are, but the next time he'll bring a note from them. At that very instant, I don't care who they are. The important point is that they're daughters of Israel. Even though I've done so much for everyone, I can't add another person without the homeowner's agreement. But I know from Volodka, our rescuer, that there's another bunker with Jews in it not far from us, which Volodka set up, and he cares for them the same as he cares for us. I send them a letter via Volodka:

> Brothers and sisters! In Radzivilov, our town, there are two young girls wandering around whom I don't know. We must help them so they don't fall into the murderers' hands at night.

[page 272]

> They're surrounded by great danger, and we Jews must use our strength to help them. I'm willing to take one of them to our bunker, and I believe that you'll also agree to give one of them shelter. With this, we will all remain alive.

Soon an answer comes, and I write to the girls without even knowing them:

---

[*] *Note in original:* A Ukrainian platoon under Banadranko's command.

My dear girls, you don't know me. You can go with this man without fear. He looks poor, but he's a righteous man. God will help and lead you in peace.

Volodka Kobit doesn't waste a moment. That very night, he goes to get them. It turns out that they're Binyamin Likhtman's daughters. Our meeting is a shock, and we cry bitterly. I'm very happy that I can help rescue then. One stays with us until liberation. And the other pretty girl stays in the second bunker with Yitschak Vaynshteyn, Simche Simogran, Hirsh Kiperman, and their families.

Volodka Kobit sits by the radio listening with great anticipation to the latest Russian victories on the fronts. He comes to us immediately to share his joy that our liberation day is indeed coming soon. Suddenly we hear artillery fire from far away; it can be heard from all sides. The Germans run like poisoned mice from place to place and shout, "Hurry, hurry, the Ruskies are coming!" Our savior Volodka can't go home yet, so he stays with us and waits for the Germans' retreat and liberation by the Russians.

The Germans release their last command: that all gentiles must leave the village because it is now the front line. The German staff is stationed in our house; we stay cautiously in the bunker with no way to leave. Bombs explode over our heads. The earth shakes violently below us. We see for ourselves the lives buried under this landslide. It continues like this for a few more days, and still we can't leave. In the meantime, we're gripped by hunger and thirst.

In the middle of the night, Volodka decides to go outside. After a few seconds, he returns with the good news: the Germans have withdrawn, but we still can't leave because the Russians haven't yet occupied the village. More days pass until we hear the noise of vehicles and the rumble of tanks, and at the same time, we hear the sound of the Russian language. It's hard for us to believe that we can be happy and that this is our liberation day. While we're being liberated, Radzivilov, our town, is also being liberated.

We take our leave of the landlord, on top of the bunker, and thank him for the great kindness that he has shown us and all the goodness he has bestowed on us during the terrible days we endured.

[page 273]

And we, all of us who are still alive after the great destruction, set out to our town, Radzivilov, especially with our true savior and leader Volodka. We breathe the thick air, and we enjoy the clear blue sky, the blazing sun's rays, and a strong wind embracing and comforting us. Finally, we are free! We can begin to live our lives again.

We arrive in Radzivilov. We see the destruction of the Jews' houses. We hardly recognize the Jewish town before us. The Jews' houses are occupied by non-Jews, gentiles from the neighboring areas having settled in them. There's no trace of the displaced Jews. Everything is strange to us; there's no one to talk to and no one willing to talk. Only our rescuer's family welcomes us, receiving us in their house with joy. Our lives are a fairytale to their brothers and sisters. Volodka arranges a great feast, offers toasts, and we drink to the living, to life, to redemption, and to our liberation! We exchange blessings and well wishes for success in life renewed, Volodka Kobit with a cup of schnapps in his hand:

> My dear children who have clung to life! You know very well what I did on to rescue you ... Never forget your savior, Volodka Kobit!

During this gathering, I'm able to gather the exact details about my sister. They tell me about how the "holy" priest Langin Taranovski unexpectedly handed over my sister, Sime Oks, and her child. Her husband was held in jail by the police all night, knowing he'd be expected to poison himself. Sime Oks and her child were taken away by the city's murderer, Damko, who killed them. They tell me about the most tragic moment, when the child Liusik cried, "Mama, Mama, why do they want to kill us?" Tears choke me. My heart breaks within me, human pain.

I am compiling this for the benefit of the "holy and gentle" priest Taranovski with his great cross on his heart, who teaches morality and religion and preaches verses from the Bible, such as "Thou shalt not murder!" And he becomes a beast who cruelly sheds human blood. And for the simple and gentle gentile, Volodka Kobit, who was known as the biggest thief in the city and who revealed his good human, compassionate, and loving heart, with no thought of the danger that might swallow him, on behalf of the Jews, tortured and sentenced to death for no crime of their own. I can't find an answer to this. The heart bleeds, and deep sadness is all around ....

Let us never forget what the German murderers did to us.

[page 274]

Let us never forget, because those of us who are still alive after the great catastrophe and the terrible extermination of six million Jews aren't half-dead, sick, broken, and shattered like a tree severed from its roots. We must document the terrible tragedy we endured to pass on to the next generation, so that they will read and remember everything that the cruel Hitler beasts did to the Jewish people during World War II.

Those of us who survived until liberation day wandered like strangers in the town where we were born and grew up. There was no one to maintain order, no future whatsoever. We encountered here and there only remnants of the great families, wrapped in sorrow and sadness. And we felt that we couldn't even begin to rebuild our lives in the place where our brothers' and sisters' blood cried out from every wall. Every piece of earth .... Circling us were preying wolves who pitied us because we clung to life. We traveled on, on from the killing fields, through villages, cities, and towns, and came to the land of our yearnings, the Land of Israel, in which each one of us began life anew and built his home and family.

[page 275]

The Likhtman daughters also survived with us, content to reestablish a home and family. To our great sorrow, both sisters succumbed to illness. Dvore suddenly became severely ill. A few days before her death, she said to me, "Sheyndele, you protected me from the Germans' hands, but now your hand is too short to save me; my fate is sealed." She died before her time. May her memory be forever with us.

We, the Holocaust survivors, descendants of Radzivilov, continue to gather at my home to talk about various things, without ever forgetting for a single moment what we endured. We bring to light the memories beyond the horror, the place where we left our dear loved ones forever. May their memory be a blessing.

The Boy Liusik Oks

Sime Oks

Shlome Vaser and His Family*

Shlome Vaser

His Daughter Yokheved

Shlome Vaser was born in 1888. It is not known how he died. His daughter, Yokheved, who was called Sonye, was educated at the Tarbut School in

---

* Translated from Hebrew by Elizabeth Kessin Berman.

Radzivilov and later went to the University of Lvov. She was murdered by the Germans in Lvov in 1941.

[page 276]

Shlome's brother, Duvid Vaser, was killed in a group of young people after the Germans conquered the town.

Sore, his sister, Moshe Halperin's wife, who was murdered in Radzivilov, miraculously survived, went to the United States, and died there in 1963.

The other sister, Shlome's wife, lives in Akko.

The Story of Sore Halperin's Rescue*

Along with her whole family, Sore endured life in a pit in the forest with the aid of a peasant, Ivan Krug. The Germans were aware that there was a group hiding in a pit, and they surrounded the place and commanded everyone to come out. If not, they would all be killed. Everyone obeyed the order and emerged, and they were shot immediately on their exit. They were left there without even being buried.

Sore recovered, and in the dead of night remembered what had happened. She saw everyone lying dead and, with her last bit of strength, began to crawl to one of the peasants' houses. He brought her inside his house, bandaged her wound, and later brought her to Brody, to her husband's brother, Rofa. He brought her to hospital, where they operated on her throat, and she survived. But she had to leave the hospital and find a hiding place. She wandered in the fields until one day she encountered a peasant coming home from work, who took pity on her. He brought her to his cellar, where there were already a woman and her daughter. Each day, the peasant brought bread and soup. She remained there until liberation day.

After she emerged from the basement, she ran toward the town. On the way, she ran into Mrs. Ite Gun, and together they went on to Dubno after they did not recognize anything in Radzivilov. Sore stayed there for a couple

---

* Translated from Hebrew by Elizabeth Kessin Berman.

of weeks, then went on to Poland, and from there through Stuttgart, Germany, to the United States.

Life was terrible during the Nazi regime, and she was immersed in the memory. She grew ill, became an invalid, and died in 1963.

Yiddish Section

From the Past

[page 278]

**R' Yosef Royzman Blesses Shlome, Leyb Ayzen's Son,
at His Bar Mitzvah**

Radivil in My Memory ...[*]

Duvid Sheyn

It is with a pounding heart that I go about putting to paper my feelings about the town of my birth, Radivil. For every person, the place where his crib stood is dear, and of course it becomes almost holy after the passage of decades of time, and certainly more so after our great catastrophe.

I can see Radivil as lively as the town was in my very early years. In our family, they used to joke that I remembered things that happened before I was born. I don't know whether that is true, but the landscape, the environs, the customs permeated me even in my very young years.

It seems to me that to have an exact portrait of Radivil, one needs to see it from two points of view: a Radivil as a border town with a lot of customs houses, or *tamozshnia,* as it is called in Russian. In czarist times, there were six first-class *tamozshnias*, and Radivil was one of them. From Russia toward the west went great exports of agricultural products—of grain, poultry, and eggs. Dozens of families were employed in these lines of business, and they lived a nice life. Various products came from outside, through Brody (or Brod, as the Jews called it), and a huge number of people in Radivil worked for the customs agents who collected the customs. This was an extensive production, and many people worked in its service, earning good wages and living a fine life.

Twice a day—in the morning between 10:00 and 12:00 and in the evening from 6:00 to 8:00—the train station boiled like a kettle, with trains coming and going. There was a huge movement of passengers, and a few Jews were always among them—small-time shipping clerks. There were also a few semi-official jobs, but Jews made a living, and an honorable one. Besides

---

[*] Translated from Yiddish by Tina Lunson. *Note in original:* This article was found, unfinished, in the estate of Duvid Sheyn, of blessed memory.

the train, there was also the little border, as we called it: Radivil lay just four kilometers from the Austrian border, and from that border it was five kilometers to Brody. So the distance between Radivil and Brody was only nine kilometers. Jews drew a livelihood from there, too, but a poorer one. A certain number of Jews would come every day with a sad-looking nag, arriving in Radivil from Brody, bringing in a few items of linen and smuggled lace or linen shawl, as they were called, and other goods like that. They took a hen, a few eggs, things like that, back with them. There were no great successes here, of course, but this was their livelihood, and they managed with that. We called these people *shegernikes* or *shergenitses,* although no one knew what the word meant.

I must add that because of the border, a border patrol troop and a Cossack unit were stationed in Radivil. And, of course, there were contractors, and that was a livelihood for quite a few families. All in all, a prosperous town with a quiet business and cultural life.

The second "pillar," so to say, of Jewish life in Radivil was "Moshe Mendil Ginzburg." He had justly earned his immortality in the memory of all Radivilers, and he was an important chapter in our book. His usual place of residence was Sankt Peterburg (today Leningrad), but his aged mother lived in Radivil, and he was closely bound to her. He also had a brother and his family (Shmuel Mes) there and many friends. Ginzburg, or simply Moshe Mendil, came almost every year to visit his family, and then there was a holiday mood in the town.

[page 281]

Although his aged mother—Rosye, of blessed memory—used to give to charity with a generous hand, and there were families who literally lived on that support, the donations had an even larger character when Ginzburg was in town. One could really say that he had simply "stood people on their own two feet."

The abovementioned two factors were practically the foundation of the town's economic life. But it also happened that this not-so-big town had quite a few developed industries. Shmuel Mes (one of Ginzburg's nephews) founded a button factory. There was a chair factory (they were called Viennese chairs) that belonged to Zindel Zaks. Two factories produced lights: Goldgart-Liberman and Stroyman-Brandvayn, and there was a beer brewery.

The outward appearance of the town gave witness to its prosperity. There were fine houses, kept in good order, not only on the main street, Lipova, but scattered throughout the entire town. There were, especially in view of the smallish population, many coaches—or *veyezdn,* as we called them—with coachmen in beautiful, colorful dress. All this gave the town a local color of prosperity, and we didn't have the typical Jewish poverty. Of course, there was still small percentage of paupers.

There were two clubs in town: a social club, "Grozshdanski," in Mokhan the pharmacist's home, and the Shakhmat Club in Yone Sheyn's home. But these by far didn't exhaust the cultural life of the town. Before World War I, there were already many types of Zionist activity, *shekel* sales, distribution of shares in the Colonial Bank, distribution of the Zionist press, and foremost, of course, was *Hatsefira,* but also other publications in Hebrew. One must keep in mind that in Radivil, despite its smallish population, there was a large ration of Hebrew teachers. There was Sender Sforim, of blessed memory, whom we used to call Sender the Reader, because he was the Torah reader in the Great Synagogue; there was R' Ayzik Shtof, a person with inborn pedagogical abilities; and Katz (I do not remember his first name), who was a more modern teacher; and Binyamin Finkelshteyn, of blessed memory; and Avigdor Melman (who used to be called Avigdor the Writer).

[page 282]

**Group of Teachers and Students from the Elementary School
under the Leadership of Avraham Zats**

Schoolchildren on a Hike

He mostly taught girls. In later years Avraham-Yehuda Polak came from Berestechko (in Radivil he was known simply as Avraham-Yehuda). Avraham-Yehuda and Binyamin Finkelshteyn conducted pioneering work in the area of disseminating the Hebrew language, and they established courses for adults. That was an important part of Zionist work, as it was carried out at that time.

A large number of children were sent to continue their studies in the larger cities nearby—Dubno, Kremenets, Rovno, and so on, but there were many cases when parents sent their children off to more distant cities so they could study in special Jewish schools. I myself, for example, traveled to Warszawa and studied at the Krinsky business school for gentiles; Moshe Golgard's children studied at Kogan's high school in Vilna.

The Government Jewish School before World War I

After the outbreak of World War I, Kogan's school moved to Yekaterinoslav (Dnepropetrovsk), and I received my diploma there. And there was even an instance when a boy was sent to the Herzl school in Tel Aviv. There was a drive to education as well as to sociopolitical activity. I want to say that the intellectual level of the Radivil population was in general very satisfactory, especially among the youth.

Polish Elementary School

If one takes into consideration the relatively small population (... Jewish residents), there were two free government public schools: one for boys and one for girls. Besides the opportunity to study at the general school in town, the crafts school, and a private high school for girls operated by its owner, Mrs. Svirska, one can certainly say there was no young person who should not have an elementary school education.

[page 285]

It gave a further push toward an interest in literature and political-social questions. Then in this little community, there were, besides Zionists, also parties with other political directions, like the Bund, Labor Zionists, and others. They weren't highly regarded in town—they were called "the black shirts," but they read and discussed, and if not for their political leaning, they would have kept more backers. There was a curious incident described in town about a Bund follower who had truly devoted herself to the work of the party with heart and soul: in an argument with her "oppositional" mother, she had shouted, "*Okh un vey,* that [Czar] Nicholas is my father, and you are my mother!"

I must also mention praise for the teachers in town, who had a definite influence on Radivil children's first steps in life. One can say almost for certain that by far the largest number of youth started with cheder, that is, with an elementary *alef-beys* teacher.

Elementary School under the Leadership of A. Zats, 1923

[page 286]

There were two—Mikhel the Teacher, of blessed memory (with whom I studied), and Zalman Hirsh (one of his grandchildren is here in this country). After R' Mikhel the Teacher, the other boys my age and I went to R' Yisrael-Yone, where we studied the Five Books with Rashi. On the same level also stood Aba the Teacher's cheder, but it was considered more modern—a kind of reformed cheder. After that I went, again with all the others of my age, to Mordekhay Naftali's (the second cantor at the Great Synagogue). With him, we were already studying Bible. Then I went to an advanced teacher, a special teacher, so to speak—a higher-level study situation where one learned the special trope for Talmud. I continued studying with him in the summer months while I was home from Warszawa for the summer break. I may have omitted a name, because I remember best the ones I studied with. But I do remember another two names of respected teachers, and those are R' Aharele, who spent his last years in the poorhouse, the makeshift "hospital" for the poor, and whose former students—more correctly, his former students' families—supported him. I remember him because my older brother Abish was also one of his students, and I used to visit him as a messenger for packages from our home. I also remember the teacher from the higher level, R' Itsik Leyb. He lived near the Great Synagogue, beside the house of Rabbi Itsikel the righteous, of blessed memory.

I turn now to institutional activities. Social aid in Radivil occupies a separate chapter. All the fine institutions that Ginzburg built had their own budgets, and even if Ginzburg supported them with a certain sum, then an equal burden was laid on the population. Just as the economically secure stratum of the Jewish population—and there were quite a few—was happy to manifest its opportunities, in town they created a style of justice not only in their own homes but also in sustaining the institutions. I'll use the the poorhouse as an example. We all know what a poorhouse looked like in Jewish towns, but the Radivil poorhouse was an exception.

[page 287]

The poor actually did have good oversight, as far as that can be said about a poorhouse.

As a border town, Radivil also had a specific border social question. A heavy stream of emigrants passed through Radivil on their way to America. They stole across the border in Radivil, and from Brody they were free to get to Hamburg or Antwerp. In those towns, there were Jewish aid agencies that helped the emigrants reach their goals. But there were many sick people among them, especially those with eye diseases, and the admitting countries were very meticulous about not letting them in. So quite a few of them were sent back. They would be taken to the border near Brody, and then the Austrian police would bring them to the police in Radivil, and from there they were accompanied by troops back to their places of residence. The older generation understood very well what that meant, "going with the troop." They used to drive people from one village to another on foot (wagons were only for the old and sick who were literally unable to walk), and in each village the sheriff turned the group over to the next sheriff, who accompanied them to the next village, and so on to their village.

A Group in Radivil Welcomes Sirota

[page 288]

It was simply a death march. Especially tragic was the situation of children when they had let the whole family through except for one child who was sent back. The item of social aid was therefore difficult, because we had to have more means. These travelers had to be given money so they could buy food along the way, and also provided with train tickets. Besides that, they had to sign a written document that they would go back to their hometowns. And here it must be mentioned that that the whole population took part in this activity, and a large part of the aid was provided by ordinary people. They took people in to spend the night, helped them with food supplies, and took them to the train for no fee. I recall that in our house, we kept a little girl of six or eight years for a long time, until correspondence led to a grandfather in the Zhitomir area who could come to take her home.

Also, religious life in Radivil played a large role. Although there were no Hasidim in the real sense of the word, as in the Polish towns and villages, everything with us was done in strict traditional stateliness.

We can begin with the Great Synagogue. According to received reports, it had stood for 104 years; that is, it was built in 1811. In 1915, during World War I, it was blown up on an Austrian officer's order for some strategic reasons. After the war, the synagogue was rebuilt with Ginzburg's support, but it never achieved its former splendor. It was a perfect example of a type of wooden synagogue that was rarely encountered. It was of colossal size, having the height of a four-story building, with a splendid Holy Ark and a large reading platform in the center. Its woodwork was majestic, massive, with colossal brass candelabra. At the sides of the Holy Ark were two seats, closed on the sides and with roofs—we used to call them *budkelekh* [cabins]. These were the seats of honor.

[page 289]

The Cemetery

In one such *budkele* sat the government rabbi, the Kazioni rabbi; and in the other, the "new" rabbi. The synagogue windows were artistically painted with images from the Bible, and the soffit was decorated with the 12 zodia-

cal signs. It was truly a holy temple. Particularly etched in my memory is the synagogue on holidays, especially the Days of Awe. The solemn quiet of Kol Nidre, the serious faces of the observant Jews, created an atmosphere of dread and trembling, a feeling that one was truly presenting oneself for the Day of Judgment. And then the cantor—Yankel the Zvihiler (he came from Zvihil–Novograd Volynskiy)—slowly ascended the reading platform in his majestic figure with the broad, white beard, around him a significant choir, everything suspenseful, everything tense, and then, like thunder, the sexton (Shmuel Shames, of blessed memory) clapped with his mallet and one could hear the powerful bass voice of Yankel the cantor—Kol Nidre ....
[page 290]

Of course, the Kol Nidre was a solemn moment in all Jewish towns and villages, but for such a small community as Radivil, it had a greater range and a greater majesty.

I started with the Great Synagogue, but there were also many study halls in town, first of all the Spanish Study Hall (near an old cemetery that was evidence that Jews had lived in Radivil for hundreds of years and had come here after the expulsion from Spain). Some of the so-called "aristocrats" prayed in the Spanish Study Hall.

We had the Great Study Hall, the Barani, the Ostrer *kloyz*, the Tailors' Study Hall, and also a series of study halls with various rabbis. The study hall of Rabbi Chayim the righteous, of blessed memory (the "old" rabbi), at Rabbi Itsikel's, at Rabbi Yosele's, of R' Levi the righteous, of blessed memory. There was also the Rabbi's Study Hall. There was a Trisk *kloyz*, an Olik, an Ostrer, the Barani Study Hall, the Zamd Study Hall, and a study hall called Zisye Kop's (I do not know where the name comes from). So one can see that there were a large number of study halls in town besides the Great Synagogue, and all were always well attended.

So we must conclude that Radivil was, among the hundreds and hundreds of Jewish small towns, a certain oasis based on a quiet, honorable economic lifestyle, from shipping, merchandising, artisanry, and the free professions, with a multibranched cultural life. All this is the Radivil from the time up to World War I in 1914, with all the influences and events of that era.

The Radzivil Synagogue and the Ark That Was Struck by Lightning[*]

The Great Synagogue in Radzivil was famous throughout all of Ukraine for its extraordinary architecture and rare originality.

[page 291]

Although it was a wooden synagogue, it was built very high, with magnificent handcarved cornices and turned balconies, and spiral stairs leading up to the women's synagogue and even higher up to the windows of the four-cornered carved spire at the top of the roof. There was a round "hat" over the spire that looked like a huge satin skullcap. Inside, the soffit was painted with the 12 zodiacal signs. The walls were adorned with unusual paintings based on verses from the Bible, such as "The mountains skipped like rams, the hills like young sheep," "Our hands were spread like the eagles of the heavens," "He made my feet like a doe's feet," "Horse and rider are thrown into the sea," and others.

And just like the paintings, the citations themselves were painted in splendid color combinations. The letters were large and beautifully illuminated. It was clear that the anonymous artist loved the graphic arts very much, as was noticeable in the other verses and prayers written in the calligraphy with which he had adorned all four walls of the unique synagogue.

It is written in the Radzivil Jewish community register that in the time of the righteous R' Itsikel of Radzivil, Velvele of Zbarazh—son of Yechiel-

---

[*] Translated from Yiddish by Tina Lunson. *Note in original:* Extract from the book *Yidishe etnografie un folklor fun Avrom Rekhtman: zikhreynes vegn der etnografisher ekspeditsie, ongefirt fun Sh. Anski* [Jewish ethnography and folklore by Avrom Rekhtman: Memoirs of the ethnographic expedition led by Sh. Anski].

Mikhel of Złoczów—came to Radzivil for a Sabbath and prayed in the Great Synagogue.

The Great Synagogue

[page 292]

He loved the synagogue very much and could not praise it highly enough. After the Sabbath, when he left, while saying his goodbyes, he blessed the town, as was his custom, and also blessed the synagogue that it should never be destroyed and that no fire should ever touch it.

It turned out later that his blessing was completely fulfilled.

It was in 1883, the Sunday beginning the week for the Torah portion *Va-etchanan*, at ten o'clock in the morning, that a hellish fire broke out. The fire came from a butcher's house, where he was frying chicken fat. The day was sunny and hot, and the flames engulfed almost the whole town. Most of the Radzivil houses were wooden, and some with straw roofs were the first to catch fire. They quickly burned to their foundations. The other houses, those of brick, held out longer before they also caught fire. The fire raged for two whole days. The Radzivil residents, kith and kin, with the few possessions they had been able to save, gathered in the cemetery, which was a distance from the town. The whole town was wiped out then; the fire had destroyed everything except the wooden synagogue. It was not even touched by the fire.

All the other holy places, such as the Husiatyn *kloyz*, the Trisk *kloyz*, the Rabbi's Study Hall, the Barani Study Hall, all the study halls that were connected to the Great Synagogue—they were all obliterated by the fire. But by some miracle, the old wooden Great Synagogue remained whole, untouched. The fire had no power over her.

Eyewitnesses related afterward that they had seen with their own eyes how, while the conflagration was flaring all around, crowds of white doves had flown in from every direction. The doves stayed over the whole roof of the synagogue, flapping their wings. and did not allow the fire to come near.

***

The elders in Radzivil know to tell about another remarkable event that took place later, with the same blessed synagogue.

[page 293]

This happened 10 years after the Great Fire.*

Even then, Radzivil had been rebuilt, with the help of our Jewish brethren—kindhearted people, children of kindhearted people. Jews were again involved in trade and successful in making a living. The community council decided—to memorialize the great miracle of the synagogue being saved from the fire, and also because it was the repository of the Torah scrolls saved from the other holy places that had not been spared—to make a new, large Holy Ark that would accommodate all the scrolls.

The heads of the community traveled to Kremenets and brought a famous woodcarver from there who was widely known in all Ukraine as a skilled Jew.

The artist-carver worked for a whole year on the Holy Ark and turned out to be an extraordinarily capable craftsman who created a rare work of art:

---

* *Note in original:* Because terrible fires happened rather often, it was usual in small towns to number the years according to the number of fires: so many years after the first fire, so many years after the second fire, and so on.

carved lions and leopards, deer and does, eagles, doves, small and large creatures, and all kinds of flowers. Experts came from distant towns especially to look at the Holy Ark and wonder at its structure and fine carvings.

And the carver, when he had finished his work, etched into the Holy Ark—far underneath—his name: "Ozer son of R' Yechiel, a masterpiece."

Five months after the Holy Ark was finished, on the first day of Shavuot, at two o'clock in the afternoon, there was a sudden cloudburst of rain, with thunder and lightning. A lightning bolt broke out over the synagogue and split the spire cover on the roof, came into the interior of the synagogue, and burned out the name of the carver underneath, including "a masterpiece."

It happened that a short time later it was learned that the same carver had previously created similar carvings in a Catholic church.

[page 294]

People saw a kind of desecration of the holy in that, and it became clear why a bolt from heaven had burned out his name along with "a masterpiece."

During the Expedition's visit to Radzivil, there was already no vestige of the old synagogue. The millionaire Moshe Ginzburg—known by the title Baron, who had been born in Radzivil and became a millionaire during the Russo-Japanese War—generously supported his hometown Radzivil and built a series of buildings for benevolent institutions. At the same time, he also rebuilt the old synagogue and completely "modernized" it, both from the exterior and interior. The old brass candelabra and chandeliers were discarded, and electric lights were installed in their place. The walls bore no trace of the bygone paintings. And so every trace of the onetime heritage of the old-fashioned beauty and majesty of Radzivil's blessed old synagogue was erased.

Comments[*]

Rachel Gurman

Radivil was not called "Radzivil" but "Radzivilov-Volyn" until World War I. Later, under Polish authority, the town was called "Radziwilow Kolo Brodow," and Jews called the town simply "Radzivil." That is also what it is called in a chapter of Sholem Aleichem's story, "Motl, son of Peysi the Cantor." Among other things is written, "Radzivil is big as a yawn, and you could steal across the border there."[†]

The old synagogue was blown up by the Austrians during World War I, for some strategic aims.

[page 295]

The synagogue disturbed the military's perspective on this so-called brother folk.

When I went back to Radzivil after World War I, I was told that a certain young man had taken photographs from a hidden location during the war and photographed the Austrian officer while he was transferring the ordnance to blow up the synagogue. I then sent the photograph to Vilna, to YIVO, and a copy found its way to Mr. Zagoroder. Of course, after the synagogue was blown up with dynamite, there was only an empty site left, and there could not be any semblance of the walls of the synagogue.

It is not correct either that "they discarded the old candelabra and chandeliers," as the author of the book, H. Rekhtman, would have it. It is not his fault; he did not receive the correct information, but again my own family said that after the synagogue was blown up, the candelabra and chandeliers still remained. However, Zelig Fershtut—who was in Radzivil during the entire Austrian occupation—told me that the Christian residents constantly stole into the site of the former synagogue because they believed

---

[*] Translated from Yiddish by Tina Lunson. *Note in original:* At the request of Mr. Ts. Zagoroder, I have revisited the chapter of the book *Yidish etnografie ...* by Rekhtman, where Radzivil's Great Synagogue was discussed.

[†] *Translator's note:* "Yawn" and "border" sound similar in Yiddish.

that the Jews had buried their fortunes there. Of course, any remains of the melted and broken chandeliers or other valuable objects were probably re-purposed.

And the history of the building of the new synagogue is a little disjointed. The truth looks entirely different. When the first families returned to Radzivil and looked at the empty site, they first thought about putting up some kind of temporary synagogue. Then my father—Moshe Sheyn, of blessed memory—went to Antonovitsh, the mayor (he was a colonel in the border patrol before the war), to persuade him to give any town barracks remaining from the former military hospital to the Jews for a synagogue.
[page 296]

Antonovitsh consented to the request, and I have the full right to say that my father and Zelig Fershtut, of blessed memory, hammered together the wooden barracks for a synagogue.

Sometime later, when life had normalized a little, a committee was creat-ed (it seems that Shmuel Fidel, of blessed memory, was the head), and with a little community money and the $10,000 that M. Ginzburg, of blessed memory, had sent, they erected the new synagogue; but there was no means with which to furnish any decorations. And not because anyone, heaven forbid, wanted to "do away with its previous splendor."

My Town, Radzivil, in the Past*

Leyb Ayzen

Radzivilov was a former border town for Russia, in Galicia. It was nine kilometers away from the well-known city of Brody.

It was a town like all the little towns in Volhynia, with its assorted Zionist organizations: Pioneer, Youth Guard, Gordonia, Betar, General Zionists, and others. There were philanthropic organizations, an orphans' committee, an old-age home, a guest house, a food bank, and others. It is worth men-tioning and recognizing some of those who devotedly educated our youth in

---

* Translated from Yiddish by Tina Lunson.

the Zionist spirit. Without undue words of praise, our town possessed an educated and aware youth in the full sense of the word, and by 1912 the first pioneers from our town had already immigrated to the Land of Israel.

I would like to recognize and mention those who stood at the head of those devoted Zionist leaders in our town at that time.

[page 297]

Home for Invalids

Bathhouse

Chayim Kremen

They used to call him "the fiery Zionist." Back when many of our youth did not understand the task of Zionism, he literally fought against all the opponents who were waiting in the Diaspora for the Messiah .... He himself did not seek to come here and see with his own eyes that the struggle was not in vain. His followers and students built the Land in the way he used to present it in his lectures at Zionist gatherings in our town.

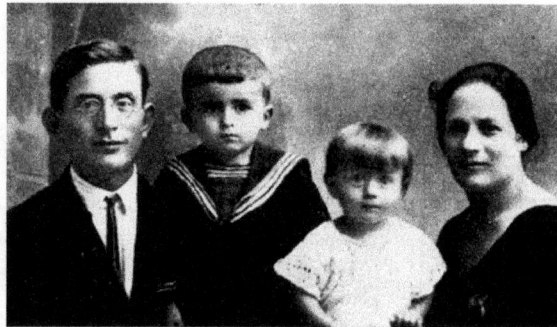

Chayim Kremen; his wife, Rive; his son, Zalman; and his daughter, Golde

Dovid'ke Sheyn

He dedicated his best years to seeing a better and more educated Zionist youth in our town. Heart and soul, he did not forget his townspeople until his last breath. Already in Israel, he initiated the creation of a memorial book for the tragically murdered martyrs of our town.

His sudden death took him away from us before his time.

The Zagoroder Family

Everyone knew the first Zionist family in our town.

Menashe Zagoroder's door was open to all the various messengers from the Land of Israel and to representatives from headquarters in Warszawa, the first gathering of the funds: the Jewish National Fund and the Foundation Fund. He also gave several lectures to spread Zionist thought among the Radzivilov residents. In addition, he was the representative of all the Yiddish and Hebrew newspapers that appeared in Poland and abroad.

He was a loyal and devoted Zionist. He also taught his children, who grew up in the Zionist spirit in the full sense of the word, and they all immigrated to Israel. His son Tsvi is to this day an active, faithful Zionist, a dedicated leader of the Radzivilov Emigrants Organization. Few of our fellow townspeople appreciate the value of his assignment—taking stubbornly on himself and seeing through the production of our yizkor book—the only commemoration of our martyrs.

Zionist Activist Group: Standing, from right: Teacher Ginzberg, Tsvi Zagoroder, Dvore Lebov, Fronye Goldgart, Sore Balaban. Seated, from right: Roze Sitner, Zlate Kagan, Roze Lizak, Bronye Balaban, Tsvi Goldgart.

Dovid'ke Goldgart (Zahavi)

As I remember him, he was one of the best leaders and teachers of Pioneer youth in our town. He gave away his youth, time, and energy to be a guide and teacher for aware and Zionist young people who would be ready to immigrate to the Land of Israel.

At the same time, I will also list from memory all the Zionist families and leaders of the Zionist organizations in our town:

Zagoroder family
Moshe Goldgart family
Balaban family
Mekhil Korin family
Moshe Tesler family

Yoel Lerner family
Gelman family
Beyrish Goldgart family
Soybel family
Yozik Zaks family

Pioneer chapter: Standing, from right: Duvid Fik, Gutman, Meler, Gun Gutman, Kurtsmer, Nudler. Seated, from right: Kupershteyn, Ginzburg, Marder, Krasnopoler, Kurtsmer, Varshevski, Bregovski.

Shumker family

Kitayksher family

Sigan Veltsye family

Royzman family

Manis Kiperman family

Chayim Kremen family

Vaynshteyn family

Grobshteyn (Saley) family

Fishel Margolis family

Feldman (Gilboa) family

Nachman Margolis family

Binyamin Sirota family

Yitschak Mikhel family

Vayl family

Chait family

Stroyman family

Yechiel-David Grobshteyn family

Avraham Zats family

Yankel Daniuk family

Poltorak family

Landis family

Zeylik-Hersh Fishman family

and others

Study Halls in Radzivilov*

R' Eli Vitels' Study Hall

The Great Synagogue (Ostra *kloyz*)

Rabbi Levi's Study Hall (Great
   Study Hall)

Rabbi Itsikel's Study Hall

Rabbi Chayim's Study Hall
   (Spanish Study Hall)

Rabbi Duvid'l's Study Hall

Uliki Study Hall (Turiysk *kloyz)*

Barani Study Hall
   (Little Synagogue)

Magid's Study Hall

Zamd Study Hall

Zisye Kopf's Study Hall

Tailors' Study Hall

Primary Teachers in Radzivilov

R' Moshe Roytman

R' Asher the Teacher

R' Mikhel the Teacher

R' Zalman Hersh the Teacher

R' Eli Brizgal (Bak

R' Shmuel Sinerekhes

R' Beyrel the Teacher

R' Tovye the Teacher

R' Motsel the Teacher

---

* Translated from Yiddish by Tina Lunson.

† The remainder of this section was translated from Yiddish by Ellen Garshick.

Elementary Talmud Teachers

Shaul the Teacher

Itsik Leyb the Teacher

Aba the Teacher

Duvid Marder

Dudye the Teacher

Moshe Tarnopoler

Avraham Lerner

Yoel Lerner

Yisrael the Teacher

Members of the Radzivil Drama Club before 1928

Shmuel Sher

Eli Chomut

Boskc Brandvayn

Sluve Kremer

Boris Koltun

Chave Ayzen

Zeyde Fershtut

Feyge Grinboym

Leyeke Polem

Melekh Shtern

Nachman Nudel

Yankel Shrayer

Mikhel Shpizel

Rivele Mandel

Monike Stirt

Feyge Faktor

Matis Tsukerman

Tovye Yakira

Avraham Koyfman

Royze Ayzen

Members of the New Drama Club

Shmuel Fershtut

Meyshe Grinblat

Leyb Ayzen

Hersh Poms

Avraham Groysman

Yitschak Furman

Shertsel Zats

Manes Kiperman

Leyb Zays

Itsikel Nudler

Rochele Fik

Yechezkel Royzman

Esterke Groysman

Nekhe Tsinayder

Yoske Stirt

Chane Polem

Leyzer Groysman

Serke Treybitsh

Yosel Karant

Boris Kaltun

[page 303]

Radzivilov Characters*

Leyb Ayzen

Boris Yefimovitsh Koltun

Everyone knew him for his library of various theater pieces. It was no easy thing to borrow a play from him to perform. First one had to make a sacrifice—a watch and two *zlotys*—and sign an obligation document, and count the pages to be sure there was not, heaven forbid, a page missing. Besides that, all the books were marked with a stamp and with a special Russian inscription:

> This is my book, as God is my witness,
> whoever steals the book, may doom befall.
> Those who did not know, read this:
> Boris Yefimovitsh Koltun, Ogrodova 22.

Yosele Peysi-Rudes

Not everyone remembers him. He was a provincial, and not everyone understood what he said. He lived in the Lodging for the Poor charity's old-age home. When Yosele approached the management with the request that he be sent to a health resort, he got the response that only the very weak and crippled were sent to a resort. A brilliant idea occurred to Yosele: he had a pair of shoes made, of which one had a high heel, and he learned to limp on one foot so that he appeared to be a "real" cripple. The home then sent him to a health resort.

Pinye the Tailor

He was a small-time artisan and a big-time pauper, burdened with a large family, with children, each one smaller than the other, who thought only about food. Chane-Keyle, his wife, had to help earn their living. She fought hard to bring a loaf of bread into the house, and that was almost gone with the first portion.

---

* Translated from Yiddish by Tina Lunson.

Chane-Keyle was a frequent visitor at her neighbor Rachel Milder's, who helped her with anything she could, and Chane-Keyle poured out her bitter heart to her. In their great poverty, Chane-Keyle brought a fresh little soul into the world each year. And when Rachel Milder tried to persuade her that in such a situation she had enough children, she naively answered, "What other pleasure does my Pinye have from me besides that?"

The Woman from Kazimierz

She had four sons and a daughter, each taller than the last, all shrewd grain merchants, and they all sputtered when they spoke. They knew nothing about love or romance. The marriage brokers banged on the doors; they were respectable matchmakers. But the sole respondent was always the mother, and when the broker Yekele Shteynberg presented a match with a dowry of $1,000, the mother replied, "For that money, he can take sick leave with me for a couple of years."

No one fought against the tax collection authority harder than the woman from Kazmierz. Every time the authorities came to inspect and the house was full of grain, she stopped up the chimney so that there was so much smoke that no one could breathe inside, and the inspector had to stand out in the street and write down what she dictated to him.

Malkele Yuntsikhes

She was a woman of marriageable age, but not so young, she was over 30, and would always say, "Whoever wants to get married should come to me." To my knowledge, up until the war, nobody came.

When the Russians arrived in 1939, Malkele dealt in several forbidden items, such as whisky, soap, and other things. Seeing through the window that someone was on the way to search her house, she quickly put the soap among the bedclothes and hung them outside to air; she covered the bottles of whisky with piles of dirty laundry. She herself stood sweating and scrubbing clothes with all her strength, singing a song all the while. The end of the story: after seven hours they had found nothing.

[page 305]

Binyamin the Water Carrier

Not everyone knew him; he lived in the cellar of the Kitas's house and had a wife named Dvorele, with nochildren. He was also blessed with his family, a mother-in-law named Chakentekhe. She was a Jewish woman not to be dismissed. She always slept with her daughter ....

Binyamin himself was very reticent and shy. And when Dvorele went for a stroll on the Sabbath with her husband and met her friends, she presented her husband, saying, "Introduce yourself. Put out your hand and say 'Binyamin.'"

That saying was widely repeated in Radzivil.

Motele Savory

He was an errand boy, an orphan. Good people had concerned themselves with doing the commandment of making a wedding for Motele and Rachel, who had fallen in love at first sight—at the wedding at Shintsiuk's, through the window. The wedding went off very well. The author of these lines was a participant and also took part in the wedding preparations, and later the circumcision, too, was attended by a large congregation. When R' Yosel Shochet looked around and saw that the fine sawdust was missing, Motele was sent to bring it. He returned very quickly, but instead of fine sawdust, he had brought farina meal.

R' Shaye Fishkes

He was always merry, happy with everything. He loved to fulfill a commandment. When Motele Savory was married, Shaye was the main person to see that everything was done just right. He went around with his horse to gather all the necessary food and equipment that people were providing for the event.

And when Shaye made a wedding for his daughter to a certain Zanvele from Brody, there was no end to his joy. He celebrated for a whole week and could not be parted from his bottle.

Then, when Shaye was seen two weeks later, with his head bandaged and two black eyes, and people asked him, "Shaye, what happened?" he answered, "I went to see my son-in-law on the Sabbath ...."

R' Moshe Chadash

He was the sexton at the Barani Study Hall. He also went around with the charity box for the Burial Society, and for the Radivil householders, he distributed invitations to weddings and circumcisions.

During the same week that Leybish Porochobnik made a wedding for his daughter, Leybish Kozultsik's mother died. As Moshe finished his rounds with the charity box, he remembered the tickets to the wedding that were still in his pocket. Seeing Fayvish Norban in the street, he shook the "give for the commandment of burial" box and called out "Leybish Porochobnik and his wife invite you and your family to the wedding canopy on Friday ...."

R' Moshe-Aharon the Cemetery Man

He was also a sexton, at the Magid's Study Hall. A kind and sincere Jew in every regard. He had to put up with a lot of trouble from his beadle, R' Binyamin, who constantly squabbled with him. R' Moshe-Aharon would stand at the reading desk with his snuff in his hand, quietly listening to the abuse, smiling and not answering a word. And when people would say, "R' Moshe-Aharon, why aren't you saying anything?" he would answer, "Bring me a receipt from Beyrel-Volf and I will talk with him."

Everyone knew that Beyrel-Volf gave out the receipts from the Burial Society ....

R' Yankele the Sexton

You always saw him happy, with a smile on his face and with some witticism. He led the food-for-the-poor institution, collecting money to help people in need.

He was a frequent visitor at Dubtshak's. And when Dubtshak told him of his difficulties in getting his wife and son out of Russia, Yankele took it upon himself to make it happen. He disappeared from Radivil for two weeks, ostensibly to travel to Truskawiec.

[page 307]

He crossed the border with a smuggler, and with great pains he was successful in bringing back Dubtshak's wife and son.

This was sensational for us in the town in those days.

Sore-Beyle the Butcher Woman

Not everyone knew her—she was literally a saint. By day she worked in a butcher shop; at night she mended galoshes. She did not give heed to this world. Offering a free loan service was her main commandment. The poor customers at the butcher's already knew that Sore-Beyle would be sure there were a few *zlotys* to travel to the fair to buy a few things. And when she didn't have money to lend, she took her own silver candlesticks to Gitil to pawn. That's how she was able to perform the commandment of a free loan service.

Every Friday, you could see Sore-Beyle going around with her huge apron, collecting pieces of challah for needy families.

Tsile Badaker

I lack sufficient words of praise to say about the noble woman Tsile Badaker, who faithfully gave to the poor strata of our town. Not everyone knew her, but this writer came to her more than once in a pressing situation to request support for someone in need. She didn't even ask whom it was for; she just gave with a generous hand to anyone who turned to her for help. Besides that, Tsile Badaker took part in and helped all the philanthropic institutions in our town.

Beyle-Rive Vaynshteyn

This woman was like a mother to the Pioneer youth in our town who used to gather in her crowded home on Pochayev Street to talk over various problems, make presentations, and discuss Zionist topics. One always felt a warm atmosphere there. She demonstrated such devotion and faithfulness to the youth that other mothers could not conceive of or understand it.

She was always happy, with a smile on her face, until her immigration to Israel with her entire family.

M. Grinberg, a landsman, an important man in Richmond, America, builds an estate in Israel.

Episodes*

Leyb Ayzen

Funeral for the Living

Our stories took place not only in Radzivil but also in the city of Brody, in 1928.

Death notices suddenly appeared on walls along the streets of Brody that the great merchant Mr. D. had passed away, a sudden death, and that the funeral would be held at three o'clock in the afternoon.

The story began with a Jewish tinsmith who lived in a cellar with his wife and five children in need and want, who couldn't pay the required rent to the building proprietor, Mr. D.

[page 309]

The then-active professional union of the Brody working class involved itself in the matter and intervened with Mr. D. about ameliorating the eviction of the abovementioned neighbor, but without results. One fine morning, the Jew was sitting outside with his family, without a roof over their heads.

To protest the rich man's dealings, it was decided to hold a funeral for the living: they brought the bier from the cemetery and, with a large gathering of people, led the funeral procession through Leshnev Street, Market Street, Gold Street, and Lemberg Street up to the house where the person in question resided. An even greater crowd assembled there, some in the know and some not, to pay their last respects. Photographers worked with all kinds of equipment to take more pictures, which they would sell among the crowd. Arriving at Mr. D.'s house, a special cantor from the movement intoned the meomorial prayer, "God, Full of Mercy."

A delegation of three members of the professional union negotiated and got 1,000 *zlotys* from Mr. D., which in those days was a good sum of mon-

---

* Translated from Yiddish by Tina Lunson.

ey. Besides that, a lot of photographs were sold, and all of that went to arrange an apartment and job for the poor tinsmith.

This event was quite a sensation at that time, in Brody and all its environs.

The World to Come, Sold for a Sack of Flour

Anything can happen in the world, including to us in Radzivil.

The story I am describing here took place in the 20th century, when culture for us was at a high level.

One cold Sunday, when all the shopkeepers and merchants were gathered in the Barani Study Hall—not only to pray but just to have a chat about politics and in general hear how Jews were faring in the world—they talked over various things, complained about problems that had nothing to do with Jewish folk, until as usual they came around to the topic of the world to come.

The participants, freethinking Jews who had no worries about making a living, could enjoy discussing it.

[page 310]

The grain merchant, Mr. B.T., wants to show that there is indeed a world to come, and one only has to be over 120 years old to merit it. There is also the Great Overseer, God, who pays every person for good or for bad. The shopkeeper, Mr. H.K., doesn't agree with Mr. B.'s conclusions and proposes that he sell his portion in the world to come for a sack of wheat flour. Mr. B.T. agrees. They shake hands on the deal, and Mr. B.T. counts out 33 *zlotys* (the value of a sack of wheat flour).

The congregation joked, made fun, and laughed at this great trick, and H.K. of course considered it very wise, telling his mother about the finalized transaction. His mother almost fell into a faint, and she demanded that he go right back and nullify the agreement. It was quite difficult to convince Mr. B.T. to sell the double share of the world to come, but others got involved, and with much effort were able to annul the deal for two sacks of flour.

The flour was distributed among the poor folk, and the town residents could not forget the big trick for a long time.

Anything Can Happen

Among the few wealthy people of our town Radzivil, Leybish Prochobnik, of blessed memory, holds a special place. Of course, he did everything in his power to keep his only son, Mikhael Prochobnik, from falling into gentile hands, and he got him exempted from military service. When Mikhael stood for the draft, the military doctor Rabtshenko from Dubno was persuaded to inscribe one word—*nyezdolni*, not suitable—for the price of $100.

Leybish Prochobnik and His Wife

[page 311]

At the same time, something grievous happened: there was a gentile in town with the same name, Mikhael Prochobnik, and with his luck, he was released first. The error was soon cleared up, but it was too late.

Behind closed doors, Leybish Prochobnik had to give another $100 to the scoundrel, and it would remain a secret.

But the news spread through the town like lightning.

A few days later, the gentile came with his hat in his hands to thank him, saying, "Thank you, Mr. Prochobnik, sir, for your kindness."

The people of Radzivil certainly remembered that one.

A Pauper with a Starched Collar (A True Story)

That is how this Jew—certainly from Lvov—looked. He wandered into our town, not, heaven forbid, to beg for a dowry, but to collect money for the "poor brides" fund—in order to make a wedding for his own daughter.

Arriving in Radzivil, he set up his first meeting with me, at the recommendation of Beyrel Lober. He greeted me very politely, said his family name with a smile, and faced me directly: "I haven't come to you for dowry funds, but to request your help in getting several addresses for flour brokers, because I come from that line of work, too. Now that I need to marry off my daughter, I must turn to my associates, who will help me out of a tight spot."

That was the introduction of a Jew, an intelligent pauper with a starched collar and a stately appearance who spoke with a German accent. Obviously, it did not take me long to put together such a list; the Jew went around to the mills, calling each by his family name on the list so as to make a better impression. Our townspeople presented themselves well and gave generously.

[page 312]

He came back to my house and ate a good lunch of soup that he'd ordered earlier. Then my guest lay down for a little rest. When he got up, he was interested to know whether there was a study hall nearby and whether wealthy people prayed there. He prayed with great intent, almost like a rabbi, and did not forget to observe the congregation. He did not speak with anyone, received a few greetings, kissed the *mezuzah,* and went home. Dinner was prepared according to his order. After the meal, he led me into a chat about the days before World War I and after the end of the war. He began,

"As a young man in '14, I started dealing in cattle, even though I was a tailor by trade. It went very well for me, but the war interrupted my plans. During the war, I supplied meat to the military, and that was good business. I think that here in town there are many butchers. Would you be so kind as to give me their addresses?"

I put together a list of all the butchers.

The second day, after eating a hearty breakfast, my guest went out to all the butcher shops, spoke with the butchers like an expert tradesman, and once again came back with a good sum of money. In the evening, he again directed our conversation to the same theme. He further related,

"When the revolution broke out in 1917, I was a great believer in the working class, but in time I was persuaded and lost my sympathies for their Marx-Engels program because I come from a religious family. Then I went back to my old trade, tailoring, until 1922. I believe that there are many tailors here in town. If it's not too difficult for you, give me the addresses of my former colleagues, and I'll visit them."

And the third evening, we talked about the time after the war and the current situation in Poland (he was also well versed in politics). Realizing that this was all tied to his money collecting, I now wanted to hear his fake stories. He told me more with great earnestness:

[page 313]

"I could see that there was nothing much to gain from tailoring, and my God-favored wife was against it, so I gradually began dealing in bookkeeping supplies. I was good at that line of business, and it took off, I made a good living at it. Most unfortunately, my wife died after a terrible illness, and I was left with two daughters and a son. Perhaps there are sellers of bookkeeping supplies here? I hope you can do me the favor of giving me their addresses."

I wrote it out again and believed from his invented stories that I was putting fellow tradesmen together.

After working over the bookkeepers' suppliers, he rested for several hours. After, that he suggested that we go for a walk. He spoke again about his stormy past, how he'd worked at Frenkel's mill as a bookkeeper and how, after the Great Fire, he was left totally at sea. "Having nothing else to turn to, I became a cantor in a small synagogue. The trustees were not happy about my past, so I had to leave the post I'd held for that short time. Meanwhile, I got my daughter engaged to a very fine young man and a good tradesman in the wood business. Perhaps I can align myself with him, because my blessed father had a sawmill before the war, so I'm also skilled in that line of work. These border regions are known for their huge forests. Aren't there sawmills around here? Perhaps it would be possible to visit them? I've promised my daughter a dowry as well as a trousseau, and that has forced me to travel the world to collect the money. I think that with God's help I'll leave your town after the Sabbath. Of you, good man, I have only one request: could you please find a few couples who can put together a few *zlotys*. It will be considered a good deed for you, because it's not appropriate for me to go from door to door, except as a failed merchant."

I tried asking whether it had been rewarding for him to come to our town, and he answered calmly that 250 *zlotys* was a very good take for a few days in a town like this. He strongly praised all those who had helped him, and me above all others, because I was the master of ceremonies and he was celebrating the wedding .... And he went on, "I'll go talk with the gentlemen at the Barani Study Hall again. I believe they'll be sympathetic and help me out in my current difficult situation. On Sunday, I'm going to Dubno—perhaps you have friends in that town?"

Sunday morning, my guest left our town, taking his leave with many thanks and adding an invitation to the wedding. Mr. Beyrel Lober, of course, came to ask about provisions for the guest he had brought me; whether I was satisfied or not, one had to pay. He promised to bring me more guests.

This story stayed in my memory and taught me to recognize people not by their appearance or character but by their speech and narrative.

[page 314]

Names and Nicknames in Radzivil*

Leyb Ayzen

Abe Rupture

Avraham Handy

Avraham Little Mercy

Avraham Chitrik

Avraham Pigtail

Aharon Bird

Atyek*

Ayzik Joker

Itsi Kozik

Itsi Painter

Itsi Head/Brain

Itsikel Harmless

Alte Stocking Cap

Eli Goat

Eli Cabin

Eli the Naked

Arke Point

Asher Calm Down

[page 315]

Yaneke

Yosele Peserode

Yosele Tsaliuk

Yosel Tshulies

Yosel Tsizis

Yosel Shot

Lander Tongue/Flap

Leyb Raven

Beyrish the Cheerful

Duvid I Forget

Hersh Casino

Hershele Shantsiuk

Hershel Chopper

Hersh Dumpling

Vove Kakinsh

Veve Stromp

Chune Firefighter

Cantor Little Demon

Chayim Leyb Puzzle

Chayim Kutsik

Moshe Fitsi-Tate

Nute Jumper

Nute Mandiyadie

Niegramatne Advacat

Nisye Kutsiperik

P. Ch. D.

Patsyekh

Podhajce [a town]

---

* Translated from Yiddish by Ellen Garshick. Some nicknames remain untranslated.

Leyb Mak	Feyge Bird
Leyb Dunai	Woodpecker
Leyb Panes	Fish Carcass
Leyb Tomcat	Ladies' Heel
Leybishe Carriage Master	
Leyzerel Fellow Traveler	Kazmierz [a town]
	Carriage
Motele Bellybutton	Pain in the Carriage
Motel Bibke	Kradikhe
Motele Whatchamacallit	
Mote the Cow Laugh	Rachel Zshukevekhe
Menashe Cherry	
Menashe Whip	Shaye Toot
Mendel Sponge Cake	Shaye Loshek
Mordekhay Lenzik	Shie Angel
Mordekhay Suitable	Shlome Potato
Moshe New	Shlome Sheep
Moshe Tsherdinek	Shmuel Sinai
Moshe Advisor	Moshe Counselor

Names from Towns and Villages

Avraham Sosover [from Sasów]	
Itsi Sestratiner [from Sestryatin]	Avraham-Yehuda Berestechker [from Berestechko]

[page 316]

Itsik-Leyb Truvetser [from Turovets]	Yechiel Parniativner [?]
	Yisrael Kripitser [from Krupets]
Binyamin the Dubner [from Dubno]	
	Leyb Baratiner [from Boratin]
Dvore Beremeler [from Boremel]	
Duvid Harachover [from Gorokhov]	Motye Baranier [from Baranye]
Dudye from the Grobelke [?]	Moshe Tarnopoler [from Tarnopol]
Dudye Poloner [from Polonnoye?]	Moshe Tisliver [?]
Velvel Leksinitser [?]	Kalman Sitner [?]
Chave Mervitser [from Muravitsa]	Shie from the Krish [?]

Chayim Yanivker [from Janów]   Shalom Chotiner [from Khotin]
                                      Shalom Chelemer [from Chelm]

[page 317]

Death and Destruction*

[page 318]

[Blank]

---

* Translated from Yiddish by Tina Lunson.

[page 319]

Forever in My Memory

Moshe Korin

Ever remaining in memory,
forever in my thoughts,
the recent past
gone by not long ago.

And I see it like today:
There lived a shtetl
full of Jews old and young
and lovely children, full of grace.

And I see the lovely picture
of Nature, wood and stream,
oh, how beautiful, how rich
you are staying in my mind.

Something I don't want to believe—
that none of it is there for me now.
That the people, dear and fine,
are no longer in this life.

The murderous hand of tyrants
mercilessly, in bestial ways,
slaughtered people, all those
still dear to us today.

When we think about it now
how did it come to pass,
how did this ever happen,
it rends the heart with grief and tears.

[page 320]

I still cannot believe it now
that people could suffer so much,
that ones so alive in every sense
awaited death day in, day out.

One fine day in the month of Tishri—
most beautiful day of the year—
everyone was led to a grave
that had been dug for them there.

They all went, old and young,

poor and rich, all equal
in their sentenced fate,
led along by bandits.

Children clung to mothers,
fathers held mothers' hands;
in the first row, community leaders,
the Rebi with the Torah and its escorts.

That entire sorrowful march
I see in my mind like today,
and will never forget it
until the end of my life.

Ever remaining in memory,
forever in my thoughts,
the recent past
gone by not long ago.

Kries-Borokhov, May 1966

[page 321]

R' Itsikel's Last Journey*

Related by Yitschak Rudman (Mordekhay Branyer's son) and recorded by Avraham Blum

"I am going, and you may all come along with me—it is all according to heaven." These were Rabbi Itsikel's last words as he was being taken by the Gestapo murderers to the slaughter with 1,200 women, children, and elders.

The murderers permitted him—for their bloody joke—to dress in his fine clothing, as if for a holiday, in a prayer shawl and his silk coat and hat, just as though to fulfill God's commandments—the rabbi marched quietly with measured steps, accompanied by Fishel and Duvid Margulis and Itsik and Nechemye, Grin's sons, who were also going along that eternal path.

The rabbi went brave and refined, as if he were going to welcome the slaughter, and murmured a prayer—perhaps "Walking in the shadow of death, I am not afraid, because you are with me"—and perhaps he protested that he and his lambs were being led to the slaughter while God was silent: "The heavenly Judge does injustice Himself." Approaching [the village of] Leviatin, two huge pits waited to swallow them. The Ukrainian thieves ordered them to undress and go into the pits, a crack of machine guns, a wailing scream of death, a curse for the murderers, and a *shema yisrael—* and the half-dead bodies of our dearest were buried half alive.

The 1,200 people were from ghetto number 1, located on Starvak Street; the second ghetto was on Butcher Street and had the same unfortunate fate as the first ghetto some six months later—with the happy exception of a few people, among whom is the teller—Yitschak Rudman!

---

* *Note in original: Radzivilov Volhynia Progressive Association,* Journal No. 20, 1951, New York.

Review[*]

Yitschak Vaynshteyn is the author of *The Destruction of Radzivilov*, the sole and very important document about the destruction of the Radzivilov Jewish community.

In offering his testimony, Vaynshteyn partly repeats some details he described in *The Destruction of Radzivilov,* but he relates many new details, and especially the recent part of the testimony, which concerns the final period before and after liberation.

Before the war, Vaynshteyn was a merchant, operating large businesses, and was a prominent resident of Radzivilov.

An intellectual with an uncompleted higher degree, he was transformed into a slave laborer in a sawmill during the Soviet and then German occupation.

A person with a realistic orientation, he had but one goal for himself: to save himself and his family. In the testimony, he tells exactly how he succeeded in extracting himself, his wife, and his children from the jaws of death.

For the entire time of the German occupation, he did not push to take on a comfortable position in the *Judenrat* or police, although he had many opportunities to do so.

Characteristic is his reply to the first head of the *Judenrat*, Viderhorn, when the latter invited him to take over his post: "I have been a giver my whole life, not a taker. I won't be an instrument of the Gestapo, and I can't take away the last bites from the Jews."

As an illustration of the above remarks, it is worth relating that Vaynshteyn had asked that certain things not be published: when his younger brother Siunye confided in him that he wanted to join the Jewish police in

---

[*] *Note in original:* From documents at Yad Vashem—9-101/1906; recorded by Mr. Alperovich, May 1962.

order to make his life easier, "I slapped him hard three times and said, 'Your foot will never dare to cross the threshold of that vile gang. Don't you dare soil your face and tarnish our family's good name.'"

[page 323]

In telling about this incident, Vaynshteyn cried hard, and it was some time until he recovered himself.

Vaynshteyn also asked that the following fact not be published: when he worked as an accountant for the Soviets, he did not pay enough attention to the Soviet rules and was denounced. He received as sentence the harsh punishment of being deported to "the white bears" [Siberia]. As a former "bourgeois," they played him up as a saboteur, and it was only thanks to the outbreak of the war that he remained in Radzivilov.

Vaynshteyn was one of the few surviving Jews from the Radzivilov ghetto. And a good thing he was, so that in 1948 he wrote down everything about the life and destruction of the Radzivilov Jewish community while it was still fresh in his memory.

In my many visits with Vaynshteyn, I became more closely acquainted with that noble man, who commanded such respect.

Assessing the importance of giving his declaration to Yad Vashem, he demanded several times that I read the writings and check that the facts were correct.

The last time I visited him, I suggested that he put together a map of the Radzivilov ghetto, and he asked me to help him correct it along with a couple of other Radzivilovers so that together we could assemble an accurate map of the ghetto.

Vaynshteyn is a new arrival. It was barely a year ago that he came to Israel from England. He left one of his sons there. One son is here in the Land.

To my question about his plans and the future, Vaynshteyn replied that first he was going to attend an *ulpan*, and then he would think about his goals.

Names in the Testimony

Jews:

Moshe-Duvid Balaban	Avraham Vaynshteyn
Yisrael Balaban	Hersh Linder
Shlome Vaser	Dubtshak—optician
Yakov Boym	Dr. Veber
Milder brothers	Yakov Kitas
Manye Vaynshteyn	Duvid Margules
Siunye Vaynshteyn	Sasha Boym
Noach Grinshteyn	Zalman Goldshmid
Leyb "Rakhentses"	Simche Semigran
Rabbi Yitschak Lerner	Tsvi Kiperman
Viderhorn	Mandel
—First chairman of the Jewish Committee Hersh Lizak	Yakov Goldshteyn
—Second chairman of the Jewish Committee Yakov Furman	Treybitsh
— Chairman of the *Judenrat* Porokhovnik	Sheyndel Zats
	Batye Goldenshteyn

Non-Jews:

Tushakovski	—Ukrainian
Mateyko	—Mayor
Misha Zaleski	—Police commandant
Tushakovski	—Sawmill director
Marianna	—Peasant
Gorski	—Lawyer
Fayshula	
Mitka	
Pietro	
Lina	

Towns Mentioned in the Testimony

Poland	USSR	Germany	England
Radzivilov	Vinnitsa	Hofgeismar bei	Nottingham

		Kassel	
Kremenets			
Brody			
Dubno			
Rovno			

Testimony

Address: Tel Aviv, 37 King George Street, Bet Hachalutsot

Date and place of birth: Kremenets, Volhynia province

Occupation: Merchant

Family members perished in World War II:

Parents:

Father—R' Shmuel-Zev Vaynshteyn, born 1879, died in the Radzivilov ghetto, May 30, 1942.

Mother—Miryam-Rachel Vaynshteyn (Bernshteyn), born 1881, died in the Radzivilov ghetto, May 30, 1942.

Brothers:

Avraham Vaynshteyn, born 1901, died in Vinnitsa, end of July or beginning of August, 1942.

His family: wife—Ester Vaynshteyn, daughter Ronye and son Yitschak. All died in the Radzivilov ghetto.

Eliezer (Siunye) Vaynshteyn, born 1910, died end of December 1942 in Berezets, Kremenets district, with his wife and mother-in-law.

Yitschak Vaynshteyn Recounts

Recorded by Y. Alperovitsh, May 1962

Because I have written more broadly about Jewish life in Radzivilov before World War II (see my memoir, *The Destruction of Radzivilov*), I will limit myself here to some short remarks on that theme.

[page 326]

Our family moved to Radzivilov. My father was a man of substance and ran very large enterprises. Between the two world wars, my father had a big mill and an abundant livelihood.

My father was a very progressive Jew and gave his children a secular education.

I studied in a cheder in my childhood years. Later, until the outbreak of World War I 1914, I studied in the Jewish Primary School in Kremenets, and later in the High School of Commerce in Kremenets. I also graduated from a Ukrainian state gymnasium and studied mathematics and law at Lvov and Kraków universities. Unfortunately, I had to interrupt my studies to help my father in his business affairs.

In 1926, I opened a shop in Radzivilov, selling desks and haberdashery. I operated that business until World War II broke out in 1939.

In 1933, I married Batye Goldenshteyn, born in Brody. Our elder son, Yosef, was born in 1936 (he now lives in Israel). Our second son, Shimon, was born in 1938 (he now lives in England).

Before the Polish era, until around 1936, the Jews in Radzivilov—as in all the other towns in our area—earned a living. There were Jews in various categories: merchants, craftsmen, retailers. Each was occupied with his issues, some with labor and some with commerce. After 1936, when the wave of anti-Semitism flooded Poland, the Jews' situation changed greatly: the Polish government opened Polish shops and incited the Polish and Ukrainian population against the Jews, but no open excesses took place.

When the Polish-German War broke out on September 1, 1939, there was chaos in the town: it was clear even in the first days of the war that the Polish army was not strong enough to oppose the German army. Many refugees came into our town from western and central Poland.

[page 327]

Every day we expected the Germans to take Radzivilov. The fear among the Jews was great. But, luckily, the Soviets took Radzivilov on September 19, and the Jews breathed more easily.

Life under the Soviet Occupation

As soon as the Soviets took Radzivilov and set up their administrative apparatus, they began to nationalize all the big shops, sawmills, and mills. My father had three partners in his mill: Moshe-Duvid Balaban, his son Yisrael, and Shlome Vaser. It goes without saying that the mill was nationalized.

When the Soviets began to deport the former *osadniks** and other Polish officials, they also deported Jewish families to Siberia—including my father's two partners, Yisrael Balaban and Shlome Vaser. Besides that, they also drove out Yakov Boym, the sawmill proprietor, Nisel Bukshteyn, the Milder brothers, Vaser, Halbershtat, and others.

I quickly evaluated the situation and decided that the best thing would be to give up my shop willingly, before the Soviets took it by force. I turned the shop over to the Soviets and went off to work as a representative to the Soviet cooperative as an accountant, later as an economist. In my business, the Soviets placed the Ukrainian Tushakovski as manager. But Tushakovski began to deal in the black market; that is, he sold a lot of merchandise on the side and put the money in his own pocket.

I must remark that before the outbreak of the Polish-German war, I had an employee in my business named Manye Vaynshteyn. Before the Soviets, she was an important activist and was elected into the leadership of the professional unions.

Manye Vaynshteyn knew well what kind of merchandise and how much of it we had in the shop. She also knew about the black marketeering conducted by the new shop manager, Tushakovski. She openly reacted to the district attorney in the Party's offices. But it did not help. Tushakovski was not removed from the post, and he remained the shop's proprietor until he had sold all the merchandise.

---

* *Translation editor's note:* An *osadnik* (Polish for settler) was a veteran of the Polish Army or a civilian who was given or sold state land in the territory ceded to Poland by Polish-Soviet Riga Peace Treaty of 1921.

As I have mentioned already, I went to work as an accountant, later as an economist, in the Soviet cooperative management. The central cooperative management had some 20 departments in town and some 30 in the villages around it.

When the Soviets introduced internal passports in 1940, they did not forget about the former "bourgeois"—rich people received a passport with a "paragraph." Those *"paragraphshtshikes"* expected to be deported any day and be sent off to the "polar bears." My father and I were included in that category of former "bourgeois." Apparently, the Soviets did not agree that I—as a former merchant with property—should be working in such a responsible post in the Trade Cooperative, and I was released from my job.

Having no other alternative and wanting to *"proletariatize"* myself, I went to work as a laborer in the sawmill that had belonged to Yakov Boym, whom the Soviets had deported to Siberia. My brother, Siunye Vaynshteyn, Goldberg (now in Israel), and others also went to work in the sawmill. I worked in the sawmill until the German-Soviet War began on June 22, 1941.

The Soviets took my father's house. He and my mother moved to a small room across from the Great Synagogue, not far from his former partner, Moshe-Duvid Balaban.

The Soviets rearranged everything according to their own style. The left-leaning elements, both Christians and Jews, worked along with the Soviet administration. It was hardly worth mentioning missing foodstuffs or clothing. The delivery of food items into the shops was not something to rejoice about. At every shop there were huge lines—*"otshereden."* The crowd was not charmed with such "procedures" but agreed with the idea that it was better to have the Soviets than the Germans. In any case, no one was expecting pogroms.

[page 329]

Life under the German Occupation

War broke out between Germany and the Soviet Union on June 22, 1941. The German army advanced quickly, and the Germans approached Radzivilov. The Jewish population began to panic. The Soviets fled amid great chaos. Some Jews tried to flee on horseback, some on bicycles. But the Germans bombed and cut off the roads, and people were forced to turn back.

The German army occupied Radzivilov on June 29. The Ukrainian population received the Germans with great joy, and they promptly organized a Ukrainian self-administration headed by Mateyko, who had declared himself an ethnic German.

The Ukrainians began to steal everything from the Jews. Besides that, they pointed out Jewish houses to the Germans so they could rob them. A wild terror began. The Ukrainians surrendered to the Germans those Jews who had been active with the Soviets. Among the first victims was Manye Vayn-shteyn, whom I mentioned earlier.

I want to say that before the Germans came into Radzivilov, my two brothers and I, with the assent of our families, had decided to flee because it was said that the Germans would capture men in particular. But as I have stated, fleeing was not possible. Even Grinshteyn, who had his own horse and wagon, was forced to turn back after he left because the Germans had already run ahead.

The First Decrees

The German authorities officially recognized the Ukrainian self-administration, and the Germans gave the administration broad powers.

At the beginning of July 1941, the German regional commissioner from Dubno appointed a German commandant in Radzivilov. Several SS officers came along with him and instituted the German command. The command promptly issued several anti-Semitic orders:

[page 330]

1. Jews must wear white armbands with blue stars of David.

2. Jews are forbidden to leave the city without permission.

There was a death penalty for not following these orders.

The Jews understood immediately that Jewish life would be outlawed, but with just these orders it would not be ended.

On the July 15, 1941, a group of Gestapo men arrived and asked the Ukrainian administration for two lists: (1) especially harmful Jews and (2) propertied Jews.

For the first list, the Ukrainians counted the Jews with whom they had previously had personal accounts and former Soviet activists, such as Manye Vaynshteyn and others.

For the second list, they counted especially wealthy Jews and also those who had turned over their possessions to Ukrainians for safekeeping—hoping to get rid of them that way. Among others, the second list included Zalman Leviton, Shimon Marder, Duvid Vaser, Ester Grinsman, the Chomut brothers, and so on.

On the same day, Gestapo drove a group of Jews out to the Brody forest with whips in order to dig a pit, not far from the train line between Brody and Radzivilov. The Jews were later shot. We heard about this from a survivor, Leyb Rakhentses, who managed to escape.

The next morning, a band of Ukrainians went into the Great Synagogue, threw the Torah scrolls out into the street, and set them on fire. They forced the town rabbi, Rabbi Yitschak Lerner, to dance around the fire.

The First Jewish Committee

In view of the tense situation, a Jewish committee was organized. It was to be a liaison with the German authorities so that Jewish life would not be destroyed. Viderhorn served as the head of the committee.

Viderhorn was a Hungarian Jew who knew German well, and Hungarian and other languages too. Although he was an assimilated Jew, he had a pure Jewish heart and a clear conscience.

[page 331]

Viderhorn headed the committee, thinking that the Germans would deal with representatives from an organized Jewish body and would to some degree restrain the Ukrainians. After a while, when Viderhorn was convinced that the committee was only a tool in German hands to press the Jews for money and valuables and to help the German authorities carry out their orders, he removed himself from office, wanting to keep his conscience clear.

Viderhorn was a personal friend of mine. He had earlier turned to me to take his place as president of the committee. I answered him, "Don't you know me, that I with my character won't and can't be a compliant conduit for German orders." I rejected his proposition. Then Viderhorn sent me the commandant of the Ukrainian police, Misha Zalevski, a school friend of my brother's, thinking he might convince me. I answered the commandant:

"My whole life I have been a giver and not a taker. And I can't take the last bit of bread from the mouths of the Jews."

"So whom should I appoint?" the commandant asked.

In the end, when he saw that he would get nowhere with me, he designated Hersh Lizak as president. But he was not the right candidate, and a few days later Yakov Furman was designated as president.

The Radzivilov *Judenrat*

The Germans wanted to broaden the legal powers of the committee and so ordered that the committee reorganize itself as a *Judenrat*.

Yakov Furman, the president, was the appropriate candidate for such an institution.

As a person, he was an egoist with a strong character; he kept his own accounting: because of the general catastrophe, he wanted to improve his own life and that of his family.

As president, he thought, he could save his own life; it was not important what he did—as long as he stayed alive. Of course, Furman was far from any sentimentality and was an obedient instrument for the Gestapo.

The *Judenrat* worked with diligence. All orders from the German authorities were fulfilled without delay.

The *Judenrat* began to pump the possessions out of the Jewish population. In handing the contributions over to the Germans, he did not forget to leave certain sums of money and valuable articles for himself.

The Jewish police were an obedient tool of the *Judenrat*. They used to drive Jews from their houses to their work, requisition various valuables, and play other such games.

Further Decrees

Decrees came one after another. (I have written more about them in my memoirs; see *The Destruction of Radzivilov*.)

On December 20, 1941, there came an order from the commissar of the Dubno area to exchange the white armbands for yellow patches. On February 2, the Gestapo ordered the surrender of wedding rings.

The *Judenrat*, on the Gestapo's order, ordered some workers to be gathered and sent them to the labor camp in Vinnitsa. They were later killed there. The sole survivor from Radzivilov, Porokhovnik, tells about this. Also among those deported to Vinnitsa was my younger brother, Avraham Vaynshteyn.

On March 5, 1942, a lot of farm wagons filled with peasants and Germans drove into town. The Jews thought some kind of action was being planned. Many Jews went into hideouts, whoever, wherever they could. Later it appeared that they had been preparing for a burglary action. The Germans and Ukrainians went from house to house and took everything that had any value at all.

The aforementioned mayor, Mateyko, directed the burglary action.

The Ghetto

A decree came on April 9, 1942, that in the next 24 hours the Jews must leave their residences and move into the quarters designated for them in the alleyways of the poorest Jewish section.

At that time, it was ordered that all Jews in the vicinity of Radzivilov leave their homes and move to Radzivilov, into the ghetto. As it happened, the Radzivilov ghetto already had a registered population of 2,600 souls.

The *Judenrat* had no easy task in meting out the places. The area was small, and people quarreled. Besides that, people slept in attics, in cellars, wherever they could.

Because of the extraordinary crowding, terrible sanitary conditions, and poor maintenance, a number of diseases spread through the ghetto. Epidemics were an everyday occurrence. Jewish and Ukrainian police guarded the ghetto, which was fenced in with barbed wire.

Provisions

The Jews had to go to various kinds of work outside the ghetto. Each could bring along something to eat. In addition, they had to do business with the Christian population. There were several ways to smuggle food into the ghetto. The Jewish police did business with the Ukrainian police. Some peasant friends used to toss food packages over the barbed wire. Later, the situation became much worse, when the police began to persecute the Christians who approached the barbed wire.

[page 334]

When I went out to work at the sawmill, I would bring in food for my family. Marianna was an elderly Christian woman, and the times had not changed her. She was a friend to the Jews and, disregarding the severe penalties that awaited her, she helped us in any way she could.

Dividing up the Ghetto

The Germans ordered the *Judenrat* to divide the ghetto into the "useful" and the "not-useful."

The "useful" would need to get special "permits" and live in the part of the ghetto that, among ourselves, we called "Korea."

The "not-useful" did not get any permits and had to live in the area "by the river."

When the *Judenrat* started to put together the list of the "useful," there was a rush for permits. In the process, all the means disappeared, and not without the *Judenrat*'s help. It turned out that many "useful" people did not get permits, and specialists who had responsible work had to move "by the river."

Of the 2,600 Jews who lived in the Radzivilov ghetto, only 400 received permits. The other 2,200 were designated for immediate destruction.

The idea that the "not-useful" would be killed was confirmed by a report from Rovno and its environs that the Jews there who did not have permits had been shot.

So 440 lucky "permittees" remained in "Korea"; 2,200 went off "by the river."

My younger brother Siunye and I got permits, thanks to the intercession of director Tushakovski, who provided proof that we were employed at the sawmill.

My parents did not get any permits, of course, and were moved from the "Korea" side to the "river" side, where we had been earlier for a short time, but now I had my permit in my pocket.

[page 335]

The Liquidation of the Ghetto "by the River"

The misfortune came completely unexpectedly. We barely succeeded in getting out, my wife and our two sleeping children in our arms. We ran to the ghetto gate. The police were not going to let us through, but I was able to show my work permit. After a lot of cursing, they let us through.

When we got over to the "lucky side," the nervousness of the Jews there was palpable. Everyone was on guard.

Groups of SS men encircled the "not-useful" ghetto on June 29, 1942. The action began. Armed from head to foot, they went from house to house and drove everyone out into the street. Anyone they found hiding, they shot on the spot.

Everyone was driven to the synagogue courtyard, where men were separated into one group, and women and children into another. Among those men were the rabbi of Radzivilov, Rabbi Yitschak Lerner, of blessed memory; my father, Shmuel Vaynshteyn, of blessed memory; Yisrael Reyf; Hirsh Linder; and many other important proprietors from the town, of blessed memory.

Those who had been shot were loaded onto peasant farm wagons and taken to the forest. The men were taken to the train under armed guard. Later someone saw that they had turned around to the direction of the "clearing" by the forest, which led to the "Radzivilov forest." Pits had been prepared there, dug by Russian prisoners of war.

At the pits, they were surrounded and ordered to undress completely, and the SS began shooting with machineguns. No matter who got a bullet and who didn't, they were all thrown into the pit and then shot through with the machineguns.

After the Germans had finished shooting the men, they came back into the ghetto and repeated the same thing with the women and children.
[page 336]

They led them along the same path as the grave for the men, where a grave was ready for them.

Two graves, one next to the other, located at the "clearing" in the "Radzivilov forest."

Thus the Germans liquidated the "not-useful" ghetto.

I lost my dear parents in that action. After that action, the Germans drove a group of people from the "useful" ghetto to wash off the bloodstains. I was among that group. At the first opportunity, I ran off to my apartment, where my parents had been. I searched for them in the hideout that I had made earlier and camouflaged for them. I hoped that they had succeeded in hiding. But nothing. They were killed along with all the Jews in the liquidation of the ghetto.

The "Useful" Ghetto

After the liquidation of the "not-useful" ghetto, I was left with my wife and two sons. The *Judenrat* and the Jewish police went wild in the ghetto.

Physically and morally shattered, having lost their nearest ones, everyone asked the question: what next? How long would we be allowed to live? Each person understood that the Germans had not granted life for long, so each person began to seek a way out. Fleeing into the forest was impossible because the Christian population was anti-Semitic and would turn Jews over at every opportunity.

Plans were hatched about how to dig hideouts. Anyone who knew a "good" Christian hoped for his help. Jews became secretive. Each hid his plans from the other. People began to fabricate "Aryan papers" for hefty prices. I managed to get such papers for myself and my wife, who at that time worked as an interpreter for a Christian attorney, Gorski. She went to the post office frequently. Once she was badly beaten by Commandant Krause for walking around in town.

[page 337]

The Liquidation of the Second Ghetto

Bitter days drew closer. Reports reached us that the Germans were preparing to murder the children in the ghetto. We began to fear leaving the children in the ghetto when we went out to work. So we decided that each of us would take one child to work with us.

I took one son with me. When I arrived at the sawmill to work, I hid him among the boards. My wife did the same with the other son.

At that time, news reached us that the complete liquidation of Volhynia Jews was underway.

At the end of September 1942, news spread that the Russian prisoners of war were digging more pits. No doubt remained for anyone that the pits were being dug for us. We did not wait; we had to decide what to do.

A group of Jews put together a list of the previously mentioned Jews and a list of the living ones, wrote it on parchment, placed it in glass jars, and buried it in the vicinity of the Great Synagogue, in order that someone, someday, would know about the destruction of the Radzivilov Jewish community.

On September 29, 1942, the German and Ukrainian police began to gather around the ghetto. Feeling the danger, I was able to take one child and tell my wife to do the same—take the other child—and to meet at an arranged place in the former "not-useful" ghetto. And so it was: we met in an attic above a little room.

While the ghetto was surrounded, a group of Jews—not seeing any other way out—committed suicide by poisoning themselves. Dr. Veber had made poison injections for the pharmacist Dubtshak and his wife and later for Yakov Kitas and his wife, Sashe Boym and his son, and Duvid Margules and his wife.

[page 338]

Finally, Dr. Veber injected his wife, his only child, and then himself with doses of poison. Zalman Goldshmid committed suicide by hanging himself. That is how the group of Jews who did not want to be murdered by the Germans died.

The Germans tore into the ghetto, and just as they had done four months before, they drove—this time men, women, and children together—to those pits at the clearing.

True, before the slaughter, a couple of hundred Jews succeeded in running away, but some of them were caught, brought back, and shot.

I must remark that at the liquidation of the "useful" Jews, they brought the former president of the first committee, Viderhorn, in a car. The Germans offered him (unofficially) an opportunity to flee, but the noble man with the clear conscience refused and was murdered along with his parents, wife, and two children.

We Flee to Brody

At that time, I was sitting hidden in the attic with my wife and children. But we could not sit there for long. The only way out was to flee to Brody, where my wife had a sister.

Some Jews who had managed to flee before the action had already set out for Brody. Some were felled by bullets along the way.

When my family and I left the attic, I went to the peasant Fayshula, who lived in the vicinity of the "not-useful" ghetto. (After the liquidation, the Christians were allowed to return there to the empty ghetto to their former apartments.) The peasant did not let us in, but he advised us about the way to Brody, across the river. One could not go via the bridge because it was being guarded by the police.

At the bridge, I met a group of Jews that included the rabbi's son, Rabbi Duvid'l Rotenberg. First, I carried both children across in my arms, then my wife. The water was as high as my neck. A Christian, seeing our situation and that we were wet, took us into his house. We stayed there until it was night.

[page 339]

The husband gave us a piece of bread, and we went across the river a second time. In the morning, we arrived safely in Brody.

In Brody

In Brody, the situation for Jews was not so dangerous. A few Jews even lived in their houses with their families. For security, my wife and I separated, each with a child, so we would not all be together. Around that time, the Radzivilov police came down to Brody looking for Jews who had run away from Radzivilov.

It was there in Brody, six days after we fled, that we knew the exact details about the liquidation of the "useful" ghetto, about which I have just written. The liquidation took place on October 6, 1942.

My wife and one child had relocated in her sister's home. When I went to visit her, I saw that the nephew was sweating and looking for a place to hide. I discussed with him the idea of taking us into his hiding place, too.

A third action was being prepared in Brody at that time. It was already the end of October 1942. Before the action, we all went to a familiar peasant, a Ukrainian, and he hid us in the attic of a sawmill.

The action happened during that time. Hiding in the attic, we observed how the Germans caught the Jews, stuffed them into trucks, and took them off someplace. We saw that the Jews were half-naked, and when a policeman wanted to free one of his Jews from the truck, he dragged him from the truck half-naked and unconscious.

In the Attic Hiding Place in the Brody Sawmill

There were 12 of us Jews hiding in the attic. Not even the sawmill director himself knew we were there. During the action, when German police were looking everywhere for hidden Jews, they also came into the sawmill to search, but the director went out and assured them that there were no Jews in the vicinity of the sawmill.

[page 340]

The police went away.

We could not stay in the attic for long. There was no food. Besides that, there was a small child among us. Once, when the child had to empty his bladder, he "moistened" a worker in the sawmill—a peasant. The peasant thought it was rain from the roof, so he came up to the attic to see where the rain was coming in. I saw that it was bad; he could see all of us in the attic and reveal our hideout. I had a flask of whisky with me. I went out to him with the flask of whisky and said, "You see us sitting here, 12 Jews in hiding. Our fate is in your hands. You can give us all away to the Germans, and then we're lost. But if you believe in God and you have a clean conscience and a humane heart—you'll forbid yourself from doing so. Consider it well before you send us to our deaths. Our fate is sealed, but meanwhile we have a spark of hope that we might survive." The peasant took the flask of whisky and did not betray us to the Germans.

We Leave Our Attic

I made an assessment of our situation, and sitting in an attic in Brody was not a plan for us, so I figured out how to leave Brody.

While I was still in the Radzivilov ghetto, I had discussed with one of the "big shots" where we could be hidden. The "big shot" was Simche Semigran. He and Tsvi Kiperman's family had left the ghetto in time and hidden with peasants they knew. I had lost contact with him. But he had given me the name of a Christian, Mitka, who would care for me the same as for them. But where was this Mitka?

I asked the Christian who had hidden us in the attic to put me in contact with Mitka from Radzivilov, according to the code I had been given. The peasant did so, and a little while later Mitka arrived.

[page 341]

But he explained to me that he could not take me and my family, but only me alone for now, and that he could take my family across later. I agreed to that. Mitka contacted a peasant who settled me in his wagon and drove me to a farmhouse in a field about halfway between Radzivilov and Dubno. Later, the peasant did indeed bring my family to me in one piece. I had also proposed that the peasant drive the Mandel family to us as well, but they did not want to risk it and refused my suggestion.

In a Fresh Hiding Place

The peasant and I began digging a hole in a stall where a cow was kept with a goat and a pig. We dug the hole in the place where the pig was kept. We dug it two meters long, one meter wide, and more than one meter high. That hole would have to be our home, the hiding place for four people.

We set up a wooden cone, hammered together with boards. When the peasant or his wife had to bring out food to us, they would lift up the cone and hand the food to us. From time to time, I would take one child, leave the hole, and sleep at the peasant's house in order to stretch out my body.

A big dog stood watch in the yard, and when the dog started to bark, we knew someone was approaching the hut, and we quickly crept back into the hole. We paid the peasant well for hiding and feeding us.

Although our hideout was in a farmhouse, wandering Jews stumbled onto it from time to time, seeking food. Once, such Jews remarked on my sleeping son to the peasant. Mrs. Peasant said that he was her sister's child, but when the child woke up and asked her to take him to the outhouse, the Jews knew that he was a Jewish child.

[page 342]

Once, a Jew asked the peasant's wife if she would let him stay overnight. She would not take him in. I refused my food and asked her to give it to that Jew. She gave it to the Jew to eat but told him to leave at once.

We Leave the Hiding Place

And so my family stayed put in the hideout for seven months. In May 1943, we had to leave because a neighboring peasant woman had accidentally noticed my wife. The peasant who was our keeper soon also wanted to be rid of us, but he was decent, and he transported us back to Mitka. Mitka showed us to a new temporary address not far from where Semigran and Tsvi Kiperman had been hiding. It was not far from the Radzivilov Jews' mass graves.

In a New Place

At our new keeper's, we were placed in a big hideout in a barn full of grain. From there, I sent the peasant Petra to find out the fate of my father-in-law, Yakov Goldenshteyn, in Brody.

Yakov Goldenshteyn was an electro-technician and one of the few surviving Jews after the liquidation of the Brody ghetto. I sent two messengers to him and his wife; unfortunately, they did not find Goldenshteyn. He had been caught and shot. The peasant did bring his wife to us. She had been hidden by a Christian named Lina (the Christian is now in Israel).

This was after the Germans' defeat at Stalingrad. We knew the Germans would stable horses in the barn where we were hiding. We would have to leave directly. According to a gentlemen's agreement, we went on to Semigran and Kiperman's hideout.

[page 343]

There were already 12 people there. It was very crowded. Besides, Semigran was ill with tuberculosis. Because of the crowding, I did not want to stay in that hideout, fearing that we could all be infected with tuberculosis. I was forced to find a new place.

At that time, the Russians were getting closer. The Russian army was already three kilometers from our place. That is where the front was. I went out to look for a new hideout and met Treybitsh (now in America) and Sheyndil Zats (now living in Tel Aviv). They showed me a place where we could hide in a cellar.

Liberation

I left my wife and children in Semigran's hideout and went by myself with an 18-year-old peasant to find the new hideout. The peasant was also hiding from the Germans. He was afraid he would be deported to Germany.

During that time, the Russians moved forward, and Semigran and Kiperman's hideout, where my wife and children were hiding, was captured by the Russians.

The village passed from hand to hand seven times. Many were killed on both sides. When I heard Russian being spoken, I went out with the peasant. The Russians forced us to bury the dead. I asked him to come later and make an announcement, since my wife and children were waiting for me. And he did. When he said my family was waiting for me, the Russians released us.

But getting to the hideout where my family was, was no simple task. The Germans had organized a counteroffensive, and the road was shot up. The Russians retreated. I asked the Russian soldiers not to leave me and to take me with them in a wagon because I had no more strength to go on. But they refused.

Gathering my last strength, hungry and weary, I went back in the direction of the hideout where my wife and children were.

[page 344]

When I got there, I could not find my family or the others there. Other peasants there were awaiting the outcome of the battle. There were partisans. They asked me to go into the hideout so I would not be noticed by the neighbors. I obeyed them and went into the hideout.

Inside, I was attacked by insects and flies, and they bit me all over. I realized that my wife and the others—Kiperman and Semigran—had left for Radzivilov. I knocked on the proprietor's door, and he opened the hideout for me. After great pains, I arrived several hours later in Radzivilov, which had been freed by the Russians.

In Radzivilov, not far from the Great Synagogue, I found an empty apartment with the few saved Jews: Semigran and his family, Kiperman and his family, Treybitsh, Sheyndil Zats Oks, and a niece, Feldman. Every day, some hidden Jews came back into Radzivilov.

After Liberation

The Soviets signed up all the men to be firefighters. Radzivilov returned to the same administration that it had had before the war.

The Soviets began to deport Ukrainians and Jews to Siberia. I saw that I, too, could be deported to Siberia and turned to a non-Jew, a former school chum of my brother Siunye, who had become manager of the finance department, and asked him to take me on as a worker. He replied that he would not take on a former bourgeois in a Soviet institution. I persuaded him that we should turn to the Party secretary about my case. The secretary gave his permission. I started work.

In a few days, there was an announcement that someone should be sent to take a course in Kharkov.

[page 345]

I agreed to travel to the course under the condition that my family be moved to Rovno. The Soviets agreed.

When I finished the three-month course in Kharkov, I returned to my family in Rovno. I was sent to work at the regional finance committee. I was given housing in a former Jewish house. I lived in Rovno until the deportations to Poland began.

After the end of the war, I went to Poland and settled in Beuthen, where I lived until the summer of 1946. Then I moved to Germany and settled in Hofgeismar bei Kassel. There, I worked in a camp where there were 2,500 Jewish refugees.

In the refugee camp, I was chosen as one of five judges in the court that resolved various conflicts among the refugees, administration, and so on. We had no dealings with the Germans.

In November, my family and I moved to England and settled in the town of Nottingham. For the first six years, I worked as a hatmaker. Later, I opened my own business.

In 1953, my wife died at the age of 50.

My older son, Yosef, immigrated to Israel in 1956. The younger son, Shimon, remained in England.

I came to Israel in August 1961.

[page 346]

Survey and Remarks

Interviewer: Y. Alperovitsh

Yechiel Porokhovnik was 17 years old in 1941, when the war between Germany and the Soviet Union broke out.

Son of a proletariat family (his father was a wagon driver), from his earliest youth he had helped his father earn a living for the family.

He was a member of Young Pioneer in Radzivilov, dreaming of going for pioneer training and later immigrating to the Land of Israel. The war destroyed all his plans.

In the first days of the German occupation, the Ukrainian fascists shot his brother Avraham because of his relationship to the Soviet activists. He swore over the fresh grave of his murdered brother to avenge the spilling of his brother's innocent blood. Later, when the Germans murdered his entire family—parents, brothers, and sisters—he saw only one goal for himself: vengeance.

Yechiel Porokhovnik used every form of battle against Nazism during the Hitler occupation: he fought in bunkers, with partisans, as a "forest Jew," and later in the Soviet Army. He did not put his weapon down until he lost his right leg.

He was among the first young people in Radzivilov who tried to organize the ghetto into an armed rebellion against the enemy. After the murder of the Radzivilov Jews, when he had lost his family, he fled to Brody, and while sitting in a bunker with other Jews there, he made contact with partisans and organized the Brody youth in the ghetto, some of whom escaped into the forest. He was never alone in his struggle. He always gathered around him a group ready with weapons in hand to defend Jewish honor and pride.

He was one of the first Jewish youths from the Brody area in the ranks of the partisans. He participated in all the most dangerous operations against the Germans and the Ukrainian gangs.

Even while he was laid up in a peasant hut for six weeks with a bullet through his leg, he was still afire with the fight. He gave his comrades the instructions and guidance they needed.

He was one of three delegates from the partisans who went to negotiate with the leadership of the Ukrainian Nationalist Division about holding their fire, so that they were not fighting against each other.

In the heat of battle, he was always one of the first in the most dangerous positions. He witnessed the deaths of his fellow partisans who fell near him, and he fought the enemy with even more fire and wrath. To his credit are no small number of German and Ukrainian casualties.

He was the organizer of a successful operation to get food for 40 Jews found in a bunker in Brody, whose stomachs were swollen from starvation. The eyes of the disbelieving Jews turned to him, and they saw him as their knight. Later, when the bunker was discovered by the Germans, he found a clever way to get the Jews out to the forest, killing several Germans along the way.

Fate would have it that after all the losses his partisan troop suffered, he was left alone. Weapon in hand, he wandered around the forest, persecuted by local Ukrainian gangs and Germans. While fleeing a German who had been pursuing him, he killed him.

As soon as he was free, he joined a Soviet military detail and was promptly sent to the front. He was awarded three military distinctions for heroic acts: Red Banner, Red Star, and the order Slava First Class, as well as many other medals.

He was among the first to voluntarily present himself to head up a group of soldiers to gather intelligence. Only when he lost his left leg in heavy fighting did he interrupt the battle, but he was satisfied that he had fulfilled his vow.

After the war and now an invalid, missing a leg, he did not rest. Arriving back in Radzivilov, he refused repatriation to Poland in order to find the murderers of his family and the Radzivilov Jews. After long searches, he found some, whom he turned over to the NKVD, and when they received their sentences, he finally rested.

In 1957, he used a second opportunity to leave Russia. He arrived in the Land that same year by way of Poland with his Russian wife and two daughters.

It was not easy to be absorbed into the country. His Russian wife—to whom he had described the land as wonderful and amazing—was quickly disappointed at not finding a warm environment there, and she left to return to the Soviet Union.

They parted on good terms: they divided the children. The wife took the younger daughter, and the elder stayed with him.

Life was hard for him. He worked in a factory and came home tired. His daughter, who was now 16 years old, ran the household. She cooked and washed and went to school in the evenings.

He stayed in contact with his wife and daughter in the Soviet Union. He received gifts from them, and he sent packages to them from here. He regretted that it had come to this, that his family had been torn apart. He missed his wife and daughter. His daughter here naturally missed her mother and sister.

To my question of whether he contemplated reuniting with his wife and child, he did not give a clear answer. He said, "It would have been better for me if my wife had refused to make me go this hard way, but we have gone our separate ways because of it, because she couldn't acclimate to this land and I couldn't oppose her decision to leave the land."

[page 349]

"My daughter and I went with them to Haifa. And only then, when the ship was leaving, did I understand that I had made a great mistake." I took his answer to mean that the family would reunite in the end. What other way could there be? I suspect that in the end he will take his daughter and leave the Land and return to his wife and child.

His testimony vividly reflects the difficult struggle for survival of the Jews of Radzivilov and Brody during the Nazi occupation.

Y. Porokhovnik provided the names of friends who gave their lives in the struggle with the bloody enemy. We also find important information about the Radzivilov Jews' participation in the partisan movement, and Porokhovnik corroborates with many facts the Ukrainian bandits' active participation in the murder of the local Jews.

Testimony

Date and place of birth: 1924, Radzivilov

Vocation: Factory worker

Address: Holon, Hatanim Street 24 Apt. 4

Family members killed in World War II:

Parents

Father: Yakov-Moshe Porokhovnik, born 1885, killed in Radzivilov ghetto during the liquidation of the second ghetto, October 1942.

Mother: Yehudit Porokhovnik (née Yergis), born in 1895, killed with his father during the liquidation of the second ghetto, October 1942.

Brothers: Gershon Porokhovnik, born 1914, killed in the Radzivilov ghetto during the liquidation of the second ghetto, October 1942.

[page 350]

Shmuel Porokhovnik, born in 1918, killed on the Front, date unknown.

Avraham Porokhovnik, born in 1922. One of the first victims in Radzivilov, shot by the Germans in the first days after their occupation.

Sister: Toybe Porokhovnik, born in 1912. Killed with the parents during the liquidation of the second ghetto, October 1942.

Yechiel Porokhovnik relates:

As a child, I studied at the Tarbut school and later at the Polish public school. I was in school until the Polish-German war broke out in September 1939.

Most of the young people in Radzivilov frequented the local Zionist youth groups. I, for example, was a member of Young Pioneer. At the meetings, we would talk about the Land of Israel. Every one of us dreamed of going to a pioneer training camp and then immigrating to the Land of Israel, but the war ruined all our plans.

My father, Yakov-Moshe Porokhovnik, was a partner in a mill in Radzivilov. He had a team of four or five horses and used to transport flour from the mill to the flour merchants. Like my brothers, I helped my father in this work.

When the Polish-German war broke out and the Russians marched into Radzivilov in September 1939, I went to work as a laborer in a sawmill and worked there until the German-Soviet war began, in July 1941.

Before the Soviet period, certain changes had taken place in Radzivilov. The larger enterprises, such as the sawmill, [grain] mills, bakeries, shops, and artisan workshops, had been taken into the government domain. Various artisan cooperatives (artels) were organized.

[page 351]

The Soviet authorities engaged mostly people with a pro-Soviet attitude from the laboring masses for work details in various establishments and institutions. Also, many Ukrainians expressed their eagerness to help the Soviet authorities. Among such Ukrainian activists were no small number of great anti-Semites, who exploited their hatred for Jews at every opportunity.

There were a significant number of Jewish refugees from Poland in Radzivilov. From their families who had remained under the Germans, they had already heard about their ill treatment under the Germans. A large proportion of the refugees signed up with the Soviets to be returned to their families, and the Soviet military later registered them all to be deported to Russia; thanks to that, they survived.

When the German-Soviet War broke out on July 22, 1941, chaos ensued. The refugees worried that the Germans would throw the Jews into a ghetto and that it would be terrible. Young people began to flee, especially Jews who had actively helped the Soviets. The Soviets did not manage to mobilize at all; they did not have any time, and the Red Army ceded in disarray. The Jews fled to Kremenets and from there to the border. But the Russian border patrol would not let anyone through, and they were forced to return to the town. Only a few succeeded in getting through.

The First Days of the German Occupation

My brother Avraham and I were among those who had fled Radzivilov. I returned home, and my brother stayed in Kremenets. He had been active for the Soviets, and it was understood that he could not return to Radzivilov.

[page 352]

When the Germans arrived in Radzivilov, the Ukrainians put together a list of the Jews who had been active in the former Soviet establishment, and naturally my brother was on the list.

The Ukrainians who had previously worked with the Soviet authorities quickly changed their colors and went heart and soul to help the Germans. Then began the robbery of Jewish possessions. They had established a self-determination government and received broad powers from the Germans. They began to settle accounts with Jews that they had had an eye on, taking special revenge on former communists, Soviet youth members, and ordinary Soviet activists.

My Brother Avraham's Death

As I mentioned before, my brother Avraham had stayed in Kremenets and did not return to Radzivilov. The Ukrainians broadcast a rumor in Kremenets that the Jews had killed a Ukrainian in the Kremenets jail and called for revenge against the Jews. My brother was among those Jewish arrestees in the Kremenets jail, whom the Germans had arrested along with other Kremenets Jews. A crowd of a few hundred Ukrainians in a wild frenzy, armed with axes, knives, and clubs, stormed the Kremenets jail and created a bloodbath. They beat dozens of Jews to death. My brother managed to escape from the jail at the beginning of the pogrom and came home to Radzivilov.

There were two German officers lodged at our house, and we thought our lives were more secure because of that. But when the Ukrainian police began to search out and arrest former communists and Communist Youth members, they of course had my brother Avraham's name on the list, and late one evening they came to take him away.

I was sleeping along with my brother Avraham when the Ukrainian police knocked on the window to be let inside. My brother and I got dressed and were preparing to run out through the back door. My father went to open the door.

[page 353]

Just at that moment, my brother began to run, but the house was surrounded by police. At that moment, as he tried to tear through the door, the police opened fire on him. He fell dead on the spot. I wanted to run right after him, but seeing that my brother was already dead, I remained where I was.

My brother's death shattered us. The news spread like lightning through the town. He was one of the first Nazi victims in Radzivilov. His dead body remained by the steps to our house.

The German officers who lodged with us did not let us take my dead brother into the house, motivated by the idea of starting an investigation against the police who had not had any right to shoot, according to their reckoning, a person who had not stepped over the threshold of the house. But the following evening the police came and took my brother's dead body to the sand pits outside the town and buried it there.

Early in the morning, we found my brother's grave. My father went to the police and asked for permission to take my brother to the Jewish cemetery, but the Ukrainian police commander, Zalewski, even though he had been a friend of my father's before, denied permission. Then we took a chance and, on our own initiative, dug up my brother, transferred him to the Jewish cemetery, and reburied him in the proper Jewish way. Others were at the reburial, among them our Dov Grinshteyn (who now lives in Ramat Gan).

Even as we were still covering the grave, the police arrived and arrested all of us. Later they released everyone except me. They tortured me for a few days, beating me so that I would confess that I was a Communist Youth member, but I did not confess. Seeing that they could not get anything out of me, they let me go home, too.

[page 354]

I swore on my dead brother's grave to take revenge on the fascists, Ukrainians, and Germans, and later I did indeed make good on my vow.

I want to emphasize that on the night when the Ukrainian police shot my brother, the police also shot 30 to 40 Jews from Radzivilov, mostly former Soviet activists. Among those shot was Yakira, who had been a rabbi in Kozin before the Polish times.

The Germans Show Their Ugly Face

We passed the first week of the German occupation under the savage terror of the Ukrainian police. Later, a detachment of Gestapo showed up and set up an administration in town, and a fresh cycle of robberies, offenses, and murders began.

First off, the administration issued an order that the Jews must wear a white armband with a blue star of David. Jews were forbidden to walk on the sidewalks or to have contact with the Christian population.

About two or three weeks after the Germans marched into town,[*] they commanded the whole Jewish population, young and old, to assemble in the market square. Something was going to happen. The Germans sorted craftsmen and noncraftsmen separately. The market square was surrounded by Germans and police. At the same time, roving gangs robbed Jewish

---

[*] *Note in original:* About this same fact, Yitschak Vaynshteyn says that this was on August 28 and not a few weeks after the Germans entered the town, as Porokhovnik tells it.—Y. A.

houses of whatever they liked. Then something happened: everyone was released and felt they had gotten off with just fear. The Jews returning home found that their houses had been looted. The reason they were released was never known.

The Germans systematically demanded contributions from the Jewish Committee they had established: money, gold, and valuables. In addition, the Germans demanded Jews for various hard labor jobs.

[page 355]

The Germans gathered a few dozen craftsmen and transported them to Vinnitsa. There they worked in a camp. Among those shipped off were my uncle Nechemye Porokhovnik (he died on February 27, 1961, in Israel); both of the Barash brothers, who were carpenters; two of the Beregovski brothers; Volf Kaplan (now in Chelyabinsk, Russia); and others that I do not remember now. Only a few ever returned from that camp. All the others died there in Vinnitsa.

Two Ghettos: For the "Useful" and for the "Not-Useful"

The Germans ordered that a ghetto be set up for the Jews in Radzivilov. So they designated a special area, where the poor Jews had previously lived. The ghetto was fenced in with barbed wire and guarded by Ukrainian and Jewish police.

After the ghetto was created, the Germans divided the Jewish population into two categories: "useful" and "not-useful." The useful workers, craftsmen and professionals, received special passes, and they were permitted to take their families and live in the area that we called "Korea"; the not-useful—old folks, women, children, and sick people—did not receive passes, and they lived in a separate area "by the river." I cannot say how many Jews lived in the ghetto.

At first, I worked in a sawmill; later I went to work with my brother Gershon in a mill. Our family had always been involved with flour and grain. My brother Gershon and I received passes as useful workers, and we took our family and went to live in the ghetto for the useful. I even had permission to go outside the ghetto, because I worked in the mill, which was located on the "Aryan" side.

That life was not easy but we coped with it.

[page 356]

The Liquidation of the "Not-Useful" Ghetto

In total, the "not-useful" ghetto existed for a couple of months. At the end of June 1942, at dawn, when everyone was sleeping, the ghetto was quickly surrounded by Germans and police. All those who did not have work passes were told to take a few valuable things, and they were all stood in long lines. Sick people who could not walk were placed in wagons or trucks. One family, Leybush Kaziultshik and his son Chayim, balked at going, and the Germans simply shot them where they stood. The Germans also shot some others who refused to go. They took the dead bodies with them.

All the Jews from the "not-useful" ghetto were led under heavy guard to a forest not far from the village of Leviatin, not far from the old stadium. Pits had already been dug out there, and everyone was shot.

That day, that is, the day of the action, I was working with the horses at the mill. The gentile men told me exactly how the "action" was carried out. In the evening, Pietro Kostiuk and I rode out on horseback to the pits. The people in the pits were still tossing about, the earth was heaving, and blood spurted from the ground. It is hard to say whether anyone managed to run away from the execution, but I think that one boy—Ruven Zeyger (who now lives in the Soviet Union)—did succeed in escaping from the pits. People said that the Jews were forced to undress completely and lie in layers on top of one another, to be shot through with machine guns one group after another until they were all dead. Thus were murdered the largest number of Radzivilov Jews.

The Youth Try to Organize

After the Germans had liquidated the "not-useful" ghetto, the Jews understood that it would not be long until the Germans liquidated the useful Jews, too.

[page 357]

Reports reached us that here and there in Volhynia, the Germans were killing the entire Jewish population without differentiation.

A group of young people in the Radzivilov ghetto organized themselves: the Fayfel brothers—Shalom and Pinchas (Pipa) (Shalom was killed after the second action, and Pinchas lives in Vienna); Chayim Royzen (now in America); Simche Yakira (Siunye) and others. The leader of the group was Asher Tsherkovski. I joined the group, too.

We used to meet and discuss how we might get weapons, what forms of resistance, and so on. Each of us thought that if the Germans wanted to liquidate the ghetto, we should put up an armed resistance. We also had to organize the other young people and flee to the forest to fight the Germans as partisans.

The Liquidation of the Second Ghetto

Five months had not passed since the liquidation of the "not-useful" ghetto when the news suddenly reached us that the Germans were about to completely liquidate the Razivilov Jews.

We had already heard that the Jews in Brody were living comparatively better than those in other towns. So when things became uneasy and people felt that the days of ghetto life were numbered, a lot of Jews fled to Brody. Most were young, especially those who were not tied to families.

In a few days, I think the end of October 1942—that is, after some of the Jews had succeeded in escaping to Brody—the ghetto was suddenly surrounded by police and Germans, and just as in the first action, all the Jews were driven to the site across from the earlier mass graves. Prepared pits, already dug out, were waiting, and the remainder of the Radzivilov Jews were shot. The Germans had dug two pits but filled only one. The second pit is still empty to this day.

It is said that at the second action, the Germans wanted to leave Vider-horn, the interpreter, alive, but he refused and wanted to perish with his family.

My parents, brothers, and sister were killed in the liquidation of the second ghetto.

I Flee to Brody

The night before the second action, I fled to Brody with my friend Genye Rayzman. The Germans had created a border between Brody and Radzivilov that divided Volhynia and Galicia, as it had been before World War I.

Many Jews who were running away from the Radzivilov ghetto toward Brody were caught and promptly shot.

My friend Rayzman and I arrived in Brody without incident. I will say that the Brody *Judenrat* did not accept the fleeing Radzivilov Jews in a friendly way.

Each time the Gestapo demanded workers from the Brody *Judenrat*, the *Judenrat* presented only Radzivilov Jews. Especially brutal and vexing to the Radzivilov Jews in the Brody ghetto were the *Judenrat* president's representative, Tsverling, and a Jewish policeman, Rubin.

Once when the Germans demanded a group of Jews from the Brody *Judenrat* to send out (you didn't know whether to work or to death), the Brody *Judenrat* put my friend Chayim Feldman on the list of those to be sent out. Mendel Tsverling was riding in the same train car. They talked about cutting a hole in the car while they were on the journey and escaping through the hole. And that is what happened: they cut out a hole near the door with a saw and opened the door, and many succeeded in jumping from the car and turning back to Brody.

When my friend and I arrived in Brody, we did not want to go into the ghetto.

[page 359]

We communicated with a friend of ours, Henekh Tishker, and with him, we dug out a bunker in his former residence. There were 30 men in that bunker, most of them young, among them five from Radzivilov: myself, Chayim Feldman, Leyb Kripitser (who was murdered), Yakov Paritski (who now lives in England) and Simche Zats (who lives in America).

The Bunker in Brody

The bunker was well made, equipped with everything we needed. There were two exits, both camouflaged. From the bunker, we kept in contact with friends in the ghetto and in other hideaways in the city.

As I have already said, the bunker was located in Henekh Tishker's former apartment. A Christian who lived there provided us with food. We were in the bunker for about half a year. We understood that we could not stay in the bunker for long, so we made plans to leave the bunker and go to the forest. We already knew that the partisans were based about 30 kilometers from Brody, in the Leshniov forest.

I Set Up Contact with the Partisans

I left the bunker, and in a few days' time I arrived safely in the Leshniov forest. I succeeded in finding a group of armed partisans, mostly former Russian prisoners of war, Poles, and a few Jews. At first, they did not trust me. They interrogated me, and after I had stayed with them for a few weeks, they gave me a revolver and an assignment: go into the Brody ghetto and bring a troop of young people back to the partisans. The group of partisans numbered 20-odd men and required high-quality recruits, in order to develop the partisan movement that was fighting two enemies—the Germans and the Ukrainian nationalists.

[page 360]

I Lead a Group of Jews out of Brody and into the Forest

For the first time, a friend from Lvov (whose family name I forget) and I went out armed, off to Brody to lead a group of Jews out to the forest. The Lvov friend went into the Brody ghetto to bring a group of Jews out, and I went off to the bunker to bring all the Jews to the forest. Both groups had to meet at one place. When I was already sitting in the bunker, we suddenly heard a shout from the Germans: "*Juden raus*!!" As I already said, there was an extra exit from the bunker. The Jews turned to that exit and wanted to run away. The Germans at that point started to chop out a bunker window that had been walled over. I quickly shouted, "Wait, don't go out!" I then shot three bullets in the direction where the Germans had chopped at the walled-over window.

The Germans could not make a judgment about the shots; it caused them some confusion. They thought that there was a well-armed group of partisans in the bunker. They ran off. I was first to run out and fired off several shots after the fleeing Germans and police. I ordered everyone to run after me.

Using the fleeing Germans' confusion, I succeeded in leading all 28 Jews through the city. I led them through side streets, past the cloister, toward to forest. So we got through the city of Brody safely and arrived in the forest.

The Lvov friend who went into the Brody ghetto to bring out a group of youths was caught during the night by the police, who conducted a sudden raid and killed him.

The Heroic Deed of a Radzivilov Youth

I want to mention that while I was sitting in the bunker in Brody, we had a case in which one Radzivilov youth—Hersh Marder, who escaped on his own from the Radzivilov ghetto—and had already fought as a partisan with a weapon in his hands, was caught by the Germans.

[page 361]

They brought him to the Brody jail. The Brody jail was guarded by firefighters.

While sitting in jail, he was able to hide his revolver. Once when they were taking him to an interrogation, to the interrogation judge, he shot his guard along the way and ran off to the Brody ghetto.

When the Germans learned about it, they came into the Brody ghetto to search for him. The Germans let the Ukrainian police and firefighters take revenge on the Jews for shooting the guard.

The bandits rampaged in the Brody ghetto for half an hour, and many Jews were killed. That was in the beginning of 1943.

The Death of a Polish Provocateur

When we were in the bunker, at the moment when the Germans started shouting "*Juden raus!*", Tishker recognized the voice of his neighbor, the Pole Yantshin, in the German shouting. After we had left the bunker in one piece, we decided to clean out the provocateur Yantshin before we went to the forest.

Tishker, Chayim Feldman, Simche Zats, Leyb Kripitser, and I turned back to Brody and went to Yantshin's apartment. Tishker—who was Yantshin's neighbor—called him out of his home. When Yantshin was outside and realized that there were four more people besides Tishker, he was frightened. Tishker said to him, "So since the Germans discovered the bunker and the people in the forest, we need food. I propose that you bring out food for the people who were in the bunker."

Yantshin answered, "In my house I have only pork and some other food, but my neighbor has just baked bread, so I suggest you go in to the neighbor and get some bread, and meanwhile I'll bring out some pork." (We knew that there were a lot of Germans drinking whisky at the neighbor's house where he was sending us.) We told Yantshin, "You go to the neighbor yourself and ask for bread."

[page 362]

(We realized that he would happily go to the neighbor and tell the Germans about us.) When Yantshin returned to the doorway, I shot him as he came out, putting several bullets in him (only I had a revolver). I laid out that despicable being where he stood. We fled immediately.

When the Germans heard shooting in the street, they ran out of the house, opened fire, but we had already escaped. Yantshin lay dead. We had finished our game.

The Jews' Friend, Sakovitsh

I will take this opportunity to say a few words about Sakovitsh, a friend to Jews.

While we were in the bunker in Brody, Tishker kept in contact with a well-known Lithuanian man, Sakovitsh. He was a communist and a great friend to Jews. Indeed, he was the main supplier of food for the 28 Jews who were holed up in the bunker. He organized a network of Jew-friendly peasants who systematically delivered food to him for the Jews. Sakovitsh would give the food to one of Tishker's neighbors, and she would hand the food over to us. I will tell you more about Sakovitsh later.

We Lead 20 Jews out of the Brody Ghetto

In the forest, in spring 1943, the news reached us that the Germans were preparing to liquidate the Brody ghetto. In all of Volhynia, there were no more ghettos at that time, and all the cities and towns in Volhynia, except for Brody, were already "*Judenrein*" ["clean of Jews"].

A friend and I went off to the Brody ghetto and were successful in getting 20 Jews out and bringing them to the partisans before the liquidation.

During the liquidation of the Brody ghetto, some Jews succeeded in escaping, and they later joined us.

[page 363]

Our detachment grew to about 100 men, in large part Jews. We had five Razivilov Jews in our detachment: myself, Feldman, Leyb Kripitser, Yakov Paritski, and Simche Zats.

My Partisan Activities

Our partisan detachment was the only one that operated in the neighborhood around Brody. We fought Germans and Ukrainian nationalists. We had no contact with any central partisan headquarters and dealt according to our own discretion and at our own responsibility. At the head of our detachment stood a former Russian Army captain, who had escaped from the fortress in Brisk (I do not know his family name, but his pseudonym was "D. Tovarishtsh").

Our detachment was divided into four groups, with 25 men in each group. Each group had its commander. I was a commander of one such group. All five of the Radzivilov Jews I listed above were in my group.

As the Leshniov forest extended for some 15 to 20 kilometers and German wagon trains and gendarmes used to pass through it, we used to attack small groups of German gendarmes and police (we did not attack the larger groups). We carried out local operations, organizing food and weapons. The main partisan stronghold was based about 100 kilometers from us, in the area of Polesia. We did not, as I stated before, have any ties with them.

The Ukrainian Nationalist Division

The German-sponsored Ukrainian Nationalist Division was active in our area, calling itself *Ukarainskaya Dobrovoltsheskaya Divizia*. The division fought against the Red Army and skirmished with the Russian partisans. The division was a military formation under the direction of the S. D.

The Germans trained them in order to send them to the front, but they did not want to go to the front and wanted to proclaim an independent Ukraine.

[page 364]

They were scattered throughout the forest and later fought against the Germans.

We also had our people in the division. Zaluzshny, a Ukrainian, was stationed in division headquarters. In fact, he was a friend of the partisan movement. From him, we learned about their operative plans against the partisans.

Ukrainian Division headquarters did not know our actual strength, and they even wanted to establish a connection with us, knowing that we were fighting against the Germans—the common enemy.

Our commander sent out a three-man delegation on a mission to the Division, to say that we should not fight one another. I was one of the three men in the delegation.

The Ukrainian Division headquarters was located about 10 kilometers from the town of Leshniov, 30 kilometers from Brody. Our negotiations brought good results: We spoke together about not fighting one another. Our and their groups operated without restraint in the same areas.

Zaluzshny explained his intent to get the Ukrainian Division leadership to talk with us about unification. He informed us that we should be careful. In the report we submitted to our commander after the two-day deliberation with the Ukrainians, we also informed him that Zaluzshny had warned us that the Ukrainian headquarters was agreeable to stopping war operations between us, with the intent of learning about our actual strength, seizing our weapons, and later wiping us out.

That warning from Zaluzshny was later confirmed, and thanks to him, we gradually prepared ourselves for an eventual unexpected attack from the Ukrainians.

The question of providing food for our detachment was a very difficult one. In the area where we were operating, so as not to incite hatred on the part of the peasants, we did not want to take their products by force, something that would cause a panic among the local population, and they would not treat us as partisans but as plain bandits.

[page 365]

That would also give the peasants an opportunity to help the Ukrainians wipe us out. For all these reasons, we were forced to operate on an economic basis in distant places. That stretched and fractured our not-so-great strength.

Our military intelligence group established contact with several local Poles, who later became our comrades, and they informed us about the local population's mood.

After various successful and unsuccessful operations, our detachment had suffered great losses. In September 1943, 2,500 Germans suddenly had us surrounded. They blocked us in, and we had no chance to tear out of their circle. Probably someone had reported us. We resisted the attacking enemy with our last bit of strength. We suffered great losses in the heavy battle. The commander of our detachment was killed. From our entire detachment, there were only 11 partisans left—8 Jews and 3 Russians.

I Am Wounded

I was badly wounded in the leg during one of the battles with the Ukrainians. I took four bullets and was laid up for six weeks until I came back around to myself. I was laid up at a known Pole's house, under the supervision of my dear friend Chayim Feldman, who did not leave my side for one minute.

During that time, as I lay wounded, our group carried out various tasks in the Poniekowice area.

[page 366]

Our acquaintance Zaluzshny's sister lived in the Poniekowice area; she was also a friend to Jews and was completely devoted to the partisans. She informed us that two Ukrainian leaders were in that area and pointed out where they were staying.

The Death of Radzivilov Youth Leyb Kripitser

We worked out a plan for how to liquidate the two Ukrainian leaders. Already knowing where they were, I sent out our group under the leadership of Mikolay Martshenko, a peasant from Zhitomir (I was still lying wounded) to kill the Ukrainian leaders.

After our group successfully arrived at the place where the Ukrainians were located, they surrounded the house, and bursting in, they shot the two Ukrainian leaders. After that bit of work, they went back to the Zaluzshny woman to spend the night.

The local Ukrainians, who saw how our group had killed the Ukrainian leaders, went spying and saw the whole group go into the Zaluzshny house.

That was a mistake. They promptly informed the Germans at the Brody garrison, who came immediately and surrounded the Zaluzshny woman's house.

Four of the people from our group were killed in heavy fighting—two Russians and two Jews. Commander Martshenko was killed. Leyb Kripitser was badly wounded, and under heavy fire from the Germans, his friends carried him out of the house and brought him to us, where Chayim Feldman and I were. But when they arrived, Leyb Kripitser was no longer alive. He had died along the way. We hid him in the forest. So died one of the best from Radzivilov, Leyb Kripitser.

We who remained were a group of six people. Three were killed in later battles. We were left as a group of three—Chayim Feldman and me, and Eliahu Valakh from Brody.

[page 367]

We Turn Back to Brody

Once we were down to a group of three, it did not make any sense to stay in the forest. We were persecuted at every turn and step, and had no chance of survival.

Eliahu Valakh had a sister in Brody who was hiding in a bunker along with 40 other Jews. We decided to go back to Brody and search out the bunker. Eliahu Valakh knew the location of the bunker, but the entrance was well disguised.

The Bunker in Brody

The bunker was in the very center of Brody, in a large, four-story house. There were a lot of Poles and Ukrainians living there. The Germans later learned that there was a bunker behind the house and that Jews were hiding out there, but they could never find the entrance to the bunker, and they did not want to blow up the whole house.

The bunker had been planned earlier by a Jewish engineer. Inside, it was a two-story living space with electric lights. There was running water and a sewage line.

When we arrived at the location of the bunker, we were able to locate the entrance because of our partisan experience. A few Jews came out to bring back food. We stopped the people, who were terrified and wanted to go back into the bunker. Eventually we all went in together. A horrible scene was revealed to us: 40-odd Jews lay half swollen from hunger and unable to move at all.

Eliahu Valakh's sister quickly recognized us and was very happy that we had come. A Radzivilov Jew, Itshe Lerner, was also in that bunker.

We had gone into the bunker with weapons. While sitting in the bunker for a few days, we began to make a plan for what to do next, how to make our existence possible.

[page 368]

I made efforts to contact our friend and sympathizer Sakovitsh, a peasant with whom we had been in touch before, in Tishker's bunker, and with Yanek Stakhovski, a school friend of Tishker's.

We were able to make contact with them, and they agreed to help us with food within the limits of their possibilities.

The food they provided for us was not at all enough to feed 40-some people. After a stormy meeting, we decided that the group of youths, 12 people, should carry out a partisan operation.

The Brody Jews who were staying in the bunker told us that there was a rich Ukrainian living on Train Street in Brody who had two stores of food products.

A Successful Operation

On Sylvester Night 1943–1944, I led a group headed to the Ukrainian's. We knocked on the door and were let into the house. I spoke perfect Ukrainian (I had learned it well in the forest) and said, "We've come from the Ukrainian Underground Movement. You are ordered to supply us with everything, including medicines, food, and clothing. I'll give you time to assemble these things. Meanwhile, we'll take everything we need. We'll come back for the medicines at an appointed deadline. If you speak to anyone about this—you'll all pay with your lives, and your house will go up in smoke."

The Ukrainian and his family were terrified. We took everything we possibly could. The Ukrainian, of course, did not stop us and offered no resistance. We also took his radio. We returned to the bunker after our successful operation, laden with good food. When the Jews recognized how much food we had brought, they all kissed us.

[page 369]

The people were happy that they could satisfy their hunger.

We set up the radio and heard that the front was nearing Sarny. The joy was great, but not for long.

The Germans Discover the Bunker

My friend Chayim Feldman and Eliahu Valakh's sister went out of the bunker to arrange something. At that moment, they noticed a group of armed Germans. The Germans chased them, wanting to detain them. They were lost and did not know what to do: run back to the bunker and tell everyone, or save everyone and give themselves up to the Germans? They chose the first: jump back into the bunker. The Germans opened fire, and Chayim Feldman was wounded in the leg. He ran up to me and told me briefly what had happened: the Germans had discovered the entrance to the bunker. There was no time to ponder. I shouted, "Everyone get out of the bunker through the emergency exit!" Since Chayim Feldman was wounded in the leg, I could not leave him there, of course. I carried him out of the bunker in my arms. Everyone had gotten out by way of the emergency exit. Luckily, we noticed two peasants driving an iron sled. As I had a weapon, I commandeered the sled from them, set Feldman in the sled, and drove off to Sakovitsh, who gave him first aid.

When the Germans tore into the bunker, they did not find anyone there, but destroyed it with grenades.

When we arrived at Sakovitsh's and he saw so many Jews, he said he could not hide so many Jews, and was also afraid of being informed on by his neighbors, who could easily find out that he was hiding Jews, and he and his family would pay with their lives.

[page 370]

He was right. I decided to take the wounded Chayim Feldman and the group of Brody Jews away.

The Death of My Friend Chayim Feldman

At night, I led the group through the neighborhood of the former Brody ghetto. At that time, the front was nearing Brody, and German positions were set up all around the city. Not far from the site of the Brody ghetto, we ran into a group of armed Germans, who saw us and opened heavy fire on us. We withdrew to the ruins of the ghetto. But completely unexpectedly, we also ran into Germans in the ghetto territory. I set Feldman on a sled; the Germans opened fire on us. I shot back. At that moment, Feldman sprang up from the sled on one foot and disappeared someplace. We hid under the ruins of the ghetto. Later, we looked for Feldman for a long time, but did not find him. The Germans were running and shooting without stopping. Feldman was probably captured, because he could not have run on one foot. I did not hear any more from Feldman. He was certainly killed then.

The loss of my best friend Chayim Feldman was the greatest loss of my life. We were loyal friends from childhood on, and as I have remarked, when I was wounded in the leg, Feldman stayed by my side for six weeks. I did the same for Feldman, but in that cursed minute I lost him forever.

The Death of Lize Kober

When the Germans opened fire on us in the area of the Brody ghetto, our group scattered. There remained only Eliahu Valakh and his sister, and also a Brody girl, Lize Kober.

[page 371]

That same night, we went into a cellar, and we decided to sit out the day in the cellar, leave Brody in the morning, and return to the Leshniov forest. We decided that Valakh's sister would go to the peasants we knew and bring us some kind of food. We would wait for her in the cellar.

We were noticed by some gentile men, and they turned us over to the Germans. Sitting in the cellar, we heard voices outside in Ukrainian pointing out the location of the cellar where we were lying in hiding. We saw that we could not wait long. We left the cellar. Lize Kober and I ran in one direction, and Eliahu Valakh ran in another. The Germans opened fire on us as we ran. At that moment, Lize Kober fell. She had taken a bullet and was bleeding badly. She said to me, "Run, save yourself, I am already lost." She remained lying there and died. This was in January 1944.

The Germans Chase after Me

I was running by myself, leaving behind the wounded Lize Kober. The Germans chased after me, shooting on every side. I ran several dozen meters. I dashed into a destroyed house, the Germans after me. I stood still behind a column in the building. When the first German ran in, I shot him and laid him out on the spot. I leapt up to the second story of the building and shot downward. The Germans were after me. I crawled down from the second story to the street and mixed in with the crowd.

I debated what to do. I decided to go back to Sakovitsh. I knocked on his door. He came out. I told him that I was alone. Sakovitsh told me that people in town were saying that some partisan had shot a German. I told him the whole story. Sakovitsh advised me, since it was not too late, to leave his house, as it was systematically spied on by both Ukrainians and Germans.
[page 372]

The Death of Zaluzshny, the Jews' Friend

Having no other alternative, I set out for the Leshniov forest. Zaluzshny lived near there. I went to him, but to my great astonishment I found the house open. Inside, everything was demolished, broken. No one was in the house. I went over to other Poles that I knew and did not find anyone there either. I later found out that the Poles were afraid to spend the night in their houses, because the Ukrainian bandits were also attacking the Poles and murdering them. A Pole told me that a few days earlier, the Ukrainian

Nationalists had killed Zaluzshny and his whole family because of his contacts with the partisans.

Alone in the Forest

I became a forest person. All alone, without family, without colleagues, without friends. It got very bad for me. Death lurked at every step and turn. I wandered from place to place for several months. At night I would knock on a peasant's door for something to eat. Finally, the Ukrainians traced me, but I had been careful and succeeded in escaping their claws.

Liberation

It was March 15 or 20, 1944. I was a vagrant alone in the forest. Suddenly I heard Russian spoken. I thought that it was Ukrainian Nationalists. I tried to take cover, but they saw me. I decided to resist them, come what may, and aimed my revolver. The Russians raised their rifles at me, ready to shoot. I spoke to them in Russian. At first, they took me for a German spy.

[page 373]

They took me to their headquarters, and along the way, they beat me. They were the avant garde of the Soviet Army.

After a detailed interrogation, I explained who I was, and I asked them to take me into their detachment, because I wanted to fight the Germans to take revenge for my murdered family's spilled blood. They wanted to send me into the back country, but I convinced them that I was determined to remain on the front. In the end, they added me to their detail, the 192nd Tashkent Division, 194 Strelkovi Regiment.

As a Fighter in the Soviet Army

The Soviet Army drove the Germans west, liberating Jews in towns and villages. The retreating Germans put up a bitter resistance.

In spring 1944, the offensive was renewed in our sector, and our detail approached Brody, liberating Gorokhov and Radziechów along the way.

In the battles to liberate Brody, many thousands of victims fell on both sides. The city of Brody defended itself against the German army with many

Panzer tanks. Our army spent a whole month in fierce battle for the liberation of Brody. Later, an order arrived from General Headquarters to stop the offensive.

I Am Awarded for the First Time

Some six kilometers from Brody lies the village of Konyushkov. The village stands on top of a hill, and the Germans were shooting at us from there.

Our detail had received an order to bombard the village, which was held by the Germans. The point changed from hand to hand five times. The sixth time, when our detail was off in battle, the commander of the Rote Company was killed. Of the entire Rote, we were left with four soldiers and two machineguns.

[page 374]

We decided that we would not leave at any price and would hold the point. The Germans tried to attack us several times, but without success. We courageously defended it for 24 hours until fresh troops arrived. Thanks to our brave conduct, the point remained in our hands.

All four of us were awarded the Slava Order First Class. We kept fighting until the winter offensive was called off.

Until the summer offensive was renewed—that would be in July 1944—we were sent to fight in the Brody region. During that time, I excelled many times, and the Soviet leadership wanted to send me to officers' school. This was July, 13, 1944. But that same day, we learned that the summer offensive would begin the next day, July 14, 1944. I did not agree to being sent back to the interior for officer training, and I requested to remain at the front. I wanted to carry out my vow: to take revenge for my murdered family. I did not want to leave my position as long as it was possible to stay.

I Am Honored a Second Time

On July 14, the renewed summer offensive began for our division. At dawn, when everyone was impatient after the long waiting period, we went into battle. Within half an hour, our artillery, tanks, aviation, and other sections were all spitting fire and bombing the German positions. After the bombardment, all the other details went on the attack. The Germans responded to our infantry with heavy fire from machineguns and bazookas.

Our battalion could not push forward. Then I noticed the site from which the Germans were raining fire on us. I turned to the battalion commander, Bayev, and asked for permission to silence the German machinegun. The commander gave his agreement. I crept toward the point of the fire and, along with my assistant, Arlov, opened fire from behind.

[page 375]

This caught the Germans completely by surprise. We destroyed the machinegun nest. Then our battalion could move forward without difficulty. For that operation, I was awarded a second time, with the order of the Red Star. Our 192nd Tashkent Division liberated Brody and other cities, towns, and villages. We turned back in the direction of Lvov.

I Lose My Right Leg

From the July 14 to 7, we did not come up against any resistance. Near Lvov, we encountered strong German forces that were defending the city.

Wanting to know what kind of strength the enemy possessed, Gretshko, the commander of our detachment, proposed that we send out some volunteers who could spy out the situation. Not many people volunteered, but I announced myself as a volunteer.

The commander assigned me a platoon of soldiers, and I led the platoon in the espionage mission. The Germans were shooting from all sides. I received an order: penetrate the enemy's position and fix their points of fire. When we closed in face to face with the Germans, a bitter battle began. Many fell on our side, dead and wounded.

I suddenly felt a strong impact in my right leg. It started to burn, and I was pouring blood. I lay on the battlefield for three hours, losing blood. The stretcher-bearers could not reach me. The Germans continued to shoot up the area even though it was very close to the German position. Finally, our detachment succeeded in pushing the Germans out. The orderlies found me and carried me to the nearest field hospital in critical condition.

My right leg had been shot through with bullets, and the left leg was also wounded. At the field hospital, a surgeon promptly amputated the right leg, high above the knee. That was July 17, 1944.

I Am Evacuated to the Interior

After my leg had been amputated, I was taken to a military hospital in Rovno. I lay there for two weeks. The German advance bombed Rovno heavily, and all the seriously wounded were evacuated by medical train to the Caucasus. I was in critical condition the whole time.

Not having been transferred to Caucasus and being in such bad condition, I was sent by the surgeon by medical train to a military hospital in Rostov. It was hospital number 4656. They put me directly into isolation, and none of the medical personnel believed that I would survive the crisis.

I lay in that hospital for nearly a year. Within that time, I regained my strength. I met another member of my battalion in that hospital, too, who had been wounded by the Vistula River. He told me that after I had been wounded on the battlefield, many people in our division talked about me, singing my praises, and he told me I had been raised to the highest award, the Order of the Red Banner.

Greetings from Radzivilov

I also met one of our Radzivilov boys, Mendel Vaynshteyn (now in Russia), in that hospital. He had signed out of the hospital earlier and gone back to Radzivilov. Later, he came back to the hospital and let me know that a few survivors of the destruction of the Radzivilov Jews had returned to Radzivilov. Among them was my uncle Nechemye Porokhovnik (my father's brother, who died in Haifa on November 27, 1961).

Mendel Vaynshteyn also told me that all the Radzivilov Jews wanted to leave Russia and repatriate to Poland. Then I decided to sign myself out of the hospital and return to Radzivilov. The wound was still fresh and was not completely healed. The doctor refused to release me from the hospital. I appealed to the hospital chief, a Jew, Major Yakov Kelman. I explained to him why I wanted to be released from the hospital. He understood completely and issued an order that I be released.

While I was in the hospital, I married Gertrude Kalishnikova.

Return to Radzivilov

I arrived in Radzivilov on April 28, 1945, and there met my uncle Nechemye and all the other Jews who had saved themselves from death. They were all gathering to go back to Poland. My uncle and I decided not to return to Poland: I wanted to take revenge on the Ukrainian bandits who had murdered our family and caused so much trouble for the Jews.

I decided to take it upon myself to search out some Ukrainian murderers and turn them over to the NKVD.

After strenuous efforts and searching, I located some murderers, among them the commander of the city police in Radzivilov, Michal Zuleski; his representative, Jefimczuk; a collaborator with the SD, Tushakovski; and the commander of the regional police, Zudanowski. They all took part in the murder of the Radzivilov Jews and were sentenced by a Soviet military tribunal to 25 years of hard labor.

Besides the "heads," some "smaller" policemen, such as Demko and others, were also sentenced.

After they had all been sentenced, I felt that I had fulfilled my vow—I had carried out my humane duty.

[page 378]

After the War

After the war, I worked for a few years in Rovno, Rovno district, until 1949. Our daughter Irit was born in 1946, and our second daughter, Tova, was born in 1949.

In 1949, it was proposed to me that I go to work as director of the processing of raw materials in Radzivilov. I worked at that post in Radzivilov for more than half a year, but I could not live in Radzivilov. My dear family and all the other Radzivilov Jews had been killed there. I requested a transfer and was sent to work in Zdolbunov. I worked in Zdolbunov from 1951 to 1954. In 1954, my wife and I decided to move to the Urals. We settled in the city of Chelyabinsk. I lived there until 1956. During that time, I received a letter that saying that repatriation to Poland was being renewed. My family and I decided to go back to Poland.

In February 1957, we left Russia and came to Poland with the aim of traveling to Israel, where my uncle Nechemye lived, having arrived in the Land in 1948.

In Poland we settled in Breslau and lived in that city for seven weeks; at the end of April 1957, we left Poland and entered the Land.

Arriving in Israel, I first lived with my family for 10 months in Shaar HaAliya; later the Jewish Agency moved us to Holon.

Now I am an invalid, and I work in the Globus factory in Tel Aviv.

For the sake of information, I would like to add at the end that the chief gendarme in Radzivilov was Krauser.

[page 379]

Song of Our Sorrow

Leyb Ayzen

Spring comes, not far from Summer,
the sun illumes with her warm rays,
the birds in the trees sing their praises to God,
I see the woods, the fields, the meadows
decked out with grasses, flowers, all kinds of colors,
reminding me now of my *shtetl*
of Jewish life until death.

Every lane, house, and masonry building
in our hearts is enveloped in eternal sorrow.
We no longer see all our own
who were torn away forever...
The trees in my shtetl blossom on,
generously giving their fruits,
no longer waiting for the Jewish blessing.

Time forgets quickly, it happened only yesterday.
And yet our memory is so small ...

Review[*]

Interview by Y. Alperovitsh

Ite Gun was 55 years old when the war between Germany and the Soviet Union began. During Hitler's occupation, and especially during the last period before liberation, she was often on the brink of destruction, and it is a miracle that she escaped death.

Ite Gun came from a wealthy family. Her father was a merchant and operated large businesses. As a child, she studied in a Russian school. After her marriage in 1905, she also ran businesses with her husband. They had a big matzo factory and a shop selling household utensils.

After her husband's death in 1920, she ran the businesses alone until 1939, when the Soviets entered Radzivilov.

She lived very well, giving her two daughters a good upbringing and education. She ran a beautifully organized home. The businesses were going well. The Radzivilov Jews remember her as very rich and much valued by the Jewish and non-Jewish populations.

A smart woman, energetic and with an objective outlook on events, it was thanks to her very sensible characteristics that she was able to survive the Hitler occupation.

In fact, for her, the German occupation was a continuation of the suffering and pain she had gone through in the Soviet period. As soon as the Soviets arrived in Radzivilov, they seized her business and also turned her matzo factory into a bakery. She—the former proprietor—was sent back to work as hired labor in the bakery.

The Soviets tricked the former "bourgeois" woman at every step and turn.

---

[*] *Note in original:* From Yad Vashem document 3-147/1908.

[page 381]

She got a passport with a paragraph indicating that she was a citizen of the second category and a candidate to be shipped to Siberia with her family.

She had many sleepless nights. Any knock on the door late at night reminded her that the NKVD might be coming to arrest her. And being afraid was fundamental: the Soviets had deported a couple of dozen "bourgeois" from Radzivilov, and Ite had no grounds to prove that she was an exception. She was soon sentenced for being away from work for more than half an hour without permission.

By the time the Germans entered Radzivilov, she was physically and spiritually broken.

The Ukrainians did not forget that she had been a wealthy woman. They often came into her home and took everything that they wanted. For the Germans, too, her house was a good address for robbery. She did not sleep for whole nights, and as in the Soviet era, she expected a knock on the door.

The Radzivilov *Judenrat* and police embittered her life, especially the president, Yankel Furman, who constantly demanded money, gold, and valuables for himself and the Germans.

Twice she eluded death, one time on the eve of the liquidation of the Brody ghetto. In both cases, she and her family were rescued by the peasant Pietro Moroz.

The period between fleeing the Brody ghetto and liberation was the most difficult for her and the most dangerous of the German occupation.

She was 17 months without a roof over her head, and spent several months with her grandchild in a hole in an old tree. She was out during the day—she did not spend the night there. She slept in the snow in the forest and in the fields under the open sky. She was happy when she had the chance to spend a night in a hog pen, sleeping in a trough that the hogs ate from.

She was in an area where Ukrainian bandits, police, Germans, and blood-thirsty peasants lurked everywhere.

You had to possess a lot of courage, energy, and a realistic orientation in order not to fall into their claws. And she was not alone. She had a nine-year-old grandchild with her—the only one of her family remaining—for whom she had to find food and whose fate she had to concern herself with.

Gradually, she reached the edge of death herself. Physically and spiritual-ly broken, losing her last bit of strength, she fell into apathy, indifferent to any-thing that might happen. Yet each time she saw that her indifference was putting her grandchild at risk, she mobilized a last bit of strength and braved all hardships.

A Jewish woman who had lived her whole life in good material circum-stances, far from physical labor and from nature—forest, field, rivers—had to wander around for 17 months alone over fields, forests, rivers, in snow and freezing weather, in the mud, always hungry and ragged.

Now she is 76 years old, living in Tel Aviv with her daughter, who came to the Land in 1925.

Telling of her survival during the days and nights causes her great sad-ness and pain. It is difficult for her to manage it, and giving testimony takes enormous effort.

Her memory does not serve her well anymore, and I used every possible means to help her concentrate in order to recover answers to the questions posed.

A few years ago, she received a letter and a photo from the grandchild that she saved. He lives in the Soviet Union and has a wife and a child. He studies at the Rovno Conservatory.

She will not let the photo out of her hand; she holds it as a sacred relic.

To preserve her voice, I will make a recording, which will be a good keep-sake for her family, the Radzivilov Organization, and Yad Vashem.

Names Mentioned in the Testimony

Jews:

Aharon Gun—husband

Sheyntshe Norban—daughter

Tsipore Yenai—daughter

Chayim Norban—son-in-law

Zalman Leviten—bookkeeper

Suretski

Shlezinger

Yakira—rabbi

Sunye Zilberman

Yankel Furman—*Judenrat* president

Yakov Shrayer

Itshe Treybitsh

Salke Putshnik

Barash—Brody *Judenrat* president

Shmuel Sherer—nephew

Shlome Gun—nephew

Non-Jews:

Anya Chaykovska—maid

Mateyko—mayor of Radzivilov

Pietro Moroz—peasant/farmer

Places Mentioned in the Testimony

Brody

Dubno

Beuthen

Radzivilov

Olevsk

Testimony

Date and place of birth: 1886, Radzivilov

Address: Tel Aviv, King David Hwy. #6

Family members who perished in World War II:

Daughter: Sheyntshe Norban (Gun), born in 1908, killed in Radzivilov along with her husband and five-year-old daughter.

In addition, she lost many relatives.

Ite Gun relates:

I was born in Radzivilov. My father was a Jewish merchant and had a confectionery business. In my youth I attended Russian high school in Brody. In 1905, I married Aharon Gun (who died in 1920). We had two daughters.

My daughter Tsipore Yenai, who now lives in Israel and with whom I now live, immigrated to Israel in 1925.

The second daughter, Sheyntshe Norban, married Chayim Norban and lived with me, along with her husband and daughter, until they were killed.

For the entire Russian and Polish era, I had a business for household utensils. Besides that, I had a big matzo factory, and every season I sold matzo all over Volhynia. I operated those businesses until the Bolsheviks arrived in town. In 1920, my husband died, and I proceeded to operate the businesses myself. After my daughter Sheyntshe was married, we ran the businesses together.

I was a wealthy woman and had a fine, ordered life. I had a beautiful house, handsomely furnished, and I educated my children. Everything went well until the war between Poland and Germany began in 1939, and a few weeks later the Bolsheviks arrived.

When the Soviets came to Radzivilov, we wealthy people lived in fear, to tell the truth. Early on, they had shipped a number of rich Jews off to Siberia, and every day I, too, expected to be deported along with my daughter, son-in-law, and grandchild.

When the Soviets began to issue passports, all the former merchants were given passports with a "paragraph." And of course, I and my daughter and son-in-law received passports with a paragraph.

I saw at once that it would be best if I willingly gave up my businesses; since I had a matzo factory, I had a location with a big oven. Plus, I had a large stock of flour in a warehouse.

When handing over the matzo factory, I simply asked them to allow me to work there as an assistant. They agreed. They confiscated all the flour and turned the matzo factory into a bakery, and started bringing in flour to bake bread for the population. Given that I was working for them as an assistant and that the flour warehouse was at my house, the Soviets made me responsible for the flour. I had signed receipts for receiving so much flour for a sum of 4,000 rubles. The flour was beginning to be used to bake bread, so there was less and less flour. I did not have documents to show how much flour had been taken out of the warehouse. I could see that the Soviets were going to ask me later where the flour went. I set off to the accounting office to ask for my signed receipts back. Along the way I met a Jew who was a representative for the Soviets. He asked me, "Where are you going during your work hours?" I related why I had to go to accounting. Then he replied, "You're away in the middle of your work, you've made a mistake." He denounced me to the court.

[page 386]

At the sentencing, he said that since I was a former bourgeois and had sabotaged the work, he would take 25% of my pension of 120 rubles a month for a period of six months. And if there were a repetition—that is, if I left work again without permission—I would be put into prison.

The Soviets also wanted to take my house, but I managed to avoid that decree. My son-in-law worked as a laborer.

I want to tell you that before the Soviets, there were shortages of products. Hundreds of people stood in lines in front of the shops for a piece of bread and other products. But since I worked with them in the bakery, I was concerned with bread, and I used to help other Jews.

I have to tell you that right as the Soviets were coming in, some of our small-time Jews began collaborating with the Soviets, wanting to take revenge on the formerly wealthy. They caused us wealthy people a lot of problems. Those Jews also called up the wrath of the Christian population and intensified the anti-Semitism. Later, when the Germans came in, the Christians took revenge on all the Jews.

As I have already said, we lived in fear. I figured each day that I would be arrested and sent to Siberia. The Soviets, meanwhile, were busy deporting former Polish officials—and the administrators and all those with the "paragraph" on their passports were left in peace for the time being.

During the Soviet occupation, I took in two young men from Stanislau who were fleeing from a German camp. I gave them a separate room, and something to eat and drink. The boys were educated—one was a teacher of German, and the second taught mathematics. One was named Sukhetski, and the second one's family name was Shlezinger. The young men later helped me with the Germans, but I will tell you about that later.

[page 387]

And so I lived in fear and fright of the Soviets until war broke out with the Germans.

Life with the Germans

The Germans arrived at the end of June 1941. At first, the Ukrainians went wild, beginning first of all with scoffing at the Jews, who were "communists, communist youth, and activists for the communists."

When the war with the Germans began, all those who had been "big shots" with the Bolsheviks tried to run away, but fleeing was not possible. The Germans sped ahead and forced them to turn back to Radzivilov.

The Ukrainians went wild. They went house to house robbing, taking every-thing they could carry away.

The Germans ordered all the Jews to wear the Star of David on their arms, and later on the shoulders as a yellow patch in front and in back.

The First Jewish Victims in Radzivilov

The Germans took about 30 Jews. They were told to dig pits in the forest, and then they were shot. Among those shot, I recall, were Zalman Leviten, who worked in the mill as a bookkeeper; the rabbi Yakira; and a boy from our street, Sunye Zilberman.

The Germans Mock the Jews

Once Gestapo officers came to my house. They ripped out the shelves, took the best pieces of furniture, and went into my warehouse where the flour was kept, and which the Soviets had brought in.

The Germans ordered my son-in-law to take a sack of flour and put it into their automobile. My daughter and I helped my son-in-law load the sack of flour into the automobile. Later the Germans said to my son-in-law, "Go wash yourself, and wash the place over your heart really well, because pretty soon we're going to shoot you."

[page 388]

This time we were really suffering from fear. You can imagine what we went through until the Germans left the house.

One time, a German came in and started to search around the house, and I could see that he wanted to get up into the attic. Up there was a closed writing desk. He broke up the desk, took some other things, and left the house.

It was terrible. I did not close an eye for whole long nights. Any rustle I heard from the street made me sure that the bandits were coming to us.

Once there was an incident when my son-in-law was standing near the house without a Star of David on his arm. Two Ukrainians came along and noticed him. They took him to the local commandant, beat him badly, and then threw him into the cellar. I followed after him there. On the way, I met a familiar peasant who had become a policeman, and I told him what had happened. I begged him to help me. He did indeed promise to help me free my son-in-law. He calmed me down and said, "Go home, Ite. Your son-in-law will come to you soon." And so it happened: a short while later my son-in-law was freed. and we were still suffering in fear.

In the Ghetto

This was, I think, around Passover 1942. The Germans ordered all Jews in Radzivilov to leave their houses and gave a deadline of one day to move into the ghetto. We were happy that all the Jews would be together, and thought perhaps the fear would not be so great. All the Jews brought what they could with them. I brought whatever I was able, including a lot of food products and wood—enough to last several years.

The Germans did not come into the ghetto often. My son-in-law worked outside the ghetto, and he used to carry messages from the Germans and had permission to move freely around the town. He was out in the town the whole day and came home to spend the night with us.

[page 389]

For 13 years before the war, Anya Zaykovskaya, a housemaid, worked for me; she was a peasant and very devoted. When the ghetto was fenced in with wire, she would come to the wire every day and bring us something to eat. Every Thursday she brought me a chicken for the Sabbath. Once, she was caught at the fence by a Ukrainian policeman while she was giving me food. He beat her and would have taken her to the commandant's office. She begged him to let her go. He warned her that if he saw her by the ghetto fence again, she would pay for it with her life. The peasant had worked for me some 10 years before. I gave him 50 marks and he let her go, but she was afraid to come again.

In the ghetto I lived in a room with 11 people. The crowding was bad, but at least food was taken care of. I had brought a supply of food, and besides that, my son-in-law brought some food in from the town every day.

The *Judenrat* and the Police

I have to tell the truth: I suffered more from the *Judenrat* and the police than from the Germans. The president was Yankel Furman—a coarse Jew, an ignorant and vile person. The Jewish police along with the *Judenrat* tore pieces out of us. Especially from the Jews who had possessions. They demanded money, gold, and other things for themselves and the Germans.

Yankel Furman wanted my son-in-law to work for the *Judenrat,* but he refused. I could never have imagined before that Jews could so bad to Jews, so brutal, without any reason. They could tear the last bite from your mouth.

The Germans really did demand money, gold, silver, and silver goblets from the *Judenrat* daily, and the Jewish police collected it all. I gave away everything I had. There were a few Jewish policemen in the ghetto who ran rampant.

[page 390]

Later they divided the ghetto into "useful" and "not-useful" parts. The workers received special passes. The nonworking, old, and ill did not get passes.

My son-in-law had a pass, and he was allowed to include my daughter and their two children on it. I did not work and did not have any pass.

Later, when they separated out all those who did not have passes, I did not go with them and stayed with my daughter. We understood that the day would come when all the "not-usefuls" would be shot.

When the news reached us that the "not-useful" Jews from Dubno, Rovno, and the surrounding areas were being killed off, we knew we were right.

Before the "action," Yankel Furman, the president, came to me and said, "Ite, you don't have a pass, and you have no right to live here in the ghetto. You must simply go over to 'that' ghetto." Yankel Furman already knew that in a few days "that" ghetto would be liquidated, so he wanted me to be killed there as well. I understood that going over to that ghetto meant death.

The Liquidation of the "Not-Useful" Ghetto

News reached us that the Germans were gathering to liquidate that ghetto. The Jews there were living in terror. And the Jews who did not have passes and lived in hiding in the "useful" ghetto were trembling. I did not have a pass either. What to do?

I have already told you that before the Soviets came, I had taken in two young Jewish men. The boys were now well situated with the Germans. One worked as a translator, and the other in a German office. They had promised to help me. They wanted to get an empty, blank pass and fill it in themselves, but they could not find any blanks.

[page 391]

Sukhetski told me that he was even prepared to make his pass over for me.

When the Germans surrounded the "not-useful" ghetto and led away the Jews to be shot, Sukhetski said, "Don't be afraid. I'll come and spend the night with you. You hide under the chest. When the Germans go in to the house and find me there, they'll stop searching."

On that day of the liquidation, I hid under the chest. They took all the Jews from that ghetto far outside the town and shot them. I languished in terror.

I Remain in the Ghetto

On that day of the liquidation of the other ghetto, several Jews escaped during the "action," and we hid them in the ghetto. They related how the Germans and Ukrainians had dragged old and sick people out of the houses, loaded them onto farm wagons and trucks, and drove off with them. Those who resisted were shot on the spot.

The Germans had promised that they would not bother the useful Jewish workers. The rabbis were among those who were fed false illusions that the workers and their families would not be liquidated. But realistic people felt that the German assurances were worth nothing. Each person sought ways to save himself. Some dealt with known people, good peasants, who for good pay would hide them. Happy was the one who had such a well-known gentile.

The proprietor of the house where I lived in the ghetto sometimes asked the mayor of the town, Mateyko, who was a friend of hers, how long we would live in the ghetto. The mayor answered, "You'll eat the summer fruit, but not the winter fruit." We well understood the meaning of the words.

[page 392]

We Flee the Ghetto

The date for the liquidation of the Radzivilov ghetto drew closer. Peasants came into the ghetto and told us that more pits were being dug. The Jews did not believe it. They interpreted it to mean that the non-Jews were creating a panic so the Jews would hide their money and gold with them. The Jews convinced themselves that the pits were for storing potatoes for the winter. The Jews believed these illusions because in Brody at that time, there was still a ghetto, and the Jews there were not doing too badly. And how was Radzivilov a lesser town than Brody? the Jews asked themselves.

I had a friendly peasant in Pietro Moroz. We were good friends with him. He had told me, "Don't be afraid. When it becomes necessary, I'll hide you and your family with us." Yet my son-in-law asked, "How long can you hide out with a gentile, and what if the war goes on for a long time?" But there was no better way out.

The time came when a lot of police and Germans entered the town. We understood: they were going to liquidate the remaining Jews of Radzivilov. We decided to leave the ghetto as long as it was not too late. I discussed it with my son-in-law and daughter, that we would flee separately so we would not be noticed and would not arouse suspicion around us.

My son-in-law and daughter went first with their children. Later I left the ghetto. I went to a peasant friend and hid there. Eventually I let Moroz know where we were so he could come sometime later and take us with him. Our family members met at the peasant's. Moroz came at night and took us with him.

I must add that when we left the ghetto, Itshe Treybitsh's family, with two children, left just after us. They said, "Where you go, we'll go, too. Do as you will, we won't be far behind."

[page 393]

When the peasant Moroz saw that another family was dragging along behind us, he told me he was prepared to hide my family, but no one else. But what to do with the Treybitsh family? Because of them, Moroz would not take us into his home either, and he left us in the forest. He was simply afraid of trying to hide so many people.

In the Forest

While we were in the forest, the Jews in the Radzivilov ghetto were slaughtered. Rumors spread among the peasants that, about three kilometers from Brody, there were Jews in the woods who were carrying a lot of money.

After a while, a peasant with an axe approached us and asked, "What are you doing here in the forest?" I did not hesitate and answered that we were just resting here, that we were on our way to Brody. I said that so the peasant would not think we would stay there in the forest. I gave him 100 marks, and he went away. Later another gentile came, and then the first one again.

Moroz arrived, and we told him the story about the gentiles. He agreed to drive us to another place. The Treybitsh family went with us. The new place was not far from Brody. Moroz assured us that no one would bother us there. He promised to bring us food.

The new place was a field of cut hay, belonging to a wealthy owner. At that time, there were still stalks of uncut hay in the field, and in the morning, peasants arrived to cut them. We were afraid the peasants would see us and report us to the Germans. When Moroz arrived, I told him this was not a place to stay, and I did not see any other way than to go back to Brody, where at the time Jews were still living.

[page 394]

Moroz brought us food, and another peasant undertook to drive us to the border for money. (The border between Germany and the [Polish] General Government was near Radzivilov.)

In Brody

We arrived in Brody in one piece. The situation of the Jews in Brody was already very poor. There was nothing to eat. The Germans had systematically extorted all the money, possessions, and foodstuffs from the Brody Jews under the threat of death. There was no ghetto there yet.

Some of the Jews had made hiding places for themselves. I met a Jewish friend, and he related the situation to me.

In Brody I found Salke Putshnik, my brother's sister-in-law. She took us in and gave us food and money. Later we moved to another apartment. Five weeks later, the Brody ghetto was created. You ask me, when was that? It seems to me that it was Passover 1943, but I don't remember exactly. But our apartment was figured into the territory of the ghetto.

In the Brody Ghetto

It was very bad. There was nothing to eat, and it was not possible to leave the ghetto to bring in something to eat. And we did not have any good friends in the Brody ghetto. Some informed on me to the *Judenrat* for being a rich woman, and the *Judenrat* demanded that I surrender money and gold to them. No one would believe that I did not have any money. But since I did not have anything to hand over, the *Judenrat* wanted to arrest my son-in-law. We hid him.

When the Jewish policemen came to take my son-in-law, they did not find him. In their anger, they arrested my daughter. They held her for eight days and threatened us, saying that if I did not give up the money and gold, they would not free her.

[page 395]

The president of the *Judenrat* in the Brody ghetto was Barash, someone I knew. I appealed to him to free my daughter. He answered, "Send me your son-in-law, and I'll free your daughter." There was no alternative, so my son-in-law presented himself to the *Judenrat*. They set my daughter free at once, and later they also freed my son-in-law.

Some time went by, and things were very bad for us. We did not have any money, and there was no way to buy any food. Around that time, the Germans demanded that the *Judenrat* assemble young men for military drills. All the young men reported, among them my son-in-law. The Germans gathered more than 300 men, marched them away to a camp in Olevsk, and shot them all. That is how my son-in-law was killed. That was at the beginning of 1943.

The Liquidation of the Brody Ghetto

After my son-in-law's death, I remained in the Brody ghetto with my daughter and two grandchildren. The time for the liquidation of the Brody ghetto was approaching.

Suddenly, completely unexpectedly, the Germans surrounded the ghetto. My daughter and grandchildren and I hid between two fences during the "action." A nephew of mine, Shmuel Sherer, also lay hidden with us. He said, "Let's run away from here." At night, we escaped from the burning ghetto and went back to the peasant Moroz.

When Moroz saw us, and saw that I had brought another group of Jews, he refused to let us into his house, and we stayed in the woods. There were eight of us.

[page 396]

The Death of My Daughter and Grandchild

Then the woods where we were located were surrounded by Germans and police. They began to draw closer to us. When they saw the Germans, my nephew, my daughter, and both grandchildren started to run away, but I stumbled and fell down. The Germans did nothing to me and chased after my nephew, daughter, and grandchildren. The Germans caught my nephew with his wife and their two children and shot them on the spot. Later, they caught my daughter and one grandchild and shot them. My grandchild

Siunye, a boy of nine, succeeded in hiding, and the Germans did not notice him.

I lay there until night. The deaths of my daughter and grandchild and of my nephew and his family had totally devastated me. I lay and waited for death. It was all the same to me. In a few days Moroz came. He found me in the woods. He told me that he had found my grandchild Siunye. I was very happy that one grandchild had been saved.

We Hide Out in a Hole in a Tree

Moroz could not take us into his house, as his wife would not allow it. There was no alternative but to hide us in a hole in an old tree. We settled in there. At night Moroz brought us food.

I must tell you that getting us to the tree was not simple. There was a stream around the tree. Moroz drove up to the stream with a horse, swam across the stream, and brought us food.

It is very difficult for me to tell you what I have experienced, and I am tired now. I will tell you a shortened version.

It happened that peasants had killed six Germans. The Germans had gone wild, going into peasants' cottages, robbing them, and beating them. The Germans also went into Moroz's house. It had been reported that Moroz was hiding a couple of Jews.

[page 397]

They immediately shot his wife, and Moroz himself barely got away with his life. They burned his house, and he went to stay with a nephew.

I lost such a good peasant in Moroz. There was no one who could bring us anything to eat.

Without a Roof over Our Heads

There was no other way but to go from house to house begging for something to eat. The peasants were inclined to be very anti-Semitic. But I had some good luck, in that they did not turn me over to the Germans or kill me themselves. My grandchild and I spent the nights in the snow. Hungry and ragged, we trudged from house to house begging for a piece of bread. Whole days went by when we did not have a bite to put in our mouths. I felt that my strength had already left me. Often, I would spend the night with my grandchild in a trough where the pigs were given their food in the stall. I said to my grandchild, "My child, I will not live through these troubles; you are still young, go and save yourself." But he would not hear of it. He did not leave me and wanted to share my fate with me, notwithstanding his mere 10 years.

By now I had completely lost my strength. But we had to keep changing our location. I crawled on my knees for four kilometers until we reached a village. I lay down and pleaded for death.

That is how I suffered for 17 months in the forest until liberation. The hardest part was the last three or four months.

Liberation

The front finally approached Radzivilov. That was spring 1944. I had gone to a peasant woman to beg for something to eat. The woman had not been willing to let me into her house before, but when she perceived that the Soviets were already nearby, she was completely different. She gave us food and allowed us to stay overnight. When I wanted to leave in the morning, she did not let us go and again asked us to stay.

[page 398]

A peasant came in and said the Russians were there in the village.

The retreating Germans set fire to the village. My son and I left the village and went into the forest. A peasant went by with a wagon full of hay. He set my son up on the hay, and I kept walking. The Russian soldiers caught sight of my grandson along the way. They gave him food and let him come over to me. He told me that the Russian soldiers wanted to take him with them. He went off with them. They dressed him in a military uniform. He came to me several times and said, "*Bobeshi*, you cannot educate me, you cannot feed and clothe me, I will go to study at the *suvorovskoye utshilishtshe*" [a military school for boys]. I was happy. He became "the son of the people," and the soldiers loved him.

After Liberation

I went back to Radzivilov. My house had been burned. I met a few Radzivilov Jews. I stayed there for a few days and went to Dubno. In Dubno, I found my nephew Shmuel Gun, my husband's brother's son (who now lives in Tel Aviv). I stayed with him until 1946. That year, we went to Poland through the repatriation. We lived in Beuthen for one year. From Poland, I traveled to Austria. I was in the camps until 1948.

I arrived in the Land in 1948 and lived with my only daughter, Tsipore Yenai.

A year ago, I received the news that my grandson Siunye was alive. At Passover I received a letter from him with a photo, a picture of him with his wife and son. He lives in Vladimir. His wife is a teacher, and he teaches in the Rovno conservatory. I treasure his photo like the eyes in my head.

My Experiences

Sheyndil Oks

Compiled by Leyb Ayzen

The Polish-Russian War

In 1939, a war broke out that ignited a fire over the whole world. The Hitler army advanced at a fast pace, occupying the captured Polish provinces. At the same time, the Soviet army came "to help Poland" and liberated Ukraine according to the agreed-on borders. My husband, Leyb Zats, along with many others, was then mobilized by the Russians. I received letters from him but did not know where he was stationed. After some time, I received the news that my husband was near the town of Lutsk-Kivertsy with others from Radzivilov. Some other women and I decided to visit our husbands. Our surprise visit to them was a disappointment—they had been shipped out deep into Russia.

Radzivilov, our little town, was full of refugees fleeing various towns where Hitler had already set foot. They related the cruelties of the first days of the Hitler authorities, but no one believed the murderous hand could reach so far as here. But the day was coming.

In 1941, on June 22, the war between Russian and Germany broke out. Cities and towns were taken very quickly, and the refugees' warnings were realized. Each day, new orders were issued. Jews began to think about how to save themselves. They began to seek out good gentiles they knew, something rare to find. My sister, Sime Oks, was lucky: she found the best place. She carried all her possessions to the famous priest, Langin Taranovski, who was a good friend of hers.

The gentiles from the town and surrounding villages were having a swell time; they came every day with sacks to fill up with Jewish possessions, which they stole unhindered. And the horrible experience began, the stormy era of World War II, in which Jewish life was in chaos. The town authority was taken over by the Germans' hangers-on: Ukrainian nationalists under the supervision of German SS officers. Taranovski the priest became the mayor. The ethnic German Mateyko was a top leader, along with other Ukrainian bandits.

The First Decree

All town residents must hang thick curtains on their windows so as not to allow the tiniest light to shine out. Disobeying carries the death penalty. The first victim was Avraham Yitschak Chomut, who unintentionally parted a curtain. A German noticed and shot him on the spot. They did not wait long before gathering a group of innocent people and killing them in the Brody forest. A melancholy overtook the town. The danger made everyone tense. The German administration and the Ukrainians began to take their revenge on the Jews.

Another strange decree: Jews must wear a white band with a sewn-on Star of David on their arms. Later they change it to yellow patches. A Jew should be recognized from a distance.

All the Jews, men and women alike, must turn in their wedding rings, fur coats, and best clothing, all according to the decree!

Once they'd relieved us of our belongings, they went after our souls. They created two ghettos for us, enclosed by barbed wire, and drove us out to work every day under police guard. A short time went by, and rumors reached us that the Rovno ghetto had been liquidated and no Jew was left alive. Not everyone wanted to believe the sorrowful report. Many people came to Sime Oks to learn some news, because she was friends with Taranovski the priest, who was now our "provider."

[page 401]

His once good friend's wife, Buretski the priest's daughter, used to pop into the ghetto to chat with my sister. All the Jews believed she would stay alive because the priest and his wife and father-in-law, Dr. Buretski, had assured her they would save her. My sister would also hop out of the ghetto to the priest's home to hear the news, because Jews couldn't read newspapers or listen to the radio, so she was the only source of news. The Jews in the ghetto waited impatiently for her to come back, often alternating waiting places to learn some news. But to our great regret, one day she came back from the priest's with the sad report that we innocent Jews were condemned to death.

This was right before Shavuos. Our holiday would fall on the same day as the Christian holiday. We hid indoors, angry, thinking, what help will come? We look out to the street; our hearts are torn seeing how everything is alive and blooming. The gentiles go around dressed up in stolen Jewish clothes and laugh at the world. Along the highway that divides the two ghettos, little gentile boys stroll, throwing stones, sticks, spitting, sticking out their tongues and shouting, "Go on Jews, you've lived long enough!" We look up at heaven and hope to God that perhaps a miracle will happen soon, as in all the times when Jews were in trouble, and a prayer was murmured in the stillness, "One and only God, give us strength to endure the trouble that must come." The sun goes down, night comes. It's dark in the houses; it's forbidden to light them, and the windows must be hung with thick curtains so that the light from the moon and the stars doesn't illuminate our mournful situation ....

We doze in the darkness and don't forget to keep watch, because no one knows what might happen. We remark on projectors that light the other side of the ghetto. Suddenly, we're surrounded by the bestial murderers with rubber truncheons in their hands, shouting, hitting, and chasing the Jews out of the ghetto. The sick, the old, who can't go quickly, they shot on the spot. They threw little children like balloons, playing with them, until they fell dead.

[page 402]

The young and middle-aged, they set in rows six across, a big herd of sheep with a few armed Germans and Ukrainian murderers. Outside the town, near Suchodol, pits had already been dug. They murdered them all there and threw them into the pits, some alive, not shot at all.

And thus did our dear fathers, mothers, sisters and brothers, children, go unknowingly, innocent, to the slaughter. And we, Jews left alive for the time being, knew very well that the dark day would come and the same would happen to us. There was no hope, no redemption for Jews.

After the liquidation of the first ghetto, the site was left scattered with the various things left by the victims: clothes, shoes, little pieces of clothing from the dear, innocent children. Tossed aside, a few holy books from which Jews had prayed and believed that there would be a miracle from heaven. But the miracle did not happen.... The small number of surviving Jews started to look for gentiles they knew who might be prepared to make bunkers for Jews.

Among the survivors of the first ghetto were two sisters, Leyele and Zelde Charash, and their mother, Dobe. They had hidden in an attic. Later, there came an order to clean up the former ghetto site. Under police watch, people were sent from the second ghetto for this forlorn work. The two sisters and their mother joined in with the workers and set to work. With quiet weeping and broken hearts, they assembled all the things of the just-recently murdered sisters and brothers, sorting them according to precise German orders. The earth shook, the heavens screamed, a black chimera lay over our heads. Who knew what else we'd have to go through, and perhaps the living were envious of the dead?

Every day the Jews were driven to various work assignments and begged God that they would come back alive.

[page 403]

One fine day, the German judge's uncle, Volodka Kobit, came into the ghetto (I note that Sasha Kobit was the German judge in our town). He visited us and offered his help to save us. Knowing Sasha Kobit as a teacher who used to visit our house often, I was very happy to go with him. My brother did not trust him; he warned me that Sasha Kobit is no teacher now but a German judge, and Volodka Kobit, you already know, is the biggest thief in the town. He'll make you his first assignment. You're naïve, and you think you can believe everyone. We'd do better to go with Yashke Gopman; he knows a lot of gentiles who have prepared a big bunker for his whole family. They like him a lot: he'd worked for years with the forest ranger, Vladek, and another gentile, Vasil, in the Chotin forest. Gopman says that's an iron bridge, the only place where we'll live through this and take revenge for our murdered brothers and sisters.

Night falls, and we set out. I go with my brother, Yakov Oks, his wife, and his daughter, Zore. And with Yakov Gopman and his family. He's our guide. He knows the whole area. After a few hours, we arrive at the indicated place. We're crawling on all fours among the thick branches. Gopman had forbidden the proprietor to toast the fact that we made it safely through this way. Meanwhile, we're happy. The bunker is comfortable, and we can talk and walk around freely in the woods. The bunker is well camouflaged. The good gentile Vasil does well by us. There's no lack of food. He brings good news every day, that the Germans will lose the war. The Russians are advancing, and soon we'll be liberated. But today, none of us should go out of the bunker because young boys are pasturing the cows, and they might notice us and turn us in. He goes away. The Jews in the bunker say this is not a gentile but an angel. I don't believe it, and I try to go out of the bunker. Gopman gets very angry and calls for me to come back. Leaving the bunker, I get furious: I can see in the distance that we're surrounded by SS men and Ukrainians, with weapons poised.

[page 404]

I can't manage to scream "Jews, save yourselves!" My brother, who ran behind me to call me back, could have run away, but he wanted to save his wife and child. Someone calls out "Halt!" but I run breathlessly. In the distance, I hear my brother shouting "Zorunye, my child, run!" Solitary, lonely, I run alone in the night darkness through the dense forest. There's no longer anyone with me. How am I? Where am I? Whom do I have to live for?

Whom can I be useful to? Alone as a stone, where should I go now? Who needs me? Everything lost, no trace remains....

No, I need to go back there and see my dearest ones murdered with my own eyes. Yes, Sheyndele! I talk to myself half out of my senses—you're going there to be killed yourself.... There's Gopman's "angel" Vasil, the murderer who turned us all over to the SS men. I know everything, but I'm pushed on by an unnatural strength, I must go, I go not knowing any direction, a step forward, and a step back, almost in the same place. Angry, faint, I fall down in the forest and pass out.

The Horrifying Tragedy

The loud barking of dogs wakes me from a deep sleep. I think something must have happened, there must be murderers around with dogs, who are jockeying for our souls and seeking fresh victims. But I'm not afraid of death anymore; I have no one to live for. I go further and notice how a pack of dogs is tearing pieces from the dead human bodies.... I arrive at the site of the murder and see my great calamity: everyone from the bunker is lying dead. My brother and his wife are among them. My heart is rent with pain. I pull the hair out of my head. But all for nothing. But where is my brother's child? I don't see her among the dead; I go into the forest and shout *Shema yisroel,* Only God, is this possible? Can it be that the child is alive? Be in the murderer's hands and still live?

[page 405]

Would she, as a child, have so sharp an idea in her brain as to lie alive among the dead and save herself that way? No, it couldn't be.

Night falls; I'm alone among all my own dead. I don't sleep; I talk to them from the pain in my broken heart and my shattered spirit. There's no consolation for me. Day begins to dawn.... I stand up for the day-to-day struggle for existence.... Alone, solitary, I turn myself around. My mind works quickly. I consider nothing now except my child. And maybe, not knowing the danger, she ran back to the gentile, to the murderer? I must run so as not to be too late. I wander among the woods, the fields; my thoughts weary me, maybe I might really find the child, my consolation. It is very hard for me to find the house of our gentile murderer. Finally, I see in the distance a house in whose yard the figure of a child is playing about. I lose my indifference; it is no human power that propels me. The skies open for me. A great miracle has happened under the heavens.... I hear my child's voice, "Shendeniu, you're alive?" "Yes, my dear, I'm alive. Now I have someone to live and fight for!"

Our joy is indescribable. We cry and laugh and forget our situation for a few minutes. I thank God, who has given me back my lost treasure. My child strokes my face with shaking hands. I have some consolation. Then the murderer was standing there with wild eyes and an ironic smile, and looked at the scene of the tragic meeting. His thought is decisive: "You won't be happy for long." I'm forced to carry on a conversation with him, that he was right when he warned us not to go out of the bunker; if I'd obeyed, we'd all still be alive. The murderer was happy with my understanding ... but now he says, now no one will come to me looking for Jews. You can sit easy because the war is coming to an end, and the reckoning will come. He prepared some food for us, and drink, and made a place for us in a room. Now, he said, he was going to Radzivilov, he'd be back at night and would call us into the house to wash up a little. His kind words did not surprise us.
[page 406]

In the angel, I had seen the image of a murderer. Now I realized he was traveling into town to denounce us. After he left, we decided to escape. We went out into a field far from his house and found a hideout among the ricks of harvested straw. Not sleeping so we could hear every rustle. Suddenly, we heard the loud barking of dogs. In the distance, in the night stillness, we heard the murderer Vasil calling my name in Russian: "Sonya! Sonya!" We both sit frozen, holding on to each other, hardly breathing, hearts pounding. We hear the cursing voices of the policemen, who run around like wolves. They shoot in every direction. We lie in great fear and murmur a quiet prayer, not knowing whether anyone could help us. They don't achieve their goal this time. After that great tumult and shooting and barking of dogs, we just sat in fear and didn't move from the spot, didn't talk to one another. After a few hours had passed and stillness prevailed in the area, the roosters began to crow; we knew that day was starting and we mustn't stay in here. We must run further. But where? The roads are impossible for us. Death pulled at every step and turn, but we must keep fighting and running wherever our legs will carry us. We'll go to a gentile and ask for bread. This is a big risk. We go slowly, avoiding the villages so as not to be noticed by gentiles who might recognize us. Night falls. We spend the night in a gentile cemetery. We lie the whole night in fear of the dead as well as the living persecutors. Dawn comes. We go further. We see a house in the distance. We head in that direction. A gentile with a murderous glint in his eyes approaches us. He signals us not to ask for bread, but calls us straight into his barn, then turns to us with these words: "You're still alive?" He raises his ax over our heads to put an end to us. I scream out with a voice not my own: "One minute! I want to talk to you about something, and if you don't like my suggestion, you can do with us as you like. Hear me out, dear gentile: we're going around the villages and looking for a hiding place. We were in Baranye with a gentile, and we have a lot of gold.

[page 407]

"If you agree, we can stay with you until the war ends. We'll give you everything. Drive with us to the village; we'll turn everything over to you, and we'll stay with you." The murderous gentile became softer; he liked the plan. He brought us bread and water; he also agreed to go to Baranye with us. We came to a river. He carried the child over first, then me. He showed us where to go. We agreed that he'd wait for us by the river until our return. He told us we shouldn't be there for too long. Walking in terror, we arrived in Baranye. Gentiles who knew me before the war took us in with tears of joy in their eyes. They told us to go right up to the attic so that a neighbor wouldn't notice us. They brought us food, they calmed us with words of consolation, that we would live to see things get better, but that they were afraid to keep us. They told us Radzivilov was clean of Jews. Only in Brody was there still a ghetto, and there were a lot of Radzivilov people there. We can't think for long; we decide to go to Brody so we could be with all the Jews, who would be with us, too. We have no strength to wrestle and torment. I talk to the gentile and ask him to be our guide. I see that he's terrified and at the same time very kind, he wants to help us. He explains that the border is heavily guarded by German patrols. We understand everything, but we must go, we have no choice. The good gentile goes to a neighbor who knows the roads well and asks him to help transfer the "illegal goods." The child and I change into long peasant clothes, kerchiefs on our heads and baskets on our arms. The two good gentiles, one in front and the other behind, carry a big can to purchase fuel oil in Brody. Not far from Brody, we stop under a tree for a while. They go to check the area. When the Germans move farther away, we cross the border without incident and safely reach Brody. Arriving in the town, the tumult was huge, Jews running around, hiding in the forest, fields, and bunkers. Each day there were actions; Jews were killed. It was the same scene I had already experienced more than once. We meet some relatives there.

[page 408]

They take us in very warmly, and we perceive the taste of our onetime home. Others from Radzivilov come over and give us the news that my sister's son, Izi Viser, is still alive. I'm dizzy with joy but in my heart think, who knows how long we'll exist? Our friends, Brody residents, prepared a bunker long ago. They were certain they would survive.

On a certain day, when I met with some Radzivilov gentiles who used to come to Brody for fuel oil, I noticed Volodka Kobit among the gentiles. Earlier, when he was in the Radzivilov ghetto, he'd offered to rescue us. My brother didn't trust him at all. Since his nephew, Sasha Kobit, was once my good friend and often came to our house to visit, I used this opportunity to send a letter through his uncle with a plea that only he could help and save me from certain death. It appears that my clever letter struck a chord in a stony heart, because the next morning, Volodka Kobit came to take us with him, with the assent of Sasha Kobit. People were simply envious of us. In those hellish days, that's called happiness.

First came Raye Kestler of Kremenets to ask to go with us. And my nephew, Izi Viser. Volodka Kobit waited one whole day: when it had gotten quite dark, he told us to gather in the road. I offered to take our friends from Brody with us, but, unfortunately, they didn't trust in our leader. They only wished that we'd get through in one piece. In the middle of the night, we cross the border without any disturbance. Volodka Kobit takes us right into his home. We all settle, stuffed into the attic, but it's very dangerous to stay here, we must find another place. Turns out that "good gentiles" have carried news to the Germans that Volodka Kobit is hiding Jews. One night, the house was surrounded by Germans, who searched in every corner. They tormented and beat Volodka, but he didn't confess to anything. To our good luck, we were in a temporary bunker not far from the house.

[page 409]

Since Volodka was now suspect, he must transfer us to another place until another bunker can be located. It's impossible to describe what Volodka Kobit did for us; it all involved the death penalty for him. Volodka himself didn't take that into account. His goal was to rescue us so we could survive, and he helped many Radzivilov Jews in several bunkers.

The danger grows from day to day. The Germans issue a stern decree: any gentile who helps a Jew will receive the death penalty. Not considering that, Volodka Kobit goes among the villages looking for a place for us, knowing all the bunkers where Jews are hidden. He took us to the village of Gai Leviatinski. There we met up with Ayzik Treybitsh and his family, whom we stayed with until liberation. Volodka and the gentiles made a new bunker for us. We couldn't settle in easily there either, because the Ukrainian police made inspections from time to time and looked for Jews, but we didn't lose hope. Volodka came every day and brought us good news and comforted us, saying we wouldn't have to suffer long now. He always reasoned with the gentiles that those who helped the Jews now would be blessed and rewarded for their humane deeds.

Time passes. Volodka comes and delivers the recent good news that the Russians are advancing and the Germans are having a reversal. One fine morning, Volodka comes and tells us that two young girls who had been hiding in various places were wandering around in Radzivilov. They are in grave danger from both the Germans and the roving gangs. He doesn't know who they are now, but the next time he comes, he'll bring a note from them. I don't care right now who they are; the point is, they are Jewish children. Not considering that I've paid well for everyone, I can't take more people into the bunker without the agreement of the proprietor of the house. Knowing earlier from our savior Volodka that there's another bunker of Jews not far from here that he takes care of as he does us, I send them this letter through him:

[page 410]

"Sisters and Brothers!
In our town of Radzivilov, there are two girls wandering around who are unknown to me. Our duty is to help them; they shouldn't fall, heaven forbid, into the murderers' hands. They're in grave danger. We're the only ones who can save them. I'm prepared to take one of them into our bunker, and I believe that you'll also find the understanding to save one of them, too. On the virtue of such deeds, we'll all hope to stay alive."

At the same time, I sent a letter through Volodka to the unknown girls:

"My dear unknowns! You may go with this person without fear. His appearance is poor but his soul is that of a saint. God will help him to bring you safely through the way."

Volodka Kobit didn't wait long. He went out that very night to bring them. It appeared that these were Binyamin Lekhtman's two children. The encounter was heartrending, with quiet weeping. I was happy that we'd succeeded in saving them. The elder, Dvore, stayed with us until liberation; the younger, Yafe, stayed in the second bunker with Yitschak Vaynshteyn, Simche Simogran, and Hersh Kiperman and their families.

Volodka Kobit sits by the radio and listens with great suspense to the Russians' latest victories at the fronts. He soon comes to us to share his happiness that we'll be liberated very soon. Suddenly, we hear cannon fire in the distance; they're bombarding from every side. The Germans flee like poisoned mice from one place to another and scream, "Faster, faster, the Russians are coming!" Our savior Volodka can't yet go home; he sits with us and waits for the Germans' defeat and liberation by the Russians.

The Germans give their last order: that all gentiles leave the villages because that's now the front. German headquarters occupies our house. We remain in the bunker, imprisoned, unable to go outside.

[page 411]

The bombs whistle over our heads, literally an earthquake. We think we'll simply be burned alive in the bunker. This goes on for several days. We can't leave the bunker after all. We can't endure the hunger and thirst.

In the middle of the night, Volodka decided to go outside. In a few minutes, he came back with the good news that the Germans had retreated, but we were forbidden to go out because the Russians hadn't yet taken the village. A few days went by, and we heard the rumble of trucks and tanks. Also the Russian language. We couldn't contain our great joy; we couldn't believe that we were free. Our town, Radzivilov, was liberated at the same time. We bid farewell to the proprietor of our bunker and thank him for his great accomplishment and the humane heart he's shown for us, to be with him in the most horrible days of our lives. All of us survivors of the great destruction set out for our town, Radzivilov, with our faithful rescuer and guide, Volodka. We can breathe freely, the air is pure for us, the sky is blue, the sun sends warm rays, a little breeze soothes us and comforts our beings. At last we're free! We must begin a new life.

We arrive in Radzivilov. We see the ruins of Jewish houses. The once-Jewish town is not recognizable. The Jewish houses are occupied by gentile neighbors. No trace of Jewish life remains. Everything is strange to us. There's no one to talk to, to tell, but our savior's family takes us in. They take us into their house with great joy and pleasure, like their own sisters and brothers. Volodka made a big feast, with whisky to drink a toast for our liberation, with the best wishes and further success in life. He turned to us, holding the glass in his hand:

"My dear surviving children! You know very well what I've done for you so you could survive, so you should never forget your rescuer, Volodka Kobit." [page 412]

And sitting there at the table, I was interested to know the details of my sister's final days. They told me about the "holy" priest Taranovski, how out of the clear blue sky he drove out my sister, Sime Oks, and her husband and child. Her husband was held overnight by the military, knowing what awaited him. He poisoned himself. They turned Sime Oks and her child over to the town murderer, Demko, for him to kill. They relate the tragic moment when the child Liusik kept screaming "Mama, Mama, why do we have to die?" Tears choke me, my heart is even more broken, a dull pain presses on me....

I draw a parallel between the "holy, kindly" priest Taranovski, with a cross over his heart, which predicates morality and religion based on verses from the Bible—thou shalt not kill!—who is transformed into an animal in human form; and the kindly, simple gentile Volodka Kobit, who had a reputation in town as the biggest thief and who demonstrated such a humane, good heart, ignoring the danger it placed him in. I can't answer that for myself. My heard is broken, my soul bloodied....

Our account with the Germans will never be closed, because the surviving Jews after the murder of six million are also half dead, sick, broken like a tree whose roots were chopped off. Our task is to describe the sorrowful tragedy of our past for the young generation. They should read and remember what the Hitler beasts did to the Jewish people in World War II.

With this opportunity to describe my experiences, it's worth mentioning two fine people: the first, a Bukhari Jew in the person of a Russian officer; and the second, a well-known priest (formerly a Jewish boy).

After the liberation, while we were in town, gentiles came to tell us that in a village located not far from Radzivilov, there were Jewish children who had been saved by good gentiles.

[page 413]

Full of fear and knowing about the Ukrainian bandits who had carried out the death details along with the Germans, I was afraid to go to the village alone in search of the Jewish children. By chance, I knew a Russian officer by the name of Rubin, who came from Bukhara. A national Jew in the full sense of the word. He helped release Jewish children from gentile hands at some self-sacrifice. It was not an easy assignment, because the Russian authorities weren't so interested in such activities. It had to be done on the sly, but his nationalism forced him and pushed him to carry it out with great success. I traveled with him to several villages, collecting some Jewish children from the gentiles without any resistance.

Among others, we were able to save Sheyndele Shrayer (now in Israel) and others whose names I do not remember. And so were rescued a lot of Jewish children who didn't even know their parents. I'm not capable of estimating the value of that person's willingness to sacrifice.

In leaving the town of our birth after liberation, our savior, Volodka Kobit, accompanied us with his entire family. He wished us success in continuing our lives and told me quietly: "They know my nephew Sasha Kobit did a lot for me. He also knew I was hiding Jews, even though he was a judge for the Germans. He's away from Radzivilov now, afraid of the Russians. I ask you, if you ever meet up with him and if he ever needs your help, help him any way you can."

His request was fulfilled shortly.

Wandering from town to town, we arrived in Kraków and settled in a transit camp, where we lived in very bad conditions. On the second day, the door opened, and, unexpectedly, in came Sasha Kobit. I was surprised by his sudden visit. He didn't look like the proud German judge; he was unfortunate, with eyes that pleaded for mercy. He was restless and upset.

[page 414]

He spoke only a few chosen words: "Your debt now, Sheyndele, is to save me."

I asked him to sit and to tell me what had happened. He told me briefly what had happened up to his coming here and asked me to help him leave Kraków.

The news spread quickly through the camp that Sasha Kobit, the former German judge, was here among those he had prosecuted. So, many wanted to hand him over to the police. Not everyone knew of his true past. I, on my part, promised to help him. His desire was to get to Czechoslovakia. I soon found out from some Jews that there was a famous priest (a former Jew) here who helped anyone who needed it. I went to him personally. He received me very well, asking me about all the particulars relative to my visit. I told him everything, though with some caution. He told me to do what was necessary as quickly as possible. Soon I accompanied Sasha Kobit to the train. He took his heartfelt leave with many thanks for this valuable help, saying he'd never forget it.

I'll never forget what I saw with my own eyes in Brody, at the home of my relatives, the Tiger family from Leshnev Street, during the time in the ghetto. Sitting in the house, sunk in my own problems, with roiling thoughts about my survival, singing suddenly interrupts my troubled mind. I hear the call of a familiar voice:

Play gypsy on your fiddle,
once again that sad little song.

A shudder goes through all my limbs. I quickly open the door and stand there, speechless. I recognize our Avraham Groysman as a beggar. I see a thinned-out, hardly human figure with its hand stretched out, begging for alms. His once-rosy cheeks are the color of flour. And his misty blue eyes seem restless. But the sound of his voice reminds me of my school friend.

[page 415]

He recognizes me and lets out a bitter cry and says to me in a broken voice, "Sheyndele, I have no alternative, otherwise I would die." I beg him with tears in my eyes, "Avraham, don't sing! Your song cuts my heart and touches my open wounds." Poor thing, he stands lost, his lips silent, shaking his head. I ask him into the house, give him some food. We talk about things, and both are happy with this sad meeting, but he can't promise me that he won't sing anymore. His words echo in my ears even now: "This is my livelihood, I mustn't liquidate myself. The murderers won't take my spirit or voice from me until the last moment of my life." Those were his words before leaving our house.

And a few minutes later, I heard him again in the distance with this song:

Green leaves, green as grass,
tell me God, why
oy, oy, people plague us so.
What has been must be no more,
red is blood and red is wine.
Green leaves,
green leaves.

We, the survivors after liberation, go around like strangers in the town where we were born without a "good morning," without a future. We meet solitary survivors from big families. We feel we are superfluous. We decide to leave the town because we're walking around among wolves who pity us because we're survivors.... We travel farther through various countries and cities until we arrive in our longed-for land, the Land of Israel, where each of us builds his home and creates a family.

The surviving Lekhtman sisters are happy with their homes and families, but to their great regret, the happiness of both sisters is destroyed forever.
[page 416]

Our Dvore became suddenly ill and had no hope of recovering. Two days before her death, she said to me, "Sheyndele, you saved me from the Germans, but now no one can help me; my fate is sealed."

The good, clever Dvore is taken away from us before her time. We'll never forget her!

Still to this day, town survivors gather with me in my house. They talk, and we spend good time in one another's company and don't forget to mention and tell about the life of our tragic past, how each of us lost our dearest and most loved.

Honor their memory!

How I Stayed Alive

Told by Etye Albert (Zlotnik) to Leyb Ayzen

In 1941, shortly after the capture of our town, Kozin, where I last lived, my husband became one of the first victims killed, leaving me alone with two children. In the ghetto in 1942, I learned from a member of the *Judenrat* that the Kozin ghetto would be liquidated on October 6. I took my two children and whatever else I could and fled. I succeeded in crossing the river that separated the ghetto. I set out for the village of Ivashtshukes. A gentile there took me in and put me up for two weeks. After taking all my possessions from me, he violently drove me out, saying, "It's a sure thing you'll be killed, so you don't really need anything."

So I began wandering from village to village with the two children, searching for someone who would have pity and give me a hiding place, but with no results. I began to struggle for my existence, hiding out by day and at night in gentile horse stables so as not to be seen, God forbid, by any human eye.

[page 417]

In the village of Sofievka, when going to a gentile by night to beg for food, I was hidden by a Ukrainian policeman who happened to be there at the house. He soon told me, "You'll never escape from my hands!" My children started to cry and plead. That bandit had pity and told us to get out. We ran breathlessly, thinking we'd be shot, but for luckless people we had some luck, that our torment was to wander in the darkness until late at night. We settled in a stall at the house of a certain Czech named Hulmar, whom the gentiles called "the Jewish rabbi," may his name be mentioned for good, because it's thanks to that Czech that I stayed alive, having no chance and no means at all to pay him.

I want to mention his fine wife, Helena, who was like a mother to me, cooking food and even washing me from time to time. She sympathized with my pain, calming me and giving me hope. It's hard for me to remember every detail, but this I can tell:

At night I had to go over to another Czech settlement, Stiskalubka. I stayed there for a while with a certain Czech, Anso, a poor gentile for whom I had to go begging. To thank me, he hid me. That was until 1942.

In 1943, we already had no place to hide, and we went to the pitch makers. It was frightfully cold outdoors; we were tired and broken. We staked our lives and went to a Czech's house. Seeing us, he told us to leave his house. His noble wife, Manye Blekh, seeing our condition, stood up for us and said to her husband, "If you want to drive out this woman and the children, you'll then have to come to their defense." The man was silent, and we stayed there.

That year, my little six-year-old son, Yankev, was killed by Ukrainian bandits.

After further wandering and more experiences of hunger and want, completely broken after my son's death, it was the same to me to live or die.
[page 418]

As fate would have it, we'd stay alive to tell about this, which we can never forget.

At the beginning of 1944, we suddenly heard terrible shooting. In terror, we looked through the window to see Russian intelligence. One of them turned to us, asking in Russian if there were many Germans in the village. In my great surprise, I didn't know what to answer. My heart was full of joy, but my joy was mixed with my great sadness that my second son, nine-year-old Hershele, had been killed before the liberation, and this did not merit rejoicing after so difficult an ordeal. The village, us included, was liberated within an hour. We received a warning from the Soviet Army that we should leave the village so as not to fall victim to bandits. So then I went all alone to Dubno. On the way, I met Sheyndil Oks. We were happy to talk and cry ... I met other Radzivilovers. Each one had to tell his experiences.

So life is stronger than death. We're now in our own land and gather from time to time with other survivors from our town, and we don't forget to recall the horrible experiences of the past, how we lost one third of our folk. All of our tellings should serve as a tombstone for our dearest and most beloved, who were killed for no reason.

[page 419]

Remnants of Radzivilov in Camp Luntz, 1947. Seated (right to left): Ite Gun, Duvid Balaban, Yosel Royzman, Gutman-Kisis. Standing: Sheyndel Oks, Yankel Poritski, Zine Oks, Leye Charash, Borya Hofman, Zelde Charash.

[page 420]

[Blank]

[page 421]

R' Avraham Danik and His Family, of Blessed Memory

Feyge Danik, Perished in the Ghetto, 25 Tishrei 1942

**Standing, left to right: Bat-Sheve Shpitsgluz (née Danik),
Dochya Mess, Polya Shternberg, Zina Vaysberg.
Sitting: Mochya Fayfel, Meta Mess, Niunye Segal.**

I Will Remember Them ...

May the memory of the people of our town, the Jews of Radzivilov, ascend, holy and pure men, women, and children, who were killed, murdered, strangled, and butchered as martyrs by the dirty Nazis and their henchmen, may their names be cursed. May the martyrs' names be magnified and sanctified, and may their memory be blessed.

[page 423]

List of Radzivilov Martyrs

Okiman	Keyla
Oks	Hilel, Rivke, Yakov, Hinde
Eydsis	Beyrel, Rachel-Leye, Liove, Mordekhay, Moshe, and Miryam
Ayzen	Shlome, Chayke, Ester, Chane, Zisel, Mordekhay
Ayzenberg	Tsipe, Roza, Genye
Albert	Hershel, Bronye, Sore, Bat-Sheve, Yakov
Albert	Anshel, Rivke, Rachel, Fayvel, Feyge
Albert	Avraham, Chave, Gerel, Rachel
Alperin	Avraham, Moshe, and Chane Perel
Alperin	Moshe, Soni, and his wife Sore (née Veser)
Bodeker	Tsila, and Bela and her daughter
Boym	Bolya, Pesye, Nina, Mindel
Boym	Shashe, Sonya, Yuke, Fime
Boym	Mishe
Bumaznik	Duvid, Simche, Yitschak, and their families
Bukshteyn	Yosef, Chaye, Nisen, Rachel, Yafe
Betlin	Moshe and his wife, Avraham, Feyge and their families
Betlin	Aharon and his family
Biber	Avraham, Tsila, Yafe, Mordekhay
Baytsh	Yente, Shalom, Ruven, and their families
Binik	Batye and her family
Binik	Nachman and his family
Binik	Matel and his family
Birenberg	Shmuel and his wife Yehudit (née Luzman)
Balaban	Yakov, Feyge, Hershel, Nute, Sonye, Menye, Malke
Baltsh	Leybish and his family
Blekh	Yechiel, Kalman, and their families
Blekhman	Mendel, Leyzer, their mother, and their families

[page 424]

Bender	Roze
Bankir	Chaye, Dobe, Leyb, Rivke, Beyle, Leye
Bespoysnik	Duvid, Meir, Yosil, and their families, and their son

	Moshe
Berger	Bine, Gershon, Mekhil, Eynekh, and their families
Berger	Volf and his son Nute
Beregovski	Beyril, Velvel, Godel, Sheyndel, Shlomi and his wife
Berger	Sore, Herts-Leyb, Chane
Bardiger	Yitschak, Chane, and their children
Broida	Golde, Leye
Bronshteyn	and his family
Brizgal	Yosef and his family
Beren	Meir, Golde, Moshe
Brandvayn	Yosef, Boske, and Venes
Brandvayn	Yechiel and his family
Barnash	Yitschak, Feyge (née Plem), and their children
Bernshteyn	Leybish
Bershtler	Ratsye
Barash	Shmuel, Nute, Avraham, Rive, Malye, Malke, Chasye
Guterman	Leon and his wife Fradel (née Bershtler)
Goldenberg	Meir and his wife, and their daughter Golde
Goldfarb	Volf and his family
Goldfarb	Yechezkel and his family
Goldfarb	Yisrael and his family
Goldfarb	Zeyde and his family
Goldshmidt	Zalman, his wife Bela, their daughters Ester and Rachel
Goldshmidt	Yisrael, Chave, Meri and her son
Goldshmidt	Moshe, Boske, Tsvi, Rivke, Yisrael
Gorin	Moshe and his family

[page 425]

Gurman	Tovye
Geyer	Chayim and his family
Gintsburg	Mentsye,Avraham, and their families
Gelman	Mendel, Menye, Zine
Gelman	Nachman, his wife Fredel (née Magid), their children Yitschak, Reyzel
Gelman	Sore, Rivke, and Zusa
Geler	Binyamin, his wife, and their son Hershel
Geker	Yisrael Moshe, Yakov, Shmuel, Feyge, Tsviye, Shule
Geker	Ide

Gervits	Yakov and his family
Grobshteyn	Yitschak, Moshe-Efraim, their mother, and their families
Grosman	Avraham and his wife Brandel
Grosman	Eliezer and his family, and his sister Ester
Grinboym	Neta and his family
Grinboym	Feyge and her family
Grinblat	Masye and her family
Grinblat	Moshe, Chane, Zisel, and their families
Grinshteyn	Menichayim and Ite
Grinshteyn	Noach, Dvore, Feyge, Rivke
Gertsberg	Shmerel and his family
Gertsberg	Lazer, Reye, Ede, Matel
Gertsenshteyn	Roze and her sister
Gershgorn	Mendel, Menashe, Yosef, and their families
Dubtsak	Avraham, his wife, and their son Musye
Dubrovidker	Moshe and his wife Freydel (née Lekhtman)
Doniuk	Avraham and his family
Dishel	Moshe, his wife, and his sisters

[page 426]

Hofman	Duvid, Yakov, Eliezer, Froike, Yisrael, Reyzel, their daughter, and their families
Hofman	Hersh and his family
Hofman	Mendel and his family
Horenshteyn	Nachum and his family
Halbershtet	Yone and his wife
Halbershtet	Motye and his family
Halbershtet	Yehoshue
Hemer	Mikhael, Tove
Herman	Ene and Bele
Vusitser	Zalman and his family
Viderhorn	and his family
Vayntroyb	Moshe, his wife Fride, their children Zuzye and Yitschak
Vaynshteyn	Shmuel, Dov, Avraham, Sonye, Eliezer, Miryam, Rachel, Ester
Vaynshteyn	Yitschak (son of Avraham), Ronye, Batye wife of Yitschak Vaynshteyn

Vaynshteyn	Etel, Malke
Vayner	Tsesye, Chayim, Moshe, Nusye, Beyrel, Tsviye
Vayner	Yehoshue and his family
Vayner	Tovye and his family
Vaysberg	Rive, Zine
Vayser	Ptechihu, Libe, Chane, Sheyndel
Vilinger	Moshe and Sore's children
Vaysman	Pinchas
Vitser	Zelig and his family
Valdman	Feyge, Simche, Motel, Rachel, Keyle, and their families
Valdman	Yechezkel, Yente, Feyge, Chaye
Valigura	Leyb and his wife
Valigura	Yitschak, Shlome, Yisrael, Mikhel, and their families
Vaser	Avraham, Pesye, Rachel, Golde, Yitschak, Shimon, and their families

[page 427]

Vaser	Shlome, Yokheved, Sonye, Duvid, Chaye
Vaserman	Yitschak and his family
Veber	Dr. and family
Veksler	Shimon, Duvid
Varshavski	Velvel and his family
Varshavski	Duvid and his wife
Varshavski	Yisrael, Itsel, Yakov, Bine
Varshavski	Azriel and his family
Varshavski	Moshe and his family
Zolotov	Alter and his family
Zukenmakher	Moshe and his family
Zeydel	Yitschak, Yehudit, Yehuda, Brokhe, Elihu, Moshe, Blume
Zilber	Meir, Batye, and their children
Zilber	Ronye, Gitel, and their family
Zilber	Nachman, Bat-Sheve, and Rivke
Zilberman	Boris, Reye, Yosef
Zilberman	Velvel and his family
Zinger	Eliezer and his family
Zinger	Beyrel, Manye, and their children
Zinger	Manye, Sheyntsi
Zamberg	Rachel

Zats	Sore-Beyle
Zats	Chaye-Hinde, Pesye, Zisel, Malke, Ester, Mindel, and their families
Zats	Ruven, Leyb, and their families
Zats	Simche, Sheyndekl, Leyb, Aba, Chane, Rachel, Sosel, Manye, Moshe,
Zaks	Dobe, Viktoria, Saba, and his wife
Zaks	Yashke, Liove, their mother (Sanikha)
Zerker	Mali

[page 428]

Chomut	Avraham-Yitschak, Chetsel, Elihu, Aharon, and their families
Chomut	Yehuda-Shalom, Moshe, Yosef, Hershel, Ester, Rachel, Chaye
Chomut	Yakov and his wife Dvore (née Charash) and their children
Chomut	Chaye-Leye, and her husband Avraham Rudman (from Pochayev)
Chait	Chaye-Tove, Leyb, Moshe, Yakov, Rive, Sore, and their families
Chenoiner	Leybish, Chayim, Shepsel, and their families
Chaset	Dr. and family
Charash	Mordekhay and his wife Dobe
Charash	Zalman, his mother, and his sisters
Turtsin	Moshe, Chaye, Leye, Yakov, Elihu
Taykh	Kalman, Brokhe, Moshe, Reye, Chaye, Peye, Sore
Tishelman	Betsalel and his family
Tenin	Peye, Sore
Tesler	Avraham, his sons Hirsh and Yitschak, and his daughters Etel and Leye
Tesler	Chasye, Simche, and their children
Tesler	Moshe and his family
Tesler	Shimon and his family
Teper	Chave, Yitschak-Meir, Beyrel, and their brothers
Treybitsh	Yitschak, Feyge, Menye, Gavriel
Treybits	Arye, Kresye, Rivke, Yoel, Tove, Leyb, Golde
Treybits	Ayzik, his wife Genye, and their children
Treybits	Moshe and Dine, Gavriel, and their daughter Dvore

Treybits	Arye and Dobe, Avraham and Serke
Treybits	Meir and Batye, their son Beyril, and their daughter Chane
Treybits	Yoel, Feyge, Tsirel
Treybits	Leyb and his wife Golde, their children, and their parents Beyrel and Ruchinke
Treybits	Keyle, Rachel
Treyger	Avraham and his family

[page 429]

Treyger	Yosef, his wife, and his daughter
Treyger	Moshe, Mintsi, Avraham-Leyb, Motel, and their families
Yuger	Beyrel-Volf and his wife
Yakira	Tovye and his family
Yakira	Ayzik-Ber and his family (rabbis)
Yaroslavski	Pesach, Sore, Gdalyahu, Feyge, Yehudit
Lebov	Bentsion, Frime, Dobe, Menye, Shlome
Lobar	Beyrel, Feyge, Tovye, Zanvel, Rachel, Mintse, Chaye
Luzman	Kalman and his wife Chane
Luybrovski	Akiva, Sore, Yosef, and Rachel
Levitan	Zalman and his family
Lustig	Shmuel, Ratsye, Shalom
Lopatin	Moshe and his family
Liberman	Pinchas and his family
Lidechover	Hirsh and his family
Lizak	Moshe and his family
Lizak	Hersh and his family
Lindner	Elihu and his family
Litsman	Beyrish, Sore, Shlome-Volf, Yosi
Likhtman	Binyamin and his wife Leye
Likhtman	Gutye and his wife, and their sons and daughter
Likhtman	Entsye and Perel
Lemelman	Beyrish, Feyge, Leye
Landis	Asher, Zelig, Rochtsye, Avraham, Hershel, Gite, Malke
Lerner	Yehuda and his wife Malke-Leye
Lerner	Beyrish and his wife Reyzel
Lerner	Yoel and his family

[page 430]

Lerner	Yisrael, Batye, Fayvish, Shifre, Yehoshue, Zusye, Yakov, Rachel
Lerer	Ayzik, Babtsye, Malke, Beyle-Rive
Magid	Nachum, Batye, their children Rozel, Duvid, and Leyb
Motshan	Yitschak and his family
Motshan	Siome and his family
Mikhel	Yochanen and his family, and his mother, the rabbi's wife
Milder	Hersh, Avraham, Meir
Mitsnik	Mendel, Ester, Rive (née Magid), and three children
Mitsnik	Meir, Chane (née Magid), their children Duvid and Yosi
Mitsnik	Eliezer, Mikhel, and their families
Meler	Shimon and his daughter, Yosef, Yehoshue, and their families
Mandel	Yakov and his family
Mandel	Yisrael, Feyge, Natan, Avraham, Golde, Zalman-Hersh
Mandelker	Avraham, Eysye, Frime, Shaye, Feyge
Mandelker	Yosef and Simche
Mes	Kostye, Gutye, Meti, Moli, Yozye, Adalye, Dosye, Asye
Mafshit	Yitschak, Beyle, Yosef, Rozye, Yakov, Ruven, Yokheved
Margolit	Fishel and his family
Margulets	Dr. and his wife (Kremenitska)
Marder	Shimon and his family
Marder	Shlome and his family
Meshoret	Hersh and his family
Meshoret	Duvid and his wife
Nudel	Reyzel and her family
Nudler	Leyb, Yitschak, Yisrael, and their families
Nuymark	Shmuel, Mikhel, and their families (including Tanchum, Mikhel's son

[page 431]

Nirenberg	Beyrel, Reyzye, Yudel
Nerben	Fayvish and his family
Nerben	Chayim and his family
Salop	Avraham, Metye, Beyle, Nusye, Volf, Yisrael, and their families

Salop	Dobe
Segal	Nekhe, Azriel, and their families
Segal	Shmuel and his wife Leyeke (née Polem) and their children
Segal	Volodye, his wife Chave (née Halbershtet), and their children
Segal	Binyamin and his family
Segal	Malke
Segal	Akiva, Sore, Pesye, Godel
Stirt	Polye, Fime, Yosef
Stirt	Berke and his family
Sigen	Voltsye and his wife, and son Chayim and his family
Simenovits	Avraham son of Avraham and his family (a convert)
Simogren	Mordekhay, his wife, and his son Simche
Sis	Zelig and his family
Sirota	Mendel, Azriel, Yudel, Moshe, Kalman, Mikhel, Libe, Rive
Smiter	Golde and her mother
Smiter	Beyle, Etel, Chayke, and their families
Smiter	Yitschak, his wife Sore, and his son Yisrael
Spirt	Zeyde, Chaye, Liusye, Muski, Meir
Spektor	Chayim, Batye, Leyb, Duvid, Pinchas, their sister, and their families
Spektor	Duvid, Etye, Yitschak, Rivke, Ahuve
Polem	Eliezer, Feyge, Golde
Polem	Elimelekh, Chaye, Chane, Avraham, their sister, and their families
Fudim	Hilel and his family

[page 432]

Fudim	Yosef and his wife
Potikhe	Meir, Etel, Malke, and their families
Futerman	Elihu, Tove, and Ekev
Poltorak	Zkharyahu, Adil, Beyril, Zev, Avraham-Leyb, Tove, Yosef
Poltorak	Yehudit, Feyge, Hershel, Chaye-Elke
Poltorak	Pinye, Chane-Keyle, and their families
Poms	Volf, Golde, Chane, Chayke, Aharon, Hersh-Leyb, and their families
Porochovnik	Duvid, Yakov-Meir, Avraham, Yakov-Moshe, Meli, and their families

Porochovnik	Yakov-Yosi and his wife Chane
Porochovnik	Neta and his family
Porochovnik	Leybish and his family
Porter	Beni, Nechame, Mikhael
Poritske	Freyde, Golde, Hinde, Beyle, Todres, and their families
Fidel	Eliezer and his family
Fidel	Shmuel and his family
Pitrushke	Falik and his family
Faygenboym	Nute and his family, and his sisters Feyge and Beyle
Faygenboym	Shlome and his family
Fild	Asher-Zelig, his wife Sore, and their children
Finkelshteyn	Beyrel, Gitel, Munye
Finkelshteyn	Gitel, Tsvi, Moshe, Yekhil, Chaye, Dudye, Moshe, Gitel, and Yesheyahu
Fayfel	Hersh and his family
Fayfel	Moshe and his family
Fik	Moshe, Libe, Duvid, Yente, Fride, Rachel, Leyb, and their families
Fik	Elihu and his family
Fish	Volf, Tove, Menye
Fishman	Gershon, Grinye, Avraham
Fishman	Zelig-Hersh and his family (who married into the Noach Sheyn family)
Feldman	Shalom and his family

[page 433]

Feldman	Velvel and his family
Feldman	Hersh and his family
Feldman	Chayim, Munye, Rachel, Yakov
Plotki	Tsvi, Ite, Dov
Fleyshman	Fishel and his family
Fleyshman	Shmay and his family
Felman	Chayim, Freyde, Beyle, Yehoshue, Brontsye and her son Yosi, Moshe, Sore, and Ester
Felman	Refal, Eti-Gitel, Berel, Meir, and Chane
Plem	Shalom and his family
Plem	Simche and his family
Petsenik	Leyb and his family
Petsenik	Yakov, Shmuel, Sore, Malke, and their families
Faktor	Shimon and his family

Faktor	Fishel and his family
Parizer	Yitschak and his family
Parizer	Lemel and his family
Parizer	Moshe and his mother
Presman	Leyb and his family
Presman	Yisrael, Munye, Yakov, Hershel, Kehas
Fershtut	Zelig and his family
Fershtut	Rachel (Shukevekhe)
Fershtut	Shmuel, Sheyve, Gisye
Tsukerman	Matis and his wife Leye
Tsinayder	Duvid, Nesye, Rivke, Chayke, Neche, Leyb, and their families
Tsirlis	Yosef, Sheyndel, Malke, Shule
Tsirlis	Yakov and his family
Cherniak	Mordekhay, Moshe, Yechezkel, Feyge, Fride, Hinde, and their families

[page 434]

Cherniak	Yekutiel and his family
Cherkeski	Asher and his wife Risye (née Royzman)
Karaulnik	Yechezkel and Chane
Karaulnik	Shimon, Rivke, Ester, Brayndel, Yehuda
Karent	Yosef and his family
Kagan	Duvid and his wife
Kagan	Mendel, Shifre, Avraham-Leyb, Leyzer, Hershel, Shimshon, Rachel, and their families
Kozultsik	Leybish, Chayim, Yitschak, his wife, and their daughter
Kotler	Ayzik, Dvore, Chayim, Gavriel
Kutshmer	family
Koyler	Yosef and his family
Koyler	Yakov and his family
Koyfman	Shmuel and his family
Koyfman	Avraham and his wife
Koltun	Boris and the whole family
Kupershteyn	Meir, Pinchas, Ite, Ester, Rivke, Malke
Korin	Mikhael, Rivke
Korin	Yitschak and his wife Frenye (née Goldgert) and their

	daughter Nene
Korin	Aharon-Yosef, his wife Lola (née Teler), Izyu, and Chayim
Koren	Yitschak and his family
Koren	Feyge, Chayim and his family
Kornits	Efraim and Feyge
Kornits	Hershel, Tsviye, Ite, Dvore, Gitel
Kitas	Yakov, Brandel, Yitschak (Izi)
Kisis	Meir and his family
Kiperman	Hinde, Yehudit, Menis

[page 435]

Kiperman	Chayim, Grine, Seyril, Aharon
Kliger	Yakov, Ido, Leyb, Neche
Kletser	Leyb, Uli, their mother Leye, and their sister Sore
Kantor	Tove
Keselman	Hersh and his family
Keselman	Yitschak, Yosef, Meir, Moshe, Rivke, Sore, and their families
Kaplan	Yitschak, Hene, and their children Avraham and Brokhe
Kaplan	Ayzik and his family
Kaplan	Shimon and his family
Krauze	Perel, Feyge, Yehudit, Motel
Kroyze	Chave, Shalom, Mordekhay, and their sister and families
Kroyt	Ayzik, Tove, Rachel, Kunye, Feyge, Simche, and their families
Kroyt	Meir, Roze, Bat-Sheve, and their families
Kroyt	Binyamin and his family
Krokhmalnik	Eli, Moshe, and their families
Krusman	Moshe and his family
Kriger	Moshe and his family
Kriger	Beyrish, Zisel, Munye, Yisrael, Gitel, Leye
Krips	Avraham, Moshe, and their families
Krishtal	Leyb and his family
Kremen	Chayim, his wife Rive, their children Zalman, Golde, Menashe
Kremen	Meir, his wife Tove, their daughter Ester-Leye
Kremer	Golde and her daughter Keyle
Kremer	Miki and his wife Rive
Kremer	Tsviye

Krants	Mitsye and his family
Krants	Hertsel and his family
Kiperferd	Yosef and his family
Kiperfereld	Avraham, Gershon, Yeshayahu, Yitschak, and their families

[page 436]

Keselman	Avraham and his family
Krasnopoler	Moshe, Chane, Leye, Hinde, Yitschak, Leye [sic] and their families
Kashket	Yisrael and his wife
Rudman	Shimon, Fride, Mikhael, Mordekhay, Ester, Yone, Yehudit
Rudman	Rachel, Perel, Shaye
Rozenbaum	Yisrael and his family
Rozenbaum	Zigmund and his family
Rozenblum	Mishe and his family
Rozenfeld	Yosef, Malke, Sore, Bat-Sheve, Dine, Dvore
Rotenberg	Duvid the rabbi, and his wife and children, his mother Leye, his brother Yosef
Rotenberg	Sisters Sore and Tserni
Royzman	Avraham, Yakov, Yechezkel, Risye, Suye, Sheyve, Reyze, Kenye, Liove
Royzen	Yakov, Yosef, and their families
Royzen	Shimon and his family
Rostster	Duvid, Gitel, Ede, Roni
Rushtin	Reyzel and her son Volf
Rayzer	Vove and his family
Reyf	Yisrael and his wife
Rishnivker	Yisrael, Sime (née Oks), and their children Hilel and Gitel
Rakov	Shlomke and his wife, and their son Duvid and his wife
Shvarts	Yosef and his wife
Shochet	Eliezer, Yitschak, Chayke, and their families
Shumker	Yosef and his family
Shumker	Eliezer, Chayke (née Shtis), and their children
Shuster	Yisrael and his family
Shurtsel	Ruven and his family
Shteynberg	Yekel and his family

Regrettable Omissions from the
List of Radzivilov Martyrs

Tviot-Shor   Ben-Tsion, Shimon, Sime, Leye

Please add on page 437.—Printer

————

From the table of contents, by Yakov and Bat-Sheve Daniuk, "Life Is More Powerful Than Death," pages 421A–421E.

Shtis	Monish and his family, his mother, and his brother Zalman
Shtirnberg	Moshe, Bine, and their sons
Shtern	Yakov and his family
Shternberg	Yakov, Leye, Leyb
Sheyn	Elke
Sheyn	Noach and his family
Shif	Menashe and his sister Kreyntse
Shpiglman	Leyb, Velvel, Elikim, Shlome, Sore-Libe, and their mother
Shpizel	Mikhel
Shpitsgluz	Moshe, his wife, and their daughter
Shapira	Moshe and his wife Chaye, their sons Yakov, Zev, and Duvid
Shrayb	Yakov and his family
Sherer	Shmuel and his family
Batt	and his family
Binik	Batye and her family
Bernash	Leyb, Zlate, Manye, Rivke
Gonik	Ben-Tsion, his wife Sore née Balaban, and their children
Gintsburg	Zisel, Moshe, Neche, Yitschak
Grobshteyn	Yechiel-Duvid (ritual slaughterer); his wife Bat-Sheve; their daughters Eydel, Brokhe; their sons Yitschak, Moshe, Efraim
Grobshteyn	Yitschak
Daniuk	Yisrael and Feyge (from Torgovitsa)
Vaynshteyn	Zev
Zinger	Nisen, Chaye-Beyle, Shifre, Brayne, Rivke

| Chait | Sime and her daughter (Moshkit) |
| Yakira | Brokhe |

[page 438]

Lechman	Yesheyahu and his family
Fudim	Shmuel, Yente, and their family
Pantis	Yosef, Leye, Ele, Moshe, Shimon, and their families
Koren	Roze
Koren	Sore and their son Avraham
Knubel	Chayim-Leyb and his family
Keselman	Leyb and his family

Late additions before printing.

Photographs in Memoriam

[page 440]

Elke Sheyn née Barats, died in the Holocaust, 13 Sivan 5702 (1942)

Yone-Nisen son of Avraham Abish Sheyn, exiled to the Austrian army in 5765 (1915); burial place and fate unknown

Moshe son of Yone-Nisen Sheyn, died 11 Kislev 5685 (1924)

Yente Valdman, daughter of Moshe Sheyn, died in the Holocaust, 25 Tishrei, 5703 (1942)

Yechezkel, son of Shraga Fayvel Valdman, son-in-law of Moshe Sheyn, died in the Holocaust, 5703 (1942)

Chaye, daughter of Yechezkel and Yente Valdman, died in the Holocaust, Tishrei 5703 (1942)

Tovye, son of Yitschak Dov Gurman, grandson of Moshe Volke Sheyn, fell with the partisans

Feyge, daughter of Yechezkel Valdman, died in the Holocaust, Tishrei 5703 (1942)

Beyrish Lemelman

Feyge and Leye Lemelman

Rochtse Landis

Tsvi Landis

[page 442]

Mikhael Koren and his wife Rive

Mrs. Vaynshteyn and her sons

Group of Radzivilovers with Fayfel

**Yisrael Goldfarb and his wife, Reyzil;
Nachman Zilber and his wife, Bat-Sheve**

[page 444]

Korin family in Radzivilov, 1936

Korin family wedding in Radzivilov, 1938

Yitschak Korin and family (second from right: his sister Leye, who lives in Israel)

Godel Segal

Ayzik Korin, died in the Spanish Civil War, 1937

[page 446]

Yakov Royzman

**Yakov and Hershele—
the Zlotnik children**

Yudel Nirenberg

Zkharye Poltorek

Yosef Mafshit

Itsi Mafshit and his wife, Beyle

[page 448]

Libe Oks-Viser

Dvore, mother of Roze Koltun-Yanait

Peye and Ruven—children of
Metye Grinblat

Brayndel, wife of
Avraham Groysman

Mordekhay and Etel Ayzen

Ozer Shadkhan and his wife, Beyle-Rokhtse

R' Yochanen, son of Rabbi Levi
Mikhel, died 25 Tishrei 5703 (1942)

Rabbi Levi Mikhel, died 7 Kislev
5687 (1926), may his memory
be for a blessing

Bele Zinger

R' Leyzer Mehgrobelke, grandfather
of Yafe and Nachman Margalit

Shifre and Brayne Zinger

Ben Tsion Lebov and his wife, Fride

[page 452]

Noach Grobshteyn and his family

[The gravestone reads:
A great leader has fallen

To the soul of a just and upright
man, generous, our teacher the rabbi
Menashe
son of Asher Zagoroder

Died 13 Sivan 5687 (1927)

May his soul be bound up in
the bond of eternal life.]

[The gravestone reads:
Mrs. Memtsi Zagoroder

Our dear mother Mrs, Memtsi
Zagoroder daughter of Barukh Tsvi,
of blessed memory, 17 Adar 5694

March 4, 1934

May her soul be bound up
in the bond of eternal life.

Her sons and daughters will
mourn her forever.]

Menashe Zagoroder

Memtsi Zagoroder

[page 454]

Miryam, wife of R' Yosef-Mendel
Grobshteyn (Saley)

Chane Teres (Tersi),
1888 (Radzivilov)–1966 (Israel)

[The gravestone reads:

Tsipore daughter of
Shlome Zagoroder

May her soul be bound up in
the bond of eternal life.]

Akiva Vaserman, died in Yagur

Name Index

The page numbers in this index refer to those in the **original book** (presented in [brackets] in this translation). An asterisk (*) indicates a woman's married surname.

Name Index for This Translation

This Name Index references page numbers for this English translation

G

534

540

546